Beyond Deep Blue

Monty Newborn

Beyond Deep Blue

Chess in the Stratosphere

 Springer

Prof. Monty Newborn
School of Computer Science
McGill University
McConnell Engineering Building
University Street 3480
H3A 2A7 Montreal Québec
Canada
newborn@cs.mcgill.ca

ISBN 978-1-4471-6073-1   ISBN 978-0-85729-341-1 (eBook)
DOI 10.1007/978-0-85729-341-1
Springer London Dordrecht Heidelberg New York

British Library Cataloguing in Publication Data
A catalogue record for this book is available from the British Library

Printed on acid-free paper

Springer is part of Springer Science+Business Media (www.springer.com)

Preface

Thirteen years have passed since IBM's Deep Blue stunned the world by defeating the human world chess champion at that time, Garry Kasparov. The purpose of this book is to initially reconsider Deep Blue's achievement and then to survey subsequent milestones in the world of computer chess. Following Deep Blue's retirement, there has been a succession of better and better chess engines, that is, computing systems programmed to play chess. Today, there is little question that the world's best chess engines are stronger than the world's best humans. We have seen a steady progression of talent, from Deep Blue to Fritz and Junior and Shredder to Hydra and Zappa and Rybka and .... There are now a number of chess engines better than the world's best human.

Each of the 21 chapters in the book — except the final one — covers a milestone of some sort. There are 20. The first chapter looks back at Deep Blue's matches with Garry Kasparov in 1996 and 1997. Ten other chapters are concerned with the ten World Computer Chess Championships that have taken place: in 1999 and then yearly beginning in 2002 and ending in 2010. Three chapters are concerned with man–machine matches: between Fritz and Kramnik (2002), Kasparov and Deep Junior (2003), and Fritz and Kramnik (2006). Three historical matches between the leading engines each occupy a chapter: Hydra versus Shredder in 2004 in Abu Dhabi, Junior versus Fritz in 2007 in Elista, and Zappa versus Rybka in 2007 in Mexico City. Lastly, there are three chapters covering the three most recent Internet Chess Club's Computer Chess Tournaments held in 2008, 2009, and 2010. These three events are each covered in late chapters and are included to give the reader a few more games between the leading engines in recent years. The final chapter makes a number of general observations.

There have been other important competitions for chess programs in recent years. These include, in particular, the yearly Dutch Computer Chess Championships, the International CSVN Tournaments, and the International Paderborn Computer Chess Championships. Games from these competitions are not presented in this book, though pointers to them appear in the references.

Information on the computing systems used in the competitions is given in most chapters. Of interest are processor speeds, memory sizes, and the number of processors used. You should be able to see the correlation between the progress in technology and the improvement in the engines.

In 1975, I published my first book entitled *Computer Chess*; it surveyed developments in the field to then. Three books, coauthored with David Levy, followed: *More Chess and Computers* in 1980, *All About Chess and Computers* in 1982, and *How Computers Play Chess* in 1991. These books surveyed the period when computers were rapidly developing and the programs were reaching grandmaster level. *Deep Blue: Computer Chess Comes of Age* was published in 1997; it covered the overall history of computer chess, focusing on Deep Blue's first encounter with Kasparov. *Deep Blue: An Artificial Intelligence Milestone* was published in 2003 and covered the story of Deep Blue, focusing on the Rematch. As said previously, this current book surveys the years since the two Deep Blue versus Kasparov matches.

Initially, I started out to write a book focusing on the three man-machine matches that constitute Chaps. 4, 5, and 8 to show that Kasparov's problems in 1997 were repeated in the three major contests in 2002, 2003, and 2006. However, as I gathered material and began to write, it became clear that the real story was the chess engines, themselves, and their steady improvement to the point now where there is little question whether man or machine is best. The issue is which engine is best now, how good it is, and, perhaps, how much better it can get.

This book may be most appreciated by chess players and aficionados of the game. A total of 118 games are included, mostly between the top engines. The games of 17 different engines are included. Analysis of the games is a risky business, as criticizing a player whose strength surpasses the world's best players is often a mistake. However, there is an attempt to examine the play nevertheless. One could write pages of analysis on each game, but a choice was made to include more games than extensive analysis. If one were to write a book about great poets or artists, it would be necessary to include examples of their writings and paintings. And here, too, the games of these great men and machines tell the story. The games are not necessarily the best games played. Our purpose is to provide a comprehensive history of their play, good and bad and mediocre.

With each game, the opening used is specified as given on the chessgames.com Web site. A tree of the openings to a depth of ten moves is given in Appendix 1. Some games have the time taken for each move, the score assigned to the move by the search engine, and the expected reply. This information is included for historical purposes and to give additional insight into the capabilities of the engines. Most often when the time indicated for a move is zero seconds, the move was thought out on the opponent's time.

There have been many games played between the top grandmasters and the top computers in recent years, but only those involving Kasparov and Kramnik are presented. Omitting those played between Hydra and British Grandmaster Michael Adams in 2005 in London was a difficult decision as the match perhaps marks the first major match in which a top grandmaster was really taken to the cleaners by a chess engine. All the games presented in this book appear in a number of places. It is their publication in one place, showing the great progress made from year to year, that distinguishes this book.

I would like to thank Frederic Friedel of chessbase.com for permission to use a number of photos. Similarly, I would like to express thanks to IBM and to the Deep

Blue team members for permission to use a photo of their team. Gian-Carlo Pascutto, Amir Ban, Bob Hyatt, Tord Romstad, Anthony Cozzie, Chrilly Donninger, Frans Morsch, Jeroen Noomen, Stefan Meyer-Kahlen, Vasik Rajlich, Zach Wegner, and Johannes Zwanzger also provided greatly appreciated background information and photos for this book, and I extend my thanks to them.

October 2010   Monty Newborn

Contents

Deep Blue Establishes Historic Landmark

On May 11, 1997, IBM's Deep Blue stunned the world when it defeated the best human chess player – possibly the best human chess player ever! – on planet Earth, Garry Kasparov, in the final game of their six-game Rematch, thereby winning the match by a 3.5–2.5 score. The victory gave Deep Blue the right to call itself the world's best chess player. But was the claim legitimate? Was Deep Blue really better than Kasparov? Was the victory a one-time fluke? Would Kasparov – or one of his kind – set the record straight in the coming months or years? We'll see in the following chapters. But first, let's review Deep Blue's two matches with Kasparov beginning with its victory in the Rematch.

The IBM Deep Blue Versus Kasparov Rematch, held May 3–11, 1997, took place in New York's Equitable Center, located at 52nd Street and Seventh Avenue,

The IBM Deep Blue Team, 1997.
Top row: Murray Campbell, Jerry Brody, Feng-Hsiung Hsu, Joe Hoane;
Bottom row: Joel Benjamin, Chung-Jen Tan.
(Photo courtesy of IBM Corporation)

M. Newborn, *Beyond Deep Blue: Chess in the Stratosphere*,
DOI 10.1007/978-0-85729-341-1_1, © Springer-Verlag London Limited 2011

adjacent to the city's world-famous Theatre District. Kasparov and Deep Blue faced each other in a TV production studio on the building's 35th floor, while an audience of 500 followed the games one floor below ground level on large closed-circuit TV screens. By the final game, people around the world were glued to their TVs watching half-hourly reports on CNN. The event had become the largest Internet happening in history to that time with millions following the games on IBM's website.

Leading up to the final game, each side had won one game; they had played to three other hard-fought draws. The match was tied at two-and-a-half points apiece. Deep Blue had the white pieces in the final game, giving it better chances than if it had the black ones. Except for winning the first game, Kasparov failed to have his way with his opponent thereafter. He lost the second game, being uncharacteristically befuddled by Deep Blue's play. He was unable to win any of the next three games despite seeming to have chances. He might have best settled on playing for a draw in the final game and on splitting the $1.1 million prize. But he evidently preferred to gamble on a line of play he thought Deep Blue wouldn't understand, one that involved a sacrifice by Deep Blue leading to a position in which it would dramatically self-destruct. However, the game didn't go according to his plans. Tactical complications arose in which Deep Blue consistently came up with better moves than Kasparov anticipated. The world champion resigned on the 19th move, thus losing the greatest chess match in history.

Even though Deep Blue won the match, few were ready to accept the fact that it was the better player. Certainly Kasparov wasn't. The match was only six games, and Kasparov was only one point behind at the end. In tennis, you have to win a game by two points! World championship chess matches usually consist of many games, with more than half ending in draws. Six games were far too few to decide something so important.

Leading up to the match, Kasparov was unhappy that he didn't have access to games played by Deep Blue since their ACM Chess Challenge match in Philadelphia, February 10–17, 1996. He had planned to study them so that he could have some idea what to expect. The Deep Blue team argued that there weren't any games to give him. They contended Deep Blue had only played scrimmage games with several grandmasters, primarily Joel Benjamin, but also Miguel Illescas, Nick DeFirmian, and John Fedorowicz. IBM had acquired the services of Benjamin and these other top players following the Philadelphia match to add high-level expertise to the team. Murray Campbell, the team's top chess player, played at the level of a strong Expert, and Feng-Hsiung Hsu, the main brain behind Deep Blue was a couple of levels weaker; others involved in the project were weaker yet. To rival the world's best player, the team felt the need for help from significantly stronger individuals. Along with scrimmaging with Deep Blue, these players also helped with Deep Blue's opening book, which was under constant modification even during the match. The less of the book that Kasparov saw, the better. But the reality was that while Deep Blue had been improved during the year leading up to the Rematch, the great majority of its code was unchanged and its style of play was pretty much the same – some improved positional play as a result of improvements in the scoring function, and improved tactical play as a result of using a system that searched twice as fast. However, not seeing recent Deep Blue games was most likely less of a handicap than Kasparov imagined.

During and following the match, Kasparov questioned the play of the computer, suggesting that some of its moves were inconsistent with his understanding of how computers were programmed to play. The implication was that Deep Blue was somehow receiving help. Kasparov seemed to have psyched himself out over these concerns, and his supporters contended his frustration affected his play. However, in most sporting contests, the psychic plays a big part. World class athletes often play with all kinds of distractions taking place. In baseball, some catchers jabber incessantly, trying to annoy the batter. When winning, an athlete can often handle distractions that would otherwise be a problem. Kasparov's concerns were never substantiated, and Deep Blue's victory stands today as one of the great scientific achievements of the twentieth century. In 2003, the movie, *Move Over: Kasparov and the Machine* appeared with Kasparov playing himself. The gist of the movie continued with the theme of suspicion, and while enjoyable, brought forward no new evidence to suggest Deep Blue was assisted during the games.

At the press conference following the final game, Kasparov said, "I personally guarantee I will tear it to pieces" in a third match. Several days later, he appeared on Larry King Live and told his host that he was willing to play the computer "all or nothing, winner take all." He had won the ACM Chess Challenge with a 4–2 score and now, after losing this one, he stood even with his opponent. Another match was appropriate. Of course, the loser of the third match, if it were Deep Blue, would be entitled to a fourth match, no? And then what?

Over the coming months there were talks between IBM and Kasparov, though no concrete action was agreed upon. The Deep Blue team spent a good deal of that time traveling the world and telling the story of their chess engine to IBM supporters and chess enthusiasts. Then some time near the end of the summer of 1997, IBM made a decision to retire Deep Blue. Perhaps the computer giant saw little to gain by continuing the project. Defeating Kasparov one more time had the potential of giving IBM more bad publicity than good. IBM evidently preferred to present an image of working alongside the human race rather than battling it! Moreover, the company must have felt the odds of a victory in the next match were in its favor. But outside IBM, there was great disappointment when the news came out. James Coates of the Chicago Tribune bemoaned the decision in his October 12, 1997, article:

> The geniuses who built a computer that whipped the world's best player fair and square in May need to learn here in October the first lesson that every back room poker player and pool shooter learns from the git go. I'm talking about the rule of threes. Say we're playing 9 ball or ping-pong, and you wipe me out. I ask for a rematch and barely beat you. Then I say bye-bye, I'm the better player and now I'm going home? Legs have been broken for less.

Not long after IBM decided to retire Deep Blue, the team broke up. Hsu left IBM, initially setting out to design a new Deep Blue equivalent to take on Kasparov; he is now with Microsoft's Research and Development in Beijing, China. Some time after leaving IBM, Hsu went as far as approaching Kasparov to set up a third match, but neither the new machine nor a match ever materialized. Murray Campbell stayed on at IBM and now manages the Intelligent Information Analysis Department at IBM's T. J. Watson Research Center. Joe Hoane, who was responsible for the software that coordinated the many processors on which Deep Blue ran, left shortly after the Rematch. Most recently, he was with Sandbridge Technologies in White Plains, New York. Jerry Brody, whose responsibility was assisting with the hardware, retired. Chung-Jen Tan, the boss of the gang, is now the director of the E-Business Technology Institute (ETI) of the University of Hong Kong where he also holds the position of Visiting IBM Chair Professorship. Deep Blue, itself, the computer – better, the computing system – is currently in two museums, in the Smithsonian Museum in Washington, D.C., and in the Computer History Museum in Mountain View, California. How is that possible, you ask? Well, the SP2 on which Deep Blue ran consisted of two cabinets. One cabinet is now in the Smithsonian, and the other is in the Computer History Museum.

Now, back to the issue of the legitimacy of Deep Blue's victory. A year before the Rematch, the ACM Chess Challenge went to Kasparov, 4–2. But recall, the match was tied after four of the six scheduled games and maybe not as one-sided as some chess aficionados like to imagine. In Game 5, Kasparov chose to avoid his favorite Sicilian Defense, having been unable to win with it in the first and third games. This implicitly showed some recognition of and respect for his opponent's strength. Instead, he played the Four Knights Opening. Then out of nowhere, on the 23rd move, he offered a draw to his opponent. And why? Deep Blue thought it was behind by three tenths of a pawn, and the team was surprised by the offer. The rules of play permitted the team to decide whether or not to accept the draw, the only decision that could be made by humans on behalf of the computer. Kasparov was a bit short on time – about 20 minutes to make the next 17 moves, about a minute a move, in contrast with the rate of play that allotted three minutes per move on average. So, perhaps, he was playing it safe here, feeling he could defeat Deep Blue in the final game with the white pieces. However, given his inability to win a game other than the second to this point, his approach had potential risks.

The Deep Blue team huddled to discuss the offer. It huddled so long that Deep Blue played its 24th move, effectively rejecting the offer. If it had accepted, the match would have been tied going into the final game. Imagine, after five games and going into the final game, the match would have been dead even if the Deep Blue team had accepted a draw offer in a position in which the computer, itself, felt it was behind!

In the final game, Kasparov successfully led Deep Blue down a line that it didn't understand, and he slowly choked it to death. The ACM Chess Challenge thus ended with two Kasparov victories, convincing most of the top chess players that Deep Blue had a long way to go before it would reach Kasparov's level. But with a final score of 4–2, Deep Blue can be given credit for giving Kasparov an excellent run for the money – $400,000 specifically – that he carried away.

Chess players, both human and computer, are assigned ratings and categories based on their performance in formal competitions. Those rated over 2500 fall into the category of grandmasters, 2200–2500 are international masters, while 2000–2200 are experts. Kasparov, at the time of the two matches was rated approximately 2850. The difference in ratings between two players is correlated to the probability of the higher rated player defeating the lower rated player as shown in the table below. The table shows that if one player wins two thirds of the points against an opponent, then he would be expected to have a rating advantage of about 125 points. Of course, six games don't give enough data for a definitive conclusion about the rating difference between Kasparov and Deep Blue.

Percentage of points won for given rating advantage

Rating advantage in points	Percentage of points won
0	50
25	53
50	57
75	60
100	64
125	67
150	70
175	73
200	76
250	81
300	85
400	92
500	96
600	98

Following the third game of the 1996 match, Kasparov gave Deep Blue credit for playing "in the 2700 range," although he observed that its strength varied widely from move to move, from as high as a "rating of 3000 to maybe 2300." It is not clear what he would have said following the final game after winning the last two games.

Deep Blue clearly improved from the first match to the second. Given that Deep Blue used a faster computing system with improved software for the second match, one might argue that during the ACM Chess Challenge, it performed just above the 2700 level and, during the Rematch, essentially at Kasparov's level. The point to be emphasized and contended in this chapter is that the 1996 match was fairly close, closer than generally recognized, and that the 1997 match saw the two stand essentially equal, although Deep Blue was the winner.

So the two Deep Blue versus Kasparov showdowns ended with one victory each. Kasparov, himself, held the title of World Champion three more years, relinquishing it to the third "K" in the series: Karpov, Kasparov, and then Vladimir Kramnik. Kasparov continued his chess career for several more years, remaining the top rated chess player. He officially retired in 2005 to devote his time to Russian politics where he became a vocal critic of the current Russian Prime Minister Vladimir Putin.

The computing system on which Deep Blue ran was the most powerful system ever used by a chess engine. It consisted of two six-foot racks containing 30 RS/6000 computers. Each of these contained 16 special chess-processor chips designed by Hsu, giving Deep Blue 480 processors searching in parallel for the best move to make.

Although the 480 processors did not yield the theoretical speedup over a single processor system of 480, the speedup was nevertheless significant.

Perhaps the most amazing aspect of the two matches was how Deep Blue's play was criticized, how it managed to exhibit bugs of all kinds, and yet obtained a score of 2–4 in Philadelphia and won the Rematch with a 3.5–2.5 score. In spite of a number of crashes and in spite of many moves criticized by the experts, Deep Blue won the Rematch. Amazing! It should be kept in mind that Deep Blue, when it played Kasparov, had played a small number of games when compared to the number played by other leading engines, such as, in particular, Fritz. With thousands of users, the programmers of the commercial engines received feedback from their users that far surpassed the effectiveness of the testing done on Deep Blue. Deep Blue's computer rivals were more solid with many more games under their belts and far more testing and debugging. One of the big shortcomings of Deep Blue – this wasn't really a bug – was its time control algorithm. Deep Blue was designed to play considerably faster than necessary as it had lost a few games leading up to the Kasparov matches on time. Rather than fix the time control algorithm to safely use all available time, the programmers designed in a big safety factor. If Deep Blue had consumed all available time, it would have played even stronger. If doubling processor speed leads to approximately a 100 point rating improvement, then taking twice the time should produce the same effect. While Deep Blue's powerful computing system was a big factor in its victory, its fragility was a major liability. In the succeeding years, far less substantial computing systems would play chess as well as Deep Blue and better yet.

The twelve games from the two matches follow, with the analysis especially pointing out Deep Blue's bugs and criticized moves, and the source of the criticism. In addition, of interest are comments made that suggest one side or the other is ahead or winning. Some of the annotations and comments that follow were extracted from the referenced books and papers and from Deep Blue logs on the IBM website.

ACM Chess Challenge, 1996: Scorecard

Name	Game 1	Game 2	Game 3	Game 4	Game 5	Game 6	Total pts
G. Kasparov	B0.0	W1.0	B1.5	W2.0	B3.0	W4.0	4.0
Deep Blue	W1.0	B1.0	W1.5	B2.0	W2.0	B2.0	2.0

IBM Deep Blue versus Kasparov Rematch, 1997: Scorecard

Name	Game 1	Game 2	Game 3	Game 4	Game 5	Game 6	Total pts
Deep Blue	B0.0	W1.0	B1.5	W2.0	B2.5	W3.5	3.5
G. Kasparov	W1.0	B1.0	W1.5	B2.0	W2.5	B2.5	2.5

The ACM Chess Challenge, February 10–17, 1996, Philadelphia

ACM Chess Challenge
Game 1, February 10, 1996
Deep Blue (W) versus Garry Kasparov (B)
Sicilian Defence: Alapin Variation. Barmen Defense Modern Line (B22)

With Kasparov at the table and the 3:00 PM hour signaling the start of the game, Deep Blue became temperamental, exhibiting the first of a number of technical problems. It was cured quickly, but it did suggest there might be other stumbles coming, as was the case [Glitch #1].

1 e4 c5 2 c3

Both players opened with their favorite moves. Deep Blue chose to continue with the Alapin Variation of the Sicilian Defense.

2 ... d5 3 exd5 Qxd5 4 d4 Nf6 5 Nf3 Bg4 6 Be2 e6 7 h3 Bh5 8 O-O Nc6 9 Be3 cxd4 10 cxd4 Bb4 11 a3 Ba5 12 Nc3 Qd6 13 Nb5 Qe7

Some thought Kasparov would test Deep Blue's willingness to play for a draw here: if he had played 13 ... Qd6 and Deep Blue replied 14 Nc3, Kasparov would have concluded that the engine's contempt factor was programmed to play for a draw in fairly equal positions. But Kasparov's curiosity about this issue wasn't as strong as his interest in playing on and testing his opponent in other ways to prepare him for later games. Yasser Seirawan, one of three commentators at the match, felt Kasparov would use the first two games to learn what he

could about Deep Blue's decision-making procedures and priorities. According to Seirawan who got word straight from the Deep Blue team, Deep Blue would indeed have gone for the draw if Kasparov had played 13 ... Qd6.

14 Ne5 Bxe2 15 Qxe2 O-O 16 Rac1 Rac8 17 Bg5 Bb6 18 Bxf6 gxf6 19 Nc4 Rfd8 20 Nxb6

Perhaps Kasparov learned something about Deep Blue's scoring function here. Deep Blue liked to double and isolate its opponent's pawns. It had managed to do so here and on its earlier 18 Bxf6.

20 ... axb6 21 Rfd1 f5 22 Qe3 Qf6 23 d5

Position after 23 d5.

Again, Deep Blue's scoring function was occupied with weighing the tradeoff of its d-pawn for Kasparov's pawn on b3, giving Kasparov an isolated, though, passed, pawn on the d-file but doubled pawns on the f-file. Seirawan said his "belief in Black's position was growing." In Michael Khodarkovsky and Leonid Shamkovich's book, Kasparov said that he "was stunned" by Deep Blue's move.

23 ... Rxd5 24 Rxd5 exd5 25 b3 Kh8

Position after 25 ... Kh8.

Kasparov plotted an attack on Deep Blue's king, either mistakenly underestimating Deep Blue's looming attack or feeling he had no better alternative.

26 Qxb6 Rg8 27 Qc5

Deep Blue found one strong move after another, stalling Kasparov's kingside attack.

27 ... d4 28 Nd6 f4 29 Nxb7

The blood pressure of those watching jumped through the roof on this move. Could Deep Blue actually grab this remote pawn with Kasparov pushing his

pawns down the engine's throat and blasting away at its king with more and more attackers?

29 ... Ne5 30 Qd5 f3 31 g3 Nd3 32 Rc7 Re8 33 Nd6 Re1 34 Kh2 Nxf2

Both sides slugged away at one another like two Japanese sumo wrestlers, pulling and pushing each other near the edge of a high cliff: one must eventually fall off. Kasparov threatened mate-in-one and continued to do so until Deep Blue nailed down a victory. Most mortals would have been shaking in their boots, but Deep Blue stayed cool, one move ahead of its opponent to the end. Deep Blue, and chess engines more generally, are at their best when defending against checkmate in complex positions.

35 Nxf7+ Kg7 36 Ng5+ Kh6 37 Rxh7+ Black resigns.

Position after 37 Rxh7+,
Black resigns.

In the final position, Kasparov had no choice but to play 37 ... Kg6 to which Deep Blue could have delivered check on g8; 38 Qg8+ and then 38 ... Kf5 39 Nxf3 would have eliminated Kasparov's mate-in-one threat and would have left him with too many problems to consider continuing.

This game was a historical milestone; it marked the first time a world human chess champion lost a tournament game to a chess engine where the time controls were those used in human world championship matches. One remarkable aspect of the game was that Deep Blue took far less time than Kasparov to make its moves. Kasparov had only five minutes on his clock to make his next few moves to the 40-move time control, while Deep Blue had about an hour. This had ominous implications for Kasparov and for the future of the human race's efforts to stay ahead of their chess-playing creations, where faster processors come out every year or so. Time is a great equalizer of chess talent.

ACM Chess Challenge
Game 2, February 12, 1996
Garry Kasparov (W) versus Deep Blue (B)
Zukertort Opening: Grünfeld Reversed (A49)

Perhaps Kasparov had taken Deep Blue too lightly in Game 1. He may have been testing his opponent, but that doesn't mean going as far as losing to it. He almost seemed to be saying by the first game that he was going to beat Deep Blue at its own game – a tactical struggle. A lesson was learned though, and this game and subsequent ones were steered toward long-term strategic situations. The chess players of the world all felt that perhaps Kasparov would fight back in this game, take it more seriously, and show Deep Blue who really is boss. That he did!

1 Nf3 d5 2 d4

Deep Blue didn't respond immediately to Kasparov's 2 d4, as another glitch surfaced. Deep Blue was out of book, using valuable time to calculate moves that should have taken negligible time. [Glitch #2].

2 ... e6 3 g3 c5 4 Bg2 Nc6 5 O-O Nf6 6 c4 dxc4

Hsu misread the computer screen on this move and played 6 ... cxd4. After

Kasparov replied 7 Nxd4, Murray Campbell, who was watching in the IBM Operations Room and observed the mistake, rushed into the Game Room to tell Arbiter Mike Valvo of the error. The game was reset to the correct position, probably much to Kasparov's exasperation though his demeanor didn't show it.

7 Ne5 Bd7 8 Na3 cxd4 9 Naxc4 Bc5 10 Qb3 O-O 11 Qxb7 Nxe5 12 Nxe5 Rb8 13 Qf3 Bd6 14 Nc6 Bxc6 15 Qxc6 e5 16 Rb1 Rb6 17 Qa4 Qb8 18 Bg5 Be7 19 b4 Bxb4

Position after 19 ... Bxb4.

According to Khodarkovsky and Shamkovich, Kasparov's 19 b4 and Deep Blue's subsequent capture "was a small achievement, but good enough for developing a decisive advantage."

20 Bxf6 gxf6 21 Qd7 Qc8 22 Qxa7 Rb8 23 Qa4

Seirawan said, "Now the win is easy."

23 ... Bc3 24 Rxb8 Qxb8 25 Be4 Qc7 26 Qa6 Kg7 27 Qd3 Rb8 28 Bxh7 Rb2 29 Be4 Rxa2

Well, maybe not so easy. Seirawan said it has "become problematic."

30 h4 Qc8 31 Qf3 Ra1 32 Rxa1

Now, Kasparov's thrown "away the lion's share of his winning chances."

32 ... Bxa1 33 Qh5 Qh8

In analyzing the position, Raymond Keene and Bryan Jacobs say in their book, "The smoke has cleared. ... Deep Blue's position may not be lost but it is devilishly difficult to hold."

34 Qg4+ Kf8 35 Qc8+

Kasparov, in time trouble, repeated the position, knowing his opponent would be happy to do the same.

35 ... Kg7 36 Qg4 Kf8 37 Bd5 Ke7 38 Bc6 Kf8 39 Bd5 Ke7 40 Qf3

Seirawan "was beginning to doubt that the computer could save the ending."

40 ... Bc3 41 Bc4 Qc8 42 Qd5 Qe6 43 Qb5 Qd7 44 Qc5 Qd6 45 Qa7+ Qd7 46 Qa8 Qc7 47 Qa3 Qd6 48 Qa2 f5

"The last mistake," according to Seirawan.

49 Bxf7 e4 50 Bh5 Qf6 51 Qa3+ Kd7 52 Qa7+ Kd8 53 Qb8+ Kd7 54 Be8+ Ke7 55 Bb5 Bd2 56 Qc7+ Kf8 57 Bc4

Kasparov said, following the game, that he "was pretty sure I was winning" after this move.

57 ... Bc3 58 Kg2 Be1 59 Kf1 Bc3 60 f4

Seirawan said this was "a gorgeous move which seals the computer's fate."

60 ... exf3 61 exf3 Bd2 62 f4 Ke8 63 Qc8+ Ke7 64 Qc5+ Kd8 65 Bd3 Be3 66 Qxf5 Qc6 67 Qf8+ Kc7 68 Qe7+ Kc8 69 Bf5+ Kb8 70 Qd8+ Kb7 71 Qd7+ Qxd7 72 Bxd7 Kc7 73 Bb5 Kd6 Black resigns.

Position after 73 ... Kd6,
Black resigns.

ACM Chess Challenge
Game 3, February 14, 1996
Deep Blue (W) versus Kasparov (B)
Sicilian Defense: Alapin Variation. Barmen Defense Modern Line (B22)

1 e4 c5 2 c3 d5 3 exd5 Qxd5 4 d4 Nf6 5 Nf3 Bg4 6 Be2 e6

A repeat of Game 1 so far. Deep Blue previously played 7 h3 but castled this time. Deep Blue stumbled on move 5, requiring the system to be rebooted. Perhaps the change in moves from 7 a3 in Game 1 to 7 O-O here was related to this. Deep Blue Prototype crashed in 1995 at the 8th WCCC when making moves from the book, leading to its disastrous loss to Fritz in the final round. The circumstances were somewhat similar. In both cases, the engine seemed to have changed its mind from what it was thinking before the system problem came up to something different after the problem was corrected. Hsu, when commenting on the loss in Hong Kong stated the "loss is probably good for us in the long run. Book preparation will be taken far more seriously from now on." [Glitch #3].

7 O-O Nc6 8 Be3 cxd4 9 cxd4 Bb4 10 a3 Ba5 11 Nc3 Qd6 12 Ne5 Bxe2 13 Qxe2 Bxc3 14 bxc3 Nxe5 15 Bf4 Nf3+ 16 Qxf3 Qd5 17 Qd3 Rc8 18 Rfc1

Seirawan said that "Benjamin could only groan after he saw this move."

18 ... Qc4

Khodarkovsky and Shamkovich felt "Black had a slightly better position."

19 Qxc4 Rxc4 20 Rcb1 b6 21 Bb8 Ra4 22 Rb4 Ra5 23 Rc4 O-O 24 Bd6 Ra8 25 Rc6

Seirawan now "expected a draw, whereas minutes before I had absolutely believed the computer was losing its scalp."

Position after 25 Rc6.

25 ... b5 26 Kf1 Ra4 27 Rb1 a6 28 Ke2 h5 29 Kd3 Rd8 30 Be7 Rd7 31 Bxf6 gxf6 32 Rb3 Kg7 33 Ke3 e5 34 g3 exd4 35 cxd4 Re7+ 36 Kf3 Rd7 37 Rd3 Raxd4 38 Rxd4 Rxd4

Kasparov offered a draw here, but it was refused.

39 Rxa6 Drawn by agreement.

Position after 39 Rxa6,
Drawn by agreement.

ACM Chess Challenge
Game 4, February 15, 1996
Kasparov (W) versus Deep Blue (B)
Semi-Slav Defense: Quiet Variation (D30)

1 Nf3 d5 2 d4 c6 3 c4 e6 4 Nbd2 Nf6 5 e3 Nbd7 6 Bd3 Bd6 e4 dxe4 8 Nxe4 Nxe4 9 Bxe4 O-O 10 O-O

Goodman and Keene gave Kasparov credit for standing "slightly better out of the opening."

10 ... h6 11 Bc2 e5 12 Re1 exd4 13 Qxd4 Bc5 14 Qc3 a5 15 a3 Nf6 16 Be3 Bxe3 17 Rxe3 Bg4 18 Ne5 Re8 19 Rae1 Be6 20 f4 Qc8 21 h3 b5 22 f5

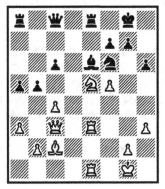

Position after 22 f5.

22 ... Bxc4

Deep Blue took a 20 minute dive while making this move. Before crashing, it was planning 22 ... Bxf5, but after recovering, it preferred 22 ... Bxc4, which turned out to be a better move. According to Khodarkovsky and Shamkovich, Kasparov's concentration was shaken by the episode and he lost "his mental focus." [Glitch #4].

23 Nxc4 bxc4 24 Rxe8+ Nxe8

Seirawan gave Kasparov credit for playing "an impressive game" thus far.

25 Re4 Nf6 26 Rxc4 Nd5 27 Qe5 Qd7 28 Rg4 f6 29 Qd4 Kh7

Deep Blue showed that it was out of ideas in a typically computer way.

30 Re4 Rd8 31 Kh1 Qc7 32 Qf2 Qb8 33 Ba4 c5

Seirawan observed "Kasparov, not only has had his advantage disappear, so had the time on his clock! He was now heading towards the precipice of defeat."

34 Bc6 c4 35 Rxc4 Nb4

Position after 35 ... Nb4.

Even Khodarkovsky and Shamkovich saw Kasparov as having problems, now, saying that the last two Deep Blue moves "not only neutralized White's attack but created counter chances."

36 Bf3 Nd3 37 Qh4 Qxb2 38 Qg3 Qxa3 39 Rc7 Qf8 40 Ra7 Ne5 41 Rxa5 Qf7

The Deep Blue team refused an offer by a tired Kasparov to call it a drawn game. Deep Blue was indicating that it held a small advantage.

42 Rxe5 fxe5

Kasparov exchanged his rook for Deep Blue's annoying knight, satisfied Deep Blue had no way to gain a victory even with a material advantage of a rook for a bishop and pawn – and expecting Deep Blue to come to the same conclusion soon.

43 Qxe5 Re8 44 Qf4 Qf6 45 Bh5

Kasparov's hand shook as he made this move. He had been under pressure to meet time control on his 40th move. Moreover, this was his fourth game of chess in five days. None had been easy games, and he was showing the strain of the battle.

45 ... Rf8 46 Bg6+ Kh8 47 Qc7 Qd4 48 Kh2 Ra8 49 Bh5 Qf6 50 Bg6 Rg8 Drawn by agreement.

Position after 50'... Rg8,
Drawn by agreement.

At the press conference following the game, Kasparov said he was "quite happy that I escaped so narrowly in the end." He felt he spent "too much time on the opening," and that led to time control problems. He thought he had a "serious advantage" in this game, but "to transfer it into something concrete, it was not easy." After four games the match stood tied at two points apiece. Who would have thought that before the match began.

ACM Chess Challenge
Game 5, February 16, 1996
Deep Blue (W) versus Kasparov (B)
Four Knights Game: Scotch Variation. Accepted (C47)

**1 e4 e5 2 Nf3 Nf6 3 Nc3 Nc6 4 d4
exd4 5 Nxd4 Bb4 6 Nxc6 bxc6 7 Bd3
d5 8 exd5 cxd5 9 O-O O-O 10 Bg5
c6 11 Qf3 Be7 12 Rae1 Re8 13 Ne2
h6 14 Bf4 Bd6 15 Nd4 Bg4 16 Qg3
Bxf4 17 Qxf4 Qb6 18 c4 Bd7
19 cxd5 cxd5 20 Rxe8+ Rxe8
21 Qd2 Ne4**

Khodarkovsky and Shamkovich felt "the
position was even" at this point.

Position after 23 … Rd8.

22 Bxe4 dxe4 23 b3 Rd8

Kasparov offered a draw here, but the
Deep Blue team debated so long whether
to accept or decline that Deep Blue made
its move 24 Qc3, nullifying the offer.
Deep Blue, though believing it had a
small advantage at this point, was out of
ideas on how to proceed, carrying out a
dance of its queen to c3 then e3 then back
to c3 over the next four moves, going
from an opportunity to draw the game to

a lost position. It couldn't see any tactical
opportunities in this tame position.
Kasparov's bishop was far stronger than
Deep Blue's awkwardly placed knight.

After four and two-thirds games, the
match stood even! Kasparov must have
been counting on having White in the
final game and winning it and the match,
or, at worst, drawing the final game and
having to be satisfied with a tied match.
In either case, there would likely be
another man–machine battle with IBM
in a year or so. Drawing here would save
energy for what would be the game of
all games.

**24 Qc3 f5 25 Rd1 Be6 26 Qe3 Bf7
27 Qc3 f4**

While Kasparov had offered a draw several moves ago, he declined to opt for it
here with 27 … Be6, gradually tighten-
ing the noose over the next 20 moves.

**28 Rd2 Qf6 29 g3 Rd5 30 a3 Kh7
31 Kg2 Qe5**

Seirawan felt "Now it is over … ."

**32 f3 e3 33 Rd3 e2 34 gxf4 e1=Q
35 fxe5 Qxc3 36 Rxc3 Rxd4 37 b4
Bc4 38 Kf2 g5 39 Re3 Be6 40 Rc3
Bc4 41 Re3 Rd2+**

Now, it was Deep Blue who sought a
draw through repetition of position –
wishful thinking! Kasparov showed he

was not interested as victory was only a few moves away.

42 Ke1 Rd3 43 Kf2 Kg6 44 Rxd3 Bxd3 45 Ke3 Bc2 46 Kd4 Kf5 47 Kd5 h5 White resigns.

At the press conference following the game, Kasparov observed that "for the first time, we are seeing something intelligent."

Position after 47 ... h5,
White resigns.

ACM Chess Challenge
Game 6, February 17, 1996
Kasparov (W) versus Deep Blue (B)
Semi-Slav Defense: Quiet variation (D30)

Kasparov could not lose the match now. But this final game brought out a number of weaknesses in Deep Blue's scoring function. They made Kasparov's life a bit easier, and he essentially coasted to victory, gradually putting a stranglehold on his opponent. He kept the position closed throughout the game, avoiding complicated tactical situations.

1 Nf3 d5 2 d4 c6 3 c4 e6 4 Nbd2 Nf6 5 e3 c5 6 b3 Nc6 7 Bb2 cxd4 8 exd4 Be7 9 Rc1 O-O 10 Bd3 Bd7 11 O-O Nh5 12 Re1 Nf4 13 Bb1 Bd6 14 g3 Ng6 15 Ne5 Rc8 16 Nxd7 Qxd7 17 Nf3 Bb4 18 Re3 Rfd8 19 h4 Nge7

Position after 19 ... Nge7.

Kasparov vividly illustrated his respect for Deep Blue's tactical play here when he was given the opportunity to play

20 Bxh7+, giving him "a strong attack" on Black's king, according to Khodarkovsky and Shamkovich, but opening up the position to Deep Blue's strength.

Hsu evidently entered erroneous information into the computer here, and Deep Blue took another dive, its last of the match. It was back on its feet in a couple of minutes. It was not Deep Blue alone that ran into problems; the computer operators added their share to frustrate Kasparov as well. This one, however, had little effect as Kasparov had matters well under control.

20 a3 Ba5 21 b4 Bc7 22 c5 Re8 23 Qd3 g6 24 Re2 Nf5 25 Bc3 h5 26 b5 Nce7 27 Bd2 Kg7 28 a4 Ra8 29 a5 a6 30 b6 Bb8

Position after 30 ... Bb8.

"Losing," said Seirawan. "Desperate," said Keene and Jacobs.

31 Bc2 Nc6 32 Ba4

Seirawan observed that "Now the game is over."

32 ... Re7 33 Bc3 Ne5 34 dxe5 Qxa4 35 Nd4 Nxd4 36 Qxd4 Qd7 37 Bd2

Khodarkovsky and Shamkovich suggested that "Black should have resigned, as it is playing practically without a rook."

37 ... Re8 38 Bg5 Rc8 39 Bf6+ Kh7 40 c6 bxc6 41 Qc5 Kh6 42 Rb2 Qb7 43 Rb4 Black resigns.

Position after 43 Rb4,
Black resigns.

The IBM Deep Blue Versus Kasparov Rematch
May 3–11, 1997, New York

The IBM Deep Blue versus Kasparov Rematch
Game 1, May 3, 1997
Kasparov (W) versus Deep Blue (B)
Zukertort Opening: Queen Pawn Defense (A06)

In this game and the five that follow, Kasparov's correctly predicted moves by Deep Blue are shown in italics.

1 Nf3 d5 2 *g3* Bg4 3 b3 Nd7

Kasparov's 3 b3 left Deep Blue out of its opening book as the world champion had evidently planned.

4 *Bb2* e6 5 *Bg2* Ngf6 6 *O-O* c6 7 *d3* Bd6 8 *Nbd2* O-O 9 *h3* Bh5 10 e3 h6 11 Qe1 Qa5

Deep Blue managed to stumble onto a small problem with its scoring function which sent its queen off to an ineffective square. One more glitch that was probably attended to by the Deep Blue team between games [Glitch #4].

12 *a3* Bc7

"A bad move that simply cuts off the retreat of the Black queen and wastes a tempo," Seirawan observed.

13 Nh4 g5

"A terrible positional concession," according to Seirawan.

14 *Nhf3* e5 15 e4 Rfe8 16 Nh2 Qb6 17 Qc1 a5 18 Re1 Bd6 19 Ndf1 dxe4

Now Seirawan felt Deep Blue wasn't doing quite so badly, saying, "Despite the previous weak play, it's not so easy to punish Black's mistakes."

20 *dxe4* Bc5 21 Ne3 Rad8 22 *Nhf1* g4 23 hxg4 Nxg4 24 f3 Nxe3 25 *Nxe3* Be7 26 Kh1 Bg5 27 Re2 a4

Seirawan contended that "White is at last ready to cash in all the positional gains that he has made. Just one more move, … and White is about ready to launch its final attack. Most observes were now predicting a merciless victory for Kasparov."

28 *b4* f5 29 *exf5* e4 30 *f4* Bxe2 31 fxg5 Ne5 32 *g6* Bf3 33 Bc3 Qb5 34 Qf1 Qxf1+ 35 *Rxf1* h5 36 *Kg1*

Position after 36 Kg1.

Could Deep Blue have held off
Kasparov's onslaught with 36 ...Ng4?

36 ... Kf8

If Deep Blue had played 36 ... Ng4,
Goodman and Keene point out that the
"situation is far from clear," while
analysis of this alternative move by
Hsu and Campbell after the match
led them to feel Deep Blue would have
had "good drawing chances." Deep
Blue's 36 ... Kf8 sealed its fate. As
badly as Deep Blue seems to have
played, it could be argued that it might
have been able to fend off a loss as late
as this move.

37 Bh3 b5 38 Kf2 Kg7 39 *g4* Kh6 40 Rg1 hxg4 41 *Bxg4* Bxg4 42 *Nxg4+* Nxg4+ 43 *Rxg4* Rd5 44 *f6* Rd1

Another bug in the Deep Blue's scoring
function surfaced here, though it had no
significance on the outcome of the game.
[Glitch #5]

Position after 45 g7,
Black resigns.

45 g7 Black resigns.

Deep Blue predicted 23 of Kasparov's
moves. It made no prediction for
Kasparov's first move, so it correctly
predicted 23 of 44 moves or 53%.

It looked like Deep Blue was in for a
rough ride. Kasparov was on a three-
game winning streak, and Deep Blue
was looking at being sent out to pasture
if it didn't do better. One could only
wonder whether Kasparov might sub-
contiously let up a bit so as not to kill the
golden calf. A close match was more
likely to lead to a third and maybe a
fourth match with increasingly larger
purses. A crushing defeat was likely to
put an end to all this.

It was quite a turnabout: Deep Blue
had essentially played even with
Kasparov for the first five and one half
games of the first match, but now it was
facing the possible end of its short
career.

The IBM Deep Blue versus Kasparov Rematch
Game 2, May 4, 1997
Deep Blue (W) versus Kasparov (B)
Ruy Lopez, Closed; Smyslov Defense (C93)

---

1 e4 e5 Nf3 *Nc6* **Bb5** *a6* **4 Ba4** *Nf6* **5 O-O** *Be7* **Re1** *b5* **7 Bb3** *d6* **8 c3** *O-O* **9 h3 h6 10 d4** *Re8* **11 Nbd2** *Bf8* **12 Nf1** *Bd7* **13 Ng3** *Na5* **14 Bc2** *c5* **15 b3** *Nc6* **16 d5** *Ne7* **17 Be3 Ng6** **18 Qd2** *Nh7* **19 a4 Nh4 20 Nxh4** *Qxh4* **21 Qe2 Qd8 22 b4 Qc7** **23 Rec1** *c4* **24 Ra3** *Rec8* **25 Rca1** *Qd8* **26 f4 Nf6 27 fxe5** *dxe5* **28 Qf1** **Ne8 29 Qf2** *Nd6* **30 Bb6** *Qe8* **31 R3a2** *Be7* **32 Bc5 Bf8 33 Nf5 Bxf5 34 exf5 f6** **35 Bxd6** *Bxd6* **36 axb5** *axb5*

Position after 36 ... axb5.

It is at this point that Deep Blue evidently confounded Kasparov with its defensive 37th move. Based on his understanding of Deep Blue's heuristics, he anticipated that Deep Blue would attempt to invade his territory with 37 Qb6. In the coming years, this position was fed to numerous chess engines by chess enthusiasts and Deep Blue's move was selected by a number of them.

37 Be4 Rxa2 38 Qxa2 Qd7 39 Qa7 *Rc7* **40 Qb6** *Rb7* **41 Ra8+ Kf7 42 Qa6** *Qc7*

Kasparov had two minutes to spare when he made his 40th move. Deep Blue had about 33 minutes.

43 Qc6 Qb6+ 44 Kf1 *Rb8* **45 Ra6 Black resigns.**

Position after 45 Ra6,
Black resigns.

With millions of people following this match move by move on the Internet while carrying out their own analyses, it wasn't long after Kasparov's resignation that doubts surfaced regarding whether he should have resigned. The following morning, the debate reached Kasparov, himself, and, that combined with his concern over how Deep Blue played some crucial moves in the game, left him quite agitated. The game, was, in fact, found to be a draw.

Strange! After three victories in a row, Kasparov resigned in a drawn position. Given how he had beaten Deep Blue in the previous three games, it wouldn't have been beyond him to have even won this game from the final position as there was lots of room for his opponent to go astray.

Deep Blue correctly predicted 29 of Kasparov's 44 moves – 66%.

The IBM Deep Blue versus Kasparov Rematch
Game 3, May 6, 1997
Kasparov (W) versus Deep Blue (B)
Mieses Opening: Reversed Rat (A00)

After the first two games, Kasparov may have had increased respect for Deep Blue's play. In both games he was pressed for time, making his 40th move with only a few minutes to spare while Deep Blue had about a half hour. And Deep Blue's opening book might have concerned the world champion, too. After trying to defeat Deep Blue with his favorite Sicilian Defense in Game 2 and finding Deep Blue's opening book well prepared, he faced a decision on what opening to play.

1 d3

Wow! Kasparov preferred not to outwit Deep Blue's book.

1 ... e5 2 Nf3 Nc6 3 c4 Nf6 4 a3 d6 5 Nc3 Be7 6 *g3* O-O 7 *Bg2* Be6 8 *O-O* Qd7 9 Ng5

Kasparov thought for almost a half hour and found himself unnecessarily behind in time.

9 ... Bf5 10 e4 Bg4 11 *f3* Bh5 12 Nh3 Nd4 13 *Nf2* h6 14 Be3 c5 15 b4 b6 16 Rb1 Kh8 17 Rb2 a6 18 bxc5 bxc5 19 Bh3 Qc7 20 *Bg4* Bg6 21 f4 exf4 22 gxf4 Qa5 23 Bd2 Qxa3 24 *Ra2* Qb3 25 *f5* Qxd1 26 *Bxd1* Bh7

The game lasted another 22 moves with neither side making any significant progress toward a victory.

27 Nh3 Rfb8 28 *Nf4* Bd8 29 *Nfd5* Nc6 30 *Bf4* Ne5 31 *Ba4* Nxd5 32 Nxd5 a5 33 *Bb5* Ra7 34 Kg2 g5 35 Bxe5+ dxe5 36 *f6* Bg6 37 *h4* gxh4 38 Kh3 Kg8 39 *Kxh4* Kh7 40 Kg4 Bc7

Kasparov had again used almost all of his allotted time while Deep Blue had almost a half hour to spare.

41 *Nxc7* Rxc7 42 *Rxa5* Rd8 43 *Rf3* Kh8 44 Kh4 Kg8 45 Ra3 Kh8 46 Ra6 Kh7 47 Ra3 Kh8 48 Ra6 Drawn by agreement.

Position after 48 Ra6,
Drawn by agreement.

A frustrated Kasparov proposed the draw; it was accepted by the Deep Blue team. Kasparov had taken 20 minutes to play his 47th move and 10 minutes to play his 48th move, desperately trying to find a way to avoid settling for a draw.

Deep Blue correctly predicted 19 of 46 Kasparov moves. The first and last move had no predictions.

> **The IBM Deep Blue versus Kasparov Rematch**
> **Game 4, May 7, 1997**
> **Deep Blue (W) versus Kasparov (B)**
> **Caro-Kann Defense (B10)**

1 e4 c6 2 d4 d6

Kasparov avoided hassling with Deep Blue's book for the second game in a row. Only in Game 2 did he give Deep Blue a chance to use its book, and that may have cost him the game.

3 Nf3 Nf6 4 Nc3 Bg4 5 h3 Bh5 6 Bd3 e6 7 Qe2 d5 8 Bg5 Be7 9 e5 Nfd7 10 Bxe7 Qxe7 11 g4 Bg6 12 Bxg6 hxg6 13 h4 Na6 14 O-O-O O-O-O 15 Rdg1 Nc7

Kasparov thought for over a half hour.

16 Kb1 f6 17 exf6 Qxf6 18 Rg3 Rde8 19 Re1 Rhf8 20 Nd1 e5 21 dxe5 Qf4 22 a3 Ne6 23 Nc3 Ndc5 24 b4 Nd7 25 Qd3 Qf7 26 b5 Ndc5 27 Qe3 Qf4 28 bxc6 bxc6 29 Rd1 Kc7

Deep Blue looked at this position for 15 minutes, its longest of the match, eventually playing 30 Ka1 expecting 30 … Re7.

30 Ka1 Qxe3

Kasparov chose to trade queens here, perhaps feeling that eliminated some of Deep Blue's strong tactical play.

31 fxe3 Rf7 32 Rh3 *Ref8* 33 Nd4 Rf2 34 Rb1 *Rg2* 35 Nce2 Rxg4 36 Nxe6+ *Nxe6* 37 Nd4 Nxd4 38 exd4 *Rxd4* 39 Rg1 *Rc4* 40 Rxg6 Rxc2

Kasparov made move 40 with four minutes to spare; Deep Blue had 25 minutes.

41 Rxg7+ *Kb6* 42 Rb3+ *Kc5* 43 Rxa7 Rf1+

Deep Blue crashed here. With one legal move, it had no effect on the move selected. [Glitch #6]

44 Rb1 Rff2 45 Rb4 Rc1+ 46 Rb1 Rcc2 47 Rb4 Rc1+ 48 Rb1 *Rxb1+* 49 Kxb1 *Re2* 50 Re7 Rh2 51 Rh7 Kc4 52 Rc7 *c5* 53 e6 *Rxh4* 54 e7 Re4 55 a4 *Kb3* 56 Kc1 Drawn by agreement.

Position after 29 … Kc7.

Position after 56 Kc1,
Drawn by agreement.

Deep Blue predicted 31 of Kasparov's 55 moves, or 55%

> **The IBM Deep Blue versus Kasparov Rematch**
> **Game 5, May 10, 1997**
> **Kasparov (W) versus Deep Blue (B)**
> **King's Indian Attack: Keres Variation (A07)**

The match stood tied at two points apiece with two games to go. This was Kasparov's last game with the white pieces. Ken Thompson was quoted in a May 11, 1997 Bruce Weber article in the New York Times saying "if he [Kasparov] loses or draws [today], the pressure will be on him in the last game, and he may have to attack when there just aren't any attacking chances." He had had a two day rest before this game.

1 Nf3 d5 2 *g3* Bg4 3 *Bg2* Nd7 4 h3 Bxf3 5 *Bxf3* c6 6 *d3* e6 7 e4 Ne5 8 Bg2 dxe4 9 *Bxe4* Nf6 10 *Bg2* Bb4+ 11 *Nd2* h5 12 *Qe2* Qc7 13 *c3* Be7 14 d4 Ng6 15 *h4* e5 16 *Nf3* exd4 17 *Nxd4* O-O-O 18 Bg5 Ng4 19 O-O-O Rhe8 20 Qc2 Kb8 21 Kb1 Bxg5 22 *hxg5* N6e5 23 Rhe1 c5 24 *Nf3* Rxd1+ 25 *Rxd1* Nc4 26 Qa4 Rd8 27 *Re1* Nb6 28 *Qc2* Qd6 29 c4 Qg6 30 *Qxg6* fxg6 31 *b3* Nxf2 32 Re6 Kc7 33 Rxg6 Rd7 34 Nh4 Nc8 35 Bd5 Nd6 36 Re6 Nb5 37 *cxb5* Rxd5 38 *Rg6* Rd7 39 *Nf5* Ne4 40 Nxg7 Rd1+

Kasparov completed his 40th move with five minutes to spare. Deep Blue had 25 minutes, maintaining the pattern of the previous games.

41 *Kc2* Rd2+ 42 Kc1 Rxa2 43 *Nxh5* Nd2 44 Nf4 Nxb3+ 45 *Kb1* Rd2 46 *Re6* c4 47 Re3 Kb6 48 *g6* Kxb5 49 *g7* Kb4 Drawn by agreement.

Position after 56 Kc1.
Drawn by agreement.

Deep Blue predicted 26 of Kasparov's 48 moves for which predictions were made, or 54%.

The IBM Deep Blue versus Kasparov Rematch
Game 6, May 11, 1997
Deep Blue (W) versus Kasparov (B)
Caro-Kann Defense: Karpov. Modern Variation (B17)

1 e4

Deep Blue stuck to its most extensively booked move.

1 ... c6 2 d4 d5

Kasparov steered away from the opening played in Game 4, implicitly implying that he hadn't found a way to improve upon it.

3 Nc3 dxe4 4 Nxe4 Nd7 5 Ng5 Ngf6 6 Bd3 e6 7 N1f3

Both sides followed standard opening theory to this point.

7 ... h6

This move was the beginning of Kasparov's attempt to suck Deep Blue into a situation that it wouldn't understand and thus misplay. However Deep Blue played quite accurately.

8 Nxe6

Deep Blue accepted Kasparov's sacrifice offer, a move Kasparov expected and that he thought was the beginning of Deep Blue's demise. The audience was electrified by this move that was played from Deep Blue's book. Moves were being made rapidly here, with both sides playing from earlier preparations.

8 ... Qe7 9 O-O fxe6 10 Bg6+ Kd8 11 Bf4 b5

Kasparov took over five minutes to make this move. The previous three had taken no more than 10–20 seconds apiece, suggesting they had been prepared ahead of time. When he finally moved, he got up from the table and walked to his lounge with the attitude of a chef who had just put his favorite recipe into the oven. Was it from here that he thought Deep Blue would fumble?

12 a4

Deep Blue's first move out of book. Deep Blue would make only seven more moves before Kasparov resigned. There was speculation that Kasparov might have been banking on Deep Blue's greedy mentality leading it to play 12 Qe2 here, going after Black's e-pawn. The move played kept pressure on Kasparov.

12 ... Bb7

Kasparov played this move in 25 seconds, then walked off to his personal lounge, then returned, then walked off again, and then finally returned when Deep Blue made its move.

13 Re1 Nd5

Kasparov took over 14 minutes to make this move. It was while considering this move that he first appeared exasperated and frustrated with his position.

14 Bg3 Kc8

Deep Blue's 14th move was calculated while Kasparov was in deep thought over his 13th move. Kasparov replied with his 14th move in short order, too.

15 axb5

Deep Blue showed that it had more in mind than a draw at this point. It could have played 15 Bh4 Qd6 16 Bg3 Qe7 leading to a draw that Kasparov would have been more than willing to accept. Kasparov walked away from the board here as if he didn't want to witness his own execution.

15 … cxb5 16 Qd3 Bc6

Kasparov appeared ready to accept defeat, looking around the Game Room for his mother, Klara Kasparova, and his coach, Grandmaster Yuri Dohokian, appearing to communicate with his mother his interest in resigning. Yasser

Seirawan suggested that he might have played "16 … Qb4 17 Rxe6 Be7 and hope."

17 Bf5 exf5 18 Rxe7 Bxe7 19 c4 Black resigns

Position after 19 c4,
Black resigns.

Some felt Kasparov's resignation was premature at this point, but he seemed to have lost his fighting spirit.

Suggest Readings

Michael Khodarkovsky and Leonid Shamkovich's book entitled "A New Era; How Garry Kasparov Changed the World of Chess," Foreword by Garry Kasparov, Ballantine Books, New York in 1997. Games from both matches are analyzed.

David Goodman and Raymond Keene's book entitled "Man Versus Machine, Kasparov Versus Deep Blue," Foreword by Patrick Wolff, H3 Publications, Cambridge, Mass., 1997. Games from both matches are analyzed.

Raymond Keene and Bryan Jacob's book entitled "Man v Machine: The ACM Chess Challenge; Garry Kasparov v IBM's Deep Blue," (with Tony Buzan), B. B. Enterprises, Sussex in 1996. Games from the ACM Chess Challenge are analyzed.

Daniel King's book entitled "Kasparov v Deeper Blue: The Ultimate Man v Machine Challenge," including an interview with Kasparov, published by Batsford, London, 1997. Games 1, 2 from the ACM Chess Challenge are analyzed as are the games from the Rematch. Games 3–6 of the ACM Chess Challenge are only briefly considered.

Bruce Pandolfini's book entitled "Kasparov and Deep Blue; The Historic Match Between Man and Machine," Simon and Schuster, 1997. Games from the Rematch are analyzed. Games from the ACM Chess Challenge only have their moves listed.

Monty Newborn, "Kasparov Versus Deep Blue: Computer Chess Comes of Age," and "Deep Blue: An Artificial Intelligence Milestone." The first book appeared after the ACM Chess Challenge and the second after the Rematch.

Yasser Seirawan, "The Kasparov – Deep Blue Match." International Computer Chess Association Journal, Vol. 19, No. 1, pp. 41–57, March 1996. The games from the ACM Chess Challenge are analyzed.

Yasser Seirawan, "The Kasparov – Deep Blue Games." International Computer Chess Association Journal, Vol. 20, No. 2, pp. 102–125, June 1997. The games from the Rematch are analyzed.

Bruce Weber, "Saturday is D-day for Kasparov," The New York Times, May 10, 1997.

Garry Kasarov, "My 1997 experience with Deep Blue," ICCA Journal, Vol. 21, No. 1, pp. 45–51, March 1998.

Open letter from Feng-hsiung Hsu http://www.chesscenter.com/twic/feng.html

Elo ratings and probabilities http://www.ascotti.org/programming/chess/elo.htm

Games from the ACM Chess Challenge, Philadelphia, 1996

Game 1: http://www.chessgames.com/perl/chessgame?gid=1070874; http://www.research.ibm.com/deepblue/watch/html/c.10.1.html

Game 2: http://www.chessgames.com/perl/chessgame?gid=1070875; http://www.research.ibm.com/deepblue/watch/html/c.10.2.html

Game 3: http://www.chessgames.com/perl/chessgame?gid=1070876; http://www.research.ibm.com/deepblue/watch/html/c.10.3.html

Game 4: http://www.chessgames.com/perl/chessgame?gid=1070877; http://www.research.ibm.com/deepblue/watch/html/c.10.4.html

Game 5: http://www.chessgames.com/perl/chessgame?gid=1070878; http://www.research.ibm.com/deepblue/watch/html/c.10.5.html

Game 6: http://www.chessgames.com/perl/chessgame?gid=1070879; http://www.research.ibm.com/deepblue/watch/html/c.10.6.html

Games from the Rematch

Game 1: http://www.chessgames.com/perl/chessgame?gid=1070912
Game 2: http://www.chessgames.com/perl/chessgame?gid=1070913
Game 3: http://www.chessgames.com/perl/chessgame?gid=1070914
Game 4: http://www.chessgames.com/perl/chessgame?gid=1070915
Game 5: http://www.chessgames.com/perl/chessgame?gid=1070916
Game 6: http://www.chessgames.com/perl/chessgame?gid=1070917

IBM's Report of the Rematch

http://www.research.ibm.com/deepblue/watch/html/c.shtml

Deep Blue's Printouts of the Games from the Rematch

http://researchweb.watson.ibm.com/deepblue/watch/html/game1clean.log
http://researchweb.watson.ibm.com/deepblue/watch/html/game2clean.log
http://researchweb.watson.ibm.com/deepblue/watch/html/game3clean.log
http://researchweb.watson.ibm.com/deepblue/watch/html/game4clean.log
http://researchweb.watson.ibm.com/deepblue/watch/html/game5clean.log
http://researchweb.watson.ibm.com/deepblue/watch/html/game6clean.log

The Dawn of the Post-Deep Blue Era

With Deep Blue retired, the new monarch of the computer chess world was up for grabs. In 1995 and leading up to the first Deep Blue versus Kasparov match, the 8th World Computer Chess Championship (WCCC) was held in Hong Kong. IBM planned to use this event to showcase the new Deep Blue and to establish formal recognition of its position at the top of the computer chess world. Deep Blue's earlier version called Deep Thought had won the 6th WCCC in 1989 in Edmonton, winning all five of its games and dominating the competition. Then in 1992, the Deep Blue team skipped participating in the 7th WCCC. The team preferred to dedicate itself to honing Deep Blue's talents against human grandmasters while aiming for the ultimate target, Garry Kasparov.

Now, while leading the field in Hong Kong and seeming to be a sure winner of the championship, Deep Blue – more specifically, an experimental version of Deep Blue, called Deep Blue Prototype – was upset in its final-round game by Fritz. Fritz ran on a far smaller 90 MHz Pentium 3 processor. The IBM engine wound up in third place, a major disappointment to the Deep Blue team and IBM. Fritz finished at the top of the pack tied with Star Socrates, each having four of five points. Fritz then defeated Star Socrates in a one-game playoff to claim the title. The computer chess pundits all recognized the IBM engine as the strongest, but it failed to capture the title. It thus played Kasparov in its two matches not as world champion, but only as the recognized world's best chess engine. Fritz, the winner in Hong Kong, reigned as world champion throughout the two Deep Blue versus Kasparov matches.

M. Newborn, *Beyond Deep Blue: Chess in the Stratosphere*,
DOI 10.1007/978-0-85729-341-1_2, © Springer-Verlag London Limited 2011

The International Computer Chess Association (ICCA), the governing body in the computer chess world, normally held a tournament to determine the world champion every three years, but the general frenzy surrounding the Deep Blue versus Kasparov matches resulted in a one year delay. It did hold three World Microcomputer Chess Championships (WMCCCs) following Fritz's win in Hong Kong – in 1995, 1996, and 1997 – though world champion Fritz was unimpressive in these events. Its programmer, Franz Morsch, entered a predecessor of Fritz, Quest, in the 1995 championship, finishing sixth. Fritz finished eighth in 1996 and 16th in 1997. There was no championship in 1998 and 1999. The two WMCCCs in 2000 and 2001 ended the series of championships for microcomputers as by then, PCs were competing on an equal footing with larger computers, and there was no need to separate computers based on size. In 1995, three other chess engines of note competed in the WMCCC: Ferret, developed in the USA by Bruce Moreland, finished third; Junior, developed in Israel by Amir Ban and Shay Bushinsky, finished 12th; and Shredder, developed in Germany by Stefan Meyer-Kahlen, finished 13th. The following year, Shredder showed its stuff for the first time when it finished in first place, followed by Ferret. A year after that, in 1997, Junior rose to the top of the pack, with Shredder finishing third, Ferret fifth, Hydra eighth, and as mentioned before, Fritz 16th.

The Fritz Team: Frans Morsch, Mathias Feist, and Alexander Kure.
(Photo courtesy of chessbase.com)

By the time the 9th World Computer Chess Championship was held June 14–20, 1999, in Paderborn, Germany, Fritz had a number of valid challengers, in particular, Junior, Shredder, Ferret, and Cilkchess. The event was held at the Heinz Nixdorf Museums Forum and co-organized by the museum and the University of Paderborn. While five rounds had been played in the previous world championship, seven would be played in this one. There had been concern that five rounds were too few to decide the championship with so many participants.

Shredder was developed by Stefan Meyer-Kahlen in 1995 as a university project. Its first major success occurred a year later when it won the 1996 WMCCC in Jakarta. It was third at the 5th French Computer Chess Championship in Paris in 1997. Shredder was programmed in C as are many chess engines.

Ferret was developed in the USA over a period of four years by Bruce Moreland in his free time. It, too, was programmed in C. When running on a 66 MHz Pentium processor, Ferret searched approximately 18,000–32,000 nodes per second. During the competition, Ferret ran on a faster 450 MHz processor and searched a correspondingly larger number of nodes. Ferret was a derivative of Moreland's open source engine GNU Chess.

Shredder's Stefan Meyer-Kahlen.
(Photo courtesy of Gian-Carlo Pascutto)

Cilkchess was a rewritten version of Star Socrates. As such, it figured to be a contender. Cilkchess ran on a large 256-processor SGI Origin 2000 supercomputer at NASA Ames.

In Paderborn, Fritz, the reigning world champion, won five of its first six games, losing only to Shredder in Round 2. It led the field by a half point entering the final round with five of six points. Just behind were Shredder, Ferret, and Junior with 4.5 points. In the final round, Shredder played Junior and won while Fritz was upset by Ferret. Fritz played with the black pieces and needed only a draw with Ferret to finish at worst tied for first place. It played the same line as it did in Round 1 when it defeated Ikarus (1: 1 e4 c5 2 Nf3 d6 3 d4 cxd4 4 Nxd4 Nf6 5 Nc3 a6); but the stronger Ferret replied 6 Be3 rather than Ikarus's 6 f3, and went on to defeat Fritz. Shredder's victory over Junior left it tied with Ferret – the two finished with 5.5 of seven points. They drew a second time in a one-game playoff for the championship. Shredder, however, was given the title of world champion on tie-breaking points, having played tougher opponents than Ferret.

That Fritz lost its title here was consistent with what had happened to all but one of the previous world champion engines. With one exception, they were all unable to successfully defend their titles. Only Cray Blitz was able to do so in 1986. Thus, in 1999, Fritz's reign ended, and Shredder was crowned the new world computer chess champion.

Chess engines have been rated for many years by the Swedish Chess Computer Association (SSDF), dating back to the middle 1980s. The ratings currently appear quarterly in the International Computer Games Association (ICGA) Journal. Prior to 2002, they appeared in the International Computer Chess Association (ICCA) Journal. In 2002, the ICCA renamed itself the ICGA. While good arguments can be made that there are better rating lists, the SSDF is the oldest and will be the one referred to throughout this book when ratings are discussed.

The table below shows the rating of the top-rated engine at two year intervals from 1986 to the turn of the century. The rightmost column shows the rating increase over each two year period. The data also shows the processing speed of the computer on which the engine was rated. On average, every year, the strongest engine's rating increased by approximately 50 points. Computer processor speeds went from 12 MHz in 1986 to 450 MHz in 2000, an increase of a factor of 37.5. This speedup would have yielded an increase in search depth of between two and three ply. In addition to speed, there was a significant increase in memory sizes by a factor paralleling the increase in processor speeds. The increase in memory sizes permitted the use of much larger hash tables. In addition, dual-processing systems and more generally, multiprocessing systems were becoming more common. The effective improvement from just the improving hardware probably added one or two additional plies to the search depth. Of course, there have been steady improvements on the software side as well, with improved search heuristics, more efficient data structures, and more knowledgeable scoring functions. These improvements also led to more extensive searches. The increased memory sizes led to larger hash tables and the incorporation of endgame databases into the engines.

SSDF top rated engine in March of alternate years from 1986 to 2000

Engine	Computer	Year	Rating	Increase
Fritz 6.0	AMD K6-2 128 MB 450 MHz	2000	2721	+132
Fritz 5.0	Intel Pentium MMX 200 MHz	1998	2589	+149
MChess Pro 5.0	Intel Pentium 80 MHz	1996	2440	+095
Mephisto Genius 2.0	Intel 486/50 66 MHz	1994	2345	+086
Mephisto Lyon	Motorola 68030 36 MHz	1992	2259	−073
Mephisto Portorose	Motorola 68030 36 MHz	1990	2332	+195
Mephisto MM4	Hitachi 6301Y 16 K, 12 MHz	1988	2137	+134
Mephisto Amsterdam	Motorola 68000 12 MHz	1986	2003	

Opening books, which were part of the earliest engines, were increasing in importance. Ken Thompson's Belle in the mid-1970s was the first to use a relatively massive book of a half million moves. The books, at least initially, helped chess engines avoid disastrous lines of play and saved time for middle and endgame game play. They had to be carefully designed so that lines in the book wouldn't end in positions that the chess engine didn't understand. This could happen if lines were added indiscriminately, without thoroughly checking out how compatible they were with the engine's style of play. Gradually, the idea of "outbooking" one's competition came into play, and it became an important theme of the post-Deep Blue era. Michael Buro's work on incorporating learning along with the opening book spread quickly to many of the chess engines in this competition.

The 1999 championship may be regarded as the first in which endgame tables were in widespread use. Those developed by Thompson in the 1980s, and more recently, by Steven Edwards and Eugene Nalimov, were used by the majority of chess engines; a few had developed their own tables.

The March 2000 SSDF Rating List showed Fritz at the top with a 2721 rating; Junior followed with a rating of 2689 and Shredder was further down the list with a rating of 2496. These ratings also suggest that Deep Blue, clearly the best of the crop when it played Kasparov, deserved a 2700 rating as an absolute minimum, and perhaps one as high as Kasparov.

Thus, at the dawn of the post-Deep Blue era, Shredder found itself at the top of the computer chess world, although Ferret, Fritz, and Junior were not far behind. They were not that far off from Deep Blue's strength as technology continued to advance and hard work by the programmers was leading to improved scoring functions, better books, bigger endgames and opening databases, and more efficient searches with fewer bugs. Deep Blue was quite ragged, with many little bugs in its code; it had played only a handful of games in its history, far fewer than engines now at the head of the pack.

While Kasparov would never get a chance to avenge his loss to Deep Blue, he and others of his ilk would soon get their chances against Deep Blue's successors. Given the data from the Swedish Rating Lists, one might conclude that the reign of the brain was coming to an end.

Data on entries to the 9th WCCC: Name, country of origin, authors, opening book, endgame tables, hardware

Name	Origin	Authors	Opening book	Endgame tables	Hardware
Shredder	DEU	Stefan Meyer-Kahlen	200 K; w/L	All 3,4,5 pc.	Intel Pentium 3 550 MHz
Ferret	USA	Bruce Moreland	<100 K; wo/L	All 3,4; some 5 pc.	Intel 4x Xeon 450 MHz
Fritz	DEU	Frans Morsch Mathias Feist	>150 K; w/L	All Nalimov	Intel 4x Xeon 500 MHz
Cilkchess	USA	Reid Barton, Don Beal, Don Dailey, Mattro Frigo, Charles Leiserson, Phil Lisiecki, Ryan Porter, Harold Prokop	24 K; wo/L	All 3,4; some 5 pc.	240 x MIPS 250 MHz
Junior	ISR	Amir Ban, Shay Bushinsky	5 M–1 M lines; w/L	All 3–5 Nalimov;	Intel 4x Xeon 500 MHz
Darkthought	DEU	Ernst Heinz, Markus Gille	50 K+ lines; wo/L	All 3,4 pc.	DEC RISC Alpha 21264 500 MHz
Rebel	NLD	Ed Schröder	400 K; w/L	None	Intel Pentium 3 600 MHz
Nimzo	AUT	Chrilly Donninger, Helmut Weigel (co-author, tuning, testing), Alexander Kure (book), W. Zugrav (hardware), Bernhard Biberle (operator), Cock de Gorter (special book)	Data Not Available	Yes; not specified	Intel Pentium 3 600 MHz
Chesstiger	GUA	Christophe Théron	350 K moves; wo/L	None	AMD K6–3 350 MHz
Hiarcs	GBR	Mark Uniache, Eric Hallsworth (book), Matthias Wullenweber (GUI, op), Erdogan Gress (GUI, op), Mathias Feist (GUI)	Data not available	All 3,4; some 5 pc.	Intel Pentium 3 550 MHz
LambChop	NZE	Peter McKenzie	1 K; wo/L	None	Intel Pentium 2 450 MHz
Francesca	GBR	Tom King	Data not available	None	Intel Pentium 2 450 MHz
VirtualChess	FRA	Marc-Francois Baudet, Jean-Christophe Weill	No data on size; wo/L	None	Intel Pentium 2 450 MHz

GromitChess	DEU	Frank Schneider	100 K; wo/L	Edwards 3,4 pc.	Intel Pentium 2 450 MHz
Eugen	SPN	Eugenio Castillo Jimenez	250 K; wo/L	Some 3 pc.	Intel Pentium 2 450 MHz
Zugzwang	DEU	Rainer Feldmann, Peter Mysliwietz, Heiner Matthias	No data on size; wo/L	Thompson's tables	512 x DEC RISC Alpha 21164 300 MHz
MChess	USA	Marty Hirsch, Sandro Necchi (book), Peter Schreiner (operator)	Data not available	Data not available	Intel Pentium 3 500 MHz
P.ConNerS	DEU	Ulf Lorenz, Heiner Matthias (book)	1 Mb; wo/L	Thompson's non-trivial 4 pc.	186 Intel Pentium 2 450 MHz
Isichess	DEU	Gerd Isenberg	Data not available	None	Intel Pentium 3 500 MHz
Diep	NLD	Vincent Diepeveen	200 K; wo/L	Data not available	Intel 4x Xeon 400 MHz
Patzer	DEU	Roland Pfister	30 K; wo/L	Most 3–4 Nalimov	Intel Pentium 2 450 MHz
Mini	USA	Larry Kaufman, Don Dailey	10 K; wo/L	KPK	Intel Pentium 2 400 MHz
Now	USA	Mark Lefler	5–6 K	None	Intel Pentium 2 450 MHz
SOS	DEU	Rudolf Huber	70 K; some learning	All Nalimov	Intel Pentium 2 450 MHz
Arthur	NLD	Walter Ravenek	Data not available	All Nalimov	Mac G3 420 MHz
Ikarus	DEU	Muntsin Kolss, Munjong Kolss	Data not available	All Nalimov	Intel Pentium 2 450 MHz
Centaur	RUS	Victor Vikhrev, Alexey Manjakhin	2 M moves; wo/L	None	Intel Pentium 2 450 MHz
Ruy Lopez	SPN	Alvaro Begue, Jose Manuel Moran	200 K ; wo/L	Edward's 3–4 pc.	Intel Pentium 2 450 MHz
XXXX2	DEU	Martin Zentner	170 K ; wo/L	Edward's 3 pc, some 4 pc.	Intel Pentium 2 450 MHz
Neurologic	DEU	Jochen Peussner	4 Mb; some learning	Edward's 3–4 pc.	Intel Pentium 2 450 MHz

Note: w/L denotes with learning, wo/L denotes without learning

Final standings of the 9th WCCC, Paderborn, Germany

#	Name	1	2	3	4	5	6	7	Pts	TB
1	Shredder	30wW	3bW	7wW	8bD	10wD	2bD	5wW	5.5	29.0
2	Ferret	20bW	14wW	10bL	24wW	12bW	1wD	3wW	5.5	28.0
3	Fritz	27bW	1wL	26bW	13wW	5bW	10wW	2bL	5.0	27.5
4	Cilkchess	21wW	24bW	5bL	12wD	11bW	6wD	10bW	5.0	26.5
5	Junior	15wW	6bW	4wW	10bD	3wL	8wW	1bL	4.5	32.5
6	Dark Thought	12bW	5wL	21bW	11wD	16bW	4bD	7wD	4.5	28.5
7	Rebel	25bW	11wW	1bL	18wW	8bL	13wW	6bD	4.5	28.0
8	Nimzo	26bD	22wW	16bW	1wD	7wW	5bL	9wD	4.5	27.5
9	Chess Tiger	10bL	13wL	29bW	22wW	14bW	19wW	8bD	4.5	23.5
10	Hiarcs	9wW	17bW	2wW	5wD	1bD	3bL	4wL	4.0	33.5
11	LambChop	18wW	7bL	15wW	6bD	4wL	24bW	16wD	4.0	27.0
12	Francesca	6wL	28bW	17wW	4bD	2wL	16wD	20bW	4.0	26.5
13	VirtualChess	24wL	9bW	19wW	3bL	26wW	7bL	18wW	4.0	24.5
14	GromitChess	28wW	2bL	18wL	23bW	9wL	27wW	25bW	4.0	22.0
15	Eugen	5bL	29wW	11bL	21wW	24bD	20wD	19bW	4.0	21.0
16	Zugzwang	19wD	23bW	8wL	17bW	6wL	12bD	11bD	3.5	26.5
17	MChess	29bW	10wL	12bL	16wL	25bD	26wW	24wW	3.5	19.5
18	P.ConNerS	11bL	20wW	14bW	7bL	19wL	21wW	13bL	3.0	25.5
19	Isichess	16bD	26wD	13bL	25wW	18bW	9bL	15wL	3.0	23.5
20	Diep	2wL	18bL	30wD	28bW	22wW	15bD	12wL	3.0	22.0
21	Patzer	4bL	27wW	6wL	15bL	30wW	18bL	29wW	3.0	20.5
22	Mini	23wD	8bL	28wD	9bL	20bL	30wW	27bW	3.0	19.5
23	Now	22bD	16wL	27bL	14wL	28wD	29bW	26bW	3.0	17.0
24	SOS	13bW	4wL	25bW	2bL	15wD	11wL	17bL	2.5	28.5
25	Arthur	7wL	30bW	24wL	19bL	17wD	28bW	14wL	2.5	20.0
26	Ikarus	8wD	19bD	3wL	27wW	13bL	17bL	23wL	2.0	25.0
27	Centaur	3wL	21bL	23wW	26bL	29wW	14bL	22wL	2.0	21.0
28	RuyLopez	14bL	12wL	22bD	20wL	23bD	25wL	30bD	1.5	20.5
29	XXXX2	17wL	15bL	9wL	30bW	27bL	23wL	21bL	1.0	21.0
30	Neurologic	1bL	25wL	20bD	29wL	21bL	22bL	28wD	1.0	19.5

#	Name	Playoff	Pts
1	Ferret	2bW	0.0
2	Shredder	1wL	1.0

9th WCCC, Paderborn
Round 2, June 15, 1999
Fritz (W) versus Shredder (B)
Ruy Lopez (C88)

Fritz, the defending world champion, was about to receive its first dose of medicine in the second round.

1 e4 e5 2 Nf3 Nc6 3 Bb5 a6 4 Ba4 Nf6 5 O-O Be7 6 Re1 b5 7 Bb3 O-O

Deep Blue had defeated Kasparov when the latter played 7 … d6 here in Game 2 of the Rematch, but Shredder chose another direction.

8 a4 b4 9 d3 d6 10 a5 Be6 11 Nbd2 Rab8 12 Bc4 Qc8 13 Nf1 Nd4 14 Nxd4 exd4 15 Bf4 Nd7 16 Nd2 Bxc4 17 Nxc4 b3 18 cxb3 Nc5 19 b4 Rxb4 20 Ra3 Qe6 21 Bd2

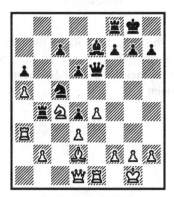

Position after 21 Bd2.

Most of the action took place on the queenside.

21 … Nxd3 22 Rxd3 Rxc4 23 b3 Rc5 24 Rxd4 Bf6 25 Rd3 Rb8 26 h3 Bb2

Position after 26 … Bb2.

Shredder's move was one more example of the unique mind of the machine.

27 Qe2 Rcb5 28 Rd5 Be5 29 Qc4 c5 30 b4

Position after 30 b4.

30 ... cxb4 31 Rxb5 Rxb5 32 Qc6

Position after 32 Qc6.

While Shredder wouldn't fall for mate-in-one, Fritz would neglect the threat of Shredder advancing its b-pawn.

32 ... h6 33 Qxa6 Qd7 34 Rc1 b3 35 Qc8+ Qxc8 36 Rxc8+ Kh7 37 Rc1 b2 38 Rb1 Rb3

Position after 38 ... Rb3.

The material is even at this point, but Fritz must now give up a bishop for a pawn.

39 Bc1 bxc1=Q+ 40 Rxc1

Shredder had an easy win from here, and its opponent could have resigned to spare the operators from carrying on for another 15 moves.

40 ... Kg6 41 g3 f5 42 exf5+ Kxf5 43 Rc6 Ra3 44 Kg2 Ra2 45 Ra6 Ke4 46 Ra8 d5 47 Rc8 d4 48 Rc4 Rxa5 49 Rb4 g5 50 Rc4 Ra1 51 Rb4 Bd6 52 Rb6 Kd5 53 Kf3 d3 54 Rxd6+ Kxd6 55 Ke3 White resigns.

Position after 55 Ke3,
White resigns.

After this loss, Fritz found itself in an uphill struggle to retain its title. Six other engines had perfect 2–0 records at this point.

Event: 9th WCCC, Paderborn
Round 5, June 18, 1999
Junior (W) versus Fritz (B)
Sicilian Closed (B23)

Junior was tied for first place with Shredder and Hiarcs when it took on Fritz in the fifth round. It came up short and this loss, along with a loss to Shredder in the final round, left Junior one half point behind Fritz, who finished one half point behind Shredder and Ferret.

1 e4 c5 2 Nc3 Nc6 3 f4 g6 4 Nf3 Bg7 5 Bb5 Nd4 6 O-O Nxb5 7 Nxb5 d6 8 Qe1 a6 9 Nc3 b5 10 d3 Bb7 11 Kh1 Qd7 12 Bd2 Nf6 13 e5 Nd5 14 Ne4 f5 15 Neg5 h6 16 Nh3 O-O 17 Qh4 Nb4 18 Bxb4 cxb4 19 Nhg1 Rac8 20 Rf2 Rc7 21 Re2 Rfc8 22 Rc1 Bd5 23 Qf2 a5 24 Qb6 a4 25 Qa5

Position after 25 Qa5.

Junior's queen had managed to hide herself in the strangest way.

25 ... b3 26 axb3 Bxb3 27 Ne1 dxe5 28 fxe5 g5 29 Qb6 e6 30 Qf2 b4 31 Ra1 Bd5 32 Qe3 Rc5 33 Qd2

33 ... Rb8 34 Qe3 Ra5 35 d4 Bf8 36 Nd3 a3 37 Rb1 Raa8 38 Rf2 Rc8 39 Rc1 Be4 40 bxa3 bxa3

Position after 40 ... bxa3.

Fritz's strong bishops and rooks along with the passed a-pawn would force a resignation soon.

41 Rd2 Qc6 42 Qe1 Rd8 43 c3 a2 44 Ra1 Qxc3 45 Ne2 Qc4 46 Qd1 Rdb8 47 Nb2 Qc6 White resigns.

Position after 47 ... Qc6,
White resigns.

9th WCCC, Paderborn
Round 6, June 18, 1999
Ferret (W) versus Shredder (B)
Evans Gambit (C52)

With two rounds to go, Ferret, Shredder, Fritz, and Hiarcs were tied for the lead with four of five points.

1 e4 e5 2 Nf3 Nc6 3 Bc4 Bc5 4 b4 Bxb4 5 c3 Ba5 6 d4 exd4 7 O-O Nge7 8 cxd4 d5 9 exd5 Nxd5 10 Ba3 Be6 11 Bb5 Bb4 12 Bxc6+ bxc6 13 Bxb4 Nxb4 14 Qa4 Qd6 15 Nc3 Nd3 16 d5 Nc5 17 Qxc6+ Qxc6 18 dxc6 Ke7 19 Rfe1 Nd3 20 Re3 Nb4 21 Nd4 Rhd8 22 Rd1 Kf6 23 a3 Nd5 24 Ne4+ Ke7 25 Ree1 Bg4 26 f3 Bc8 27 Nc5+ Kf6 28 Nb5 Be6 29 Na6 Rac8 30 Nbxc7

Position after 30 Nbxc7.

Both sides now became temporarily distracted from the tactics that had dominated the game thus far.

30 ... h5 31 h3 h4 32 a4 Nxc7 33 Rxd8 Rxd8 34 Nxc7 Rc8 35 Nxe6 fxe6 36 Rc1 e5 37 Kf2 Ke6 38 g3 hxg3+ 39 Kxg3 Kd6 40 Rd1+ Ke6 41 Rd7

Position after 41 Rd7.

Ferret, up a pawn, seemed to be in a position to win the king, rook, and pawns endgame, but Shredder's king had other ideas.

41 ... Rxc6 42 Rxg7 Rc3 43 Rg4 Kf5 44 h4 Rc1 45 h5 Rc6 46 Rg7 Ra6 47 Rg4 Rc6 48 Rg7 Ra6

Shredder proposed a draw.

49 Rg8

Not quite! Ferret, with an extra pawn, wasn't quite ready to settle for a half point.

49 ... Rb6 50 Kh4 Rb4+ 51 Kg3 Rb6 52 Kh4 Rb4+ 53 Rg4 Rb2 54 Kg3 Rb6 55 a5 Rd6 56 Rg7 Ra6 57 Rg8 Rd6 58 Kh4 Rd4+ 59 Kg3 Rd6 60 Rb8 Kg5 61 Re8 Rd5 62 a6 Ra5 63 Re7 e4 64 Rxa7 Ra3 65 Kf2 Rxf3+ 66 Ke2 Kxh5 67 Ra8 Rf7 68 Ke3 Re7 69 Rb8 Kg6 70 Rb6+ Kf5 Drawn by agreement.

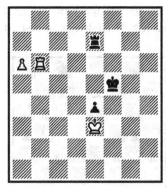

Position after 70 ... Kf5,
Drawn by agreement.

The draw left Ferret and Shredder tied for second place after six of the scheduled seven rounds. Fritz, who defeated Hiarcs, regained the lead.

9th WCCC, Paderborn
Round 7, June 19, 1999
Shredder (W) versus Junior (B)
Ruy Lopez, Worrall Attack (C86)

Fritz, with five of six points, led Shredder, Ferret, and Junior by a half point with one game to go. It seemed on its way to successfully defending its title.

1 e4 e5 2 Nf3 Nc6 3 Bb5 a6 4 Ba4 Nf6 5 O-O Be7 6 Qe2 b5 7 Bb3 d6 8 c3 O-O 9 d4 Bg4 10 Rd1 exd4 11 cxd4 d5 12 e5 Ne4 13 Nc3 Nxc3 14 bxc3 Bf5 15 Bf4 Na5 16 Bc2 Qc8 17 Bg5 Bxg5 18 Nxg5 h6 19 Nf3 Nc4 20 Bb3 Qe6 21 Nh4 Be4 22 f3 Bh7 23 f4 Be4 24 Qf2 Rfb8 25 f5 Qe7 26 Rf1 Qd7 27 f6 g6 28 Rad1 Qg4 29 Nf3 Qf4 30 Rc1 a5 31 Qe1 Qe3+ 32 Rf2

Position after 32 Rf2.

Junior seemed to have a good attack, but it traded away its primary troublemaker here.

32 ... Qxe1+ 33 Rxe1 Ra6 34 Nd2 Nxd2 35 Rxd2 b4 36 cxb4 Rxb4 37 Rc1 a4 38 Bd1 Rc4 39 Rxc4 dxc4 40 Re2 Bd3 41 Rb2 Rb6

Position after 41 ... Rb6.

Junior was about to straighten up its pawns, but the net result was that it gave too much strength to Shredder's advanced pawns.

42 Rxb6 cxb6 43 d5 Be4 44 d6 Bc6 45 Kf2 Bd7 46 Ke3 b5 47 Kd4 Kf8 48 Bf3 Ke8

Position after 48 ... Ke8.

49 Bd5 h5 50 h4 Kf8 51 a3 Ke8 52 Kc3 Kf8 53 Kb4 Kg8 54 Be4 Kf8

Position after 54 ... Kf8.

Junior's roof is about to collapse.

55 e6 fxe6 56 Bxg6 e5 57 Bxh5 e4 58 g4 Bc8 Black resigns.

Position after 58 ... Bc8,
Black resigns.

Fritz now needed to win its final game with Ferret to hold on to its title. A draw would leave it tied with Shredder, and a loss would leave it a half point behind Shredder and Ferret.

9th WCCC, Paderborn
Round 7, June 19, 1999
Ferret (W) versus Fritz (B)
Sicilian, Najdorf (B90)

Fritz's second dose of medicine was about to be delivered by Ferret. The soon-to-be ex-world champion would have to settle for tying for third place, a half point behind Shredder and Ferret.

1 e4 c5 2 Nf3 d6 3 d4 cxd4 4 Nxd4 Nf6 5 Nc3 a6 6 Be3 e5 7 Nb3 Be6 8 f3 Be7 9 Qd2 Nbd7 10 g4 h6 11 h4 b5 12 O-O-O Nb6 13 Be2 b4 14 Nb1 Nfd7 15 Qxb4 d5 16 Qa5 d4 17 Bf2 Qc7 18 f4 Bxb3 19 axb3 Rc8 20 c3 Nc5 21 Kc2 Nxe4

Fritz's pieces were well developed, though it had not yet castled, and that became a problem.

22 Bg1 f6 23 Bd3 Nc5 24 Bg6+ Kf8 25 fxe5 fxe5 26 b4 Ncd7 27 Qa2

A mate threat on f7.

27 ... Qc4 28 Qxc4 Nxc4 29 Kb3 a5 30 Bf5 Ke8 31 bxa5 Nxa5+ 32 Ka2 Nc6 33 cxd4 Nb4+ 34 Kb3 Rb8 35 Nc3 Nd3+ 36 Kc2

Position after 36 Kc2.

36 ... Nxb2 37 Ra1 Nc4 38 Ra7 Rd8 39 Nb5 Nf8 40 Kc3 Nd6 41 Nc7+ Kf7 42 dxe5

Position after 42 dxe5.

Ferret managed to win a pawn and develop a strong attack on Fritz's king.

42 ... Nxf5 43 gxf5 Kg8 44 Bd4 Rh7 45 e6 h5 46 Kc4 Rc8 47 Kd3 Rd8 48 Ke4 g6 49 fxg6 Rxd4+ 50 Kxd4 Rg7 51 Nd5 Nxe6+ 52 Ke5 Bd6+ 53 Kxd6 Black resigns.

Position after 53 Kxd6,
Black resigns.

9th WCCC, Paderborn
Playoff, June 19, 1999
Shredder (W) versus Ferret (B)
English, Four Knights, Kingside Fianchetto (A29)

Shredder and Ferret finished the seven-round competition tied for first place with five and a half points. In this long game, they played to a draw. Shredder was the only entry to finish undefeated.

1 c4 e5 2 Nc3 Nf6 3 Nf3 Nc6 4 g3 d5 5 cxd5 Nxd5 6 Bg2 Nb6 7 O-O Be7 8 d3 O-O 9 a4 a5 10 Be3 Ra6 11 Rc1 Bb4 12 Re1 f6 13 Bd2 Be6 14 Ne4 Nd7 15 Bxb4 axb4 16 e3 Bd5 17 Ned2 Qe7 18 b3 Raa8 19 d4 e4 20 Nh4 f5 21 Bh3 g6 22 Rf1 Qe6 23 Ng2 g5 24 Qh5 Qe7 25 Ne1 Qg7 26 Qe2 Nb6 27 Nc2 Be6 28 Bg2 Na5 29 Na1 Nd5 30 Rfe1 Nc3

Position after 30 ... Nc3.

Neither side had any idea how to proceed; a slugfest loomed.

31 Qf1 c6 32 Rc2 Kh8 33 Nb1 Nxb3 34 Nxc3 bxc3 35 Rxc3 Qf7 36 g4 fxg4 37 Nxb3 Bxb3 38 Bxe4 Rxa4 39 Rc5 Be6 40 Rec1 h6 41 R1c2 Rfa8 42 Rb2 Bc4 43 Qc1 Be6 44 Qf1 Bc4

Position after 44 ... Bc4.

Were they dancing to a draw?

45 Qc1 Ra1 46 Rb1 Rxb1 47 Qxb1 Be6 48 Re5 Rf8 49 Qb2 Qf6 50 Ra5 Kg8 51 Ra7 Bc8 52 Ra8 Qe7 53 Bb1 Be6 54 Ra7 Rb8 55 Bd3 Qc7 56 Qb1 Bf7 57 Be2 Kg7

Position after 57 ... Kg7.

Ferret couldn't hang on to the pawn. Shredder seemed to have the upper hand.

58 Bxg4 Bg6 59 Qb3 Bf7 60 Qb4 Kh8 61 Bf5 Kg8 62 e4 Kg7 63 Qb2 Kg8 64 Qa3 Kg7 65 Qa1 Kg8 66 Qa4 Qd6 67 e5 Qd8 68 e6 Bh5 69 Qc4 Qf6 70 e7+ Kg7 71 Qc5 Be8 72 Bg4 Qf4 73 Bf3 Kf6 74 Be2 Bd7 75 Bh5 Be8 76 Bf3 h5 77 Be2 g4 78 Bd1 h4 79 Qb4 Bd7 80 Ra3 Re8 81 Re3 Kg7 82 Be2 Qf6 83 Bd3 Rb8 84 Re5 b5

85 Bf5 Bxf5 86 e8=N+ Rxe8 87 Rxe8 Bg6 88 Re7+ Kg8 89 Rd7 Be8 90 Qe7 Qg6 91 Rb7 Qb1+ 92 Kg2 h3+ 93 Kg3 Qg1+ 94 Kf4 Qxf2+ 95 Kxg4 Qg2+ 96 Kh4 Qf2+ 97 Kxh3 Qf3+ 98 Kh4 Qf4+ 99 Kh3 Qf3+ 100 Kh4 Qf4+ 101 Kh3 Qf3+ Drawn by repetition.

Position after 101 ... Qf3+,
Drawn by repetition.

While the two drew, Shredder was awarded the title of World Champion, having played tougher opponents.

Position after 84 ...b5.

Shredder now won an exchange, but then allowed Ferret's queen to force a draw!

Suggest Readings

References on Endgame Databases

Ken Thompson, An example of QPvQ. ICCA Journal, Vol. 9, No. 4, pp. 201–204, 1986.

Ken Thompson, Retrograde analysis of certain endgames. ICCA Journal, Vol. 9, No. 3, pp. 131–139, 1986.

Ken Thompson, KQPKQ and KRPKR endings. ICCA Journal, Vol. 13, No. 4, pp. 196–199, 1990.

Ken Thompson, Chess endgames, ICCA Journal, Vol. 14, No. 1, p. 22, 1991.

Ken Thompson, New results for KNPKB and KNPKN endgames. ICCA Journal, Vol. 14, No. 1, p. 17, 1991.

Ken Thompson, 6-Piece endgames. ICCA Journal, Vol. 19, No. 4, pp. 215–226, 1996.

Ken Thompson, 6-Piece endgames. Advances in Computer Chess 8 (eds. H.J. van den Herik and J.W.H.M. Uiterwijk), pp. 9–26. Universiteit Maastricht, Maastricht, The Netherlands, 1997.

Ken Thompson, (1999, 2000) http://cm.bell-labs.com/cm/cs/who/ken/chesseg.html. 6-man EGT maximal positions, maximal mutual zugzwangs and endgame statistics.

Ken Thompson, The longest: KRNKNN in 262. ICGA Journal, Vol. 23, No. 1, pp. 35–36, 2000.

Ken Thompson, (2000) http://cm.bell-labs.com/cm/cs/who/ken/chesseg.html. 6-man EGT maximal positions, maximal mutual zugzwangs and endgame statistics.

Ken Thompson, (2000), 6-Piece database statistics. http://cm.bell-labs.com/who/ken/chesseg.html.

Ken Thompson, (2000), 6-man EGT maximal positions and mutual zugzwangs. http://cm.bell-labs.com/cm/cs/who/ken/chesseg.html.

Ken Thompson, (2001). http://cm.bell-labs.com/cm/cs/who/ken/chesseg.html. 6-man EGTs, maximal positions, maximal mutual zugzwangs and endgame statistics.

Steven J. Edwards, (1994). Endgame databases of optimal play to mate. ftp://chess.onenet.net/pub/chess/TB/... KPK.tbs/tbb/tbw

Steven J. Edwards, Comments on Barth's Article "Combining knowledge and search to yield infallible endgame programs." ICCA Journal, Vol. 18, No. 4, pp. 219–225, December 1995.

Steven J. Edwards and the Editorial Board, An examination of the endgame KBNKN. ICCA Journal, Vol. 18, No. 3, pp. 160–167, September 1995.

Steven J. Edwards, An examination of the endgame KBBKN. ICCA Journal, Vol. 19, No. 1, pp. 24–32, March 1996.

Steven J. Edwards, (1996). Summary: Chess Endgame Tablebase Results Summary. ftp://ftp.onenet.net/pub/chess/TB/Summary.gz. (31 January 1996).

Eugene V. Nalimov, (1999). ftp://ftp.cis.uab.edu/pub/hyatt/TB/tbgen.zip. Source code of the EGT generator.

Eugene V. Nalimov, C. Wirth, and G. McC. Haworth, KQQKQQ and the Kasparov-World Game. ICCA Journal, Vol. 22, No. 4, pp. 195–212, December 1999.

Eugene V. Nalimov, G. Mc Haworth and E. A. Heinz, Space-efficient indexing of chess Endgame tables. ICGA Journal, Vol. 23, No. 3, pp. 148–162, September 2000.

Eugene V. Nalimov, G. Mc Haworth and E. A. Heinz, Space-efficient indexing of endgame tables for chess. Advances in Computer Games 9, (eds. H. J. van den Herik and B. Monien), pp. 93–113. IKAT, Universiteit Maastricht, Maastricht, The Netherlands, 2001.

Opening Book Learning

Michael Buro, Toward opening book learning. ICCA Journal, Vol. 22, No. 2, pp. 98–102, 1999.

Material on the 9th WCCC

Mathias Feist, "The 9th World Computer–Chess Championship," ICGA Journal, Vol. 22, No. 3, pp. 149–159, September 1999.
Website of the 9th WCCC: http://wwwcs.uni-paderborn.de/~wccc99/gindex.html
Ferret versus Shredder, Round 6, 9th WCCC: http://www.chessgames.com/perl/chessgame?gid=1550211
Shredder versus Junior, Round 7, 9th WCCC: http://www.chessgames.com/perl/chessgame?gid=1550206
Ferret versus Fritz, Round 7, 9th WCCC: http://www.chessgames.com/perl/chessgame?gid=1550207
Shredder versus Ferret, Playoff, 9th WCCC: http://www.chessgames.com/perl/chessgame?gid=1550205

Other Reference

Website of all WMCCC from 1980 through 2001: http://old.csvn.nl/wmcchist.html

Jeroen Noomen Discusses Rating Lists

Jeroen Noomen, The revolution of 2005 and the rating lists, ICGA Journal, Vol. 29, No. 4, pp. 227–229, December 2006.

2002: Shredder Bows to Deep Junior at the 10th WCCC

3

The twenty-first century began with Shredder as world champion. Between its coronation at the 9th WCCC in 1999 and its defense of the title at the 10th WCCC in 2002, Shredder and its main rivals battled each other a number of times in various competitions. All were in Europe where computer chess engines and tournaments for them were proliferating. Before considering the 2002 world championship, an examination of these other events is in order.

The Deep Junior team: Shay Bushinsky and Amir Ban.
(Photo courtesy of Shay Bushinsky and Amir Ban)

M. Newborn, *Beyond Deep Blue: Chess in the Stratosphere*,
DOI 10.1007/978-0-85729-341-1_3, © Springer-Verlag London Limited 2011

In Feb. 9–13, 2000, in its first test as world champion, Shredder passed successfully, winning the 9th International Paderborn CCC, with six of seven points. Junior followed with five and a half points. Fritz finished with four points. Junior defeated Fritz; draws resulted when Shredder played Junior and Shredder played Fritz.

Later that year, on August 21–25, the 17th WMCCC took place in the Alexandra Palace in London. Shredder won again, winning seven of nine points. Fritz finished second with six and a half points. Neither engine lost a game during the competition. Junior finished in fifth place with five and a half points.

Shredder continued its domination of the computer chess world when it won the 10th International Paderborn CCC, held Feb 20–25, 2001. It garnered seven and a half of nine points. Fritz finished second with seven points. In head to head play, Shredder and Fritz played to a draw.

The Brain Games Network (BGN) World Qualifier Match between Deep Fritz and Deep Junior took place in Cadaqués, Spain, April 24–May 1, 2001. The winner would play Vladimir Kramnik the following year in Bahrain. Shredder's team declined an invitation to participate. Deep Fritz lost the first five games, and was losing 3.5/8.5 at the end of the first half of the match, but incredibly managed to finish even with Deep Junior at the end of the 24 scheduled games! Fritz won two playoff games and thus the right to play Kramnik. Both engines ran on dual Pentium systems running at 933 MHz. Games were played at regular tournament time controls. (More about the Deep Fritz versus Kramnik match in the next chapter).

The 1st International CSVN Tournament was held in Leiden, Netherlands, May 18–20, 2001. Fritz tied for first with Gambit Tiger. Shredder and Junior didn't participate.

Shredder's winning streak came to an end at the 18th WMCCC, held in Maastricht, August 18–23, 2001. Deep Junior ran off with championship, winning the nine-round event by two points. Shredder and Fritz, who was playing under the name of Quest, finished in a tie for second place. Shredder lost two games, one to Deep Junior and a second to Fritz (Quest). These were Shredder's first defeats in major competitions since the 15th WMCCC in 1997 in Paris. Fritz also defeated the improving Ferret as did Shredder. Deep Junior and Fritz drew.

The 21st Dutch CCC was held in Leiden, Oct 27, 2001–Nov 4, 2001. It was won by Chess Tiger, with Fritz finishing third. Shredder, Junior, and Ferret did not compete.

Shredder returned to the top of the pack when it won the 11th International Paderborn CCC, held February 27, 2002–March 3, 2002. Shredder finished with six wins and one loss. Second was Fritz, who beat Shredder in their head-to-head battle. Even though Shredder won this event, its invincibility had been cracked again.

Fritz won the 2nd International CSVN Computer Chess Tournament held in Leiden, The Netherlands, May 31, 2002–June 2, 2002. It finished with 7.5/9. Shredder finished tied for third with six points. Fritz defeated Shredder in their encounter.

Thus, between the 9th and 10th WCCCs, Shredder, Junior, and Fritz each had their moments in the sun. Shredder finished in first place in all but two of the six tournaments in which it competed. Junior dominated the 18th WMCCC and, except for losses in its match with Fritz, had the distinction of not losing a game to Shredder, Fritz, or Ferret during the time between world championships. Deep Fritz defeated Deep Junior to qualify to play Kramnik, its most significant achievement. It also defeated Shredder in their two most recent games. Leading up to the 10th WCCC, each of the three could claim to be best.

A new force was coming into play along with the new century. Chess engines, over the years had seen great progress in (1) opening books to guide the first ten or so moves, (2) search heuristics to determine moves during the middlegame and early endgame until (3) endgame database found themselves in play. Over the years, there had been great progress in all three.

Six-piece endgame databases had become a part of many chess engines. Eugene Nalimov's software had become the most widely used. Although yielding perfect play when called upon, they were, in practice, not called upon that often. Middlegame search heuristics were clearly improving, helped along by faster processors and parallel systems. For example, Junior became Deep Junior when it was moved to a multiprocessing system for the 2002 championship. Other engines added "Deep" to their names for the same reason.

But it was the increasing relevance of opening books in deciding the outcome of games that became more pronounced in this new century. Reflecting this trend has been the inclusion of the author of each entry's opening book in the ICGA Journal reports on the WCCC beginning with this 2002 event. The table on the next page gives the names along with the primary authors and the hardware used. Opening books developed by one person were sometimes used by more than one chess engine. Shredder's book was developed by the Italian chess expert Sandro Necchi. Deep Junior's book was developed by the Israeli Grandmaster Boris Alterman, Brutus and Quest's books were both developed by the Austrian chess player, Alex Kure.

Shredder, Fritz, Junior, and Ferret's final positions in tournaments between the 1999 and the 2002 WCCCs.

Event	Shredder	Junior	Fritz	Ferret
9th Int. Paderborn, Feb. 9–13, 2000	1	2	5	
17th WMCCC, London, Aug. 21–25, 2000	1	5	2	
10th Int. Paderborn, Feb. 20–25, 2001	1		2	
Brain Games Network Match, Apr. 21 – May 1, 2001		2	1	
1st Int. CSVN CC Tourn., Leiden, May 18–20, 2001			1	
18th World MCCC, Maastricht, Aug. 18–23, 2001	3	1	2	9
21st Dutch CCC, Leiden, Oct. 27–Nov. 4, 2001			3	
11th Int. Paderborn, Feb. 27–Mar. 3, 2002	1		2	
2nd Int. CSVN CC Tourn., Leiden, May 31–Jun. 2, 2002	3	1		

The 10th WCCC was held July 6–11, 2002, on the Universiteit Maastricht campus. Jaap van den Herik, Editor of the ICGA Journal and professor at the university, served as Tournament Director. It is primarily through over 25 years of hard work and dedication to his mission that the journal has become the premier publication in the field of computer games.

Summary of head to head results for Shredder, Fritz, Junior, and Ferret between the 1999 and the 2002 WCCCs (Excluding BGN Match)

Event	Result of leading engines
9th Int. Paderborn	Shredder drew with Junior, Shredder drew with Fritz, Junior defeated Fritz
17th WMCCC	Shredder drew with Fritz, Shredder drew with Junior, Fritz drew with Junior
10th Int. Paderborn	Shredder drew with Fritz
18th WMCCC	Junior drew with Fritz (Quest), Junior defeated Shredder, Fritz (Quest) defeated Shredder, Fritz (Quest) defeated Ferret, Shredder defeated Ferret
11th Int. Paderborn	Fritz defeated Shredder
2nd Int. CSVN CCT	Fritz defeated Shredder

	Junior	Fritz	Shredder	Ferret	Summary (W-D-L)
Junior		2.0	2.0		2-4-0
Fritz	1.0		4.5	1.0	4-5-1
Shredder	1.0	1.5		1.0	1-5-4
Ferret		0.0	0.0		0-0-2

Given that there has been a tendency toward longer games as the engines improved over the years, the rate of play was sped up from the previous rate of the first 40 moves in 2 hours, followed by the next 30 moves in an hour, and then all the remaining moves in 30 minutes to the first 60 moves in 2 hours and then all the remaining moves in 30 minutes. A game was thus limited to, at most, 5 hours in contrast to 7 hours in previous championships. In 2010, the time controls were tightened again to essentially limit games to lasting at most four hours. Of course, speeding up the rate of play results in a decrease in the quality of play. But it also allows the operators to live a bit more normal life, getting to sleep and eating at reasonable hours. Given the tradeoffs, eating and sleeping won out, and the level of play suffered some undetectable amount. However, countering the effect of speeding up the rate of play, the organizers increase the number of round from seven played in 2002 to nine for this event.

Data on the length of games played by the top half of the finishers against each other for each of the 16 world championships is summarized in the table on the following page. The second column gives the number of games played between the finishers in the top half. The third column gives the average length of the games that were won. The fourth column gives the average length of the games that were drawn. The fifth column gives the number of wins and draws. The rightmost column gives the time control rules used at the championship.

The data only considers games played between engines that finished in the top half. Often, many weak engines participated, and the games between them and the better engines obscure the already somewhat obscure data! It does appear that the games are getting longer and that the percentage of drawn games is increasing. The length of drawn games seems to be quite random. In general one might argue the faster moves are made, the fewer moves in the game, as errors in evaluation are more likely to occur. The data doesn't take into account the stubbornness of operators to resign on behalf of their entries, though this factor might not have changed over the years.

At the end of the scheduled nine rounds in Maastricht, Deep Junior and Shredder were tied at seven and a half points apiece. They had met in the fourth round when they were tied for first place with 3.5/4 points; Shredder made short work of Deep Junior, defeating it in 37 moves. Deep Junior caught up with Shredder by winning its fifth and eighth round games while Shredder drew both of its games. The final ninth round saw both Shredder and Deep Junior add a point to their score. Except for Shredder's loss to Deep Junior, neither engine lost a game in the competition.

Deep Junior and Shredder then played a two-game playoff at a rate of 1 hour per player per game. In the first game, Junior with Black dominated play with a brutal kingside attack, forcing a resignation on the 35th move. In the second game, Shredder made vigorous attempts to come through, but Junior defended well, eventually giving Shredder no choice but to play for a draw by threefold-repetition. So Junior became the new World Computer Chess Champion, much to the delight of Ban, Bushinsky, and Alterman!

Data on games played between engines that finished in the top half in world championships

Year	Games	Win length	Draw length	W-D	Time control rules
1974	7	50.1	–	7-0	40/2 h, 10/30 m thereafter
1977	9	45.4	70	8-1	" "
1980	10	48.0	56.5	8-2	" "
1983	18	48.7	61.3	15-3	" "
1986	16	46.9	82.0	15-1	" "
1989	19	53.4	56.6	14-5	40/2 h, 20/1 h thereafter
1992	18	68.0	63.4	11-7	40/2 h, 60/1 h, then adjudication
1995	21	53.4	53.1	13-8	40/2 h, 40/1 h thereafter
1999	33	53.8	54.4	25-10	40/2 h, 30/1 h, all/30 m
2002	28	50.0	62.3	16-12	60/2 h, all/30 m
2003	24	60.0	36.7	21-3	" "
2004	18	62.2	49.9	11-7	" "
2005	15	55.3	59.3	12-3	" "
2006	30	56.8	64.6	16-14	" "
2007	15	74.3	78.6	8-7	" "
2008	9	51.6	70.8	5-5	" "
2009	10	48.5	61.5	4-6	" "
2010	10	69.5	68.5	8-2	All/1.75 h, plus 15 s/move

Data on entries to the 10th WCCC: Name, country of origin, authors, opening book endgame tables, hardware

Name	Origin	Authors	Opening book	Endgame tables	Hardware
Deep Junior	Israel	Amir Ban, Shay Bushinsky	Boris Alterman	Eugene Nalimov	Intel Pentium 4 Dual Core 2.2 GHz/Intel Pentium 3 1 GHz
Shredder	Germany	Stefan Meyer-Kahlen	Sandro Necchi	Eugene Nalimov	AMD Dual Athlon MP 2100
Brutus	Austria	Chrilly Donninger	Alexandre Kure	Eugene Nalimov/Own	AMD Xilinx Virtix FPGA, 1 GHz
Quest	The Netherlands	Frans Morsch, Mathias Feist	Alexandre Kure	Eugene Nalimov	AMD Dual Athlon MP 2000+
Warp	New Zealand	Peter McKenzie	Based on Hudson	None	Intel Pentium 4 1.7 GHz
Diep	The Netherlands	Vincent Diepeveen	Arturo Ochoa	Own	Teras, 60 processors, 500 MHz
Isichess	Germany	Gerd Isenberg	Own book	Own	AMD 2.1 GHz
Ikarus	Germany	Muntsin & Munjong Kolss	Own book	Eugene Nalimov	AMD Athlon 2000+
ParSOS	Germany	Rudolf Huber	Own book	Eugene Nalimov	Intel Pentium 3 Dual Core 1 GHz
Goliath	Germany	Michael Borgstaedt	Erdogan Gunes	Eugene Nalimov	AMD Athlon XP 1500
Chinito	Europe	Eugenio Castillo-Jimenez, Pascal Tang	Own book	None	Intel Pentium 4 1.7 GHz
Sjeng	Belgium	Gian-Carlo Pascutto	Own book	Eugene Nalimov	AMD Athlon XP 1800
XiniX	The Netherlands	Tony Werten	Own book	Eugene Nalimov/Own	AMD Athlon 2000+
Insomniac	USA	James Robertson	Josef Zwinger	Eugene Nalimov	AMD Athlon XP 2100
SpiderChess	The Netherlands	Martin Giepmans	Based on Dann Corbitt	None	AMD Athlon XP 2000
Postmodernist	UK	Andrew Williams	Based on Dann Corbitt	Eugene Nalimov	Intel Pentium 4 1.7 GHz
NoonianChess	USA	Charles Roberson	Based on Robert Hyatt	None	Intel Pentium 4 2 GHz
Sharky	USA	John Kominek	Own book	None	Intel Pentium 3 500 MHz

Final standings of the 10th WCCC; nine rounds and playoffs, Maastricht

#	Name	1	2	3	4	5	6	7	8	9	Pts	BU
1	Shredder	7wW	9bW	3wD	2bW	4wD	12bW	8wW	6bD	11wW	7.5	38.50
2	Deep Junior	8bD	10wW	6bW	1wL	9wW	3bW	4wW	5bW	12wW	7.5	38.25
3	Brutus	11bW	12wW	1bD	4wD	5bW	2wL	7bW	13wW	6bW	7.0	33.75
4	Quest	16wW	14bW	5wD	3bD	1bD	6wD	2bL	7wW	9bW	6.0	28.25
5	Warp	15wW	6wD	4bD	14bW	3wL	7bL	12wW	2wL	13bW	5.0	21.00
6	Diep	18wW	5bD	2wL	7bD	4bD	5wW	9bW	1wD	3wL	5.0	20.50
7	Isichess	1bL	8wD	13bW	6wD	17bW	5wW	3wL	4bL	10wD	4.5	18.00
8	Ikarus	2wD	7bD	15wW	9bD	12wD	13bD	1bL	11wL	17bW	4.5	17.75
9	ParSOS	13wW	1wL	17bW	11wW	2bL	10bW	6wL	18bW	4wL	4.5	12.75
10	Goliath	12bL	2bL	18wW	11wW	6bL	9wL	16bW	17wW	7bD	4.5	11.75
11	Chinito	3wL	15bL	16wW	10bL	18wW	14bD	17wW	8bW	1bL	4.5	11.50
12	Sjeng	10wW	3bL	14wD	15bW	8bD	1wL	5bL	16wW	2bL	4.0	15.25
13	XiniX	9bL	16bD	7wL	18bW	14wW	8wD	15bW	3bL	5wL	4.0	11.25
14	Insomniac	17bW	4wL	12bD	5wL	13bL	11wD	18bW	15bD	16bD	4.0	9.50
15	SpiderChess	5bL	11wW	8bL	12wL	16wD	17bD	13wL	14bD	18wW	3.5	9.00
16	Postmodernist	4bL	13wD	11bL	17wD	15bD	18wW	10wL	12bL	14wD	3.0	6.75
17	NoonianChess	14wL	18bW	9wL	16bD	7wL	15wD	11bL	10bL	8wL	2.0	3.25
18	Sharky	6bL	17wL	10bL	13wL	11bL	16bL	14wL	9wL	15bL	0.0	0.00

#	Name	Playoff 1	Playoff 2	Pts
1	Deep Junior	2bW	1wD	1.5
2	Shredder	1wL	2bD	0.5

10th WCCC, Maastricht
July 8, 2002, Round 4
Deep Junior(W) versus Shredder(B)
Queen's Gambit Declined (D31)

1 d4 Nf6 2 c4 e6 3 Nc3 Bb4 4 f3 d5
5 a3 Be7 6 e4 dxe4 7 fxe4 e5 8 d5
O-O 9 Bd3 Ng4 10 Nf3 Bc5 11 Qe2

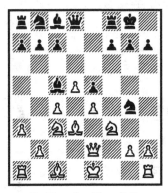

Position after 11 … Qe2.

Deep Junior was insufficiently concerned with its king's exposure. From
this eleventh move on, its king was
under pressure.

11 … Bf2+ 12 Kd2 Bc5 13 h3 Nf2
14 Rf1 Nxd3 15 Kxd3 c6 16 Nxe5
Bd6 17 Ng4 cxd5 18 exd5 f5 19 Nf2
Bd7 20 Be3 Re8 21 Qf3 Na6 22 Bf4
Bxf4 23 Qxf4 b5 24 Kc2 Rc8 25 Nd3
bxc4 26 Ne5 Nc5 27 Nxd7 Qxd7

28 Rad1 Rb8 29 Rb1 a5 30 Qxf5 Qb7
31 d6 Qb3+ 32 Kc1 Qb6 33 b4 cxb3
34 Qd5+ Re6 35 Rd1 b2+ 36 Kc2
Kh8 37 Qc4 Ree8 White resigns.

Position after 37 Ree8,
White resigns.

This win by Shredder left it alone in first
place, a half point ahead of Brutus and
Quest. However, Deep Junior would go
on to win its remaining five games and
wind up tied with Shredder at the end
of regulation play, necessitating a two-
game playoff.

10th WCCC, Maastricht
Playoff Game 1, July 11, 2002
Shredder(W) versus Deep Junior(B)
Queen's Gambit Declined (D10)

1 d4 d5 2 c4 c6 3 Nc3 Nf6 4 e3 e6
5 Nf3 Nbd7 6 Qc2 Bd6 7 Be2 O-O
8 O-O dxc4 9 Bxc4 a6 10 e4 e5
11 Rd1 Qe7 12 d5 Nb6 13 Bd3 cxd5
14 exd5 Bg4 15 Bg5 h6 16 Bxf6
Qxf6 17 Bh7+ Kh8 18 Be4 Qd8
19 h3 Bxf3 20 Bxf3 f5 21 Be2 Qh4
22 a4 e4 23 a5 Nd7 24 Qa4 Rad8
25 Qc2

Deep Junior gradually strengthened its position over the coming moves, giving Shredder little option but to resign when it did.

25 … Rc8 26 Re1 Rc7 27 Qd2 Re8
28 Qc2 Nf6 29 Bf1 e3 30 g3 Qg5
31 Kh2 f4 32 Kh1 f3 33 h4 Qh5
34 Rxe3 Rxe3 35 Kg1 Ng4 White resigns.

Position after 35 … Ng4,
White resigns.

For the second time in the tournament, Deep Junior whipped Shredder.

10th WCCC, Maastricht
Playoff Game 2, July 11, 2002
Deep Junior (W) versus Shredder(B)
Sicilian (B56)

1 e4 c5 2 Nf3 d6 3 d4 cxd4 4 Nxd4
Nf6 5 Nc3 a6 6 f4 e5 7 Nf3 Nbd7 8 a4
Be7 9 Bd3 O-O 10 O-O exf4 11 Kh1
Nh5 12 Nd4 Ndf6 13 Be2 g6 14 Bxh5
Nxh5 15 Nd5 Bf6 16 Bxf4 Nxf4
17 Rxf4 Bg7 18 c3 Be6 19 Nxe6 fxe6
20 Rxf8+ Bxf8 21 Nf4 Qf6 22 Qg4
Re8 23 g3 Bg7 24 Rg1 Qe5 25 Nd3
Qa5 26 Ra1 Qc7 27 Qe2 Qc6 28 Nb4
Qd7 29 Nd3 Rf8

Shredder, needing a win to avoid finishing behind Deep Junior, showed no interest in drawing here, avoiding 29 … Qc6.

Position after 29 … Rf8.

30 Kg2 Bh6 31 Nb4 Kg7 32 Qc4 Be3
33 Rf1 Rxf1 34 Qxf1 Qxa4 35 e5 Qd7
36 Qf6+ Kg8 37 Nd3 d5 38 Kf3 d4
39 Ke2 a5 40 Nc5 Qb5+ 41 Nd3 Qd7
42 Nc5 Qb5+ 43 Nd3 Qd5

Shredder again avoided a draw by repetition of position here as it needed to win this game.

44 c4 Qg2+ 45 Nf2 Qc6 46 Qd8+ Kf7
47 Qf6+ Ke8 48 Qh8+ Kd7 49 Qxh7+
Kc8 50 Qxg6 Qxc4+ 51 Nd3 Qc2+
52 Kf3 Kb8 53 Qe8+ Ka7 54 Qb5
Qd1+ 55 Kg2 Qe2+ 56 Kh3 Qh5+
57 Kg2 Qe2+ 58 Kh3 Qh5+ 59 Kg2
Qe2+ Drawn by repetition.

Position after 59 ... Qe2+,
Drawn by repetition.

Deep Junior forced a draw and thus took the title of World Champion away from Shredder. Unlike previously, the next world championship was scheduled for the following year, and henceforth, world championships would be held every year.

Suggest Readings

Reports on the 9th International Paderborn CCC: http://wwwcs.uni-paderborn.de/~IPCCC/ipccc2000.html

Reports on the 17th WMCCC: Tom King, "Shredder wins the 17th World Microcomputer Chess Chanpionship, ICGA Journal, Vol. 23, No. 3, pp. 165–172, September 2000. http://www.mark-weeks.com/chess/a0wm$tix.htm; http://www.grappa.univ-lille3.fr/icga/tournament.php?id=31

Reports on the 10th International Paderborn CCC: Ulf Lorenz, The 10th International Paderborn Computer-Chess Championship, ICGA Journal, Vol. 24, No. 1, pp. 42–45, March 2001. http://wwwcs.uni-paderborn.de/~IPCCC/ipccc2001.html

Reports on the Brain Games Network Qualifying Match between Deep Fritz and Deep Junior, April 24–May 1, 2001: Jos Uiterwijk (with chess annotations by IGM Karsten Müller), "The BGN World Qualifier Match Deep Fritz vs. Deep Junior," ICGA Journal, Vol. 24, No. 3, pp. 191–192, September 2001. http://www.chessbase.com/events/bgnq/

Reports on the First International CSVN CCC, May 18–20, 2001: Th van der Strom, "Report on the 1st International CSVN Tournament," ICGA Journal, Vol. 24, No. 2, pp. 115–117, June 2001. http://www.csvn.nl/index.php?option=com_content&task=view&id=26&Itemid=49

Website for all Dutch Championships; played yearly since 1981; http://www.csvn.nl/index.php?option=com_content&task=category&sectionid=5&id=24&Itemid=46

Reports on the 11th International Paderborn CCC: Ulf Lorenz, The 11th International Paderborn Computer–Chess Championship, ICGA Journal, Vol. 25, No. 1, p. 50, March 2002. http://wwwcs.uni-paderborn.de/~IPCCC/ipccc2002.html; http://www.chessbase.com/newsdetail.asp?newsid=192

Reports on the Second International CSVN CCC, May 31 – June 2, 2002: Th. Van der Storm, "Results of the 2nd International CSVN Tournament, ICGA Journal, Vol. 25, No. 2, p. 125, June 2002. http://www.csvn.nl/index.php?option=com_content&task=view&id=50&Itemid=49; http://www.computerschaak.nl/; http://www.chessbase.com/newsdetail.asp?newsid=339

Reports on the 10th WCCC: James Robertson, "The 10th World Computer–Chess Championship,"
    ICGA Journal, Vol. 25, No. 3, pp. 170–176, September 2002.
    http://www.grappa.univ-lille3.fr/icga/event.php?id=5
Website for all International CSVN CCC: http://www.csvn.nl/index.php?option=com_content&
    task=category&sectionid=5&id=30&Itemid=49
Website for Italian CCCs, 2001–2002: http://old.csvn.nl/ita_hist.html
Website for 1st Polish CCC, Lodz, September 13–15, 2002: http://old.csvn.nl/pol_hist.html
Website for Spanish CCCs: http://old.csvn.nl/esp_hist.html
Website for French CCCs, 1993-2002: http://old.csvn.nl/fra_hist.html
Website for Hungarian CCCs, 2001, 2002, 2003: http://old.csvn.nl/hun_hist.html
Website for Deep Junior and its history: http://www.robotwisdom.com/ai/deepjunior.html

2002: Deep Fritz Befuddles Kramnik, Drawing 4–4 in Bahrain

It took more than five years to again bring together the human world chess champion and, well, let's say, one of the world's best chess engines. This time the human was Vladimir Kramnik and the engine was Deep Fritz. Their eight-game match took place in Le Royal Meridiene Hotel in Manama, Bahrain, October 4–15, 2002.

Mathias Feist and Vladimir Kramnik before Game 1
(Photo courtesy of chessbase.com)

M. Newborn, *Beyond Deep Blue: Chess in the Stratosphere*,
DOI 10.1007/978-0-85729-341-1_4, © Springer-Verlag London Limited 2011

The host, Emir Sheikh Hamad Bin Issa al-Khaleifa offered a prize of $1 million to Kramnik if he won, $800,000 if he drew, and $600,000 if he lost. The match would be our first opportunity to test whether Deep Blue's 1997 victory was a one-time happening, of dubious legitimacy as some argued, or a real victory.

The Brain Games Network organized the match, initially planning to hold it in October of 2001. However the 9/11 attack in the USA resulted in a postponement. While the planning was in progress, Kramnik defeated Garry Kasparov in the Brain Games Network Match in London, October 2, 2000, through November 2, 2000, winning with a 8.5–6.5 score and giving him the right to be called world champion. He came to Bahrain with a 2807 FIDE rating.

Earlier in 2001, in April, a match between Deep Fritz and Deep Junior was held in Cadequés, Spain, to decide which engine would play Kramnik. Deep Fritz won 14–12. The match started disastrously for Deep Fritz, which lost the first five games before coming back strongly in the last ten games to draw even at 12 games apiece. Deep Fritz then won both games of a two-game playoff. Shredder had declined to participate in the selection procedure. Leading up to the Bahrain match, Fritz adopted the name of Deep Fritz when it was modified to run on multiprocessing systems. During the match, Deep Fritz used eight Pentium 3 processors running at 900 MHz while searching about 3,000,000 positions per second. These figures contrasted with Deep Blue's 200,000,000 positions per second on thirty RS/6000 computers running at 130 MHz. Each RS/6000 computer contained sixteen special-purpose chess processors designed by Hsu; in effect, Deep Blue ran on 480 chess processors. However, Deep Fritz had gone through many more years of refinement of its chess heuristics and many more years of debugging than Deep Blue. This, and the fact that computers had continued to increase in speed, suggested that Deep Fritz might be better in Bahrain than Deep Blue was in New York.

When interviewed by Chessbase before the Bahrain match, Kramnik said he had tested "Fritz on a Notebook with a 600 MHz processor. I let Fritz replay the games of Deep Blue in 1997. It was a great shock! In almost every position Fritz was suggesting objectively better variations. The chess engine is clearly stronger than Deep Blue, whatever the hardware. The developers have done some excellent work in the past years. The special version that will run on eight processors in Bahrain I think will definitely be over 2800 in its Elo performance." In the September issue of the ICCA Journal, the Swedish Rating List assigned a rating of 2763 to Deep Fritz, though Deep Fritz's true rating was probably somewhat higher.

The rules for the match differed from those governing play when Deep Blue defeated Kasparov. The longer eight-game match would yield a more credible result than the six-game match played in New York, although the more games, the more likely fatigue might cut into Kramnik's strength. Games, however, were not played on consecutive days, and that gave Kramnik better conditions than Kasparov had. In New York, Games 2, 4, and 6 were played the day after Games 1, 3, and 5, respectively, and Kasparov scored only a draw in these three games. Games were to be adjourned after 60 moves, thus potentially avoiding extended hours at the board and the consequences of fatigue. During the adjournment, Kramnik was free to use chess engines (Fritz!) to assist him in analysis. As it happened, no game lasted

60 moves. Three drawn games ended before the thirtieth move, and the average length of the eight games was a relatively short 37 moves. The rules also required the Deep Fritz team to freeze the code of their engine in advance of the match and provide Kramnik the engine for practice. Taken together, Kramnik had better conditions than Kasparov had had. Nigel Short, Danny King, Julian Hodgsen, and Mig Greengard were there to provide commentary for the match.

The first game of the match ended in a draw after only 28 moves. Only pawns remained on the board, and though Kramnik had two more than his opponent, there was no way for him to find a way to win. The second and third games were won by Kramnik somewhat routinely. At that point in the match, Deep Fritz seemed finished. Moreover, Kramnik ended a drawn Game 4 with an extra passed a-pawn, only reinforcing his domination of the match. The fifth game saw Kramnik make one of the greatest blunders of his career when he hung a knight! And the sixth game saw Kramnik gamble on a risky attack that Deep Fritz survived. Not only survive, it went on to win the game and equalize the match at three points apiece. The final two games were dull draws, resulting in a tied match.

Vladimir Kramnik versus Deep Fritz, Bahrain 2002: Scorecard

Name	Game 1	Game 2	Game 3	Game 4	Game 5	Game 6	Game 7	Game 8	Total Pts
Deep Fritz	W0.5	B0.5	W0.5	B1.0	W2.0	B3.0	W3.5	B4.0	4.0
V. Kramnik	B0.5	W1.5	B2.5	W3.0	B3.0	W3.0	B3.5	W4.0	4.0

Brains in Bahrain
Game 1, October 4, 2002
Deep Fritz (W) versus Vladimir Kramnik (B)
Ruy Lopez (C67)

---

1 e4 e5 2 Nf3 Nc6 3 Bb5 Nf6 4 O-O Nxe4 5 d4 Nd6 6 Bxc6 dxc6 7 dxe5 Nf5 8 Qxd8+ Kxd8

The queens were gone early. Was this Kramnik's anticomputer strategy? We'll see.

9 Nc3

The game followed moves well booked by both sides up to this point. Perhaps Krammik was using this game to get a feel of his opponent's strength.

9 ... h6

This game was the same as one played between Vishwanathan Anand and Kramnik (June 27, 2001; Mainz Rapid CC Champions Du, Mainz, Ger) up to this point. That game continued 10 h3 Bd7 11 b3 Kc8 12 Bb2 b6 13 Rad1 Ne7 14 Rd2 c5 leading to a 28-move Kramnik victory. Would Deep Fritz do better than Anand?

10 b3 Ke8 11 Bb2 Be7

Evidently designed to take Deep Fritz out of book, which it appeared to do.

12 Rad1 a5 13 a4 h5 14 Ne2 Be6 15 c4 Rd8 16 h3 b6 17 Nfd4 Nxd4 18 Nxd4 c5 19 Nxe6 fxe6 20 Rxd8+ Kxd8 21 Bc1 Kc8 22 Rd1 Rd8 23 Rxd8+ Kxd8 24 g4 g6 25 h4

Deep Fritz guaranteed a draw with this move. A dull game for players of such strength. Kramnik may have been satisfied with this result as he was left playing White in four of the seven remaining games.

25 … hxg4 26 Bg5 Bxg5 27 hxg5 Ke8 28 Kg2 Drawn by agreement.

Position after 25 h4.

Position after 28 Kg2, Drawn by agreement.

Brains in Bahrain
Game 2, October 6, 2002
Vladimir Kramnik (W) versus Deep Fritz (B)
Queen's Gambit Accepted, Classical (D27)

---

1 d4 d5 2 c4 dxc4 3 Nf3 Nf6 4 e3 e6 5 Bxc4 c5 6 O-O a6 7 dxc5 Qxd1

Deep Fritz willingly exchanged queens here at Kramnik's invitation. This is the second game in which queens departed quite early.

8 Rxd1 Bxc5 9 Kf1 b5 10 Be2 Bb7 11 Nbd2 Nbd7 12 Nb3 Bf8

A strange move. Perhaps Deep Fritz was satisfied having queenside castling possibilities.

13 a4 b4 14 Nfd2 Bd5 15 f3 Bd6 16 g3 e5 17 e4 Be6 18 Nc4 Bc7 19 Be3 a5 20 Nc5 Nxc5 21 Bxc5 Nd7 22 Nd6+ Kf8 23 Bf2 Bxd6 24 Rxd6 Ke7 25 Rad1 Rhc8 26 Bb5 Nc5 27 Bc6 Bc4+ 28 Ke1 Nd3+ 29 R1xd3 Bxd3 30 Bc5 Bc4 31 Rd4+ Kf6 32 Rxc4 Rxc6 33 Be7+ Kxe7 34 Rxc6

Position after 34 ... Rxc6.

A real slugfest led to a rook and six pawns endgame in which Kramnik out-maneuvered Deep Fritz.

34 ... Kd7 35 Rc5 f6 36 Kd2 Kd6 37 Rd5+ Kc6 38 Kd3 g6 39 Kc4 g5 40 h3 h6 41 h4 gxh4 42 gxh4 Ra7 43 h5 Ra8 44 Rc5+ Kb6 45 Rb5+ Kc6 46 Rd5 46 ... Kc7 47 Kb5 b3 48 Rd3

48 ... Ra7 49 Rxb3 Rb7+ 50 Kc4 Ra7 51 Rb5 Ra8 52 Kd5 Ra6 53 Rc5+ Kd7 54 b3 Rd6+ 55 Kc4 Rd4+ 56 Kc3 Rd1 57 Rd5+ Black resigns.

Position after 57 Rd5+, Black resigns.

A routine road to victory for Kramnik from here with the rooks gone.

Brains in Bahrain
Game 3, October 8, 2002
Deep Fritz (W) versus Vladimir Kramnik (B)
Opening: Scotch Game (C45)

---

1 e4 e5 2 Nf3 Nc6

The same two moves as in the first game, but Deep Fritz decided to go another direction this time.

3 d4 exd4 4 Nxd4 Bc5 5 Nxc6 Qf6 6 Qd2 dxc6 7 Nc3 Ne7 8 Qf4 Be6 9 Qxf6 gxf6

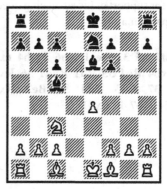

Position after 9 ... gxf6.

For the third time in three games, the queens departed the game at this point evidently much to Kramnik's delight; the engine is equally, though in this case naively, delighted with Kramnik's doubled pawns. Kramnik may have been plotting to castle queenside and use his king to support an eventual queenside pawn push.

10 Na4 Bb4+ 11 c3 Bd6 12 Be3 b6 13 f4 O-O-O 14 Kf2 c5 15 c4 Nc6 16 Nc3 f5 17 e5 Bf8 18 b3 Nb4 19 a3 Nc2 20 Rc1 Nxe3 21 Kxe3 Bg7 22 Nd5 c6 23 Nf6 Bxf6 24 exf6 Rhe8 25 Kf3 Rd2 26 h3 Bd7 27 g3 Re6 28 Rb1 Rxf6 29 Be2 Re6 30 Rhe1 Kc7

Position after 30 ... Kc7.

An innocuous move, but anticipating the need for support of his advancing queenside pawn majority.

31 Bf1 b5 32 Rec1 Kb6 33 b4 cxb4 34 axb4 Re4 35 Rd1 Rxd1 36 Rxd1 Be6 37 Bd3 Rd4 38 Be2 Rxd1 39 c5+ Kb7 40 Bxd1

Position after 40 Bxd1.

Kramnik had an extra pawn and a strategically placed king as the combatants entered a bishop and pawns versus bishop and pawns endgame. Kramnik made it look easy in winning his second straight game.

40 ... a5 41 bxa5 Ka6 42 Ke3 Kxa5 43 Kd4 b4 44 g4 fxg4 45 hxg4 b3 46 Kc3 Ka4 47 Kb2 f6 48 Bf3 Kb5 49 g5 f5 50 Kc3 Kxc5 51 Be2 White resigns.

Position after 51 Be2,
White resigns.

1 d4 d5 2 c4

Kramnik opened as he had done in his victorious Game 2.

2 ... e6 3 Nf3 c5 4 cxd5 exd5 5 g3 Nc6 6 Bg2 Nf6 7 O-O Be7 8 Nc3 O-O 9 Bg5 cxd4 10 Nxd4 h6 11 Bf4 Bg4 12 h3 Be6 13 Rc1 Re8 14 Nxe6 fxe6 15 e4 d4 16 e5 dxc3 17 exf6 Bxf6 18 bxc3 Qxd1 19 Rfxd1

The queens remained on the board a little longer this time.

19 ... Rad8 20 Be3 Rxd1+ 21 Rxd1 Bxc3 22 Rd7 Rb8 23 Bxc6 bxc6 24 Rxa7 Rb2 25 Ra6 Bd2 26 Rxc6 Bxe3 27 fxe3 Kf7

Kramnik had caged Deep Fritz's king, and though there was no way for him to win without a Deep Fritz misplay, the game continued until the 40-move time control passed.

28 a4 Ra2 29 Rc4 Kf6 30 Kf1 g5 31 h4 h5 32 hxg5+ Kxg5 33 Ke1 e5 34 Kf1 Kf5 35 Rh4 Kg6 36 Re4 Kf5 37 Rh4 Kg5 38 Kg1 Kg6 39 g4 hxg4 40 Rxg4+ Kf5 41 Rc4 Drawn by agreement.

Position after 41 Rc4,
Drawn by agreement.

At the halfway point in the match, Kramnik led with a 3–1 score.

1 d4 Nf6 2 c4 e6 3 Nf3 d5 4 Nc3 Be7 5 Bg5 h6 6 Bh4 O-O 7 e3 Ne4 8 Bxe7 Qxe7 9 cxd5 Nxc3 10 bxc3 exd5 11 Qb3 Rd8 12 c4 dxc4 13 Bxc4 Nc6 14 Be2 b6 15 O-O Bb7

16 Rfc1 Rac8 17 Qa4 Na5 18 Rc3 c5 19 Rac1 cxd4 20 Nxd4 Rxc3 21 Rxc3 Rc8 22 Rxc8+ Bxc8 23 h3 g6 24 Bf3 Bd7 25 Qc2 Qc5 26 Qe4 Qc1+ 27 Kh2 Qc7+ 28 g3 Nc4 29 Be2 Ne5 30 Bb5 Bxb5 31 Nxb5 Qc5 32 Nxa7 Qa5 33 Kg2 Qxa2 34 Nc8

Position after 34 Nc8.

One of the greatest blunders of Kramnik's career coming up! With a two-point lead in the match, could he have been subconsciously trying to avoid smashing his opponent? An overwhelming Deep Fritz defeat could potentially put off future lucrative man–machine matches for a decade. Better to keep it close, some thought, was his logic. Some also had the same thought after Kasparov, who won the first game of the Deep Blue versus Kasparov Rematch – his

third straight victory over Deep Blue – erroneously resigned Game 2. One might have thought that Kasparov didn't want to pummel his opponent and kill future opportunities with IBM. But here, Kramnik's move was a simple oversight. He evidently forgot the knight could check. And in New York, Kasparov's last thought was to go easy on his opponent.

34 ... Qc4 35 Ne7+ Black resigns.

Position after 35 Ne7+,
Black resigns.

Brains in Bahrain
Game 6, October 15, 2002
Vladimir Kramnik (W) versus Deep Fritz (B)
Queen's Indian (E15)

---

1 d4 Nf6 2 c4 e6 3 Nf3 b6 4 g3 Ba6 5 b3 Bb4+ 6 Bd2 Be7 7 Bg2 c6 8 Bc3 d5 9 Ne5 Nfd7 10 Nxd7 Nxd7 11 Nd2 O-O 12 O-O Rc8 13 a4 Bf6 14 e4 c5 15 exd5 cxd4 16 Bb4 Re8 17 Ne4 exd5 18 Nd6 dxc4

Kramnik would now sacrifice his knight while going for the jugular. Over the next ten moves, Kramnik checked Deep Fritz eight times, trading off all his attackers, and winding up fighting for

Position after 18 ... dxc4.

his own survival. If Kramnik wasn't sure this would lead to victory, he should have taken another approach. At this point in the match, he held a one-point lead. Ignoring his loss in the previous game due to a careless error, perhaps he felt confident enough to gamble a bit here.

19 Nxf7 Kxf7 20 Bd5+ Kg6 21 Qg4+ Bg5 22 Be4+ Rxe4 23 Qxe4+ Kh6 24 h4 Bf6 25 Bd2+ g5 26 hxg5+ Bxg5 27 Qh4+ Kg6 28 Qe4+ Kg7 29 Bxg5 Qxg5 30 Rfe1 cxb3 31 Qxd4+ Nf6 32 a5 Qd5

Deep Fritz, ahead in material, wanted to trade down, trading queens here. Earlier in the match, it was Kramnik who seemed to prefer to dispose of the queens to avoid tactical complications.

33 Qxd5 Nxd5 34 axb6 axb6 White resigns.

Position after 34 … axb6,
White resigns.

Commentator Mig Greengard felt Kramnik might have given up prematurely and that "this final position is very close to being a draw!!"

Brains in Bahrain
Game 7, October 17, 2002
Deep Fritz (W) versus Vladimir Kramnik (B)
Queen's Indian, Old Main line, 9.Qxc3 (E19)

The match was tied at three points apiece after six rounds.

1 d4 Nf6 2 c4 e6 3 Nf3 b6 4 g3 Bb7 5 Bg2 Be7 6 O-O O-O 7 Nc3 Ne4 8 Qc2 Nxc3 9 Qxc3 c5 10 Rd1 d6 11 b3 Bf6 12 Bb2 Qe7 13 Qc2 Nc6 14 e4 e5 15 d5 Nd4 16 Bxd4 cxd4

Kramnik managed to arrive at a closed position where Deep Fritz's tactical strength could be held at bay. The passed pawn was a thorn in Deep Fritz's side. The

Position after 16 … cxd4.

game lasted another dozen moves, but neither side saw any way to make progress.

**17 Bh3 g6 18 a4 a5 19 Rab1 Ba6
20 Re1**

Deep Fritz saw no way to make any
headway in this closed position.

20...Kh8 21 Kg2

Another directionless move.

**21 ... Bg7 22 Qd3 Rae8 23 Nd2 Bh6
24 f4 Qc7 25 Rf1 Kg8 26 Rbe1 Qd8
27 Kg1 Bb7 28 Re2 Ba6 Drawn by
agreement.**

Kramnik must have felt relieved to draw
this game anticipating playing White in

the final game. The match stood tied at
three and a half points apiece. A tired
Kramnik might make an effort to win
the final game, but he also must have felt
he would be satisfied to leave Bahrain
with an even score.

Position after 28 ... Ba6,
Drawn by agreement.

**Brains in Bahrain
Game 8, October 19, 2002
Vladimir Kramnik (W) versus Deep Fritz (B)
Queen's Gambit Declined, Orthodox Defense, Classical (D68)**

**1 d4 Nf6 2 c4 e6 3 Nf3 d5 4 Nc3 c6
5 Bg5 Be7 6 e3 O-O 7 Bd3 Nbd7
8 O-O dxc4 9 Bxc4 Nd5 10 Bxe7
Qxe7 11 Rc1 Nxc3 12 Rxc3 e5
13 Bb3 exd4**

What engine would refuse to isolate an
opponent's pawn? Kramnik was willing
to go along with Deep Fritz.

**14 exd4 Nf6 15 Re1 Qd6 16 h3 Bf5
17 Rce3 Rae8 18 Re5 Bg6 19 a3 Qd8
20 Rxe8 Nxe8 21 Qd2 Drawn by
agreement.**

Position after 21 Qd2,
Drawn by agreement.

It might be noted that in the first three games, the queens departed early in the game, and Kramnik's score was 2.5–0.5. In the remaining five games, they remained around longer, and Kramnik drew three and lost two.

Kramnik must have been happy the match was over. His result was better than Kasparov's in 1997, but if the match was meant to show that Kasparov's defeat was not legitimate, it failed.

Suggest Readings

Official site at: http://www.braingames.net/event2.php

K. Müller, "The Clash of the Titans: Kramnik – Fritz Bahrain," ICGA Journal Vol. 25, No. 4, pp. 233–238, December, 2002.

Mathias Wüllenweber, "The match from Fritz' view point," ICCA Journal, Vol. 25, No. 4, pp. 239–240, December, 2002.

T. Karlsson, "The Swedish Rating List," ICCA Journal, Vol. 25, No. 3, p. 199, September, 2002.

You will find a list of over 100 articles on the following page: http://www.chessbase.com/newsdetail.asp?newsid=538

Game 1: http://www.chessgames.com/perl/chessgame?gid=1255230; http://www.chess.co.uk/twic/event/brainb02/game2.html

Game 2: http://www.chessgames.com/perl/chessgame?gid=1255231; http://www.chess.co.uk/twic/event/brainb02/game2.html

Game 3: http://www.chessgames.com/perl/chessgame?gid=1255233; http://www.chess.co.uk/twic/event/brainb02/game3.html

Game 4: http://www.chessgames.com/perl/chessgame?gid=1255234; http://www.chess.co.uk/twic/event/brainb02/game4.html

Game 5: http://www.chessgames.com/perl/chessgame?gid=1255235

Game 6: http://www.chessgames.com/perl/chessgame?gid=1255236; http://www.chess.co.uk/twic/event/brainb02/game6.html

Analysis of Game 6 by Mig Greengard. http://www.chessbase.com/images2/2002/bahrain/games/mig6.htm

Game 7: http://www.chessgames.com/perl/chessgame?gid=1255443; http://www.chess.co.uk/twic/event/brainb02/game7.html

Game 8: http://www.chessgames.com/perl/chessgame?gid=1255444; http://www.chess.co.uk/twic/event/brainb02/game8.html

An analysis of the match by German Grandmaster Carsten Mueller: http://www.scribd.com/doc/3579/Mueller-Kramnik-vs-Deep-Fritz-2002

2003: Deep Junior Confounds Kasparov, Drawing 3–3 in New York

5

If Kramnik couldn't restore dignity to the human race in Bahrain, perhaps Kasparov could do it in his match with Deep Junior in New York, scheduled for January 26, 2003–February 7, 2003. Kasparov was approximately 40 rating points stronger than Kramnik, although the latter was now world champion, and the opponent wouldn't be Deep Fritz or Deep Blue, but an even stronger Deep Junior. In spite of Deep Fritz's defeat of Deep Junior to gain the right to play Kramnik, Deep Junior had a stronger record over recent years and held the title of world computer chess champion. Thus the showdown between Kasparov and Deep Junior pitted two even larger giants against each another than did the brawl in Bahrain.

Garry Kasparov and Amir Ban before the start of Game 5.
(Photo courtesy of chessbase.com)

M. Newborn, *Beyond Deep Blue: Chess in the Stratosphere*,
DOI 10.1007/978-0-85729-341-1_5, © Springer-Verlag London Limited 2011

The match, officially named The FIDE Man Versus Machine World Chess Championship, was sponsored by the Federation Internationale des Echecs (FIDE), and X3D Technologies Corporation. It was sanctioned by FIDE, the International Computer Games Association, and the United States Chess Federation. The prize fund for the match was a million dollars, with Kasparov receiving a half million dollars just for appearing. To the victor would go $300,000, $200,000 to the loser. If the match ended in a tie, the $500,000 would be divided equally.

The match took place at the New York Athletic Club located on New York City's prestigious Central Park South. The game room was situated on the twelfth floor while the public watched from a packed 300-seat auditorium two floors lower. FIDE arbiter Geurt Gijssen served as match arbiter. Grandmasters Maurice Ashley and Yasser Seirawan, commentators during the Deep Blue versus Kasparov match in New York, served again in this capacity.

Six games were scheduled, with a day of rest between games except the third and fourth, for which a 2-day rest was scheduled – six games over 13 days. This was better for Kasparov than the shorter match in New York in which Games 1 and 2 were played on consecutive days as were Games 3 and 4, and similarly Games 5 and 6. One day separated Games 2 and 3 and two days separated Games 4 and 5 – thus six games over 9 days. Baseball pitchers need three or four days for their arm to recover from an outing. Thoroughbred horses need a week or so between races. Kasparov's brain needs at least a day. The rate of play for each game was the same as in Kasparov versus Deep Blue matches: each player had to make 40 moves in two hours, then 20 moves in one hour, and then there was a 30 minute sudden death period for each player. A game could last a maximum of seven hours, too long for Kasparov to be at the top of his game throughout. Unlike Kramnik versus Deep Fritz, no adjournments were permitted.

During the match, programmers Amir Ban and Shay Bushinsky ran Deep Junior on a machine with four Intel Xeon 1.9 GHz processors and 3 GB of memory. In the March 2003 issue of the ICGA Journal, the Swedish Rating List assigned a rating of 2687 to a single processor version of Deep Junior running at 1.2 MHz. The chess engine used in this match was likely at least 100 rating points stronger, essentially the same as Kasparov's rating. Ban and Bushinsky, just fair chess players, received help from Grandmaster Boris Alterman on the opening book, which was becoming increasingly important for their engine's success.

Kasparov was accompanied by the same entourage as in his earlier New York match with Deep Blue: Grandmaster Yuri Dokhian, International Master Michael Khodarkovsky, his manager Owen Williams, and his mother Klara Kasparova.

Kasparov had White in the opening game and forced a resignation from Deep Junior on the 27th move. While having a strong position in the second game, he had to settle for a draw by repetition on the 29th move after Deep Junior came up with a dramatic sacrifice. In Game 3 and while playing White, Kasparov built up a strong position but found himself in time trouble and evidently overlooked counterplay by his opponent; he resigned on the 36th move. The match was thus tied at the midpoint. Deep Junior, however, had White in two of the three remaining games, giving

Kasparov a daunting task. Game 4 was the longest of the match lasting 61 moves, 25 more than any other game. Unlike the first three games where Kasparov had good positions, Deep Junior had the upper hand throughout most of the game and Kasparov was quite content with a draw. Game 5 was Kasparov's final chance to win with White, but a dramatic sacrifice by Deep Junior led to a quick 19-move draw. In the final game, Kasparov kept the position quiet and was content with a draw and $750,000 for his efforts.

Garry Kasparov versus Deep Junior, New York, 2003: Scorecard

Name	Game 1	Game 2	Game 3	Game 4	Game 5	Game 6	Total points
G. Kasparov	W1.0	B1.5	W1.5	B2.0	W2.5	B3.0	3.0
Deep Junior	B0.0	W0.5	B1.5	W2.0	B2.5	W3.0	3.0

The FIDE Man vs Machine World Chess Championship
Game 1, January 26, 2003
Garry Kasparov (W) versus Deep Junior (B)
Queen's Gambit Declined, Semi-Slav Defense: Stoltz Variation.
Shabalov Attack (D45)

---

1 d4 d5 2 c4 c6 3 Nc3 Nf6 4 e3 e6
5 Nf3 Nbd7 6 Qc2 Bd6 7 g4

7 ... dxc4 8 Bxc4 b6 9 e4 e5 10 g5 Nh5
11 Be3 O-O 12 O-O-O Qc7 13 d5

According to David Levy, this move was "a secret weapon that Kasparov and his team had developed in Mocsow especially for Deep Junior," reasoning that Deep Junior "would have little or no theory on the line and could be busted." In a game the previous year with Shredder, Shredder preferred to play 7 Be2 and went on to lose to Deep Junior. Kasparov must have felt that he could march Deep Junior down the same line and then challenge his opponent with his aggressive 7 g4, whereupon Deep Junior would have no idea how to proceed.

Position after 13 d5.

Kasparov now struck the first blow, leading to winning an exchange of a knight for rook five moves later.

13 ... b5 14 dxc6 bxc4 15 Nb5 Qxc6 16 Nxd6 Bb7 17 Qc3 Rae8 18 Nxe8 Rxe8 19 Rhe1 Qb5 20 Nd2 Rc8 21 Kb1 Nf8 22 Ka1 Ng6 23 Rc1 Ba6 24 b3 cxb3 25 Qxb3 Ra8 26 Qxb5 Bxb5 27 Rc7 Black resigns.

A beautiful game by Kasparov, giving his supporters confidence in his chances in the coming games. Little did they know that this would be Kasparov's only day in the sun, that opportunities for wins evaporated in some games, and exciting sacrifices by his opponent made life difficult in others.

Position after 27 Rc7,
Black resigns.

The FIDE Man vs Machine World Chess Championship
Game 2, January 28, 2003
Deep Junior (W) versus Garry Kasparov (B)
Sicilian Defense: Kan. Polugaevsky Variation (B42)

---

1 e4 c5 2 Nf3 e6 3 d4 cxd4 4 Nxd4 a6 5 Bd3 Bc5 6 Nb3 Ba7 7 c4 Nc6 8 Nc3 d6 9 O-O Nge7 10 Re1 O-O 11 Be3 e5 12 Nd5 a5 13 Rc1 a4 14 Bxa7 Rxa7 15 Nd2 Nd4 16 Qh5 Ne6 17 Rc3 Nc5 18 Bc2 Nxd5 19 exd5 g6 20 Qh6 f5 21 Ra3 Qf6 22 b4 axb3 23 Rxa7 bxc2 24 Rc1 e4 25 Rxc2 Qa1+

26 Nf1 f4 27 Ra8 e3 28 fxe3 fxe3

Position after 28 ... fxe3.

Everything seemed to be going very well for Kasparov up to this point. Up an exchange, a victory in the previous game, and now closing in for the kill in this game.

29 Qxf8+

A stunning sacrifice by Deep Junior that quickly led to a draw. Of course, any other move would have given Kasparov an easy victory.

29 ... Kxf8 30 Rxc8+ Kf7 Drawn by agreement.

Position after 30 ... Kf7,
Drawn by agreement.

The FIDE Man vs Machine World Chess Championship
Game 3, January 30, 2003
Garry Kasparov (W) versus Deep Junior (B)
Queen's Gambit Declined, Semi-Slav Defense: Stoltz Variation (D45)

---

1 d4 d5 2 c4 c6 3 Nc3 Nf6 4 e3 e6 5 Nf3 Nbd7 6 Qc2

This game was the same as Game 1 to this point where Deep Junior played 6 ... Bd6 and was faced with Kasparov's nasty 7 g4. This alternate move was intended to avoid this.

6 ... b6 7 cxd5 exd5 8 Bd3 Be7 9 Bd2 O-O 10 g4

Position after 10 g4.

The same provocative move by Kasparov from Game 1, initiating an attack on Black's king that all but the world's best players would have succumbed to. An exciting blood bath followed that left Kasparov short of material and time to polish off his opponent. If one can program a computer to be suspicious of gifts, here was a good test case! And equally, if one can warn humans that computers defend especially well, here was a good case, too!

10 ... Nxg4 11 Rg1 Ndf6 12 h3 Nh6 13 e4 dxe4 14 Bxh6 exd3 15 Rxg7+ Kh8 16 Qxd3 Rg8 17 Rxg8+ Nxg8 18 Bf4 f6

The storm finally came to a lull. Deep Junior had recovered its balance and had survived Kasparov's onslaught on its king fairly well.

19 O-O-O Bd6 20 Qe3 Bxf4 21 Qxf4 Bxh3 22 Rg1 Qb8 23 Qe3 Qd6 24 Nh4 Be6 25 Rh1 Rd8 26 Ng6+

Kg7 27 Nf4 27…Bf5 28 Nce2 Ne7 29 Ng3 Kh8 30 Nxf5 Nxf5 31 Qe4 Qd7

Position after 31 … Qd7.

Kasparov was in time trouble here. He must have considered the possibility of simply forcing a draw with 32 Ng6+ Kg7 33 Nf4 Kg8, but concluded that the line he played could do no worse.

32 Rh5 Nxd4 33 Ng6+ Kg8 34 Ne7+ Kf8

Position after 34 … Kf8.

It may be that Kasparov, when he played 32 Rh5, expected to reach this position, and that he then planned to continue with 35 Rxh7, overlooking 35 … Nb3+ 36 Kc2 Na1+ and eventually mate. The alternative that he chose led to an exchange of material that gave Deep Junior's passed h-pawn too big of a problem for Kasparov to handle.

35 Nd5 Qg7 36 Qxd4 Rxd5 White resigns.

Position after 36 … Rxd5,
White resigns.

At the halfway point, the match stood tied at 1.5–1.5 points. Kasparov won Game 1, seemed to have the better of it in Games 2 and 3, and could have won all three games! But – the match was dead even with three games to go and Deep Junior having White in two of them. Deep Junior had managed to overcome powerful Kasparov attacks in the last two games, drawing one and turning the tables in the other. Kasparov must have been quite frustrated at this point. For Deep Junior, it was all "ho-hum."

The FIDE Man vs Machine World Chess Championship
Game 4, February 2, 2003
Deep Junior (White) versus Garry Kasparov (Black)
Sicilian Defense: Paulsen. Szen Variation (B44)

---

1 e4 c5 2 Nf3 Nc6 3 d4 cxd4 4 Nxd4
e6 5 Nb5 d6 6 c4 Nf6 7 N1c3 a6
8 Na3 Nd7 9 Nc2 Be7 10 Be2 b6
11 O-O Bb7 12 h3 O-O 13 Be3 Rc8
14 Qd2 Nce5 15 b3 Nf6 16 f3 Qc7
17 Rac1 Rfe8 18 a3 Ned7 19 Rfd1
Qb8 20 Bf2 Rcd8 21 b4 Ba8 22 a4
Rc8 23 Rb1 Qc7

Position after 32 … Nc6.

Lots of Muhammad Ali's "rub-a-dub" by the knights. Deep Junior had managed to advance a pawn to the sixth rank and annoy the life out of Kasparov. It had two strong bishops. Kasparov's dance to this point was motivated by avoiding confrontations and waiting for a position to arise that Deep Junior wouldn't understand. Such positions are becoming harder to set up by the top players, and this game was no exception.

33 Nxc6 Rxc6 34 Kg1 h6 35 Qa3 Rdc8

Kasparov found himself in time trouble at this point and had to play quickly until completing his fortieth move.

36 Bg3 Bf8 37 Qc3 Ne5 38 c5 Nd7 39 Qxa5 Nxc5 40 Nxc5 Rxc5 41 Qa4 R5c6 42 Bf2 d5

Position after 23 … Qc7.

Kasparov kept his cards well covered! No daring attacks. No sacrifices. A completely different game than any of the first three. Meanwhile, Deep Junior slowly expanded its frontier and was now ready to challenge its opponent.

24 a5 bxa5 25 b5 Bb7 26 b6 Qb8 27 Ne3 Nc5 28 Qa2 Nfd7 29 Na4 Ne5 30 Nc2 Ncd7 31 Nd4 Red8 32 Kh1 Nc6

Position after 42 … d5.

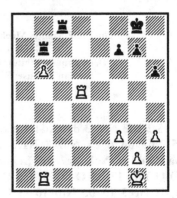

Position after 49 Rxd5.

An offering to gain space for his pieces. It was all but a sure thing that Deep Junior would bite. Material would now fly from the board with Deep Junior maintaining the upper hand, though unable to come up with a way to lower the boom.

43 Bxa6 Bc5 44 Bxc5 Rxc5 45 Bxb7 Qxb7 46 exd5 exd5

Kasparov could expect to do no better than draw from this point on.

49 … Rc6 50 Rdb5 h5 51 Kf2 Re6 52 f4 g6 53 Kg3 Kg7 54 Kh4 Kh6 55 R1b4 Rd6 56 g3 f6 57 g4 hxg4 58 hxg4 Kg7 59 Rb3 Rc6 60 g5 f5 61 Rb1 Drawn by agreement.

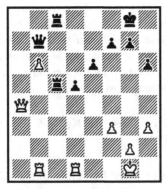

Position after 45 … Qxb7.

Deep Junior must have liked these trades, leaving it with a passed b-pawn.

47 Qa7 R5c7 48 Qxb7 Rxb7 49 Rxd5

Position after 61 Rb1,
Drawn by agreement.

Unlike Games 2 and 3, Kasparov must have gone home content with a draw. With two games to go, the outcome of the match looked like a standoff between the two superstars.

The FIDE Man vs Machine World Chess Championship
Game 5, February 5, 2003
Garry Kasparov (W) versus Deep Junior (B)
Nimzo-Indian Defense: Normal Variation. Bishop Attack Classical Defense (E48)

---

1 d4 Nf6 2 c4 e6 3 Nc3 Bb4 4 e3 O-O 5 Bd3 d5 6 cxd5 exd5 7 Ne2 Re8 8 O-O Bd6 9 a3 c6 10 Qc2

Position after 10 Qc2.

Brace yourself! Deep Junior sacrifices a bishop for a highly speculative attack.

10 ... Bxh2+ 11 Kxh2 Ng4+ 12 Kg3 Qg5 13 f4 Qh5 14 Bd2 Qh2+ 15 Kf3

Qh4 16 Bxh7+ Kh8 17 Ng3 Nh2+ 18 Kf2 Ng4+ 19 Kf3 Nh2+ Drawn by agreement.

Position after 19 ... Nh2+,
Drawn by agreement.

Kasparov had little choice here but to play for a draw by repetition. Deep Junior, unable to capitalize on its sacrifice, was delighted to draw the game and thus play the final game with an even score and the white pieces.

The FIDE Man vs Machine World Chess Championship
Game 6, February 7, 2003
Deep Junior (W) versus Garry Kasparov (B)
Sicilian Defense: Najdorf. Opocensky Variation Traditional Line (B92)

In New York, Kasparov entered the final game against Deep Blue with the score tied and playing Black. He gambled on winning in dramatic fashion, but was unable to do so. He took a very conservative approach this time,

not any different than Kramnik had in Bahrain. In the three games that Kasparov played with Black (Games 2, 4, and this one), he chose the Sicilian Defense, his favorite. Against Deep Blue, he played a Sicilian Defense in

Game 2, lost it, and then avoided it in Games 4 and 6.

1 e4 c5 2 Nf3 d6 3 d4 cxd4 4 Nxd4 Nf6 5 Nc3 a6 6 Be2 e5 7 Nb3 Be7 8 O-O O-O 9 Kh1 Bd7 10 Be3 Bc6 11 Bf3 Nbd7 12 a4 b6 13 Qd3 Bb7 14 h3 Rc8 15 Rad1 h6 16 Rfe1 Qc7 17 g3 Rfd8 18 Kh2 Re8 19 Re2

Position after 19 Re2.

Kasparov had avoided riling up his opponent thus far in a quiet, dreary encounter. In another nine moves, the game and the match would be over.

19 … Qc4 20 Qxc4 Rxc4 21 Nd2 Rc7 22 Bg2 Rec8 23 Nb3

Position after 23 Nb3.

23 … Rxc3

After managing to play a quiet game and after a good 15 minutes think, Kasparov took what would turn out to be one last swing at his opponent with this move, much to the delight of his supporters. But they were all taken aback when he then offered a draw. The Deep Junior team declined, but then made their own offer several moves later, and Kasparov quickly accepted.

24 bxc3 Bxe4 25 Bc1 Bxg2 26 Kxg2 Rxc3 27 Ba3 Ne8 28 f4 Drawn by agreement.

Position after 28 f4,
Drawn by agreement.

The commentators felt Kasparov was winning in the final position and wondered why he didn't choose to play on. But Kasparov was probably more concerned about the need to play perfect chess if he had any chance to win, and that the smallest error could cost him the match. He had made a number of mistakes in previous games that the machine took advantage of, and there was a good chance the same could happen here. Kasparov said it was "more important not to lose than it was to win." And that, along with Kramnik's standoff several months earlier and Kasparov's loss to Deep Blue in 1997, marks the third straight failure by the world's strongest humans to topple their silicon opponents. Time was not on the side of the human race.

Suggest Readings

David Levy, The state of the art in Man vs. "Machine" chess, ICGA Journal, Vol. 26, No. 1, pp. 3–8, March 2003.

K. Müller, Man equals machine in chess, ICGA Journal, Vol. 26, No. 1, pp. 9–13, March 2003.

Game 1: http://www.chessgames.com/perl/chessgame?gid=1260051; http://www.chessbase.com/columns/column.asp?pid=159

Game 2: http://www.chessgames.com/perl/chessgame?gid=1260055; http://chessbase.com/newsdetail.asp?newsid=762

Game 3: http://www.chessgames.com/perl/chessgame?gid=1260058; http://chessbase.com/newsdetail.asp?newsid=766

Game 4: http://www.chessgames.com/perl/chessgame?gid=1260271; http://chessbase.com/newsdetail.asp?newsid=771

Game 5: http://www.chessgames.com/perl/chessgame?gid=1260279; http://chessbase.com/newsdetail.asp?newsid=777

Game 6: http://www.chessgames.com/perl/chessgame?gid=1260286; http://chessbase.com/newsdetail.asp?newsid=782

Post-match interview with Garry Kasparov: http://www.youtube.com/watch?v=WWYaLg21Dss&feature=related

2003: Shredder, the Comeback Kid, Comes Back at 11th WCCC

The 11th World Computer Chess Championship took place in Graz, Austria, November 21, 2003–November 30, 2003. A beautiful exhibition hall called the Dome in the Mountain, located in the Schlossberg, a castle hill in the center of Graz, was the site of the games. For the first time the event was organized by the newly formed International Computer Games Association (ICGA), which the former ICCA had evolved into as a result of the growing links between programmers of different games. It was also the first time that a world computer chess championship was held one year after the previous one, rather than after a 3-year interval, a new practice that would continue. And, it was also the first time that the championship was coupled up with the Computer Olympiad, David Levy's creation intended to parallel the Olympic Games, but for computers.

Participating in Graz were all the major engines. Deep Junior was there to defend its title. Shredder, the titleholder from 1999 to 2002, and Deep Fritz, the winner in 1995, were there to attempt comebacks. Shredder had finished even with Deep Junior after the nine scheduled rounds at the previous world championship, settling for runner-up when Deep Junior scored 1.5–0.5 points in their two-game playoff. Shredder stood at the top of the Swedish Rating List with a 2810 rating. This marked the first world championship held with an entry rated over 2800. Deep Fritz was rated at 2762 and still riding high from its late 2002 4–4 drawn match with Kramnik. Not alone being world champion, Deep Junior had held Kasparov to a 3–3 draw in their early 2003 match. All in all, Deep Junior had to be considered the favorite here. These three engines were playing at the level of the world's best humans.

Deep Fritz and Deep Junior ran on quad Xeon 2.8 GHz processors, and Shredder on a dual Xeon 3.06 GHz processor. The local favorite, Brutus, was designed by Chrilly Donninger around a field programmable gate array (FPGA), eight of which were used, (two per computer) during the tournament. Diep ran on a 512 processor SGI supercomputer. Deep Sjeng ran on a dual AMD Opteron 242 processor at 1.6 GHz. The computers were getting more powerful!

A major upset shook up the tournament in the very first round when Ruy Lopez, who wound up finishing in last place, upset the defending champion. Deep Junior was doing well until its bishop got pinned in the middle of the board and the engine was unable to find a way to save it and the game. Deep Junior fought fiercely for the

M. Newborn, *Beyond Deep Blue: Chess in the Stratosphere*,
DOI 10.1007/978-0-85729-341-1_6, © Springer-Verlag London Limited 2011

remainder of the competition, winning eight of ten points but finishing in third place behind Shredder and Deep Fritz. Both finished with impressive scores of 9.5/11 points. Just as in the previous year, and even though 11 rounds were played, a two-game playoff was necessary to obtain a clear winner However, unlike last year when Shredder lost to Junior, Shredder came out on top this time, defeating Deep Fritz, 1.5–0.5. This was in fact the fourth world championship in a row where a playoff was necessary to determine a champion. In 1995, Fritz defeated Star Socrates in a one-game playoff; in 1999, Shredder defeated Ferret. The number of games played at these four championships increased from 5 at the 1995 championship to 7 in 1999, to 9 in 2002, and to 11 in the 2003 championship. Coincidently, a tie for first place didn't happen again at the world championship for 2004 through 2010.

Shredder had good fortune in the final round. In its game with Jonny, Shredder had the game wrapped up when a programming bug allowed a position to repeat three times. On the move at that point, Jonny announced the repetition, but its operator evidently didn't notice the declaration and simply played the move output by the engine. The tournament director ruled that the move took preference over the declaration, and the game continued. Shredder avoided repeating the position again and went on to win the game. This is one more example of an obvious bug affecting the outcome of a game, and, in this case, the world championship.

Whether Shredder was the best engine is not clear. In head to head competition among the top four finishers – excluding the two-game playoff – Deep Junior earned two points, Shredder and Deep Fritz each one and a half points, and Brutus one point. Including the playoffs, Junior still had the best percentage, 66.6%, versus Shredder's 62.5%, Deep Fritz's 50%, and Brutus's 33.3%. If Deep Junior hadn't been upset by Ruy Lopez, it would have won the tournament and kept the title. And if Jonny's operator had declared a draw, Deep Fritz would have regained the title it had lost the previous year to Deep Junior. Nevertheless, Shredder was back on top – on top of two engines that had stood even with the world's best humans only months earlier.

Data on entries to the 11th WCCC: Name, origin, authors, opening book

Name	Origin	Authors	Opening book
Shredder	DEU	Stefan Meyer-Kahlen	Sandro Necchi
Deep Fritz	NLD	Frans Morsch and Mathias Feist	Alexander Kure
Deep Junior	ISL	Amir Ban, Shay Bushinsky	Boris Alterman
Brutus	AUT	Chrilly Donninger	Alexander Kure
Green Light	GBR	Tim Foden	Own book
Diep	NLD	Vincent Diepeveen	Arturo Ochoa
Chinito	EUR	Eugenio Castillo Jimenez and Pascal Tang	Own book
ParSOS	DEU	Rudolf Huber	Own book
Quark	DEU	Thomas Mayer	Leo Dijksman
Falcon	ISL	Omid David Tabibi	Own book
Deep Sjeng	BEL	Gian-Carlo Pascutto	Jeroen Noomen
Jonny	DEU	Johannes Zwanzger	Own book
Nexus	DEU	Ralf Dorr	Own book
Hossa	AUT	Steffen Jacob	Own book
Ruy Lopez	ESP	Jose Manuel Moran and Alvaro Begue	Own book
List	DEU	Fritz Reul	

Final standings of the 11th WCCC; 11 rounds and playoffs, Graz.

#	Name	1	2	3	4	5	6	7	8	9	10	11	Points	BU
1	Shredder	16bW	6wW	2bL	5wW	4wW	10bW	3bD	7wW	9wW	8bW	12wW	9.5	67.0
2	Deep Fritz	10wW	11bW	1wW	4bL	3bD	6wW	5bW	16wW	13bW	7wW	8wW	9.5	66.5
3	Deep Junior	15wL	8bW	16wW	11bW	2wD	4bW	1wD	9bW	5bW	6wW	7bW	9.0	65.5
4	Brutus	5bW	15wW	12bW	2wW	1bL	3wL	16bD	6wW	10bW	13wW	9bW	8.5	63.0
5	Green Light	4wL	7wW	15bW	1bL	10wW	16bD	2wL	11bW	3wL	12bD	14wW	6.0	63.0
6	Diep	9wW	1bL	10wD	15bW	11wD	2bL	14wW	4bL	12wW	3bL	13wW	6.0	60.5
7	Chinito	12wL	5bL	8wW	9bW	16wL	15bW	11wW	1bL	14wW	2bL	3wL	5.0	61.0
8	ParSOS	13bD	3wL	7bL	14wW	12bL	9bD	10wW	15bW	11wW	1wL	2bL	5.0	57.0
9	Quark	6bL	16bW	14bW	7wL	13bW	8wD	12bW	3wL	1bL	11bW	4wL	4.5	62.5
10	Falcon	2bL	14bW	6bD	12wW	5bL	1wL	8bL	13wL	4wL	15bW	xxW	4.5	61.0
11	Deep Sjeng	14bW	2wL	13bW	3wL	6bD	12wW	7bL	5wL	8bL	9wL	15wW	4.5	56.0
12	Jonny	7bW	13bW	4wL	10bL	8wW	11bL	9wL	14bW	6bL	5wD	1bL	4.0	58.5
13	Nexus	8wD	12wL	11wL	16bD	9wL	14bD	15wW	10bW	2wL	4bL	6bL	3.5	55.0
14	Hossa	11wL	10wL	9wL	8bL	15wW	13wD	6bL	12wL	7bL	xxW	5bL	2.5	49.5
15	Ruy Lopez	3bW	4bL	5wL	6wL	14bL	7wL	13bL	8wL	xxW	10wL	11bL	2.0	59.0
16	List	Disq	Disq	Disq	Disq	Disq	Disq	Disq	Disq	Disq	Disq	Disq	–	–

#	Name	Playoff 1	Playoff 2	Points
1	Shredder	2wD	1bW	1.5
2	Deep Fritz	1bD	2wL	0.5

Notes: (1) Disq = Disqualified, (2) xxW = Won as a result of a "bye"

11th WCCC, Graz
Round 1, November 22, 2003
Deep Junior (W) versus Ruy Lopez (B)
Ruy Lopez Closed (C96)

This game marked the beginning of Deep Junior's problems in this championship. In the very first round, the world champion lost a game to a weak engine, in fact, the weakest of all. Ruy Lopez didn't defeat another engine in the remaining ten rounds or even draw with one! Sorta cute that Ruy Lopez defeated Deep Junior playing the Ruy Lopez.

1 e4 e5 2 Nf3 Nc6 3 Bb5 a6 4 Ba4 Nf6 5 O-O Be7 6 Re1 b5 7 Bb3 d6 8 c3 O-O 9 h3 Na5 10 Bc2 c5 11 d4 cxd4 12 cxd4 Bb7 13 Nbd2 exd4 14 Nxd4 Re8 15 b4 Nc6 16 Nxc6 Bxc6 17 Nf3 d5 18 e5 Ne4 19 a3 a5 20 Rb1 axb4 21 axb4 Qb6 22 Be3 Qc7 23 Qd4 Ra3 24 Ra1 Rea8 25 Rxa3 Rxa3 26 Qb2 Ra6 27 Rc1 h6 28 Qb3 Qb7 29 Nd4 Bd7 30 f3 Ng5 31 Qd3 Bxb4 32 h4 Ra3 33 Nb3 Ne6 34 Qh7+ Kf8 35 Nd4 Nxd4 36 Bxd4 Qc7 37 e6 Bxe6 38 Bxg7+ Ke7 39 Bxh6

It was about here that the tide turned against the world champion. Deep Junior's kingside attack led nowhere. Its bishop on c2 was under pressure over the coming moves, eventually falling on the 54th move. This left Ruy Lopez up a full bishop. When a passed b-pawn started to run, Deep Junior said "uncle."

39 ... Bc5+ 40 Kh1 Be3 41 Re1 Bxh6 42 Qxh6 Qg3 43 Qd2 Qxh4+ 44 Kg1 Ra2 45 Rc1 Qc4 46 Kh1 Kd7 47 f4 Bg4 48 f5 Be2 49 f6 Kd6 50 Kh2 Kc7 51 Kg3 Kb7 52 Qg5 Qc3+ 53 Kh2 Qc7+ 54 Kh1 Rxc2 55 Qxd5+ Kb6 56 Qd4+ Rc5 57 Re1 Bc4 58 Kg1 Bd5 59 Rc1 Qd6 60 Qe3 Bb7 61 Rf1 Qd5 62 Qf2 b4 White resigns.

Position after 62 ... b4,
White resigns.

Position after 39 Bxh6.

Deep Fritz handed Shredder its only loss of the tournament in this game.

1 Nf3 c5 2 g3 Nf6 3 c4 e6 4 Nc3 d5 5 cxd5 Nxd5 6 Bg2 Nc6 7 O-O Be7 8 d4 O-O 9 e4 Nxc3 10 bxc3 b6 11 d5 exd5 12 exd5 Na5 13 Re1 Bf6 14 Ne5 a6 15 Bf4 Ra7 16 Nc6 Nxc6 17 dxc6 Qxd1 18 Raxd1 Bg4 19 Rd3 g5 20 Bd6 Rd8 21 Ree3 c4 22 Rd5 Be6 23 c7

It may be hard to believe, but this pawn remained on c7 until move 49!

23 ... Rc8 24 Rd2 b5 25 Bd5 Bg4 26 a4 bxa4 27 Re4 Bd7 28 Rxc4 h6 29 h4 a5 30 f4 g4 31 f5 h5 32 Kf2 a3 33 Be4 Bb5 34 Rc5 Bd7 35 Ke3

Position after 35 Ke3.

Deep Fritz's king became an aggressor and led his pieces to victory in an exciting endgame.

35 ... a4 36 Kd3 Ra6 37 Bf4 Rb6 38 Kc4 Be8 39 Bg5 Kg7 40 Ra2 Rb3 41 Bxf6+ Kxf6 42 Kd5 Rb6 43 Rxa3 Ke7 44 f6+ Kxf6 45 Kd4 Bd7 46 Rxh5 Rd6+ 47 Rd5 Ke7 48 c4 Rxc7 49 Rxd6 Kxd6 50 Bd5 Ke7 51 c5 Bb5 52 Re3+ Kf6 53 Rc3 Ra7 54 c6 a3 55 Rc2 Ke7 56 Rf2 f6 57 Kc5 Bd3 58 Kb6 Ra6+ 59 Kb7 Ra5 60 c7

For the second time in this game, a pawn on c7 became a persistent feature, this time, until the game ended.

60 ... Ba6+ 61 Kc6 Bc8 62 Re2+ Kf8 63 Bc4 Ra4 64 Rc2 f5 65 h5 Kg7 66 Kc5 Ra7 67 Kd6 Ra4 68 Ke7 Ra5 69 Ba2 Re5+ 70 Kd8 Bb7 71 Rd2 Kf8 72 h6 Re8+ 73 Kd7 Re7+ 74 Kd6 Rh7 75 Rh2 Bc8 76 Ke5 Ke7 77 Bg8 Rh8 78 h7 Kd7 79 Rc2 Ke7 80 Ra2 Black resigns.

Position after 80 Ra2,
Black resigns.

With this victory, Deep Fritz and Brutus led the field each with three victories.

11th WCCC, Graz
Round 4, November 24, 2003
Brutus (W) versus Deep Fritz (B)
Ruy Lopez Closed (C92)

After three rounds, only Deep Fritz and Brutus remained undefeated. They were paired in this round. And lo and behold, Deep Fritz, which had delivered Shredder's only loss of the tournament in the previous round, lost its only game of the tournament here. Brutus consequently found itself leading the pack by a half point.

1 e4 e5 2 Nf3 Nc6 3 Bb5 a6 4 Ba4 Nf6 5 O-O Be7 6 Re1 b5 7 Bb3 d6 8 c3 O-O 9 h3 Bb7 10 d4 Re8 11 Nbd2 Bf8 12 a4 Na5 13 Bc2 c5 14 d5 c4 15 b4 cxb3 16 Nxb3 Nxb3 17 Bxb3 Nd7 18 c4 bxc4 19 Bxc4 Qc7 20 Nd2 Be7 21 Ba3 Nc5 22 Be2 Bg5 23 Rc1 Bc8 24 Rc4 Qa5 25 Nf3 Bd8 26 Bb4 Qc7 27 Qc2 Bd7 28 Bxc5 dxc5 29 Rxc5 Qd6 30 a5 Be7 31 Rc3 Bd8 32 Ra1 Rb8 33 Nd2 Qh6 34 Nc4 Qf6 35 Rf3 Qe7 36 d6

Position after 36 d6.

Brutus's advanced d-pawn cramped Fritz's game to the point where the former soon gained a winning position.

36 ... Qf8 37 Rd3 Rb5 38 Rdd1 Rb8 39 Ne3 Rc8 40 Qb3 Rc5 41 Qb7 Be6 42 Bxa6 Bxa5 43 Qa7 Bb4 44 Ra4 Rc6 45 Rxb4

Brutus won a minor piece and coasted to victory from here.

45 ... Ra8 46 d7 Rc1 47 Qb6 Rxd1+ 48 Nxd1 Bxd7 49 Bc4 Rc8 50 Ne3 h6 51 Bd5 Kh7 52 Rb1 f6 53 Qa7 Rd8 54 Rb7 Ra8 55 Qb6 Rd8 56 Rc7 Qh8 57 Qa7 Bc8 58 Bb3 Rf8 59 Qb6 Rd8 60 Qxf6 Qf8 61 Rf7 Qg8 62 Nf5 Bxf5 63 exf5 Black resigns.

Position after 63 exf5,
Black resigns.

Here was Deep Fritz, having just knocked off Shredder, giving up against Brutus, who was on its way up in the world of chess engines, with this marking its first victory of major significance.

11th WCCC, Graz
Round 5, November 25, 2003
Deep Junior (W) versus Deep Fritz (B)
Sicilian Closed (B23)

1 e4 c5 2 Nc3 Nc6 3 Nf3 e5 4 Bc4 d6 5 d3 Be7 6 Nd2 Bg5 7 h4 Bxd2+ 8 Bxd2 Nf6 9 O-O O-O 10 f4 Bg4 11 Qe1 Be6 12 f5 Bxc4 13 dxc4 h6 14 Nd5 Nb4 15 Nxf6+ Qxf6 16 Bxb4 cxb4

Position after 16 ... cxb4.

All the minor pieces were gone, and only queens, rooks, and eight pawns remained per side .

17 Rd1 Rac8 18 b3 a5 19 Rf3 b5 20 cxb5 Rxc2 21 Rfd3 Rd8 22 R1d2 Rxd2 23 Rxd2 Rc8 24 g3 Qd8 25 Qf2

25 ... Rc1+ 26 Kh2 Qb8 27 Rd5 Qc7 28 Kh3 Rh1+ 29 Kg4 g6 30 fxg6 fxg6 31 Rd2 Qd7+ 32 Kf3 h5 33 b6 Rc1 34 Kg2 Qc6 35 Kh2 Kg7 36 b7 Qxb7 37 Rxd6 Qf7 38 Qb2 Rc3 39 Qd2 Rf3 40 Kg2 Rf1 41 Rd7 Drawn by agreement.

Position after 41 Rd7,
Drawn by agreement.

A rather dull game between these two titans, perhaps the dullest in this book.

11th WCCC, Graz
Round 5, November 25, 2003
Shredder (W) versus Brutus (B)
Sicilian Najdorf (B97)

Brutus led the field with a perfect score of four wins to this point.

1 e4 c5 2 Nf3 d6 3 d4 cxd4 4 Nxd4 Nf6 5 Nc3 a6 6 Bg5 e6 7 f4 Qb6 8 Nb3 Be7 9 Qf3 Nbd7 10 O-O-O Qc7 11 Kb1 b5 12 Bd3 Bb7 13 a3 O-O-O 14 Qe2 Kb8 15 Rhf1 h6 16 Bh4 g5 17 Be1 gxf4 18 Rxf4 Rdg8 19 Bh4 Rg6 20 Rdf1 e5 21 Rf5 Rc8 22.g4 Bd8 23 g5 hxg5 24 Bxg5 Be7 25 h4 Qd8 26 Qe1 Qc7 27 h5

27 ... Rxg5 28 Rxg5 Nxe4 29 Nxe4 Bxe4 30 Bxe4 Bxg5 31 Rxf7 Rf8 32 Rxf8+ Nxf8 33 Na5 Kc8 34 Qg1 Qxa5 35 Bf5+

Hereafter, Brutus would scramble around, loosing ground with each move.

35 ... Kb7 36 Qxg5 Qc7 37 Be4+ Kb6 38 h6 Qb8 39 Qg1+ Kc7 40 Qg7+ Kb6 41 b4 a5 42 Qg1+ Ka6 43 Qg8 Ka7 44 Qd5 Ng6 Black resigns.

Position after 27 h5.

Position after 44 ... Ng6, Black resigns.

Get ready for a great bloodbath! And keep an eye on Shredder's h-pawn.

While material was even, Brutus's game was about to fall apart.

11th WCCC, Graz
Round 6, November 25, 2003
Brutus (W) versus Deep Junior (B)
Sicilian Richter-Rauzer Attack (B67)

1 e4 c5 2 Nf3 d6 3 d4 cxd4 4 Nxd4
Nf6 5 Nc3 Nc6 6 Bg5 e6 7 Qd2 a6
8 O-O-O Bd7 9 f4 b5 10 Bxf6 gxf6
11 Kb1 b4 12 Nce2 Qb6 13 g3 Rc8
14 Bg2 Na5 15 b3 Nc6 16 Nxc6
Qxc6 17 Rc1 Qb6 18 Rhf1 a5 19 f5
e5 20 c3 h5 21 cxb4 axb4 22 Rxc8+
Bxc8 23 Rd1 Ke7 24 Nc1 Bh6
25 Qe1 Ba6 26 Bf1 Bxf1 27 Qxf1
Rc8 28 Nd3 Rc3 29 Qe2 Qb5
30 Kb2 Qa6 31 a4 Qb6 32 Ne1 h4
33 Nc2 h3 34 Qe1 Kf8 35 Rd5 Bg5
36 a5 Qa7 37 Nxb4 Rc1 38 Rd1
Rc8 39 Nc2 Qc5 40 Na3 Be3 41 b4
Bd4+ 42 Kb3 Qc7 43 Rd3 Rb8
44 b5 Bc5 45 Qc3 Qc6 46 Qb4

46 ... Qc7 47 Rc3 Qb7 48 Rxc5 dxc5
49 Qxc5+ Kg7 50 Qd5 Qe7 51 b6
Rd8 52 Qb5 Qd6 53 Qe2 Qc5 54 Nb5
Qc1 55 Qc2 Qf1 56 Nc3 Rc8 57 Kb2
Qg1 58 Kb3 Qc5 59 Qd3 Qxa5

Brutus's passed pawns fell to Deep
Junior as well as the game.

60 Qe3 Rc6 61 Nd5 Qb5+ 62 Nb4
Rxb6 63 Qd2 Qf1 64 g4 Qb1+
65 Ka3 Rb5 66 Ka4 Rxb4+ 67 Qxb4+
Qa2+ 68 Kb5 Qxh2 White resigns.

Position after 68 ... Qxh2,
White resigns.

Position after 46 Qb4.

Wow!...Brutus would soon be forced to
exchange a rook for a bishop and pawn.
Though facing two passed pawns, Deep
Junior's rook versus knight advantage
eventually proved too much for Brutus.

Brutus, after winning its first four games,
had just taken its second dose of medicine from the top contenders.

11th WCCC, Graz
Round 7, November 25, 2003
Deep Junior (W) versus Shredder (B)
Sicilian Scheveningen (B80)

1 e4 c5 2 Nf3 d6 3 d4 cxd4 4 Nxd4
Nf6 5 Nc3 a6 6 Be3 e6 7 f3 b5 8 g4
h6 9 Qd2 Nbd7 10 O-O-O Bb7 11 h4
b4 12 Na4 Qa5 13 b3 Nc5 14 a3
Nxa4 15 axb4 Qc7 16 bxa4 d5 17 e5
Nd7 18 f4 Nb6 19 f5 Nxa4 20 fxe6
Nc3 21 exf7+ Kxf7 22 Bd3 Bxb4
23 Rdf1+ Kg8 24 Qf2 Ba3+ 25 Kd2
Ne4+ 26 Bxe4 dxe4 27 Qf5 Bb4+
28 Kd1 Qc4 29 Ne6 Qd5+

Position after 32 … Qc4+,
Drawn by agreement.

Shredder faced the choice of being
mated or settling for a draw.

30 Ke2 Qc4+ 31 Kd1 Qd5+ 32 Ke2
Qc4+ Drawn by agreement.

11th WCCC, Graz
Playoff 1, November 30, 2003
Shredder (W) versus Deep Fritz (B)
Sicilian Najdorf (B97)

The two playoff games were played at
the speed of all moves in 60 minutes per
side.

1 e4 c5 2 Nf3 d6 3 d4 cxd4 4 Nxd4
Nf6 5 Nc3 a6 6 Bg5 e6 7 f4 Qb6
8 Nb3 Be7 9 Qf3 Nbd7 10 O-O-O
Qc7 11 Kb1 b5 12 Bd3 b4 13 Ne2
Bb7 14 Qh3 Nxe4 15 Bxe7 Kxe7
16 Qh4+ Nef6 17 Rhe1 a5 18 Nbd4
Kf8 19 g4 Nc5 20 Ng3 Rc8 21 g5
Nd5 22 Bxh7 e5

Position after 22 … e5.

A complex position and the beginning of a good slugfest!

23 Nb5 Qd7 24 Nf5 Qxb5 25 Nxd6 Qc6 26 fxe5 Nd3 27 Re2 N3f4 28 Rf2 Rd8 29 g6 Rd7 30 gxf7 Qc7 31 Rd4 Qc6

32 Rf1 Ba6 33 Rfd1 Be2 34 Rc1 Ba6 35 Rcd1 Be2 36 Rc1 Ba6 37 Rcd1 Drawn by repetition.

Position after 37 Rcd1,
Drawn by repetition.

Position after 31 ... Qc6.

Too complex to figure out!

11th WCCC, Graz
Playoff 2, November 30, 2003
Deep Fritz (W) versus Shredder (B)
English Symmetrical (A30)

---

1 Nf3 c5 2 c4 Nf6 3 Nc3 e6 4 g3 b6 5 Bg2 Bb7 6 O-O a6 7 Re1 Be7 8 e4 d6 9 d4 cxd4 10 Nxd4 Qc8 11 f4 O-O 12 Be3 h5 13 h3 Rd8 14 Rc1 Nbd7 15 f5 e5 16 Nd5 Re8 17 Nb3 Bd8 18 g4 hxg4 19 hxg4 Nh7 20 Qd2 Bh4 21 Red1 Rb8 22 Nxb6 Nxb6 23 Bxb6 Bxe4 24 Bxe4 Rxb6 25 Qe2 Ng5 26 Rc2 Qb8 27 Kf1 a5 28 Bd5 a4 29 Qh2 axb3 30 axb3 Nf3 31 Bxf3 Qd8 32 Rc3 Qg5 33 Qd2 Qf6 34 Qe3 Reb8 35 Bd5 Ra6 36 Qd3 Qh6 37 Kg2 Qg5 38 Rg1 Qxg4+ 39 Kh1 Qd4 40 Qe2 Bf6 41 Rh3 Qa7 42 Qd2 Kf8

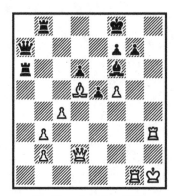

Position after 42 ... Kf8.

Shredder's king scampers to safety. The theme of the game over the coming moves was the relative safety of Shredder's king versus the exposure of Deep Fritz's.

43 Rd1 Rab6 44 Qf2 Qa5 45 Rdd3 Ke7 46 Qf1 Qa7 47 Be4 Ra6 48 Rd1 Ra2 49 Qe2 Ra1 50 Kg2 Bg5 51 Rhd3 Rxd1 52 Qxd1 Qc5 53 Qh5 Bf6 54 Bd5 Rf8 55 Qh3 Qa5 56 Qh1 Rg8 57 Be4 Rd8 58 Qd1 Bh4 59 Rc3 Qb4 60 Qh5 Bf6 61 Bd5 Rf8 62 Qh3 Qa5 63 Qh1 Qc5 64 Rd3 Qc8 65 Rf3 Qb8 66 Rh3 g8 67 Be4 Rc8 68 Qg1 Qc7 69 Qe1 Rb8 70 Qe2 Qa5 71 Bd5 Rg8 72 Qc2 g6

After a 20-move prance around the board by both sides looking for a weakness, Shredder struck. This was the beginning of Deep Fritz's downfall.

73 Rg3 Rc8 74 Qd1 gxf5 75 b4 Qa2 76 Qe2 Qa1 77 Ra3 Rg8+ 78 Rg3 Rxg3+ 79 Kxg3 Qg1+ 80 Kh3 e4 81 Bxe4 Be5 82 Qg2 Qe3+ 83 Qf3 Qxe4 84 Kg2 Qxc4 85 Qxf5 Qxb4 86 Qg5+ Ke6 87 Qd8 Qd2+ 88 Kf3 Qd1+ 89 Kf2 Bd4+ White resigns

Position after 89 … Bd4+, White resigns.

Position after 72 … g6.

Suggest Readings

Omid David Tabibi, "The 11th World Computer-Chess Championship", ICGA Journal, Vol. 26, No. 4, pp. 252–259, December 2003.

Website on the 11th WCCC, Graz, Austria, November 22–30, 2003: http://www.grappa.univ-lille3. fr/icga/event.php?id=3; http://www.chessbase.com/newsdetail.asp?newsid=1336

Games from the 3-7 rounds and the playoff games: http://www.chessbase.com/games/2003/graz03. htm; http://www.chessbase.com/games/2003/graz04.htm; http://www.chessbase.com/games/ 2003/graz05.htm; http://www.chessbase.com/games/2003/graz06.htm; http://www.chessbase. com/games/2003/graz07.htm; http://www.chessbase.com/games/2003/graz12.htm

Website dedicated to Deep Sjeng's performance in the 11th WCCC: http://www.lokasoft.nl/deep_ sjeng_in_wccc2003.html

The Austrian Chess Federation website for the 11th WCCC: http://www.chess.at/turniere/turniere2003/ chess003/

2004: Deep Junior Edges Out Shredder to Take 12th WCCC

Playing on home turf is an advantage in most sports. But in computer chess? Well, based on the results of the 12th WCCC, one has to give this hypothesis some credibility. It certainly didn't hurt Deep Junior. The Israeli program took on its main rivals, Shredder and Fritz, in its own backyard, the campus of Bar-Ilan University in Ramat-Gan, a suburb of Israel's largest city, Tel Aviv, and showed them who's best. Shredder had taken the title of World Champion away from Deep Junior the previous year; Deep Junior had won the title in 2002, having taken the title away from Shredder, who in turn had taken it away from Fritz in 2001! Until Shredder won the title in 2003, no world champion had ever lost the title and regained it later. Now, it happened for a second time in a row.

The format of the tournament was an 11-round Swiss system held July 3–12, 2004. With 14 participants, this meant that each program played all but two of the other programs. Deep Junior played all but the 12th and 14th place finishers, while runner-up Shredder played all but the ninth and 13th place finishers. Eight nations were represented: Germany, The Netherlands, USA, Belgium, France, Spain, Great Britain, and Israel. The time control was 60 moves in two hours followed by all the remaining moves in 30 minutes.

The top five finishers used four-processor HP computers based on AMD's Opteron 2.2 GHz processor. The other participants used Pentium 4 processors or AMD's Athlon 64 3200+ processors. The September 2004 Swedish Rating List had versions of Shredder, Fritz, and Junior, all rated within 20 points of 2800; the versions competing in this event ran on more powerful computers and probably would receive ratings 50–100 points higher.

Leading up to the championship, Hydra, a souped-upped version of Brutus, joined the ranks of the leading engines when it captured first place in the 13th International Paderborn Computer-Chess Championship held February 11–15, 2004. Hydra won all but one of its games, defeating Fritz in Round 3 and drawing with Shredder in Round 6. Hydra finished a point ahead of Fritz and a point and

M. Newborn, *Beyond Deep Blue: Chess in the Stratosphere*,
DOI 10.1007/978-0-85729-341-1_7, © Springer-Verlag London Limited 2011

a half ahead of Shredder in an impressive performance. Two months later, April 23–25, 2004, at the 4th International CSVN Tournament in Leiden, Shredder managed to finish a point and a half ahead of Hydra in winning that event. Hydra passed up the 12th WCCC to prepare for its head-to-head battle the next month in Abu Dhabi with Shredder, a match covered in the next chapter.

Deep Junior regained the title of World Computer Chess Champion when it gathered nine of a possible 11 points to finish a half point ahead of runner-up Shredder and two points ahead of fourth-place finisher Fritz. Both Deep Junior and Shredder finished the eleven-round championship without a loss. Fritz dropped two games, one to Falcon, a second Israeli program that finished in eighth place, and a second to third place finisher Diep, developed by Vincent Diepeveen of the Netherlands. Deep Junior, Shredder, and Fritz drew the three games they played with one another.

Deep Junior led the field throughout the tournament, though Shredder drew even after Round 9. Both drew their games in Round 10, and thus entering the final round, the two were tied for the lead. Deep Junior was paired with ParSOS and routinely won its game, while Shredder was only able to draw with Falcon. Thus Deep Junior was recrowned world champion.

Data on entries to the 12th WCCC: Name, country of origin, authors, opening book, hardware

Name	Origin	Authors	Opening book	Hardware
Deep Junior	ISR	Amir Ban, Shay Bushinsky	Boris Alterman	HP 4x ProLiant 2.2 GHz
Shredder	DEU	Stefan Meyer-Kahlen	Sandro Necchi	AMD Opteron Quad Core 2.0 GHz, Transtec
Diep	NLD	Vincent Diepeveen	Arturo Ochoa	AMD Opteron Quad Core 2.0 GHz
Fritz	NLD	Frans Morsch, Mathias Feist	Alexander Kure	AMD Opteron Quad Core 2.0 GHz, Transtec
Crafty	USA	Robert Hyatt	Peter Berger	AMD Opteron Quad Core 2.4 GHz
Jonny	DEU	Johannes Zwanzger	Own book	Intel Pentium 4 2.8 GHz, AMD Athlon 64 3200+
ParSOS	DEU	Rudolf Huber	Own book	AMD Athlon 64 3200+
Falcon	ISR	Omid David Tabibi	Eros Riccio	AMD Athlon 64 3200+
IsiChess	DEU	Gerd Isenberg	Own book	AMD Athlon 64 3400+
Deep Sjeng	BEL	Gian-Carlo Pascutto	Jeroen Noomen	AMD Athlon 64 3400+
WoodPusher	GBR	John Hamlen	Own book	Intel Pentium 4 2.8 GHz
Movei	ISR	Uri Blass	Own book	Intel Pentium 4 2.8 GHz
The Crazy Bishop	FRA	Remi Coulom	Own book	Intel Pentium 4 2.8 GHz
FIBChess	ESP	Guillermo Baches Garcia	No book	Intel Pentium 4 2.8 GHz

Final standings of the 12th WCCC, Ramat Gan

#	Name	1	2	3	4	5	6	7	8	9	10	11	Pts	BU
1	Deep Junior	6bD	11wW	3bW	5wW	2bD	10wW	9bD	8wW	4wD	13bW	7bW	9.0	65.0
2	Shredder	5bD	7wW	6bD	3wW	1wD	4bD	12wW	10bW	11wW	14bW	8bD	8.5	60.5
3	Diep	13wW	8bW	1wL	2bL	6wD	12bW	5wL	11bW	9wW	4bW	14wW	7.5	58.0
4	Fritz	10wD	9bD	8wL	13bW	5wW	2wD	14bW	7wW	1bD	3wL	12bW	7.0	60.5
5	Crafty	2wD	10bD	9wW	1bL	4bL	14wW	3bW	12wW	8bW	7wL	13wW	7.0	60.5
6	Jonny	1wD	13bW	2wD	8bL	3bD	9wW	7bL	14wW	12bD	10wW	11bD	6.5	56.5
7	ParSOS	12wW	2bL	10wD	9bD	11wW	8bD	6wW	4bL	13wD	5bW	1wL	6.0	63.5
8	Falcon	14bW	3wL	4bW	6wW	10bL	7wD	13bW	1bL	5wL	11bW	2wD	6.0	62.0
9	IsiChess	11bD	4wD	5bL	7wD	14wW	6bL	1wD	13bW	3bL	12wW	10bW	6.0	56.5
10	Deep Sjeng	4bD	5wD	7bD	12wW	8wW	1bL	11wW	2wL	14bW	6bL	9wL	5.5	62.0
11	WoodPusher	9wD	1bL	12wD	14bW	7bL	13wD	10bL	3wL	2bL	8wL	6wD	3.0	60.0
12	Movei	7bL	14wW	11bD	10bL	13wW	3wL	2bL	5bL	6wD	9bL	4wL	3.0	59.0
13	The Crazy Bishop	3bL	6wL	14bW	4wL	12bL	11bD	8wL	9wL	7bD	1wL	5bL	2.0	61.0
14	FIBChess	8wL	12bL	13wL	11wL	9bL	5bL	4wL	6bL	10wL	2wL	3bL	0.0	62.0

12th WCCC, Ramat-Gan
Round 5, July 8, 2004
Shredder (W) versus Deep Junior (B)
Sicilian Defense: Najdorf. Poisoned Pawn Variation (B97)

When this game was played, Deep Junior led the field – and Shredder, in particular – by a half-point after four rounds.

1 e4 c5 2 Nf3 d6 3 d4 cxd4 4 Nxd4 Nf6 5 Nc3 a6 6 Bg5 e6 7 f4 Qb6 8 Nb3 Be7 9 Qf3 Nbd7 10 O-O-O Qc7 11 Kb1 b5 12 Bd3 Bb7 13 a3 h6 14 Qh3 O-O 15 Bh4 Nc5 16 Nxc5 dxc5 17 e5 Nd5 18 Nxd5 Bxd5 19 Bf6 Bxf6 20 exf6 Qxf4 21 fxg7 Rfd8 22 Be2 Qg5 23 Bf3 Bxf3 24 Qxf3 Rxd1+ 25 Rxd1 Rd8 26 Rf1 Qg6 27 Qc6 c4 28 Rf2 Qh5 29 Ka2 Qd5 30 Qc7 Rd7 31 Qb8+ Kxg7 32 Rf3 c3+ 33 b3 Qd2

Shredder's attack ran out of gas, and a draw loomed at Shredder's instigation.

34 Rg3+ Kf6 35 Qh8+ Ke7 36 Rxc3 a5 37 Rc8 Rd8 38 Rc7+ Rd7 39 Rc8 Rd8 40 Rc7+ Rd7 Drawn by repetition.

Position after 40 … Rd7,
Drawn by repetition.

Thus after five rounds, Deep Junior remained at the head of the field with four points, ahead of Shredder by a half point.

Position after 33 … Qd2.

12th WCCC, Ramat-Gan
Round 6, July 8, 2004
Fritz (W) versus Shredder (B)
Sicilian, Scheveningen, Classical (B85)

Shredder trailed the leader Deep Junior by a half point when this game was played. Fritz trailed by a full point.

1 e4 c5 2 Nf3 d6 3 d4 cxd4 4 Nxd4 Nf6 5 Nc3 a6 6 Be2 e6 7 O-O Be7 8 f4 O-O 9 Kh1 Nc6 10 Be3 Qc7 11 a4 Re8 12 Bf3 Bf8 13 g4 Nxd4 14 Bxd4 e5 15 Bg1 exf4 16 g5 Nd7 17 Nd5 Qd8 18 Bg2 Ne5 19 Rxf4 Be6 20 Ra3 Rc8 21 Bb6 Qxg5 22 Rg3 Qh6 23 Be3 ·

23 ... Bxd5 24 exd5 Nc4 25 Rxc4 Rxe3 26 Rxg7+ Kxg7 27 Rxc8 Qh4 28 Qg1 Re1 29 Bf1+ Kh6 30 Qg2 Qf4 31 Qh3+ Kg6 32 Qg2+ Kf6 33 Kg1 Ke7 34 Rc7+ Kd8 35 Rxb7 Bg7 36 c3 Bd4+ 37 cxd4 Qxd4+ 38 Kh1 Rxf1+ 39 Qxf1 Qxd5+ 40 Qg2 Qd1+ 41 Qg1 Qf3+ 42 Qg2 Qd1+ 43 Qg1 Qd5+ 44 Qg2 Qd1+ **Drawn by repetition.**

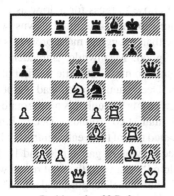

Position after 23 Be3.

The stage was set for a wild brawl at the end of which material would stand even.

Position after 44 ... Qd1+,
Drawn by repetition.

Shredder had no choice but to play for a draw. With Deep Junior winning its game with Deep Sjeng, that left Shredder one point off the lead with five rounds to go. Lots could still happen.

12th WCCC, Ramat-Gan
Round 9, July 11, 2004
Deep Junior(W) versus Fritz (B)
Sicilian, Najdorf (B90)

1 e4 c5 2 Nf3 d6 3 d4 cxd4 4 Nxd4
Nf6 5 Nc3 a6 6 Be3 e6 7 f3 b5 8 g4
Nfd7 9 Qd2 Nb6 10 O-O-O N8d7
11 Ndxb5 axb5 12 Nxb5 Ba6
13 Nxd6+ Bxd6 14 Qxd6 Nc4
15 Bxc4 Bxc4 16 Qd4

Position after 34 Ka2,
Drawn by agreement.

Position after 16 Qd4.

Deep Junior had three pawns for a knight.

16 ... Be2 17 Qxg7 Rf8 18 Bc5 Bxd1
19 Rxd1 Qc7 20 Bd6 Qb6 21 Kb1
Qa6 22 a3 Qe2 23 Rd4 Qxf3 24 Ka2
Rc8 25 c3 h6 26 Bb4 Qe3 27 Rxd7
Kxd7 28 Bxf8 Qxe4 29 Qxf7+ Kc6
30 h4 Qd5+ 31 Kb1 Qd1+ 32 Ka2
Qd5+ 33 Kb1 Qd1+ 34 Ka2 Drawn
by agreement.

Fritz chose to press for a draw as Deep Junior's bishop and three pawns were more than enough to make prospects not very good. Meanwhile, Shredder won its game to move into a tie for first place with Deep Junior; each had garnered seven points through this ninth round. In the final two rounds, Deep Junior defeated two of the weaker entries, while Shredder won its game in Round 10, but could only drawn in the final round with the other Israeli engine, Falcon. Thus, Deep Junior was crowned world champion for the second time.

Suggest Readings

Johannes Zwanzger, "The 12th World Computer-Chess Championship", ICGA Journal, Vol. 27,
    No. 3, pp. 160–167, September 2004.
Shredder versus Deep Junior, Round 5, 12th WCCC: http://www.chessgames.com/perl/
    chessgame?gid=1293621
Fritz versus Shredder, Round 6, 12th WCCC: http://www.chessgames.com/perl/chessgame?
    gid=1293628
Deep Junior versus Fritz, Round 9, 12th WCCC: http://www.chessgames.com/perl/chessgame?
    gid=1293644

2004: Hydra Slews Shredder in Abu Dhabi

8

No sooner than the 12th WCCC was over in Israel and Deep Junior had regained the title of World Champion, Hydra took on Shredder in an eight–game match in Abu Dhabi: The Abu Dhabi Computer Challenge. The dates were August 14–24, 2004. Hydra won the match with a very impressive 5.5–2.5 score, winning three games, drawing five and raising the question of which chess engine was really the best. For half a decade, Junior, Fritz, and Shredder took turns at the top. Now, there was a newcomer, possibly the best of all. The following year, Hydra essentially murdered England's Grandmaster Michael Adams, and its status grew even higher.

The Hydra team consisted of Chrilly Donninger, the main brain and lead programmer, Ulf Lorenz, a University of Paderborn researcher, in charge of testing, Muhammad Nasir Ali, in charge of the project at Abu Dhabi's Pal Group, and grandmasters Christopher Lutz and Talib Mousa. Lutz and Mousa gave advice on how to improve Hydra. They also programmed the opening book, replacing Alexander Kure, who had worked with Donninger in developing the opening book for Brutus, Hydra's predecessor.

When playing Shredder, Hydra ran on a 16 node Linux cluster, in which each node was an Intel 3.06 Xeon processor. Each processor contained a FPGA Virtex I card provided by Alpha Data Systems, Edinburgh. The cluster of computers was housed in Pal Group's offices in Abu Dhabi. In contrast, Shredder ran on an AMD Quad Opteron system with each processor   running at 2 GHz; it evaluated about two million positions per second.

Shredder's website provides the games from this event with the time to make every move recorded as well as the score assigned to the continuation found and the search depth associated with the continuation. It also gives the predicted move by its opponent when it differs from the move played, and it also indicates whether a Shredder move was played from book. The time taken for a move by Hydra was used to construe whether the move was from book.

Five of the eight games were drawn in the endgame. Three of the five drawn games ended with each side having a bishop and one, two, or three pawns. In the other two, each side had rook(s) and pawns against rook(s) and pawns. In three of the five draws, Shredder had an extra pawn but no chance to win. In summary, Hydra gave Shredder a real lesson, and while Deep Junior had claim to the world title, it might well be that Hydra was the world's best chess engine at the end of 2004.

The Openings

Seven of the eight games opened with a Sicilian Defense. All four with Hydra playing White began with the identical first five moves: 1: e4 c5 2 Nf3 d6 3 d4 cxd4 4 Nxd4 Nf6 5 Nc3 a6.

The Hydra team: Ulf Lorenz, Ali Nasir Muhammad, Dr. Christian Donninger.
(Photo courtesy of Dr. Christian Donninger)

In Game 1, Hydra then played 6 Be3 and was met with 6 ... e6. Hydra went on to win the game.

In Game 3, Hydra followed the same moves through 6 Be3, but Shredder chose 6 ... e5 rather than 6 ... e6, and managed to draw the game.

In Game 5, Hydra picked a different sixth move, playing 6 Be2 rather than 6 Be3, perhaps deciding to avoid the line that led to a draw in Game 5. However, it did no better even with this change of moves.

Going into Game 7, Shredder trailed Hydra, 4–2. Game 7 was identical to Game 5 until Shredder steered off with 6 ... e5 rather than 6 ... e6, perhaps hoping that it might do better than draw, as a win was necessary not to lose the match. However, the change also led to a draw, and assured Hydra would win the match.

Game 2 was identical to Game 1 through 5 ... a6. At that point Shredder played 6 Bg5, rather than Hydra's 6 Be3 in Game 1. If this alternative was selected to do better than Hydra's 6 Be3, it was the wrong decision. Hydra won its second game.

Game 4 was the only game that wasn't a Sicilian Defense, a Nimzo – Indian Defense that ended in a draw. The game was in Shredder's book though the 26th move. Hydra was book only through the tenth move. Nevertheless, Shredder could do no better than draw.

By Game 6, Shredder was in deep trouble, behind in the match by a 3.5–1.5 score. A Sicilian developed in which Hydra steered clear of the previous lines played, playing 2 ... e6 rather than 2 ... d6, and the game ended in a draw.

Game 8, of no consequence to the outcome of the match, followed Game 6 until Hydra played 4 Nc6 and the game was drawn.

Shredder outbooked Hydra in every game! In two games, Shredder returned to picking moves from its book after leaving it on an earlier move. In Game 4, Shredder played its first 26 moves from book! The minimum number Shredder played was eight. Hydra played between eight and thirteen. Every move from book effectively saved two minutes time for use on later moves. Playing the first ten moves from book saved about 20 minutes. Rather than playing the first 60 moves in two hours – or 2 hours per move as the rules specified – the engine could play moves 11 through 60, 50 moves, in two hours, or 2.4 minutes per move. In spite of outbooking Hydra in every game, Shredder found its scoring function indicating that it was behind in five of the eight games after the first and the fifth move out of book. On average and when playing White, Shredder was ahead by 0.05 points after the first move out of book and ahead by 0.19 points after five moves. When playing Black, it was behind by 0.32 points after one move out of book and behind by 0.16 points after five games. Game 6 was the most favorable to Shredder when coming out of book. If Shredder's score was worse than or equal to –0.16 five moves out of its book, it went on to lose the game. If not, it drew.

Hydra versus Shredder, Abu Dhabi Chess Challenge: 2004: Scorecard

Name	Game 1	Game 2	Game 3	Game 4	Game 5	Game 6	Game 7	Game 8	Total points
Hydra	W1.0	B2.0	W2.5	B3.0	W3.5	B4.0	W5.0	B5.5	5.5
Shredder	B0.0	W0.0	B0.5	W1.0	B1.5	W2.0	B2.0	W2.5	2.5

Moves played from Shredder and Hydra's book, game by game

	Game 1	Game 2	Game 3	Game 4	Game 5	Game 6	Game 7	Game 8
Hydra moves in book	10	10	12	10	13	8	12	9
Shredder moves in book	16	16	15	26	13	9	12	14

Shredder scores one and five moves out of book

	Game 1	Game 2	Game 3	Game 4	Game 5	Game 6	Game 7	Game 8
Shredder score one move out of book	+0.14	−0.70	−0.99	−0.01	−0.21	+0..62	−0.22	+0.28
Shredder score five moves out of book	−0.48	−0.45	−0.07	−0.03	+0.08	+1.05	−0.16	+0.10
Shredder's result	Loss	Loss	Draw	Draw	Draw	Draw	Loss	Draw

Abu Dhabi Computer Challenge, Abu Dhabi
Game 1, August 14, 2004
Hydra (W) versus Shredder (B)
Sicilian, Najdorf (B90)

---

1 e4 c5 2 Nf3 d6 3 d4 cxd4 4 Nxd4 Nf6 5 Nc3 a6 6 Be3 (Bg5) e6 7 f3 (Be2; 2:10m)

Shredder assumed Hydra would play 7 Be2 instead of 7 f3. Hydra thought for two minutes and ten seconds. In this chapter, moves not from book will have a time given with them. So far, only Hydra's last move was not from book. In addition, in this chapter, if Hydra didn't make the move that Shredder expected, Shedder's expected move is given. So far, Hydra's sixth and seventh moves were not expected by Shredder.

7 ... b5 8 g4 (Qd2; 19s) h6 9 Qd2 (16s) Nbd7 10 O-O-O Bb7 11 h4

To here, this game was the same as Deep Junior versus Shredder, Round 7, 11th WCCC, Graz, 2003. Shredder did better when it played 11 ... b4 and went on to draw the game. It might be noted that Hydra returned to picking moves from its book.

11 ... d5 12 exd5 (2:13m) Nxd5 13 Nxd5 (1:43m) Bxd5 14 Bg2 (4:19m) Ne5 15 Qe2 (2:41m) Qa5 16 f4 (2:02m) Qxa2 17 Bxd5 (2:19m) Qa1+ (+.14/16; 33s)

Shredder's first move out of book. It assigned the continuation found a score of +.14 points in its favor while searching to a depth of 16 plies.

18 Kd2 (15s) Bb4+ (−.31/17; 51s) 19 c3 (1:19m) Qxb2+ (−.41/19; 1:10m) 20 Ke1 (1:02m) Bxc3+ (−.43/19; 1:02m) 21 Kf1 (2:45m) exd5 (−.48/20; 2s) 22 fxe5 (2:07m)

Position after 22 fxe5.

Shredder's attack has resulted in exchanging a minor piece for three potentially dangerous passed queenside pawns. However, Hydra's advanced kingside pawns, along with one more attacker, soon put the squeeze on Shredder's king.

22 ... Qb4 (−.48/19; 2s) 23 Bf2 (Kf2; 2:19m) O-O (−.58/20; 3:59m) 24 g5 (Nc6; 9:52m) Bxd4 (−.89/20; 4:22m) 25 Bxd4 (9s) h5 (−.98/19 2:35m) 26 Kg2 (Qxh5; 14s) Rac8 (−.98/19; 3:56m) 27 Rhf1 (14s) Qe7 (−1.16/18; 2:18m) 28 Qxh5 (2:38m) Rc2+ (−1.38/18; 49s) 29 Kg3 (1:11m) Rc6 (−1.64/18; 1:19m) 30 Rd3 (2:40m) a5 (−1.90/18; 1:06m)

Shredder's pawn push was a futile attempt to stave off defeat.

31 Rdf3 (4:31m) Re6 (−2.63/17; 9:03m)

Shredder thought for 9 minutes, desperately seeking a way out of the growing pressure around its king.

32 Rf6 (2:00m) Rxe5 (−2.72/19; 3s)

Shredder had no choice but to exchange its rook for a Hydra bishop and pawn.

33 Bxe5 (2:34m) Qxe5+ (−2.72/19; 3s) 34 R6f4 (2:24m) a4 (−2.84/17; 54s) 35 Kg2 (1:42m) d4 (−3.59/18; 1:36m) 36 Rxf7 (Rf5; 1:51m) Qd5+ (−4.04/17; 3:00m) 37 R7f3 (1:46m) Rc8 (−4.23/18; 3s) 38 Re1 (Qf7+; 1:22m) Black resigns.

Position after 38 Re1,
Black resigns.

Abu Dhabi Computer Challenge, Abu Dhabi
Game 2, August 15, 2004
Shredder (W) versus Hydra (B)
Sicilian, Najdorf (B97)

1 e4 c5 2 Nf3 d6 3 d4 cxd4 4 Nxd4 Nf6 5 Nc3 a6 6 Bg5 e6 7 f4 Qb6 8 Nb3 Be7 9 Qf3 Nbd7 (Qc7) 10 O-O-O Qc7 11 Kb1 b5 (1:58m) 12 Bd3 b4 (1:48m)

Position after 12 … b4.

Hydra avoided playing 12 … Bb7 as its predecessor, Brutus, playing Black, had done when it lost to Shredder at the 11th WCCC. Deep Junior, as Black, played the same line against Shredder at the 12th WCCC. and after playing 12 … Bb7 went on to draw the game (See Chap. 7). Maybe here Hydra steered clear of 12 … Bb7, hoping to do better with 12 … b4.

13 Ne2 Bb7 (3:30m) 14 Qh3 Nxe4 (Bxe4; 2:09m) 15 Bxe7 Kxe7 (2:05m)

Shredder gave up a pawn, evidently feeling it obtained something in return with Hydra's king now unable to castle.

16 Qh4+ Ndf6 (3:29m) 17 Rhe1 (−.45/17; 1:36m) h6 (a5; 2:35m) 18 f5 (−.57/19; 2:28m) e5 (2:15m)

Shredder was about to hand over a second pawn.

19 Nf4 (–.48/20; 0s) Ng5 (4:15m) 20 Nh5 (–.78/19; 1:00m) Nxh5 (1:07m) 21 Qxh5 (–.70/18;15s) Bxg2 (2:03m) 22 Nd2 (–.74/19; 0s) a5 (Qc6; 2:30m) 23 h4 (–.80/18; 2:49m) Nh7 (1:54m) 24 Qe2 (–.95/19; 9s) Bc6 (Bb7; 2:30m) 25 Rg1 (–1.17/20; 6:13m) Rhg8 (Rag8; 2:10m) 26 Ne4 (–1.25/18; 2:26m) Bxe4 (a4; 18s) 27 Bxe4 (–1.17/16; 24s)

Position after 27 Bxe4.

Hydra had clearly gained the upper hand and controlled play now until victory was obtained on move 51.

27 ... Rac8 (Raf8; 1:58m) 28 Bd3 (–1.54/18; 3:10m) Qb6 (Nf6; 2:00m) 29 Bb5 (–1.71/18; 2:09m) Nf6 (12s) 30 Ba4 (–1.90/18; 3:08m) e4 (Rc5; 1:40m) 31 Rde1 (–1.85/18; 1:23m) Qc5 (Rc5; 3:52m) 32 Qa6 (–1.90/18; 1:16m) d5 (2:14m) 33 Rd1 (–1.19/19; 1s) d4 (1:53m) 34 Bb3 (–2.06/18; 4s) Rc6 (e3; 2:04m) 35 Qe2 (–2.53/19; 2:54m)

35 ... Kf8 (Qe5; 2:46m) 36 Ba4 (–1.19/18; 1:20m) Rd6 (Rc8; 2:23m) 37 Qf1 (–1.94/19; 1:54m) Rd8 (e3; 1:33m) 38 Qa6 (–1.95/19; 1:19m) Qc7 (9s) 39 Qb5 (–1.93/19; 1:25m) Rh8 (Rd5; 1:16m) 40 Qf1 (–1.91/20; 3:58m) Rh7 (e3; 2:00m) 41 Bb3 (–2.07/18; 2:10m) h5 (e3; 54s) 42 Ba4 (–2.41/18; 2:12m) e3 (1:47m) 43 Qb5 (–2.68/18;4s) Rh6 (1:51m) 44 Rg2 (–2.81/19; 0s) Rd5 (Ne4; 1:06m) 45 Qf1 (–3.18/17; 58s) Ng4 (53s) 46 Bb3 (–3.52/17; 49s) Rd8 (1:01m) 47 Ba4 (–3.80/18; 2:15m) Rf6 (Rb6; 1:02m) 48 Re1 (–4.60/18; 3:19m) g6 (Qe5; 51s)

A third pawn to Hydra, and a fourth and resignation coming soon.

49 Rc1 (–4.71; 1:49m) Rxf5 (1:32m) 50 Qe2 (–6.06/20; 6:50m) Qe7 (10s) 51 Bb5 (–6.06/17; 25s) Qxh4 (36s) White resigns.

Position after 51 ... Qxh4,
White resigns.

Hydra, after two victories in a row, was in command of the match.

Abu Dhabi Computer Challenge, Abu Dhabi
Game 3, August 17, 2004
Hydra (W) versus Shredder (B)
Sicilian, Najdorf Variation (B90)

1 e4 c5 2 Nf3 d6 3 d4 cxd4 4 Nxd4 Nf6 5 Nc3 a6 6 Be3 (Bg5)

This game followed Game 1 to here, where, unlike Shredder's previous 6 ... e6 that led to a loss, it tried 6 ... e5 here.

6 ... e5 7 Nb3 Be6 8 f3 (Qd2) Nbd7 9 g4 b5 10 g5 b4 11 Ne2 (Nd5) Nh5 12 Qd2 h6

Diep faired better against Fritz at the 12th WCCC just days before this event when it won with 12 ... a5.

13 gxh6 (3:29m) g6 14 O-O-O (2:26m) a5 15 Kb1 (3:48m) Nhf6 16 h4 (4:28m) a4 (–.48/19; 2:16m) 17 Nbc1 (1:48m) d5 18 Bg5 (1:32m) dxe4 (–.99/19; 13:00m) 19 Ng3 (h5; 2:54m) Qb6 (–.64/17; 1:36m) 20 Nxe4 (h5) (4:17m) Nxe4 (+.26/18; 1:56m) 21 fxe4 (7s) f6 (+.01/19; 3:38m) 22 Be3 (7s) Bc5 (–.07/16; 9s) 23 Bxc5 (3:33m) Nxc5 (+.15/20; 0s) 24 Bg2 (Qf2; 3:22m) a3 (+.11/17; 2:10m) 25 b3 (5:17m) Bg4 (+.19/21; 0s) 26 Rdf1 (Rdg1; 1:53m) Rd8 (Score not given; 13s) 27 Nd3 (2s) Qd6 (+.93/19; 1:30m) 28 Qxb4 (1:51m) Nxd3 (+1.08/21; 0s) 29 Qxd6 (1:16m) Rxd6 (+1.05/23; 0s) 30 cxd3 (1:15m) Be2 (+.94/22; 4s) 31 Rc1 (Rf2; 1:14m) Bxd3+ (+1.22/20; 3s) 32 Ka1 (17s) Rxh6 (+1.17/21; 1:13m) 33 Rc8+ (Bf3; 1:04m) Ke7 (+.84/22; 2:48m) 34 Ra8 (1:20m) g5 (+.76/21; 1:20m) 35 Rxa3 (1:18m) Rxh4 (+.98/22; 2:01m) 36 Ra7+ (8s) Ke8 (+.98/22; 2:01m) 37 Rc1 (Rxh4; 37s) Bxe4 (+.39/22; 4:23m) 38 Bxe4 (2:22m) Rxe4 (+.17/23; 0s)

Position after 38 ... Rxe4.

Hydra, down a pawn, satisfied itself with a draw.

39 Rc8+ (2:17m) Rd8 (+.00/24; 0s) 40 Rcc7 (2:40m) Rd2 (+.00/24; 0s) 41 Rc8+ (56s) Rd8 (+.00/26; 0s) 42 Rcc7 (1:23m) Rd2 (+.00/24; 29s) 43 Rc8+ (Ra8+; 1:00m) Rd8 (+.00/7; 0s) Drawn by repetition.

Position after 43 ... Rd8,
Drawn by repetition.

Abu Dhabi Computer Challenge, Abu Dhabi
Game 4, August 18, 2004
Shredder (W) versus Hydra (B)
Nimzo–Indian Defense: Normal Variation. Bernstein Defense (E59)

1 d4

Finally an opening other than a Sicilian!

1 ... Nf6 (d5) 2 c4 e6 3 Nc3 Bb4 4 e3 O-O 5 Bd3 d5 6 Nf3 c5 7 O-O Nc6 (cxd4) 8 a3 Bxc3 9 bxc3 dxc4 10 Bxc4 Qc7 11 Bd3 e5 (2:16m) 12 Qc2 Re8 (2:51m) 13 Nxe5 Nxe5 (57s) 14 dxe5 Qxe5 (1:40m) 15 f3 Bd7 (3:21m) 16 a4 Rac8 (Bc6; 3:42m) 17 e4 c4 (2:47m) 18 Be2 Nd5 (2:44m) 19 exd5 Qxe2 (1:55m) 20 Qxe2 Rxe2 (1:37m) 21 Bf4 Rc5 (3:55m) 22 Rfb1 Rxd5 (3:30m) 23 Rxb7 g5 (3:21m) 24 Kf1 Rc2 (3:10m) 25 Be3 Rxc3 (2:05m) 26 Bxa7 Rb3 (1:20m) 27 Rc7 (–.01/21; 1:43m) c3 (13s) 28 Rc1 (+.00/20; 1:21m) Rb4 (Bxa4; 18s) 29 R1xc3 (–.01/21; 4:48m) Bxa4 (1:28m)

If the game didn't seem to be drawn before this move, it certainly did now, though it lasted another eight moves.

30 Rc1 (–.01/20; 2:11m) h6 (Bb5+; 38s) 31 Bf2 (–.03/20; 1:55m) Rb2 (2:17m) 32 Be1 (–.06/22; 0s) Bb5+ (Ra2;1:41m) 33 Kg1 (–.02/20; 32s) Bd7 (Ra2; 33s) 34 h3 (–.05/21; 2:41m) Ra2 (2:03m) 35 R7c2 (–.03/23; 0s) Rxc2 (1:16m) 36 Rxc2 (–.02/25; 0s) Kh7 (f6; 1:36m) 37 Rd2 (+.00/25; 1:18m) Rxd2 (8s) 38 Bxd2 (–.02/29; 0s) Drawn by agreement.

Position after 38 Bxd2,
Drawn by agreement.

Halfway through the match, Hydra had won three of four points. Shredder's chances looked grim.

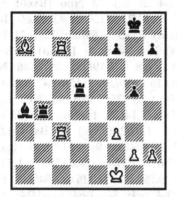

Position after 29 ... Bxa4.

Abu Dhabi Computer Challenge, Abu Dhabi
Game 5, August 20, 2004
Hydra (W) versus Shredder (B)
Sicilian Defense, Najdorf, Opocensky Variation (B92)

This was a fascinating game. From move 57, the game was drawn. However, it lasted another 40 moves in which each side tried its best to push pawns while simultaneously preventing pawn advances by its opponent and defending with bishops of opposite colors.

1 e4 c5 2 Nf3 d6 3 d4 cxd4 4 Nxd4 Nf6 5 Nc3 a6 6 Be2 (Bg5) e6 7 O-O Be7 8 f4 O-O 9 a4 Nc6 10 Be3 Qc7 11 Kh1 Re8 12 Bf3 Rb8 13 g4 Nd7 14 Bg2 (2:14m) **Nb6** (–.21/18; 0s) **15 b3** (3:56m) **Nxd4** (–.19/19; 55s) **16 Qxd4** (1:54m) **Nd7** (–.06/20; 8s) **17 g5** (2:57m) **b6** (–.01/20; 11s) **18 Bc1** (2:58m) **Bb7** (+.08/21; 0s) **19 Bb2** (4:33m) **Qc5** (+.03/22; 0s) **20 Nd5** (Qxd5; 1:08m) **Bf8** (+.00/21; 1:58m) **21 Ne3** (1:16m) **Qxd4** (–.01/21; 40s) **22 Bxd4** (52s) **e5** (–.01/21; 1:00m) **23 fxe5** (3:55m) **dxe5** (–.13/23; 0s) **24 Bb2** (1:34m) **Nc5** (–.28/21; 44s) **25 Nd5** (1:13m) **Rbd8** (–.24/20; 21s) **26 Rad1** (2:01m) **b5** (–.50/20; 44s) **27 axb5** (2:11m) **axb5** (–.50/21; 0s) **28 h4** (2:20m) **Rc8** (–.70/20; 0s) **29 Rf2** (Rfe1; 2:36m) **b4** (–.82/19; 4:41m) **30 Rfd2** (Kh2; 1.12m) **Rb8** (–1.05/19; 2:08m) **31 Kh2** (4:43m) **Rbc8** (–.99/20; 0s) **32 Kg3** (Re2; 7:49m) **Rb8** (–1.02/20; 4:20m) **33 Ra1** (Nxb4; 1:04m) **Rbd8** (–.86/19; 4:16m) **34 Ra5** (Kh2; 15s) **Bc6** (–.99/19; 1:49m) **35 Rd1** (h5; 1:35m) **Bd6** (–.79/18; 2:08m) **36 Kf3** (Kh2; 3:52m)

Position after 36 Kf3.

Hydra's king entered the fray to shore up its center, and somehow managed to go unscathed in the process.

36 ... Bf8 (–.81/18; 2:29m) **37 Bh3** (Ra7; 14s) **Kh8** (–1.53/20; 5:49m) **38 Bc1** (Ra7; 1:43m) **Kg8** (–1.65/18; 1:41m) **39 Be3** (2:09m) **Ne6** (–1.92/20; 0s) **40 Rd2** (1:57m) **Ra8** (–1.68/20; 0s) **41 Rxa8** (1:50m) **Rxa8** (–1.64/22; 0s) **42 Nb6** (Bxe6; 53s) **Re8** (–.54/21; 1:20m) **43 Bxe6** (Bf5; 1:21m) **Rxe6** (–.89/22; 22s) **44 Rd8** (22s) **Re8** (–.98/24; 1:06m) **45 Rxe8** (9s) **Bxe8** (–1.19/25; 29s) **46 Nd5** (16s) **f6** (–.89/26; 1:45m) **47 Bd2** (8s) **Bh5+** (–.89/25; 36s) **48 Ke3** (14s) **Bc5+** (–1.14/25; 1:39m) **49 Kd3** (6s) **Kf7** (–1.02/24; 39s) **50 Bxb4** (21s) **Bf2** (–.96/23; 9s) **51 Ba5** (gxf6; 1:07m) **Bxh4** (–.68/24; 1:51m) **52 gxf6** (7s) **Bxf6** (–.64/24; 50s) **53 b4** (c4; 8s) **Bg4** (–.61/24; 36s)

54 c4 (13s) h5 (–.77/24; 1:21m)
55 b5 (6s) Bd7 (–.66/23; 52s) 56 Ke2
(50s) g5 (–.97/23; 37s) 57 Nxf6 (Bc7;
9s) Kxf6 (–.24/26; 59s) 58 Bd8+
(25s) Kg6 (–.31/28; 24s) 59 Kf2
(1:35m) h4 (–.29/28; 0s) 60 Be7
(Kg2; 1:31m) h3 (–.06/25; 1:24m)
61 Kg3 (9s) g4 (–.06/25; 1:21m)
62 Bc5 (Bb4; 11s) Kf6 (–.05/23; 38s)
63 Bb4 (Ba7; 10s) Be8 (+.00/25; 37s)
64 Ba3 (Bc5; 1:08m) Bg6 (+.30/24;
1:01m) 65 c5 (45s) Bxe4 (+.30/25;
0s) 66 c6 (57s) Ke6 (+.54/24; 0s)
67 c7 (Bc5; 29s) Bb7 (+.83/22; 24s)
68 Bc5 (3:33m) Kd5 (+1.30/26; 0s)
69 Bg1 (35s) Bc8 (+1.29/25; 37s)
70 b6 (10s) Ke4 (+1.61/24; 34s)
71 b7 (8s) Bxb7 (+1.26/25; 2:23m)
72 Kxg4 (8s)

Position after 72 Kxg4.

While Shredder had an extra pawn, there
was no way it could win the game. Both
sides agreed to a draw 23 moves later.
Shredder never saw it coming based on
the score it was calculating.

72 ... Bc8+ (+1.25/25; 54s) 73 Kg3
(6s) Kd3 (+1.26/26; 41s) 74 Kf2 (9s)
e4 (+1.26/26; 32s) 75 Bh2 (6s) 75 ... e3+

(+1.26/24; 22s) 76 Ke1 (13s) Ba6
(+1.29/23; 39s) 77 Be5 (Bg3; 33s)
Ke4 (+1.32/26; 53s) 78 Bh2 (Bd6;
30s) Kf3 (+1.36/25; 1:03m) 79 Be5
(Bg1; 31s) Bc8 (1.36/24; 17s) 80 Kf1
(7s) Bd7 (+1.35/24; 13s) 81 Bd6
(Bh2; 33s) Bf5 (+1.35/24; 43s)
82 Be5 (Bh2; 35s) Ke4 (+1.20/22;
31s) 83 Bg3 (35s) Kf3 (+1.25/25; 0s)
84 Be5 (40s) Bc8 (+1.23/25; 0s)
85 Bd6 (Ke1; 29s) Be6 (+1.23/25;
39s) 86 Ke1 (28s) Bg4 (+1.23/23; 0s)
87 Kf1 (Bh2; 16s) Be6 (+1.23/22; 5s)
88 Ke1 (41s) Bc8 (+1.19/24; 0s)
89 Kf1 (11s) Bg4 (+1.19/24; 25s)
90 Be5 (Ke1; 23s) e2+ (+1.12/25;
19s) 91 Ke1 (26s) Ke3 (+1.12/25; 0s)
92 Bd6 (25s) Be6 (+1.14/24; 16s)
93 Bc5+ (10s) Kf3 (+1.13/23; 15s)
94 Bd6 (7s) Bc8 (+1.13/23; 5s)
95 Bh2 (11s) Bf5 (+1.13/24; 8s)
Drawn by agreement.

Position after 95 ...Bf5,
Drawn by agreement.

After two losses, Shredder has now
drawn three, but with three games to go,
Hydra must have been preparing the
victory celebration.

Abu Dhabi Computer Challenge, Abu Dhabi
Game 6, August 21, 2004
Shredder (W) versus Hydra(B) ·
Sicilian Defense (B54)

1 e4 c5 2 Nf3 e6 3 d4 cxd4 4 Nxd4 a6 (Nf6) 5 Bd3 Bc5 (Nf6) 6 Nb3 Ba7 7 Qe2 d6 (Nc6) 8 Be3 Nc6 (Bxe3) 9 Nc3 b5 (Bxe3; 1:42m) 10 Bxa7 (+.62/20; 2:29m) Rxa7 (2:57m) 11 Qg4 (+.51/21; 0s) Nf6 (Qd6; 2:16m) 12 Qxg7 (+.94/21; 4:16m) Rg8 (8s) 13 Qh6 (+1.14/22; 3:26m) Rxg2 (8s) 14 Qh3 (+1.05/20; 1:37m) Rg8 (1:01m) 15 O-O-O (+1.08/19; 39s) b4 (e5; 1:55m) 16 Ne2 (+.89/18; 1:48m) e5 (2:18m) 17 Qf3 (+.82/19; 1:45m) Be6 (Rg6; 2:22m) 18 h3 (+.94/19; 2:33m) Ke7 (2:49m) 19 Qe3 (+1.03/21; 0s) Nd7 (Bxb3; 3:44m) 20 Kb1 (+1.15/18; 1:24m) Qb6 (4:17m) 21 Qh6 (+1.19/21; 0s) Nf6 (a5; 4:03m) 22 Rhf1 (+1.44/18; 1:47m) a5 (2:46m) 23 Nd2 (+1.58/18; 0s)

Position after 23 Nd2.

Shredder's +1.58 evaluation of the position was its most positive of this game, and, in fact, the most positive of any

position it had in the entire match! Some credit must have been given for having castled while Hydra's king had not and could not. The evaluation dropped a full pawn after its next move.

23 ... Nd4(b3; 2:04m) 24 Nc1 (+.54/19; 16:46m) a4 (3:38m) 25 f4 (+.27/18; 1:05m) Qc5 (1:08m) 26 fxe5 (+.27/19; 0s) Qxe5 (3:28m) 27 Nc4 (−.38/19; 2:11m) Qg5 (4:14m) 28 Qxg5 (−.13/21; 0s) Rxg5 (36s) 29 Nxd6 (−.37/20; 30s) Bxh3 (1:08m) 30 Rf4 (−.37/19; 0s) Kxd6 (1:45m) 31 Rxf6+ (−.38/20; 0s) Be6 (Ke5; 58s) 32 Rh6 (+.53/18; 46s) Ke5 (2:55m) 33 Rxh7 (+.56/20; 0s) Bg4 (12s) 34 Rd2 (+.58/19; 50s) Bf3 (1:21m) 35 c3 (+.43/20; 4s) bxc3 (1:36m) 36 bxc3 (+.24/19; 2s) Ne6 (1:42m) 37 Rh3 (+.12/18; 1:23m) Rg2 (Bxe4; 1:10m) 38 Rxg2 (+.05/19; 1:04m) Bxg2 (30s) 39 Rh5+ (+.00/20; 1:37m)

Position after 39 Rh5+.

Shredder, though up a pawn, evidently was satisfied with a draw here, assigning its move a score of +.00. It also assigned a score of +.00 to a number of coming moves.

39 ... Kf4 (53s) 40 Kc2 (–.02/19; 1s) Ke3 (Bf3; 1:08m) 41 e5 (–.11/19; 1:09m) Nf4 (Re7; 10s) 42 Rg5 (+.00/21; 50s) Nxd3 (11s) 43 Nxd3 (+.00/24; 52s) Be4 (9s) 44 Rg3+ (–.01/24; 26s) Ke2 (2:49m) 45 Rh3 (–.01/27; 0s) Bf5 (1:25m) 46 Rg3 (–.01/26; 0s) Rd7 (Bg6; 43s) 47 Rg2+ (+.00/25; 51s) Ke3 (13s) 48 Rg3+ (+.00/25; 1:19m) Ke4 (7s) 49 Kd2 (+.00/24; 36s) Kd5 (10s) 50 Ke2 (+.00/22; 33s) Rd8 (Rc7; 9s) 51 Rg7 (–.02/20; 1:11m) Rf8 (Bxd3+; 8s) 52 Rg5 (+.00/19; 33s) Ke4 (41s) 53 Rg3 (+.00/20; 1s) Rh8 (50s) 54 Rg2 (+.00/21; 0s) a3 (Rd8; 2:11m) 55 Rf2 (+.25/22; 40s) Rh4 (8s) 56 Kd2 (+.19/23; 39s) Be6 (7s) 57 Nc5+ (+.08/22; 33s) Kxe5 (50s) 58 Nxe6 (–.17/23; 17s) Kxe6 (23s) 59 Kd3 (–.08/23; 4s) f5 (1:00m) 60 c4 (–.03/25; 0s) Ke5 (31s) 61 Re2+ (–.01/24; 19s) Kd6 (33s) 62 Kc3 (–.01/24; 14s) f4 (Rh8; 48s) 63 Re4

(+.00/25; 36s) Rh3+ (Kc5; 12s) 64 Kb4 (+.00/25; 39s) 64 ... f3 (14s) 65 Re8 (+.00/23; 41s) Rh1 (Kd7; 37s) 66 Rf8 (+.02/22; 27s) Rb1+ (Rf1; 48s) 67 Kxa3 (+.04/25; 1:06m) Rf1 (11s) 68 Kb2 (+.03/24; 50s) f2 (Ke5; 28s) 69 a4 (+.01/26; 46s) **Drawn by agreement.**

Position after 69 a4,
Drawn by agreement.

The fourth consecutive draw left Hydra up 4–2 with two rounds to go. Hydra assured itself to finish no worse than tied with Shredder. But a tie was highly unlikely given the treatment Shredder had received thus far.

Abu Dhabi Computer Challenge, Abu Dhabi
Game 7, August 23, 2004
Hydra (W) versus Shredder (B)
Sicilian Defense: Najdorf. Opocensky Variation (B92)

---

1 e4 c5 2 Nf3 d6 3 d4 cxd4 4 Nxd4 Nf6 5 Nc3 a6 6 Be2

To here, the same as Game 5. Shredder drew playing 6 ... e6.

6 ... e5 7 Nb3 Be7 8 O-O O-O 9 Kh1 (Be3) b6 10 Be3 (Bg5) Bb7 11 f3 b5 12 Qd2 Nbd7 13 a3 (3:14m) Qc7 (+.00/19; 2:05m) 14 Rfd1 (Rad1; 40s) Rad8 15 Qe1 (2:41m) Nc5 (–.22/18; 2:44m) 16 Nxc5 (Rac1; 3:06m) dxc5

(+.15/14; 4s) 17 b3 (Qf2; 14:52m)
Bc6 (–.01/19 3:42m) 18 a4 (Kg1;
2:48m) b4 (–.17/21; 2:38m) 19 Na2
(35s) a5 (–.16/20; 1:47m) 20 c3 (Qf2;
10s) Nh5 (–.22/19; 1:48m) 21 Rac1
(Qf2; 3:23m) Bxa4 (–.46/20; 4:53m)
22 bxa4 (1:51m) b3 (–.74/22; 39s)
23 Bc4 (55s) bxa2 (–.65/21; 54s)
24 Qe2 (40s) h6 (–.71/21; 1:30m)
25 Qxa2 (Bd5; 24s) Bg5 (–.55/21;
1:08m) 26 Bxg5 (45s) hxg5 (–.53/21;
0s) 27 h3 (Bd5; 3:02m) Qe7 (–.63/19;
2:05m) 28 Kg1 (Rb1; 1:46m) Nf4
(–.73/19; 1:39m) 29 Kh2 (Rb1; 8s)
Nh5 (–.77/19; 1:16m) 30 Rb1 (1:35m)
Nf6 (–1.01/20; 1:47m) 31 Qb3 (Kh1;
1:47m) Nh5 (–1.55/20; 2:02m)
32 Qb6 (21s) Rxd1 (–1.56/19; 1s)
33 Rxd1 (2:31m) g4 (–1.53/22; 1s)
34 fxg4 (2:25m) Qf6 (–1.65/22; 0s)
35 Qxf6 (2:19m) Nxf6 (–3.18/27; 0s)

36 g5 (Bd5; 1:18m) Nxe4 (–4.24/28;
7:51m) 37 g6 (15s) Nxc3 (–4.24/25;
1:49m) 38 Rc1 (Rf1; 2:08m) Nxa4
(–3.57/25; 1:39m) 39 Rf1 (10s) Nc3
(–3.68/25; 55s) 40 Bxf7+ (2:06m)
Rxf7 (–4.09/26; 9s) 41 Rxf7 (59s) a4
(–4.48/25; 10:56m) 42 Rc7 (55s) Kf8
(–4.47/25; 0s) 43 Rxc5 (1:23m) Nd1
(–4.94/24; 13s) 44 Rxe5 (55s) a3
(–5.03/24; 0s) 45 Rf5+ (53s) Ke8
(–5.24/24; 0s) 46 Ra5 (Rf7; 47s) Nb2
(–5.74/23; 3:18m) **Black resigns**

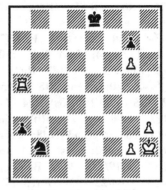

Position after 46 ... Nb2,
Black resigns.

While Shredder's knight was munching
on Hydra's pawns, Hydra's g-pawn,
bishop and rook teamed up to polish off
Shredder's chance to end the match with
an even score.

Abu Dhabi Computer Challenge, Abu Dhabi
Game 8, August 24, 2004
Shredder (W) versus Hydra (B)
Sicilian Defense: Paulsen. Bastrikov Variation (B47)

This game had no consequence on the
outcome of the match but was played
nevertheless.

1 e4 c5 2 Nf3 e6 (d6) 3 d4 cxd4
4 Nxd4 Nc6 (Nf6) 5 Nc3 Qc7 (Nf6)
6 Be2 a6 (Nf6) 7 O-O Nf6 8 Be3 Bb4
9 Na4 O-O 10 c4 Bd6 (2:27m) 11 g3
Nxe4 (Nxd4; 3:56m) 12 Bf3 f5
(2:38m) 13 c5 Be5 (5:11m) 14 Nxc6
dxc6 (7:26m) 15 Nb6 (+.28/20;
3:58m) Rb8 (11s) 16 Qc2 (+.12/20;
4:00m) Nf6 (Bf6; 1:40m) 17 Nc4
(+.16/19; 1:51m) f4 (10s) 18 Bd2
(+.21/19; 1:33m) Bd4 (10s) 19 Bxf4
(+.10/20; 2:35m) e5 (8s) 20 Be3
(+.15/20; 1:50m) Be6 (Bxe3; 1:25m)
21 Bxd4 (+..08/18; 1:58m) exd4 (10s)
22 Qe2 (+.02/19; 5:07m) Bf5 (1:59m)
23 Rfe1 (+.00/19; 3s) d3 (2:21m)
24 Qd2 (+.00/20; 0s) Qd8 (Rbd8;
2:07m) 25 Qc3 (+.48/18; 3:16m) Nd7

(Nd5; 2:01m) 26 b4 (+.52/19; 1:29m) 26 ... Qf6 (2:00m) 27 Qxf6 (+.62/21; 0s) Nxf6 (Rxf6; 1:59m) 28 a3 (+.61/20; 1:49m) Rfd8 (Rfe8; 1:19m) 29 Nd6 (+.55/20; 1:22m) Bg6 (15s) 30 Re7 (+.83/20; 1:06m) b6 (Rd7; 21s) 31 Bxc6 (+1.18/20; 3:41m) bxc5 (10s) 32 bxc5 (+.93/20; 1:52m) Rb3 (4:00m) 33 Reel (+.97/21; 0s) d2 (Kf8; 2:09m) 34 Re3 (+1.24/20; 1:27m) Bc2 (Rxe3; 2:18m) 35 Bf3 (+1.21/21; 55s) Rxe3 (2:25m) 36 fxe3 (+1.24/23; 0s) g5 (Nd7; 1:16m) 37 Bd1 (+1.09/20; 1:13m) Bd3 (22s) 38 h3 (+1.02/20; 1:20m) Ne4 (Kf8; 2:03m) 39 Nxe4 (+.70/22; 2:18m) Bxe4 (6s) 40 Kf2 (+.71/21; 50s) Kg7 (1:24m) 41 Ke2 (+.81/22; 0s) h5 (57s) 42 g4 (+.84/23; 0s) h4 (hxg4; 51s) 43 Ra2 (+.01/24; 1:45m) Bd3+ (11s) 44 Kf2 (+.08/26; 52s) Rf8+ (18s) 45 Kg2 (+.07/26; 14s) Be4+ (22s) 46 Kg1 (+.05/26; 25s) Rd8 (35s) 47 Rb2 (+.06/25; 11s) Kf6 (1:24m) 48 Rb6+ (+.06/24; 0s) Ke5 (46s) 49 c6 (+.02/24; 57s) Rc8 (Bd3; 1:05m) 50 Rxa6 (−.05/24; 1:53m) Bd3 (11s) 51 Rb6 (−.04/22; 6s) Ke4 (Rf8; 1:07m) 52 Rb7 (−.05/23; 53s) Rxc6 (36s) 53 Re7+ (−.29/24; 1:15m) Kd5 (7s) 54 Bb3+ (−.05/23; 26s) Kd6 (Bc4; 26s) 55 Re6+ (−.26/25; 49s) Kc5 (Kc7; 13s) 56 Rxc6+ (−.26/25; 44s) Kxc6 (5s)

The final phase of the game was entered. Neither side was able to do more than dance until the game ended 18 moves later.

57 Kf2 (−.51/29; 1:17m) Kc5 (Kd6; 18s) 58 Kf3 (−.50/27; 1:04m) Bf1 (8s) 59 Kf2 (−.51/28; 28s) Bb5 (1:12m) 60 a4 (−.50/30; 15s) Bd3 (1:24m) 61 Bd1 (−.32/29; 0s) Kc4 (Kb4; 38s) 62 e4 (−.26/28; 44s) Kd4 (Bxe4; 41s) 63 e5 (−.20/28; 1:02m) Kxe5 (7s) 64 Ke3 (+.00/29; 22s) Bf1 (33s) 65 Kxd2 (−.25/28; 2:47m) Bxh3 (7s) 66 Bf3 (−.08/25; 4s) Bf1 (1:14m) 67 Ke3 (−.13/25; 0s) Bc4 (Ba6; 46s) 68 a5 (−.12/27; 36s) Ba6 (Bb5; 11s) 69 Bg2 (+.00/27; 49s) Bb5 (Kd6; 49s) 70 Bb7 (−.04/27; 48s) Kd6 (1:02m) 71 Bg2 (−.01/28; 0s) Kc5 (40s) 72 Bh3 (−.04/26; 17s) Kd5 (Bc6; 25s) 73 Bg2+ (−.04/29; 0s) Kc5 (Kd6; 42s) 74 Bh3 (+.00/28; 18s) Kd5 (Bc6; 21s) 75 Bg2+ (−.04/26; 6s) Kc5 (Kd6; 43s) **Drawn by repetition.**

Position after 75 ... Kc5, Drawn by repetition.

Position after 56 ... Kxc6.

Suggest Readings

Shredder's report on the Abu Dhabi Computer Challenge: http://www.shredderchess.com/chess
   –download/games/abu –dhabi –2004.html

Shredder's version of 2005 IPCCC in Paderborn: http://www.shredderchess.com/chess –news/
   shredder –news/ipccc2005.html

Website of Hydra Chess Engine: http://www.hydrachess.com/

Article in the New Yorker about Hydra and Michael Adams: http://www.newyorker.com/
   archive/2005/12/12/051212fa_fact_mueller

A review of the New Yorker Article, by Michael Goeller: http://www.kenilworthchessclub.org/
   kenilworthian/2005/12/new –yorker –article–On –computer –chess.html

Game 1: http://www.chessgames.com/perl/chessgame?gid=1305843

Game 2: http://www.chessgames.com/perl/chessgame?gid=1302498

Game 3: http://www.chessgames.com/perl/chessgame?gid=1302500

Game 4: http://www.chessgames.com/perl/chessgame?gid=1302501

Game 5: http://www.chessgames.com/perl/chessgame?gid=1302502

Game 6: http://www.chessgames.com/perl/chessgame?gid=1302503

Game 7: http://www.chessgames.com/perl/chessgame?gid=1305844

Game 8: http://www.chessgames.com/perl/chessgame?gid=1305845

2005: Zappa Red Hot at 13th WCCC

9

Iceland may be one of the cooler countries on this planet, but Zappa was red-hot August 13–21, 2005 when it totally dominated the field at the 13th WCCC played at Reykjavik University. And if the Bobby Fischer versus Boris Spassky world championship match in 1972 was the most famous chess match in Iceland's history, this competition will go down as the strongest tournament ever played on its soil, or better, its rocks. Fischer is certainly the most famous chess player to compete in Iceland; Zappa may be the strongest player ever to compete there.

Zappa won ten of its eleven games, drawing only with Futé, the last place finisher. Futé lost all its other games. Second place went to another newcomer Fruit, developed by French computer games programmer, Fabien Letouzey. The current world champion Junior and the former world champion Shredder couldn't keep up, finishing four and three points off the lead, respectively. The twelve participants came from six different countries: Belgium, France, Germany, Israel, The Netherlands, and the USA.

Whoo! We haven't mentioned Hydra, who smashed Shredder just one year ago? Considering that performance, Hydra could arguably be considered the best of all chess engines. But the Hydra team decided to pass up this year's championship. However, Zappa's amazing performance put in doubt whether Hydra could argue it was best.

M. Newborn, *Beyond Deep Blue: Chess in the Stratosphere*,
DOI 10.1007/978-0-85729-341-1_9, © Springer-Verlag London Limited 2011

Zappa's creator, Anthony Cozzie.
(Photo courtesy of Anthony Cozzie)

Where in the world did Zappa come from? Well, to anyone who is a bit hip, it's clear the name came from Frank Zappa, prominent singer and composer whose career was cut short by prostate cancer. He died at the early age of 53. Zappa, the chess engine, followed a typical path to the top of the world of chess engines: a 13th place finish in the 2003 Internet Chess Club CCT 5, a third place finish the following year, and then a first place finish just half a year before this championship. In addition, in July of 2005, a month before coming to Iceland, Zappa knocked off GM Jaan Ehlvest, 3–1, in a 4-game match in New York. Ehlvest had a rating just above 2600. Zappa's creator, Anthony Cozzie, was a University of Illinois at Urbana-Champaign graduate student while Zappa was being developed.

After two rounds, Zappa and Fruit, two newcomers to a computer chess world championship, found themselves at the top of the pack, the only undefeated engines. Crafty had been the troublemaker for Shredder in Round 1, and the wrecker of Junior in Round 2. In the third round, Zappa became the sole leader when it polished off Fruit in a 75-move battle.

In Round 4, Zappa only managed to draw against last place finisher Futé, while Crafty pulled even with Zappa when it garnered a full point in its game with The Crazy Bishop. Futé's draw with Zappa was the only game it managed not to lose.

Thus, after four rounds, Zappa found itself sharing the lead with Crafty, both with three and a half points. Junior was a half point behind. Most notable in the fifth round was Fruit's defeat of Shredder, perhaps the landmark loss marking Shredder's decline from the top of the computer chess world, somewhat akin to Belle's loss to Cray Blitz in the 4th WCCC held in 1983 in New York.

Zappa won its game in Round 6 as well as all its remaining games. In Round 7, it played Junior. If Junior had won, it would have taken over first place, and in the driver's seat on the road to defending its title. The game followed book lines until the 20th move. On the 26th move, Zappa forced a pawn to d6 into the heart of Junior's camp. This opened the gates for an onslaught of White attackers, and a resignation by a helpless Junior ten moves later. Zappa now had six and a half points and led the field by one and a half points with four rounds remaining.

After an eighth round victory, Zappa had an impressive seven and a half points, two points better than Junior, Shredder, Crafty, Fruit, and Deep Sjeng. A ninth round victory by Zappa over Shredder, victories by Fruit and Junior, a draw by Crafty, and a loss by Deep Sjeng meant that with two rounds to go, only Fruit and Junior had a chance to finish even with Zappa. This seemed an unlikely scenario as Zappa would have to lose its final two games, and thus far, it had only drawn one of nine. Zappa's tenth round victory over Crafty sewed up the championship.

In the final round, what was anticipated before the competition began as the ultimate showdown of the tournament turned out to be an anticlimactic contest to see who would finish in third place: Shredder defeated Junior to finish with seven and a half points, three behind Zappa. Junior was a full point further behind.

Thus the world had a new computer chess champion, one that totally dominated its opponents. Zappa had just polished off upstart Fruit, world champion Junior, former world champion Shredder, Crafty, and six other respectable engines, drawing only one of eleven games. Given Junior's results with Kasparov in 2003, and Deep Fritz's results with Kramnik the previous year, it would be a fair estimate that the world's top humans would have been hard pressed to finish much higher than the middle of the field of twelve. Amazing!

Data on entries to the 13th WCCC: Name, country of origin, authors, opening book, endgame tables, hardware

Name	Origin	Authors	Opening book	Endgame tables	Hardware
Zappa	USA	Anthony Cozzie	Erdogan Gûnez	5+	AMD 64 2x2 2.2 GHz
Fruit	FRA	Fabian Letouzey	Marc Lacrosse	None	AMD 64 1x2 2.4 GHz
Deep Sjeng	BEL	Gian-Carlo Pascutto	Jeroen Noomen	5	AMD 64 1x2 2.2 GHz
Shredder	DEU	Stefan Meyer-Kahlen	Sandro Necchi	5+	AMD 64 4x2 2.6 GHz
Crafty	USA	Robert Hyatt	Peter Berger	5+	AMD 64 4x2 2.2 GHz
Junior	ISR	Amir Ban, Shay Bushinsky	Boris Alterman	5	4 CPUs
Diep	NLD	Vincent Diepeveen	Vincent Diepeveen	6	AMD 64 4x2 1.8 GHz
Jonny	DEU	Johannes Zwanzger	Johannes Zwanzger	5	AMD 64 2.6 GHz
The Baron	NLD	Richard Pijl	Carlos Pesce	5	Intel 3.0 GHz
IsiChess	DEU	Gerd Isenberg	Gerd Isenberg	None	AMD 64 2.2 GHz
The Crazy Bishop	FRA	Remi Coulom	Remi Coulom	None	Intel 3.0 GHz
Futé	FRA	Jean-Louis. Boussin	Jean-Louis. Boussin	KPK	AMD 64 2.2 GHz

Results Table for the 13th WCCC, Reykjavik

#	Name	1	2	3	4	5	6	7	8	9	10	11	Pts	BU
1	Zappa	11wW	3bW	2wW	12bD	8wW	9bW	6wW	10wW	4bW	5wW	7bW	10.5	55.5
2	Fruit	8bW	9wW	1bL	10wD	4bW	5wW	7bL	11wW	3bW	6bW	12wW	8.5	57.5
3	Deep Sjeng	9bD	1wL	10bW	4wD	5bW	7wW	11bW	6bD	2wL	12bW	8wW	7.5	58.5
4	Shredder	5wD	7bW	11wW	3bD	2wL	12bW	8wW	9bD	1wL	10bW	6wW	7.5	58.5
5	Crafty	4bD	6bW	7wW	11bW	3wL	2bL	12wW	8bW	9wD	1bL	10wD	6.5	59.5
6	Junior	12bW	5wL	8bW	7wW	9bW	11wW	1bL	3wD	10bW	2wL	4bL	6.5	59.5
7	Diep	10bW	4wL	5bL	6bL	11wW	3bL	2wW	12bW	8wD	9bW	1wL	5.5	60.5
8	Jonny	2wL	12bW	6wL	9wW	1bL	10wW	4bL	5wL	7bD	11wW	3bL	4.5	61.5
9	The Baron	3wD	2bL	12wW	8bL	6wL	1wL	10bD	4wD	5bD	7wL	11bW	4.0	62.0
10	IsiChess	7wL	11bL	3wL	2bD	12wW	8bL	9wD	1bL	6wL	4wL	5bD	2.5	63.5
11	The Crazy Bishop	1bL	10wW	4bL	5wL	7bL	6bL	3wL	2bL	12wW	8bL	9wL	2.0	64.0
12	Futé	6wL	8wL	9bL	1wD	10bL	4wL	5bL	7wL	11bL	3wL	2bL	0.5	65.5

13th WCCC, Reykjavik
Round 3, August 15, 2005
Zappa (W) versus Fruit (B)
Queen Pawn Opening (A45)

1 d4 Nf6 2 Nc3 d5 3 f3 e6 4 e4 Bb4
5 a3 Bxc3+ 6 bxc3 c5 7 e5 Nfd7 8 f4
Qh4+ 9 g3 Qd8 10 Bd3 c4 11 Bf1
O-O 12 Nf3 Qa5 13 Bd2 Nb6 14 Bh3
Nc6 15 O-O Na4 16 Rf2 Bd7 17 Nh4
g6 18 Rb1 Rab8 19 Qg4 Bc8 20 f5
exf5 21 Qf4 f6 22 Qh6 Qc7 23 Bg2
Be6 24 exf6 Rxf6 25 Bf4 Qe7
26 Bxb8 Nxc3 27 Be5 Nxb1 28 Bxf6
Qxf6 29 Nxf5 Nc3 30 Nh4

Position after 30 Nh4.

Zappa had managed to win a rook for a knight and pawn.

30 ... Qg7 31 Qe3 Nxd4 32 Nf3
Nxf3+ 33 Bxf3 Bf7 34 Qxa7 b5
35 Qb8+ Qf8 36 Qe5 Qg7 37 Qe7
Kh8 38 Rf1 Bg8 39 Re1 Qxe7
40 Rxe7 Nb1 41 Ra7 d4 42 Kf2 Be6
43 Ke1 Nc3 44 Kd2 h5 45 Rb7 Bf5
46 Kc1 Kg8 47 Bc6 Ne2+ 48 Kd2
Nc3 49 Bxb5 Nb1+ 50 Kc1 Nxa3
51 Bd7 Be4 52 Be6+ Kf8 53 Rd7
Nxc2 54 Rf7+ Ke8 55 Rf4 Bd3
56 Bxc4 g5 57 Rf6 Bxc4 58 Kxc2

Ke7 59 Rf5 Ke6 60 Rxg5 Be2 61 Kd2
Kf6 62 Rg8 d3 63 Rf8+ Kg7 64 Rf4
Kh6 65 h3 Kg7 66 Rf2 Kg6

Position after 66 ... Kg6.

Zappa's deep search, aided by transposition tables, saw that exchanging its rook for Fruit's bishop and pawn led to victory.

67 Rxe2 dxe2 68 Kxe2 Kf5 69 Kd3
Ke5 70 Ke3 Kf5 71 Kd4 Ke6 72 Ke4
Kf6 73 Kf4 Kg6 74 Ke5 h4 75 g4 Kg5
Black resigns.

Position after 75 ... Kg5,
Black resigns.

13th WCCC, Reykjavik
Round 5, August 16, 2005
Shredder (W) versus Fruit (B)
Sicilian Defense: Taimanov Variation (B46)

1 e4 c5 2 Nf3 e6 3 d4 cxd4 4 Nxd4 Nc6 5 Nc3 a6 6 Be2 d6 7 Be3 Nf6 8 f4 Be7 9 O-O Qc7 10 Qe1 O-O 11 Kh1 Nxd4 12 Bxd4 b5 13 Qg3 Bb7 14 a3 Bc6 15 Bd3 Rfd8 16 Rae1 Qb7 17 Bxf6 Bxf6 18 e5 Be7 19 Ne4 dxe5 20 fxe5 Rd5 21 Re2 Rf8 22 Nf6+ Bxf6 23 Rxf6 Rd4 24 Rh6 g6 25 Rh4 Rxh4 26 Qxh4 Qb6 27 Qf4 Rd8 28 Rf2 Rd7 29 c3 Qc7 30 Qe3 Qd8 31 Bf1 Rd1 32 Kg1 Qd5 33 Re2 a5 34 Qf2 b4 35 axb4 axb4 36 cxb4 h6 37 Re1 Rxe1 38 Qxe1 Qd4+ 39 Qf2 Qxb4

49 b4 Qb7 50 Qd2 Kg7 51 Qb2 Qb5 52 Kg1 h5 53 Ba2 Qd3 54 Qf2 Kg8 55 Kh2 Be4 56 Qb2 h4 57 b5

Position after 57 b5.

Fruit could have drawn here with 57 … Qg3+, but chose not to. It must have seen winning White's e-pawn while holding off its advancing b-pawn.

57 … g5 58 Qf2 Qc3 59 b6 Kf8 60 Kg1

White's advanced b-pawn came to a stall on b6. Shredder was out of ideas on how to make any progress in this position — not that there were any. So, since you cannot pass in chess, it simply moved its king to and fro while Fruit developed a winning position.

Position after 39 … Qxb4.

A materially even position that looks quite drawn, although we had to wait a while to see if Shredder's b-pawn would become a problem for Fruit.

40 h3 Be4 41 Kh2 Bd5 42 Bd3 Qb7 43 Qf6 Qb6 44 Qh4 Qb8 45 Qf6 Qb7 46 Bb1 Qd7 47 Qh4 Qc7 48 Qf4 Ba8

60 … Qa1+ 61 Kh2 Qxe5+ 62 Kg1 Qa1+ 63 Kh2 Qc3 64 Kg1 Ke7 65 Kh2 f5 66 Kg1 Kd7 67 Kh2 Kc6

68 Qe2 68 ... Kxb6 69 Qf2+ Kc6 70 Qe2
Kd6 71 Bc4 Qe5+ 72 Kg1 Qd4+
73 Kh2 g4 74 hxg4 fxg4 75 Qxg4
Qxc4 76 Qxh4 Qe2 77 Qd8+ Kc6
78 Qc8+ Kb5 79 Qb8+ Kc4 80 Qc7+
Kd3 81 Qd6+ Bd5 82 Qa6+ Kd2
83 Qa5+ Kc2 84 Qa4+ Bb3 85 Qd4
e5 86 Qa7 e4 87 Qc5+ Bc4 88 Qa3
Qd3 89 Qa5 e3 90 Qa4+ Qb3 91 Qe8
e2 92 Qe4+ Kb2 93 Qh4 Qc3 94 Qf2
White resigns.

Position after 94 Qf2,
White resigns.

13th WCCC, Reykjavik
Round 7, August 19, 2005
Zappa (W) versus Junior (B)
Semi-Slav Defense: Stoltz Variation. Shabalov Attack (D45)

---

1 d4 d5 2 Nf3 Nf6 3 c4 e6 4 Nc3 c6
5 e3 Nbd7 6 Qc2 Bd6 7 g4 h6 8 Rg1
e5 9 cxd5 cxd5 10 g5 hxg5 11 Nxg5
e4 12 Nb5 Nb6 13 Bd2 Bf5 14 h3
Bh2 15 Rg2 Rc8 16 Qb3 Bb8 17 Bb4
Nh7 18 Nxh7 Rxh7 19 Rg1 Rc6
20 Nc3 a6 21 a4 Nc4 22 Bxc4 dxc4
23 Qc2 Rch6 24 Qe2 Qc8 25 O-O-O
b5

Zappa was about to push an annoying
d-pawn deep into Junior's territory and
then viciously attack its opponent into
submission.

26 d5 Qb7 27 d6 Bd7 28 axb5 axb5
29 Rg5 f5 30 Rd5 Qa8 31 Kb1 g6
32 Re5+ Kf7 33 Nd5 Kf8 34 Nf6 Rf7
35 Re8+ Kg7 36 Nh5+ **Black**
resigns.

Position after 36 Nh5+,
Black resigns.

Position after 25 ... b5.

13th WCCC, Reykjavik
Round 9, August 2005
Shredder (W) versus Zappa (B)
Sicilian Defense, Dragon Variation (B76)

1 e4 c5 2 Nf3 d6 3 d4 cxd4 4 Nxd4 Nf6 5 Nc3 g6 6 Be3 Bg7 7 f3 O-O 8 Qd2 Nc6 9 O-O-O

Shredder reached this position a year earlier when playing Hydra in Round 5 of the 2004 International CSVN Tournament. Hydra had played 9 ... Nxd4. Shredder built up a strong kingside attack that led to victory. Was it hoping for the same to happen here?

9 ... d5 10 exd5 Nxd5 11 Nxc6 bxc6 12 Nxd5 cxd5 13 Bh6 Qc7 14 Bxg7 Kxg7 15 h4 h5 16 Re1 Rb8

Position after 16 ... Rb8.

Shredder now sacrificed a pawn in hopes of obtaining an advantage on the kingside, but the tactic led nowhere, worse yet, to an eventual defeat. At the level that the top engines were playing, sacrifices that don't yield a fairly quick payback are often the first step on the road to defeat. Zappa fought back, gradually gaining control of the board, advancing its pawns, and forcing a resignation on move 41. A real show of strength by Zappa.

17 g4 hxg4 18 h5 Qb6 19 c3 Rh8 20 fxg4 Bxg4 21 h6+ Kf8 22 b3 Rc8 23 Kb2 d4 24 c4 Bf5 25 Bd3 Bxd3 26 Qxd3 Qd6 27 Qd2 Rh7 28 Qg5 f5 29 Ref1 Rc5 30 Qg2 Kf7 31 Rf2 Qf6 32 Rff1 a5 33 Qa8 g5 34 Kc2 Re5 35 Kc1 g4 36 Kd1 Rh8 37 Qg2 d3 38 Qf2 a4 39 Qh4 Re2 40 Qxf6+ exf6 41 b4 Rxa2 White resigns.

Position after 41 ... Rxa2,
White resigns.

13th WCCC, Reykjavik
Round 11, August 21, 2005
Shredder (W) versus Junior (B)
Sicilian Defense: Najdorf. Poisoned Pawn Variation (B97)

1 e4 c5 2 Nf3 d6 3 d4 cxd4 4 Nxd4 Nf6 5 Nc3 a6 6 Bg5 e6 7 f4 Qb6 8 Nb3 Be7 9 Qf3 Nbd7 10 O-O-O Qc7 11 Kb1 b5 12 Bd3 Bb7 13 Rhe1 b4 14 Ne2 Rc8 15 Ned4 O-O 16 Qh3 Rfe8 17 e5

30 Bc4 Be5 31 Rf1+ Ke8 32 Nd3 Bd6 33 Kc1 Re4 34 Bf7+ Kd8 35 Kd2 Be7 36 Rf5 Rd4 37 Re5 Bf6 38 Rc5 Rd6 39 Ke2 Bd7 40 Rc4 b3 41 axb3 Bb5 42 Re4 Bxd3+ 43 cxd3 Bxb2 44 Bc4 Rd4 45 Re6 Bc3 46 Rc6 Rd7 47 Bg8 Rc7 48 Rxc7 Kxc7 49 Bxh7

Position after 17 e5.

Over the next ten moves, 14 pieces left the board; in the process, Shredder would con Junior out of two pawns, and then coast to victory.

17 ... dxe5 18 fxe5 Nxe5 19 Nxe6 fxe6 20 Qxe6+ Kf8 21 Qxe5 Qxe5 22 Rxe5 Rcd8 23 g3 Be4 24 Bxf6 Bxf6 25 Rxe8+ Rxe8 26 Bxa6 Bf3 27 Rf1 Bg2 28 Rg1 Bc6 29 Nc5 Re3

Shredder had the game wrapped up at this point, but play went on for another ten moves.

49 ... Kd6 50 Be4 Kc5 51 Ke3 Be5 52 Bh7 Bd4+ 53 Kf4 Kb4 54 Bg8 Ba7 55 Bc4 Kc3 56 Kg5 Bc5 57 Kg6 Bd4 58 g4 Kb4 59 g5 Black resigns.

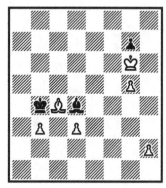

Position after 59 g5,
Black resigns.

Suggest Readings

Yngvi Björnsson and Jaap van den Herik, "The 13th World Computer-Chess Championship, ICGA Journal, Vol. 28, No. 3, pp. 162–175, September 2005.

An article by the Spike team on the Chess 960 Tournament in Mainz: http://spike.lazypics.de/mainz2005_en.html

An article on the Univ of Illinois, Urbana-Champaign Campus Computer Science website about Anthony Cozzie: http://www.cs.uiuc.edu/news/articles.php?id=2005Sep1-76

Zappa versus Fruit, Round 3, 13th WCCC: http://www.chessgames.com/perl/chessgame?gid=1366735

Shredder versus Fruit, Round 5, 13th WCCC: http://www.chessgames.com/perl/chessgame?gid=1366747

Zappa versus Junior, Round 7, 13th WCCC: http://www.chessgames.com/perl/chessgame?gid=1366739

Shredder versus Zappa, Round 9, 13th WCCC: http://www.chessgames.com/perl/chessgame?gid=1366741

Shredder defeated Hydra in 2004 with same opening used in Round 9: http://www.chessgames.com/perl/chessgame?gid=1316427

Shredder versus Junior, Round 11, 13th WCCC: http://www.chessgames.com/perl/chessgame?gid=1366761

2006: Junior, Another Comeback Kid, Wins 14th WCCC

The 14th World Computer Chess Championship was held in the Oval Lingotto, a large arena built for speed skating races at the 2006 Winter Olympics in Turin, Italy. The dates were May 25, 2006, through June 1, 2006. The tournament was hosted by the Organizing Committee of the 37th Chess Olympiad, which took place in the arena at the same time. The computer chess competition was a sideshow for the world's best human players competing in the Olympiad.

All the big boys came for a change – all except Fritz. Zappa returned to defend its title. Comeback kids Junior and Shredder were hoping to come back one more time. The powerful newcomer Rybka, was the new giant kid on the block.[1] Eighteen entrants representing Italy, USA, The Netherlands, Israel, Germany, Hungary, Switzerland, and Spain participated in the 11-round Swiss tournament. Six entrants came from the host country, though none turned out to be contenders.

Rybka came on the scene in December of 2005 when it captured first place in the 15th International Paderborn CCC in Paderborn, Germany. It finished ahead of Zappa and Shredder, defeating Zappa in the process. Two months later, it captured the first place in the Internet Chess Club CCT 8. It won eight of nine points, finishing a point and a half ahead of Zappa, Junior, and Hiarcs and, again, defeating Zappa along the way. Vasik Rajlich, the programmer of Rybka, was born in Cleveland, Ohio, with dual Czech-USA citizenship. He grew up in Prague, returning to the USA for studies, graduating from MIT. He held the title of International Chess Master. During the competition, Rybka ran on an AMD eight-processor machine running at 2.2 GHz.

Zappa ran on 512 processors of the National Center for Supercomputing Applications' (NCSA) Cobalt supercomputer, a 1024 processor machine at the University of Illinois at Champaign-Urbana. It used Intel's Itanium 2 processors running at 1.6 GHz. Zappa was searching one hundred million nodes per second, and looking three to four ply deeper than the Reykjavik version. Junior ran on an

---

[1] In the ICGSA website, Vasik Rajlich's entry is called "Rajlich." On Rybka's website, it is called "Rybka." This chapter uses the name Rybka.

M. Newborn, *Beyond Deep Blue: Chess in the Stratosphere*,
DOI 10.1007/978-0-85729-341-1_10, © Springer-Verlag London Limited 2011

Intel dual-core Xeon 5160 processor (codenamed Woodcrest) that had just been released. The 3 GHz processor gave Junior the ability to search 9.3 million nodes per second, approximately 33% more than in Reykjavik. Shredder's computing system was slightly faster than in Reykjavik where the engine used 2.2 GHz processors. Here in Turin, Shredder's AMD processors ran at 2.6 GHz.

The Swedish Rating List of June 2006 rated Rybka at 2931, almost 100 points higher than any human has ever been rated. Shredder was rated at 2819 and Junior at 2790. Zappa wasn't rated. These chess engines were pulling away from the top human competition. Rybka was rated 110 points higher than was Shredder (2821) at the time of the last world championship.

In the first round, Zappa missed out on a half point when it drew with Jonny. That gave the others hope. In Reykjavik, Zappa won ten and drew one, missing out on a half point in 11 rounds! Here, after one round, it had played to a draw.

After two rounds, Junior, Shredder, and Rybka were undefeated and were tied for the lead. Zappa was a half point behind.

In Round 3, the first game between the killers took place. Shredder defeated Rybka in an impressive game; Shredder won a rook for a bishop and pawn early in the middle game and essentially coasted to a 53-move victory from there. Junior and Zappa won their games. Thus, after three rounds, Junior and Shredder were the only undefeated entries. A half point behind, Rybka and Zappa were in close pursuit.

Junior and Shredder met in Round 4 as did Rybka and Zappa. When the round ended, nothing had changed. Both games were draws. While Shredder seemed to have the advantage throughout most of its game, Junior was able to pull off a draw.

Amir Ban and Shay Bushinsky relaxing while Stefan Meyer-Kahlen awaits
Shredder's 20th move in their two engines' Round 4 encounter.
(Photo courtesy of Gian-Carlo Pascutto)

At one point, Shredder was up three pawns. Then it was forced to give up a knight for an advancing a-pawn to prevent even greater damage. The chess engines agreed to a draw on the 59th move. Zappa and Rybka's game also ended in a draw. Their game followed the Sicilian defense, Najdorf Variation played at the previous world championship and won by Zappa. Zappa played 9 … Nxd4 rather than 9 … d5 as it had in Reykjavik, and wound up settling for a draw.

In Round 5, Rybka rejoined the leader's pack with a victory over feisty Crafty, while Junior, Shredder, and Zappa drew their games, including the game between Shredder and Zappa.

All four contenders drew in Round 6, including the game between Junior and Rybka. Shredder missed the chance to take a clear lead when it drew with Jonny. Thus after six rounds, Junior and Shredder, with 5 points, had a half-point lead over Rybka and Zappa.

Shredder moved to the lead in Round 7 when it defeated Diep, while Junior drew with Zappa and Rybka drew with Jonny. At this point in the tournament, the top four contenders had all played each other and would now take on lesser rivals.

Thus far, Jonny had played the role of spoiler, depriving Zappa, Shredder, and Rybka of victories. It had played with the black pieces against Zappa and Shredder. However, in Round 8, Jonny lost to Junior, propelling the Israeli chess engine into a tie for the lead with Shredder, who could do no better than draw with Spike. Zappa and Rybka trailed by a half point. With three rounds to go, four engines had chances to finish on top, and a tie for the championship loomed large.

In Round 9, the four contenders all won. In the penultimate tenth round, Junior and Rybka won playing White, while Shredder and Zappa drew playing Black. Junior thus found itself with a half-point lead over Shredder and Rybka. Zappa was a half point further behind.

In the final Round 11, Shredder played Chaturanga, one of the weakest entries, and romped to an easy win. Rybka, with Black, played a dangerous Ikarus, but also won. Zappa could do no better than draw with Crafty. The championship went to Junior who defeated IsiChess in an exciting game; Junior's passed pawns and rooks outmaneuvered IsiChess's defending rooks. Isichess played White as it had when it played Junior in the 12th WCCC in 2004. That time, the game ended in a draw. This time, IsiChess pursued a different opening, perhaps hoping to do better than draw. This marked Junior's third world championship, and second comeback.

Junior, Shredder, and Zappa all finished the championship without a loss. All games between the top four finishers ended in draws, with the exception of a victory by Shredder over Rybka in Round 3. It is interesting that Junior won four of its six games with Black. Shredder could win only one. Rybka also won four games with Black though it lost the tournament, perhaps, in Round 3 when playing Black against Shredder. Overall, the record of the top four finishers when playing with the white pieces was 13-8-0, while it was 11-11-1 playing with the black pieces. Clearly, playing with the white pieces was an advantage for the top engines. That didn't seem to be the case for the others. Crafty, in particular, couldn't win a game when playing White, but won all five of its games when playing Black. Three of its losses with White were against the first four finishers, somewhat explaining this irregularity in the data.

Data on entries to the 14th WCCC: Name, country of origin, authors, opening book, endgame tables, hardware

Name	Origin	Authors	Opening book	Endgame tables	Hardware
Junior	ISR	Amir Ban and Shay Bushinsky	Boris Alterman	Yes	Intel 2x2 3.0 GHz
Shredder	DEU	Stefan Meyer-Kahlen	Sandro Necchi	Yes	AMD 4x2 2.6 GHz
Rybka	HUN	Vasik Rajlich	Jeroen Noomen	No	AMD 4x2 2.2 GHz
Zappa	USA	Anthony Cozzie	Erdogan Gûnez	No	Intel 512 proc 1.6 GHz
Spike	DEU	Volker Bôhm and Ralf Schâfer	Timo Klaustermeyer	Yes	AMD 2x2 2.0 GHz
Diep	NLD	Vincent Diepeveen	Eros Riccio	Yes	AMD 2x2 2.4 GHz
Jonny	DEU	Johannes Zwanzger	Stefan Kleinert	Yes	AMD 1x2 2.5 GHz
Crafty	USA	Robert Hyatt	Peter Berger, Marc Lacrosse	Yes	AMD 4x2 2.2 GHz
Ikarus	CHE	Muntsin Kolss and Munjong Kolss	Munjong Kolss	Yes	AMD 2x2 1.8 GHz
IsiChess	DEU	Gerd Isenberg	Gerd Isenberg	No	AMD 2.2 GHz
Delfi	ITA	Fabio Cavicchio	Fabio Cavicchio	No	Intel 3.0 GHz
Chiron	ITA	Ubaldo Farina	Ubaldo Farina	No	AMD 2.2 GHz
ParSOS	DEU	Rudolf Huber	Salvatore Spitaleri	No	AMD 2.0 GHz
Uragano3D	ITA	Luca Nadei	Luca Nadei	No	AMD 2.0 GHz
Chaturanga	ITA	Stefano Malloggi	Stefani Malloggi	No	Intel 3.2 GHz
Lion	ITA	Gian Carlo Delli Colli	No Data Available	No Data Available	No Data Available
FIBChess	ESP	Guillermo Baches Garcia	Guillermo Baches Garcia	No	AMD 2.0 GHz
EtaBeta	ITA	Antonia Jeanrenaud	Antonia Jeanrenaud	No	Intel 3.0 GHz

Final standings of the 14th WCCC, Turin

#	Name	1	2	3	4	5	6	7	8	9	10	11	Pts	BU
1	Junior	11bW	9wW	5bW	2wD	6bD	3wD	4bD	7wW	8bW	14wW	10bW	9.0	70.5
2	Shredder	10wW	8bW	3wW	1bD	4wD	7bD	6wW	5bD	12wW	13bD	15wW	8.5	68.5
3	Rybka	13bW	6wW	2bL	4wD	8bW	1bD	7wD	11wW	18bW	17wW	9bW	8.5	62.5
4	Zappa	7wD	16bW	12wW	3bD	2bD	6wD	14wW	9bW	4bL	11wD	8bD	7.5	70.0
5	Spike	12wD	7bW	1wL	8bD	16wW	9bD	14wW	2wD	4bL	11wD	17bW	6.5	61.0
6	Diep	17wW	3bL	10wW	16bW	1wD	4bD	2bL	8wL	11bW	18wW	12bD	6.5	59.5
7	Jonny	4bD	5wL	14bW	12wW	13bW	2wD	3bD	1bL	15wW	8wL	18bW	6.5	62.5
8	Crafty	14bW	2wD	9bW	5wD	3wL	12bW	10wL	6bW	1wL	7bW	4wD	6.0	73.0
9	Ikarus	18wW	1bL	8wL	11bD	10wW	5wD	13bW	4wL	17bW	15bW	3wL	6.0	58.0
10	IsiChess	2bL	15wW	6bL	14wW	9bL	11wL	8bW	18wW	13bW	4wD	1wL	5.5	60.5
11	Delfi	1wL	17bW	16wL	9wD	12bD	10bW	15wW	3bL	6wL	5bD	14bW	5.5	56.5
12	Chiron	5bD	13wW	4bL	7bL	11wD	8bW	18bW	17wW	2bL	xxD	6wD	5.0	54.0
13	ParSOS	3wL	12bL	18wW	15bW	7wL	17bW	9wL	14bW	10wL	2wD	xxD	5.0	48.0
14	Uragano3D	8wL	18bW	7wL	10bL	17wW	15bW	5bL	13wL	xxD	1bL	11wL	3.5	48.5
15	Chaturanga	16wL	10bL	11bW	13wL	18bW	14wL	11bL	xxD	7bL	9wL	2bL	2.5	44.5
16	Lion	15bW	4wL	11bW	6wL	5bL	Disq.	–	–	–	–	–	2.0	28.5
17	FIBChess	6bL	11wL	15bL	18wW	14bL	13wL	xxD	12bL	9wL	3bL	5wL	1.5	49.5
18	Etabeta	9bL	14wL	13bL	17bL	15wL	xxD	12wL	10bL	3wL	6bL	7wL	0.5	50.5

Note 1: xxD indicates a draw as a result of a bye; note 2: Disq. indicates disqualified.

14th WCCC, Turin
Round 3, May 26, 2006
Shredder (W) versus Rybka (B)
Bishop's Opening (C24)

1 e4 e5 2 Bc4 Nf6 3 d4 exd4 4 Nf3
Nc6 5 e5 d5 6 Bb5 Ne4 7 Nxd4 Bd7
8 Bxc6 bxc6 9 O-O Bc5 10 f3 Ng5
11 f4 Ne4 12 Be3 Bb6 13 Nd2 c5
14 N4f3 Nxd2 15 Qxd2 c6 16 c3 Rb8
17 Qc2 O-O

Position after 17 … O-O.

A quiet game to here. Shredder would
now win a rook for a bishop and pawn
while threatening mate. From there, it
would coast to victory. Rybka had
underestimated the danger of Shredder's
coming f-pawn advances.

18 f5 Rb7 19 f6 gxf6 20 Bh6 c4+
21 Kh1 Bc5 22 Bxf8 Bxf8 23 Rae1
Bc8 24 Qf2 f5 25 Nd4 Qe8 26 Qh4
h6 27 Qh5 Qe7 28 Nxc6 Qg5 29 Qe2
Bc5 30 Nd4 Rb6 31 Nf3 Qg4 32 Qd2
Be6 33 Rb1 Bd7 34 Nd4 Be7
35 Rbe1 Bg5 36 Qf2 f4 37 b4 Qh5
38 Rd1 Bc8 39 a4 Rb7 40 b5 Bg4
41 Nf3 Be6 42 Ra1 Bd8 43 a5 Qg4
44 Qc5 Kh7 45 Qc6 Bc8 46 Qxd5
Rd7 47 Qxc4 Bb7 48 Rad1 Bxa5
49 Rxd7 Qxd7 50 Qxf4 Bxf3 51 Rxf3
Kg8 52 h4 Qe6 53 Qg3+ Black
resigns.

Position after 53 Qg3+,
Black resigns.

14th WCCC, Turin
Round 4, May 27, 2006
Junior (W) versus Shredder (B)
Sicilian Defense: Najdorf Variation. English Attack (B90)

1 e4 c5 2 Nf3 d6 3 d4 cxd4 4 Nxd4 Nf6 5 Nc3 a6

Position after 5 … a6.

Junior and Shredder had met six times before this game. In three of the games, the Sicilian Defense, Najdorf Variation, was played up to this point. In the first game, Junior (W) versus Shredder (B) in the 18th WMCCC in 2001, Junior played 6 Be3 and Shredder replied 6 … e6. Junior won that game. This time, Shredder did better when it played 6 … e5. When playing White, Shredder used this opening, too, against Junior in their two battles in the 2004 and 2005 world championship. In both games in this position, Shredder played 6 Bg5, drawing the first game and winning the second. It seems that both sides were happy playing this line whether as White or Black.

6 Be3 e5 7 Nb3 Be6 8 f3 Nbd7 9 Qd2 Be7 10 g4 O-O 11 O-O-O b5 12 g5 Nh5 13 Nd5 Bxd5 14 exd5 b4 15 Kb1 a5 16 Bb5 a4 17 Nc1 a3 18 Nd3 Rb8 19 Bc6 axb2

Position after 19 … axb2.

Through thick and thin, Junior passed on capturing Shredder's pawn on b2. The pawn served as a shield for Junior's king, and it stayed there until the end of the game. Shredder was up a pawn at this point.

20 Rhg1 Qc7 21 Rg4 f5 22 Rxb4 f4 23 Bf2 Bxg5 24 c3 Kh8 25 Qc2 Nhf6 26 Rg1 Bh6 27 Qa4 Nb6 28 Qa5

Position after 28 … Qa5.

Shredder was about to win a second pawn and be ahead two pawns.

28 ... Nbxd5 29 Qxc7 Nxc7 30 Rxb8
Rxb8 31 Nb4 Ne6 32 Rd1 e4 33 a4
exf3

Position after 33 ... exf3.

Shredder was now ahead three pawns
but Junior's a-pawn would soon become
a major nuisance, forcing Shredder to
give up a knight to remove it from the
board. After that, neither side had much
chance to win.

34 a5 Ng4 35 Rd2 Nxf2 36 Rxf2 Nc7
37 a6 Nxa6 38 Nxa6 Rb3 39 Rxf3 g5
40 Bd5 Rb5 41 Bc4 Rb7 42 Nb4 g4
43 Rd3 Bg7 44 Rxd6 Bxc3 45 Nd5
Bd2 46 Nf6 Bc3 47 Nxg4 Kg7
48 Rd5 Ra7 49 Ba2 h6 50 h4 Ra4
51 Nh2 Re4 52 Rd1 Re3 53 Rg1+
Rg3 54 Rf1 Re3 55 Nf3 Kg6 56 Bb3
Kf5 57 h5 Re7 58 Rd1 Kg4 59 Bd5
Drawn by agreement.

Position after 59 Bd5,
Drawn by agreement.

14th WCCC, Turin
Round 4, May 27, 2006
Rybka (W) versus Zappa (B)
Queen's Gambit Declined Semi-Slav (D45)

---

1 Nf3 Nf6 2 c4 e6 3 Nc3 d5 4 d4 c6
5 e3 Nbd7 6 Qc2 Bd6 7 Be2 O-O
8 O-O dxc4 9 Bxc4 Qe7 10 Ne2 e5
11 Ng3 g6 12 Bb3 e4 13 Ng5 Bxg3
14 fxg3 Nb6 15 Qc5 Qxc5 16 dxc5
Nbd7 17 Bd2 h6 18 Nh3 a5 19 Rac1
a4 20 Bc2 Re8 21 Bb1 a3 22 b3
Nd5 23 Nf4 N7f6 24 Nxd5 Nxd5
25 Rc4 f5 26 g4 Be6 27 gxf5 gxf5
28 Bc2 Red8 29 Rd4 Rd7 30 Rd1
h5 31 Bc1 Nf6 32 Ra4 Rxa4 33 bxa4
Bxa2 34 Bxa3 Rd5 35 Rxd5 Nxd5
36 Kf2 h4 37 Bd1 Bc4 38 Bb2 Nb4
39 Bd4 Nc3+ 40 Kg1 Kf7 41 Bh5+
Ke6 42 a5 Nc1 43 Bd1 Be2 44 Ba4
Kd5 45 Bf6 h3 46 gxh3 Bh5 47 h4

47 ... Kxc5 48 Bg5 Nd3 49 Kg2 f4
50 Bxf4 Nxf4+ 51 exf4 e3 52 Kf1 Kd4
53 a6 bxa6 54 Bxc6 a5 55 h3 Kd3
Drawn by agreement.

Position after 55 ... Kd3,
Drawn by agreement.

> **14th WCCC, Turin**
> **Round 5, May 27, 2006**
> **Shredder (W) versus Zappa (B)**
> **Sicilian Defense: Dragon Variation. Yugoslav Attack (B76)**

1 e4 c5 2 Nf3 d6 3 d4 cxd4 4 Nxd4 Nf6 5 Nc3 g6 6 Be3 Bg7 7 f3 O-O 8 Qd2 Nc6 9 O-O-O

Position after 9 O-O-O.

Thus far, the game followed the same line the two had played at the previous WCCC. Zappa had played 9 ... d5 and won. Here it only drew with the capture!

9 ... Nxd4 10 Bxd4 Be6 11 Kb1 Qc7 12 h4 Rfc8 13 h5 Qa5 14 h6 Bh8 15 a3 Rab8 16 Bxf6 Bxf6 17 Nd5 Qxd2 18 Nxf6+ exf6 19 Rxd2 Rc6 20 a4 Rb6 21 Rd4 Kf8 22 b4 a6 23 b5 axb5 24 axb5 f5 25 exf5 Bxf5 26 Kb2 Re8 27 g4 Bd7 28 c4 Re1 29 Kc3 Ke7 30 Bg2 Re2 31 Rg1 d5 32 Rxd5 Be6 33 Rd3 Ra2 34 Rdd1 Rd6 35 Ra1 Rf2 36 Ra7 Rdd2 37 Rxb7+ Kd6 38 Rb6+ Ke7

Shredder had the option of playing for a draw here with 39 Rb7+, but evidently preferred to play on.

Position after 38 ... Ke7.

39 Bh1 Rc2+ 40 Kd3 Rfd2+ 41 Ke3 Re2+ 42 Kf4 Rxc4+ 43 Kg3 Rb2 44 Rb8 Rb3 45 Kh2 Kf6 46 Rh8 Rxb5 47 Rxh7 Rb8 48 Bg2 g5 49 Rg7 Rh8 50 Kg3 Rxh6 Drawn by agreement.

Position after 50 ... Rxh6,
Drawn by agreement.

The game ended with equal material: each side had a pair of pawns, a pair of rooks, and bishops of the same color.

14th WCCC, Turin
Round 6, May 27, 2006
Junior (W) versus Rybka (B)
Sicilian Defense: Paulsen. Bastrikov Variation English Attack (B48)

1 e4 c5 2 Nf3 e6 3 d4 cxd4 4 Nxd4 Nc6 5 Nc3 Qc7 6 Be3 a6 7 Qd2 Nf6 8 O-O-O Bb4 9 f3 Ne5 10 Nb3 b5 11 Kb1 Nc4 12 Bxc4 bxc4 13 Nc1 Rb8 14 N1e2 O-O 15 Bf4 e5 16 Bg5 Ne8 17 Ka1 d6 18 h4 Be6 19 a3 Qa5 20 Qc1 Rb7 21 h5 h6 22 Bd2 Nc7 23 g4 Rfb8 24 g5 hxg5 25 h6 Nb5 26 Nxb5 Bxd2 27 Rxd2 Rxb5

28 Rd5 f6 29 Rxd6 Rxb2 30 Qxb2 Rxb2 31 Kxb2 Bf7 32 Nc3 Qc7 33 Rhd1 gxh6 34 Rxf6 h5 35 Rdd6 Kg7 36 Rb6 h4 37 Nd5 c3+ 38 Ka1 Qc4 39 Rb7 Qf1+ 40 Ka2 Qc4+ **Drawn by agreement.**

Position after 27 … Rxb5.

Position after 40 … Qc4+,
Drawn by agreement.

Rybka's position had reached an apex. Now Junior would make a sufficient comeback, forcing Rybka to satisfy herself with a draw 12 moves later.

Rybka had no choice but to play for a draw here as Junior was threatening to capture Rybka's bishop and then mate in a few moves.

14th WCCC, Turin
Round 7, May 29, 2006
Zappa (W) versus Junior (B)
Queen's Indian Defense: Fianchetto. Check Variation Intermezzo Line (E15)

---

1 d4 Nf6 2 c4 e6 3 Nf3 b6 4 g3 Ba6
5 b3 Bb4+ 6 Bd2 Be7 7 Bg2 Bb7
8 Nc3 O-O 9 O-O Na6 10 Bc1 d5
11 Ne5 c5 12 Bb2 Nc7 13 Rc1 Bd6
14 cxd5 exd5 15 Nc4 Be7 16 dxc5
Bxc5 17 Na4 Be7 18 Ne3 Re8 19 Nf5
Ne6 20 Rc2 Qd7 21 Qd3 Rad8
22 Rd1 h6 23 Rcc1 Kh8 24 h4 d4

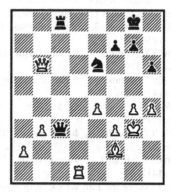

Position after 44 Qxb6.

While Zappa had three extra pawns,
Junior's pieces were positioned for an
attack on its opponent's king. Zappa had
just enough play to avoid a loss.

**44 ... Qe5+ 45 Kg2 Rc2 46 a4 Nf4+
47 Kh1 Nh3 48 Rf1 h5 49 gxh5 Re2
50 Qd8+ Kh7 51 Qb6 Qf4 52 Kg2
Qxh4 53 Qc5 Nf4+ 54 Kg1 Nh3+
55 Kg2 Nf4+ Drawn by agreement.**

Position after 24 ... d4.

Zappa won Junior's isolated d-pawn in
the next few moves and picked up two
more on moves 41 and 44.

25 Nxd4 Bxg2 26 Kxg2 Nxd4
27 Bxd4 Qg4 28 f3 Qh5 29 Qc2 Bd6
30 Bf2 Rd7 31 Nb2 Rc7 32 Qd3 Rxc1
33 Rxc1 Ba3 34 Rc2 Bxb2 35 Rxb2
Qe5 36 Rd2 Kg8 37 e4 Rc8 38 g4
Nh7 39 Qa6 Qc3 40 Rd5 Nf8 41 Qxa7
Ne6 42 Kg3 Nc7 43 Rd1 Ne6
44 Qxb6

Position after 55 ... Nf4+.
Drawn by agreement.

Suggest Readings

Jaap van den Herik and Johanna Hellemons, "The 14th World Computer-Chess Championship, ICGA Journal, Vol. 29, No. 2, pp. 83–94, June 2006.

Rybka at Paderborn, December, 2005: http://www.rybkachess.com/docs/PADERBORN COMPUTER.htm

Rybka's website: http://www.rybkachess.com/index.php?auswahl=Tournaments

Internet Chess Club ICCT8: http://www.cctchess.com/cct8/index.html

14th WCCC, Round 3, Shredder versus Rybka: http://www.chessgames.com/perl/chessgame? gid=1414964

14th WCCC, Round 4, Rybka versus Zappa: http://www.chessgames.com/perl/chessgame? gid=1415419

14th WCCC, Round 4, Junior versus Shredder: http://www.chessgames.com/perl/chessgame? gid=1415418

14th WCCC, Round 5, Shredder versus Zappa: http://www.chessgames.com/perl/chessgame? gid=1415875

14th WCCC, Round 6, Junior versus Rybka: http://www.chessgames.com/perl/chessgame? gid=1417276

14th WCCC, Round 7, Zappa versus Junior: http://www.chessgames.com/perl/chessgame? gid=1417754

Junior's report on the 14th WCCC: http://www.chessbase.com/newsdetail.asp?newsid=3277

Time may have run out on the human race in Bonn, Germany, November 25, 2006–December 5, 2006 when Deep Fritz brought Vladimir Kramnik to his knees. In 1997, Kasparov bowed to Deep Blue, 3.5–2.5. In 2002 and 2003, both Kramnik and Kasparov were unable to do any better than stand even in their respective matches with computers. With the top chess engines clearly stronger than they were during those matches, how could one imagine Kramnik would set matters straight in Bonn in The Duel: Man vs. Machine? Four years had passed since his last encounter with Deep Fritz, four years during which chess engines were improved in many aspects. And if Kramnik didn't manage to win or at least draw, one could be sure future matches were not any more likely to produce favorable results for us humanoids.

Of note, Deep Fritz was not even considered the best chess engine. There were Zappa, Junior, and Hydra; each had some claim to being the best and better than Fritz. Fritz had passed on playing in the 14th WCCC evidently to prepare for this match, but by doing so, it gave up the right to claim itself at the top of the pack.

The contest was sponsored by the German energy company RAG. It took place in the Bonn Museum's Art and Exhibition Hall. Kramnik was guaranteed $500,000, and $1,000,000 if he won. Time controls required each player to make 40 moves in the first two hours and then 16 moves per hour thereafter. Games were played on alternate days beginning November 25, 2006. During the match, Deep Fritz ran on an Intel Core 2 Duo processor while searching about ten million positions per second. More than ten million visitors on the Internet watched as grandmasters Helmut Pfleger, Klaus Bishoff, and Yasser Seirawan gave commentary.

Kramnik seems to have had chances to win the first game, but the two sides traded off pieces to the point where neither side had mating material. The second game was a classic. Kramnik made one of the greatest blunders ever played by a grandmaster when he overlooked a mate-in-one. Only several moves earlier he had passed on an opportunity to draw. The next three games were drawn, even though Kramnik had White in two of them. Under pressure to win the final game, rather than perhaps playing for a draw as he might have done in other circumstances, Kramnik fell a second time to Fritz, losing the match with a 4–2 score.

M. Newborn, *Beyond Deep Blue: Chess in the Stratosphere*,
DOI 10.1007/978-0-85729-341-1_11, © Springer-Verlag London Limited 2011

Vladimir Kramnik versus Deep Fritz in Bonn, 2006: Scorecard

Name	Game 1	Game 2	Game 3	Game 4	Game 5	Game 6	Total points
V. Kramnik	W0.5	B0.5	W1.0	B1.5	W2.0	B2.0	2.0
Deep Fritz	B0.5	W1.5	B2.0	W2.5	B3.0	W4.0	4.0

Man versus Machine, Bonn
Game 1, November 25, 2006
Vladimir Kramnik (W) versus Deep Fritz (B)
Catalan Opening (E03)

**1 d4 Nf6 2 c4 e6 3 g3 d5 4 Bg2 dxc4
5 Qa4+**

Kramnik smartly set out to recapture Black's pawn before he found himself permanently down a pawn.

**5 ... Nbd7 6 Qxc4 a6 7 Qd3 c5 8 dxc5
Bxc5 9 Nf3 O-O 10 O-O Qe7 11 Nc3
b6 12 Ne4 Nxe4 13 Qxe4 Nf6 14 Qh4
Bb7 15 Bg5 Rfd8 16 Bxf6 Qxf6
17 Qxf6 gxf6 18 Rfd1 Kf8 19 Ne1**

Kramnik seemed to have a clear edge here and winning chances with strong endgame play.

**19 ... Bxg2 20 Kxg2 f5 21 Rxd8+ Rxd8
22 Nd3 Bd4 23 Rc1 e5 24 Rc2 Rd5
25 Nb4 Rb5 26 Nxa6 Rxb2 27 Rxb2
Bxb2 28 Nb4 Kg7 29 Nd5 Bd4**

Position after 29 ... Bd4.

30 a4

Could Kramnik have won this game by playing 30 e3, followed by marching his king over to the queenside and grabbing the Black b-pawn?

**30 ... Bc5 31 h3 f6 32 f3 Kg6 33 e4 h5
34 g4 hxg4 35 hxg4 fxe4 36 fxe4
Kg5 37 Kf3 Kg6 38 Ke2 Kg5 39 Kd3
Bg1 40 Kc4 Bf2 41 Kb5 Kxg4
42 Nxf6+ Kf3 43 Kc6 Bh4 44 Nd7
Kxe4 45 Kxb6 Bf2+ 46 Kc6 Be1
47 Nxe5 Kxe5 Drawn by agreement.**

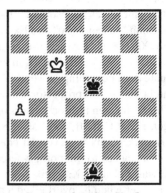

Position after 47 ... Kxe5,
Drawn by agreement.

Man versus Machine, Bonn
Game 2, November 25, 2006
Deep Fritz (W) versus Vladimir Kramnik (B)
Queen's Gambit Accepted (D20)

This game will go down in chess history with others having great blunders. This one should be near the top of the list.

1 d4 d5 2 c4 dxc4 3 e4 b5 4 a4 c6 5 Nc3 b4 6 Na2 Nf6 7 e5 Nd5 8 Bxc4 e6 9 Nf3 a5 10 Bg5 Qb6 11 Nc1 Ba6 12 Qe2 h6 13 Be3 Bxc4 14 Qxc4 Nd7 15 Nb3 Be7 16 Rc1 O-O 17 O-O Rfc8 18 Qe2 c5 19 Nfd2 Qc6 20 Qh5 Qxa4 21 Nxc5 Nxc5 22 dxc5 Nxe3 23 fxe3 Bxc5 24 Qxf7+ Kh8 25 Qf3 Rf8 26 Qe4 Qd7 27 Nb3 Bb6 28 Rfd1 Qf7 29 Rf1 Qa7

Position after 29 ... Qa7.

All was going well for Kramnik to this point. He was given the opportunity to draw by repetition with 29 ... Qd7 but passed, feeling he had chances to do better.

30 Rxf8+ Rxf8 31 Nd4 a4 32 Nxe6 Bxe3+ 33 Kh1 Bxc1 34 Nxf8

Kramnik stepped into mate-in-one! He made a classic visual error here. Overlooking the danger of pieces on the edge of the board, in this case the knight, is a common occurrence. The human mind does not give equal attention to pieces on the edge relative to those in the middle of the board. While this was a major blunder, it was the kind of blunder that even top players make. He was probably focused on forcing a pawn down the throat of Deep Fritz here.

Position after 34 Nxf8.

34 ... Qe3

chessbase.com reported, "Kramnik played the move 34...Qe3 calmly, stood up, picked up his cup, and was about to leave the stage to go to his rest room. At least one audio commentator also noticed nothing, while Mathias Feist, who was running Deep Fritz, kept glancing from the board to the screen and back, hardly able to believe that he had input the correct move. Deep Fritz was displaying mate-in-one, and when Mathias executed it on the board, Kramnik briefly grasped his forehead, took a seat to sign the score sheet, and left for the press conference, which he dutifully attended."

Kramnik's blunder here exceeded his blunder in his previous match with Fritz in 2002 (See Chap. 4, Game 2).

In the near countless number of chess positions, it's surprising how similar the position where Kramnik blundered in Game 5 of the 2002 match is with the position in this game where he blundered.

35 Qh7 Mate.

Position after 35 Qh7, Mate.

Man versus Machine, Bonn
Game 3, November 29, 2006
Vladimir Kramnik (W) versus Deep Fritz (B)
Catalan Opening (E03)

---

1 d4 Nf6 2 c4 e6 3 g3 d5 4 Bg2 dxc4 5 Qa4+ Nbd7 6 Qxc4 a6 7 Qc2

Kramnik chose 7 Qd3 in Game 1 and that ended in a draw.

7 ... c5 8 Nf3 b6 9 Ne5 Nd5 10 Nc3 Bb7 11 Nxd5 Bxd5 12 Bxd5 exd5

13 O-O Nxe5 14 dxe5 Qc8 15 Rd1 Qe6 16 Qd3 Be7 17 Qxd5 Rd8 18 Qb3 Rxd1+ 19 Qxd1 O-O 20 Qb3 c4 21 Qc3 f6 22 b3 Rc8 23 Bb2 b5 24 Qe3 fxe5 25 bxc4 Rxc4 26 Bxe5 h6 27 Rd1 Rc2 28 Qb3 Qxb3 29 axb3 Rxe2 30 Bd6 Bf6 31 Bc5 a5

Position after 31 ... a5.

Kramnik, down a pawn, had to be careful not to err here. At best he could force a draw – which he did.

32 Bd4 Be7 33 Bc3 a4 34 bxa4 bxa4 35 Rd7 Bf8 36 Rd8 Kf7 37 Ra8 a3 38 Rxf8+

A sacrifice by Kramnik that led to a routine draw.

38 ... Kxf8 39 Bb4+ Kf7 40 Bxa3 Ra2 41 Bc5 g6 42 h4 Kf6 43 Be3 h5 44 Kg2 Drawn by agreement.

Position after 44 Kg2, Drawn by agreement.

Man versus Machine, Bonn
Game 4, December 1, 2006
Deep Fritz (W) versus Vladimir Kramnik (B)
Petrov Defense (C42)

---

1 e4 e5 2 Nf3 Nf6 3 d4 Nxe4 4 Bd3 d5 5 Nxe5 Nd7 6 Nxd7 Bxd7 7 O-O Bd6 8 Qh5 Qf6 9 Nc3 Qxd4 10 Nxd5 Bc6 11 Ne3 g6 12 Qh3 Ng5 13 Qg4 Qf4 14 Qxf4 Bxf4 15 Nc4 Ne6 16 Bxf4 Nxf4 17 Rfe1+ Kf8 18 Bf1 Bb5 19 a4 Ba6 20 b4 Bxc4 21 Bxc4

Position after 21 Bxc4.

Deep Fritz entered the endgame with more active pieces than Kramnik, but this position looked more like a draw than anybody's victory.

21 ... Rd8 22 Re4 Nh5 23 Rae1 Rd7 24 h3 Ng7 25 Re5 Nf5 26 Bb5 c6 27 Bd3 Nd6 28 g4 Kg7 29 f4 Rhd8

Kramnik seemed satisfied to get out of this game with a draw.

30 Kg2 Nc8 31 a5 Rd4 32 R5e4 Kf8 33 Kf3 h6 34 Rxd4 Rxd4 35 Re4 Rd6 36 Ke3 g5 37 Rd4 Ke7 38 c4 Rxd4 39 Kxd4 gxf4 40 Ke4 Kf6 41 Kxf4 Ne7 42 Be4 b6 43 c5 bxc5 44 bxc5 Ng6+ 45 Ke3 Ne7 46 Kd4 Ke6 47 Bf3 f5 48 Bd1 Kf6 49 Bc2 fxg4 50 hxg4 Ke6 51 Bb1 Kf6 52 Be4 Ke6 53 Bh1 Kf6 54 Bf3 Ke6 Drawn by agreement.

Position after 29 ... Rhd8.

Position after 54 ... Ke6,
Drawn by agreement.

**Man versus Machine, Bonn
Game 5, December 3, 2006
Vladimir Kramnik (W) versus Deep Fritz (B)
Nimzo-Indian, 4 e3 (E51)**

Kramnik had failed to win a game thus far. He had two remaining games. He had to win one to tie the match and two to win the match. His chances looked grim, though his chances were better in this game in which he'd play with the white pieces than the next.

1 d4 Nf6 2 c4 e6 3 Nf3 d5 4 Nc3 Bb4 5 e3 O-O 6 a3 Bxc3+ 7 bxc3 c5

8 Bb2 Nc6 9 Rc1 Re8 10 Bd3 dxc4 11 Bxc4 e5 12 dxe5 Qxd1+ 13 Rxd1 Nxe5 14 Nxe5 Rxe5 15 Be2 Bd7 16 c4 Re7 17 h4 Ne4 18 h5 Ba4 19 Rd3 b5 20 cxb5 Bxb5 21 Rd1 Bxe2 22 Kxe2 Rb8 23 Ba1 f5 24 Rd5 Rb3 25 Rxf5 Rxa3 26 Rb1 Re8 27 Rf4 Ra2+ 28 Ke1 h6 29 Rg4 g5 30 hxg6 Nxf2 31 Rh4 Rf8 32 Kf1 Nh3+ 33 Ke1 Nf2 34 Kf1 Nh3+ 35 Ke1 Drawn by repetition.

Neither side was in a position to avoid the draw. With Deep Fritz playing White in the final game, there was pressure on Kramnik to avoid a draw unless absolutely necessary. But avoiding a draw here would mean a loss. So a draw it was.

Position after 35 Ke1,
Drawn by repetition.

Man versus Machine, Bonn
Game 6, December 5, 2006
Deep Fritz (W) versus Vladimir Kramnik (B)
Sicilian Defense, Najdorf Variation (B90)

Fritz would be delighted with a draw in this game, and probably set its contempt factor accordingly. Kramnik realized the difficulties he faced. In an interview following his draw in the last game, Ulf Hammarstrom, a chess Expert asked "Even showing your best game, you can't beat the computer. Is it impossible?" Kramnik replied "Well, no... It's very hard to beat the computer, but it is possible. Maybe I will be able to do this in the last game. I will tell you a little secret. I have played with this program many games (60 or so) in rapid time control, 10 minutes each. That's much harder for a man than longer time control. And I played with black every time. Well, I managed to win only twice out of the 60 games. Lots of draws. So I wouldn't be surprised if there are many draws here in this match. I knew that if I played well there would be many draws. If I play badly there will be few draws."

1 e4 c5 2 Nf3 d6 3 d4 cxd4 4 Nxd4 Nf6 5 Nc3 a6 6 Bc4 e6 7 O-O Be7 8 Bb3 Qc7 9 Re1 Nc6 10 Re3 O-O 11 Rg3 Kh8 12 Nxc6 bxc6 13 Qe2 a5 14 Bg5 Ba6 15 Qf3 Rab8 16 Re1 c5 17 Bf4 Qb7 18 Bc1 Ng8 19 Nb1 Bf6 20 c3 g6 21 Na3 Qc6 22 Rh3 Bg7 23 Qg3 a4 24 Bc2 Rb6 25 e5 dxe5 26 Rxe5

Fritz's rook is not up for grabs as a mate would follow. Kramnik knew this.

**26 ... Nf6 27 Qh4 Qb7 28 Re1 h5
29 Rf3 Nh7**

Position after 29 ... Nh7.

Kramnik's position went downhill gradually from here until Deep Junior's
a-pawn became too much to handle.

**30 Qxa4 Qc6 31 Qxc6 Rxc6 32 Ba4
Rb6 33 b3 Kg8 34 c4 Rd8 35 Nb5
Bb7 36 Rfe3 Bh6 37 Re5 Bxc1
38 Rxc1 Rc6 39 Nc3 Rc7 40 Bb5 Nf8
41 Na4 Rdc8 42 Rd1 Kg7 43 Rd6 f6
44 Re2 e5 45 Red2 g5 46 Nb6 Rb8
47 a4 Black resigns.**

Position after 47 a4,
Black resigns.

Suggest Readings

Matthias Wüllenweber, Frederic Friedel, and Mathias Feist, Kramnik vs. Deep Fritz: Computer
    wins match by 4–2, ICGA Journal, Vol. 29, No. 4, pp. 208–213, December 2006.
http://www.uep-chess.com/cms_english/index.php?option=com_content&task=view&id=2&Itemid=3
http://www.scribd.com/doc/3579/Mueller-Kramnik-vs-Deep-Fritz-2002
http://www.thechessdrum.net/newsbriefs/2002/NB_BrainGames2.html
http://www.chessbase.com/eventlist.asp?eventname=Kramnik%20vs%20Deep%20Fritz
Game 1: http://www.chessgames.com/perl/chessgame?gid=1440787, http://www.chessbase.com/
    newsdetail.asp?newsid=3507
Game 2: http://www.chessgames.com/perl/chessgame?gid=1440796, http://www.chessbase.com/
    newsdetail.asp?newsid=3509, Wikipedia article on great chess blunders: http://en.wikipedia.
    org/wiki/Blunder_(chess)
Game 3: http://www.chessgames.com/perl/chessgame?gid=1440892, http://www.chessbase.com/
    newsdetail.asp?newsid=3513
Game 4: http://www.chessgames.com/perl/chessgame?gid=1440893, http://www.chessbase.com/
    newsdetail.asp?newsid=3517
Game 5: http://www.chessgames.com/perl/chessgame?gid=1440901, http://www.chessbase.com/
    newsdetail.asp?newsid=3521
Game 6: http://www.chessgames.com/perl/chessgame?gid=1441056, http://www.chessbase.com/
    newsdetail.asp?newsid=3524

2007: Deep Junior Deep Sixes Deep Fritz in Elista, 4–2

Deep Fritz's defeat of Kramnik in 2006 marked the end of human attempts to outplay their electronic rivals – at least prior to the publication of this book. More than a decade had passed since Garry Kasparov downed Deep Blue in Philadelphia. During that time, computers became much faster and were given far greater storage capacity. Opening books were improved. Debugging produced more solid engines. Scoring functions were more sophisticated with knowledge more cleverly encoded. Search heuristics were more refined. Parallel processing systems were proliferating. One might argue that humans also improved with the top players more knowledgeable about opening theory and more aware of how to play chess engines. But the human improvement was far less than that of the computer hardware and software.

Thus, it is fair to say that 2007 marked the beginning of a new era in the chess world, an era that might be called "Chess in the Stratosphere." The strongest games henceforth would be played by chess engines. They would often make moves that the top humans would not understand. Only other engines would be able to do that. And the engines would continue to outperform the human race by about 50 rating points a year, and that improvement could be expected to continue for many years.

In 1997 when Deep Blue defeated Kasparov, Deep Blue was recognized as the best of the engines. In 2006, Deep Fritz, a chess engine that wasn't even recognized as best, knocked off the human world champion. Well, if Deep Fritz wasn't best, you ask, just who was? And who is best today? The remaining chapters of this book address this question.

It wasn't quite a year after defeating Kramnik that Deep Fritz ran up against arch rival Deep Junior in a six-game match held in Elista, Kalmykia, and entitled The Ultimate Computer Chess Challenge. Deep Junior held the title of world champion and figured to be the stronger of the two, even though in 2002 it had lost a match to Deep Fritz that decided which of the two would play Kramnik in Bahrain and also even though Deep Fritz had just knocked off the human world champion. Didn't that give Deep Fritz some bragging rites? Isn't it reasonable to assume that a chess engine that could outplay Kramnik was the best of the engines? Of course, Deep Junior stood toe-to-toe with Kasparov in 2003. We'll see!

Kalmykia's President Kirsan Ilyumzhinov, a wealthy chess enthusiast and FIDE president, hosted the match in Elista's Chess City Complex, June 6–11, 2007. The Ultimate Computer Chess Challenge was sanctioned by FIDE and by the ICGA. Games were played at a relatively rapid rate of all moves in 75 minutes plus an additional five seconds per move. A $100,000 prize fund was established, with $60,000 going to the winner and $40,000 to the loser.

Deep Fritz ran on an eight-core 2.66 GHz processor located in Hamburg. It was searching about 14 million chess positions per second, and searching to a depth of as much as 20 ply. Deep Junior ran on a 16-core 3.0+ GHz Intel Server located in London. It was searching about 24 million positions per second, and to a depth of as much as 24 ply. It might be noted that when the two chess engines played their match in 2002 for the right to play Kramnik that year, both engines were running on an 8-processor Pentium 3 system running at 900 GHz. Processor speed had almost tripled in the 5 years that had passed. In 2002, Deep Fritz was credited with searching three million positions per second.

The first two games were drawn. Then Deep Junior defeated Deep Fritz twice, the first time in a long tedious endgame and the second time when it won an exchange on the 30th move and then capitalized on a Fritz inaccuracy on the 33rd move. Two draws ended the six-game match with Deep Junior a 4–2 victor.

The match was characterized by a slew of sacrificial offerings. In the first game, Deep Fritz sacrificed two pawns. At one point in the game, Deep Junior was up two pawns, but the short 32-move game ended with material dead even. In the second game, Deep Fritz was up three pawns at one point though a draw was agreed upon with Deep Junior having a bishop to two Deep Fritz pawns. In its first victory in Game 3, Deep Junior sacrificed three pawns leading to a strong position at move 38, though it took another 38 moves to force a resignation. Two pawns were sacrificed by Deep Junior along the way to its victory in Game 4. In Game 5, Deep Junior offered a knight to build a strong attack, though Deep Fritz passed. The draw guaranteed Deep Junior the match with one game to go. In the final game, Deep Junior, finding itself in a bad position, managed to sacrifice a knight, giving it the opportunity to set up perpetual check, drawing the game and winning the match with a 4–2 score.

So, it is Deep Junior that now gets the bragging rites as the best chess engine! Deep Fritz might throw out an alibi: its computing system was clearly weaker that Deep Junior's. But the rules never said the two competitors had to use equivalent systems.

The Openings

Games 1 and 5, with Deep Junior playing White, were Queen's Gambit openings both of which ended in draws. Game 5 followed Game 1 until Deep Junior played 5 Bg5 rather than 5 e3 as it had played in Game 1. While Deep Junior was only able to draw Game 5, no better than it did in Game 1, the draw was good enough to clinch the match. A Sicilian Defense in Game 3 led to a Deep Junior victory.

Deep Fritz, when playing White, was unable to win a game. In Game 4, a game that followed the drawn Game 2 for the first 15 moves, Deep Fritz tried a different 16th move only to lose, though it was its weak 33rd move that led to its downfall. Game 6 was a Reti opening that had no bearing on the outcome of the match and was drawn.

Deep Junior versus Deep Fritz, in Elista, 2006: Scorecard

Name	Game 1	Game 2	Game 3	Game 4	Game 5	Game 6	Total pts
Deep Junior	W0.5	B1.0	W2.0	B3.0	W3.5	B4.0	4.0
Deep Fritz	B0.5	W1.0	B1.0	W1.0	B1.5	W2.0	2.0

The Ultimate Computer Chess Challenge, Elista
Game 1, June 6, 2007
Deep Junior (W) versus Deep Fritz (B)
Queen's Gambit Declined Semi-Slav (D45)

---

1 Nf3 Nf6 2 c4 e6 3 Nc3 d5 4 d4 c6 5 e3 Nbd7 6 Qc2 Bd6 7 Bd3 O-O 8 O-O dxc4 9 Bxc4 b5 10 Bd3 Bb7 11 e4 e5 12 dxe5 Nxe5 13 Nxe5 Bxe5 14 h3 Qe7 15 Be3 Rfe8 16 Ne2 Rad8

Position after 16 … Rad8.

A pawn sac? Ten of the next thirteen half-moves were captures. Both sides must have seen all this.

17 Bxa7 c5

A second sac?

18 Bxc5 Qc7

Deep Junior was up two pawns but was forced to return them.

19 Be3 Qxc2 20 Bxc2 Bxe4 21 Bxe4 Nxe4

One pawn has been given up.

22 Rfd1 Bxb2 23 Rxd8 Rxd8

The material evened up.

24 Rb1 Be5 5 f4 Bc7 26 Rxb5

Deep Junior went up a pawn again but would give it back soon, and then both sides will agree to a draw.

26 … Rd3 27 Bd4 f6 28 h4 g6 29 a4 Ng3 30 Nxg3 Rxd4 31 Ne2 Rxa4 32 g3 Drawn by agreement

Position after 32 g3,
Drawn by agreement.

Though Deep Junior had an extra pawn or so during the game, Deep Fritz was able to claw its way to a fast draw.

The Ultimate Computer Chess Challenge, Elista
Game 2, June 7, 2007
Deep Fritz (W) versus Deep Junior (B)
Gruenfeld Defense: Exchange. Modern Exchange Variation (D85)

---

1 d4 Nf6 2 c4 g6 3 Nc3 d5 4 cxd5 Nxd5 5 e4 Nxc3 6 bxc3 Bg7 7 Nf3 c5 8 Rb1 O-O 9 Be2 Nc6 10 d5 Ne5 11 Nxe5 Bxe5 12 Qd2 e6 13 f4 Bc7 14 O-O exd5 15 exd5 Ba5 16 d6 b6 17 Bf3 Rb8 18 Bb2 b5 19 Ba3 Bf5 20 Rbd1 c4 21 Rfe1 Bd3 22 Re5 b4 23 cxb4 Bb6+ 24 Kh1 Qxd6 25 Bb2 Rbe8 26 Rxe8 Rxe8 27 Qc3 f6 28 Qxf6 Qxf6 29 Bxf6

Deep Fritz went up a pawn.

29 ... Kf7 30 Be5 Rd8 31 Rc1 Be3 32 Rc3 g5 33 fxg5

Deep Fritz went up a second pawn, and a third several moves later.

33 ... Bd2 34 Ra3 Re8 35 Rxa7+ Kg6 36 Rg7+ Kf5 37 Bg3 c3 38 Bd1 c2

Deep Fritz was forced to give up a bishop for two pawns (immediately) and a third shortly.

39 Bxc2 Bxc2 40 Rxh7

Position after 40 Rxh7.

If Deep Junior was going to win, it would be necessary to do so without queening a pawn. White was up five pawns for a bishop.

40 ... Re2 41 h3 Bxb4 42 Rb7 Ba3 43 Ra7 Bb2 44 Kh2 Kxg5 45 Ra5+ Kf6 46 Ra6+ Kf5 47 Ra5+ Ke6

Deep Fritz's 47 Ra5+ showed it was proposing a draw, while Deep Junior's 47 ... Ke6 showed it prefers to play on.

48 Ra6+ Kf7 49 Ra7+ Kg6 50 Ra6+ Kh7 51 Ra7+ Kh8 52 h4

While apparently pushing for a draw several moves earlier, Deep Fritz seemed willing to play on now, passing up 52 Ra8+.

52 ... Be4 53 Kh3 Bd4 54 Ra4 Bg1 55 Bf4 Bxg2+ 56 Kg4 Bc6 57 Ra6 Rg2+ 58 Kf5 Drawn by agreement.

Position after 58 Kf5,
Drawn by agreement.

The Ultimate Computer Chess Challenge, Elista
Game 3, June 8, 2007
Deep Junior (W) versus Deep Fritz (B)
Sicilian Defense: Najdorf Variation. Poisoned Pawn Accepted (B97)

---

1 e4 c5 2 Nf3 d6 3 d4 cxd4 4 Nxd4 Nf6 5 Nc3 a6 6 Bg5 e6 7 f4 Qb6 8 Qd2 Qxb2 9 Rb1 Qa3 10 e5 h6 11 Bh4 dxe5 12 fxe5 Nfd7 13 Ne4 Qxa2

A second pawn sacrifice.

14 Rd1 Qd5 15 Qe3 Qxe5

A third pawn sacrifice!

16 Be2 Bc5 17 Bg3 Bxd4 18 Rxd4 Qa5+ 19 Rd2 O-O 20 Bd6 Re8 21 O-O f5 22 Qg3

Deep Junior, which had made a career of making sacrifices, taunts Deep Fritz with one more offering.

22 ... Nc6 23 Qg6 Qd8 24 Bc4 Kh8 25 Ng5 Qxg5 26 Qxe8+ Kh7 27 Bf4 Qg6 28 Qxg6+ Kxg6 29 Bxe6 Nf6 30 Bc4 Kh7 31 Bc7 a5 32 Ra1 a4 33 Bb5 Ne4 34 Rd3 Nb4 35 Rd8 a3 36 Bd7 Nxc2 37 Rf1 Bxd7 38 Rxa8

It was quite a brawl to this point, though the dust was hardly settling even now. Deep Junior was left with two rooks while Deep Fritz had two knights and three extra pawns.

38 ... Be6 39 Be5 Ng5 40 Rf2 Bb3 41 Rxf5 Kg6 42 Rf1 a2 43 Ra7 Ne3 44 Rxb7 Bd5 45 Rxg7+ Kh5 46 Rc1 Nxg2

For the next 38 moves, there was not a capture. Deep Junior gradually maneuvered its way to a tedious endgame victory.

47 Kf2 Nh3+ 48 Ke2 Nh4 49 Ba1 Be4 50 Rc4 Bb1 51 Rg3 Ng5 52 Rb3 Nf5 53 Kd1 Ne4 54 Kc1 Kg5 55 Rf3 Kg4 56 Ra3 Kf4 57 Rc8 Nf2 58 Rcc3 Ne4 59 Rf3+ Kg4 60 h3+ Kg5 61 Ra5 Nd6 62 Ra4 Ne4 63 Rb4 Nfd6 64 Kb2 Nf5 65 Rb5 Nd6 66 Rc5 Nb7 67 Rc4 Nbd6 68 Rg4+ Kh5 69 Rgf4 Kg6 70 Kc1 Kg5 71 Rg4+ Kh5 72 Ra4 Kg6 73 Rff4 Nc8 74 Ra5 Ncd6 75 h4 Kf7 76 Re5 Kg6 77 Kb2 Kf6 78 Kb3 Kf7 79 Ra4 Kg6 80 Ra6 Kf7 81 h5 Kf6 82 Kb4 Kf7 83 Ra7+ Kf6 84 Rd7 Kg5 85 Rxd6 Black resigns.

Deep Junior had converted its advantage into a victory.

Position after 85 Rxd6,
Black resigns.

The Ultimate Computer Chess Challenge, Elista
Game 4, June 9, 2007
Deep Fritz (W) versus Deep Junior (B)
Gruenfeld Defense: Exchange. Modern Exchange Variation (D85)

1 d4 Nf6 2 c4 g6 3 Nc3 d5 4 cxd5 Nxd5 5 e4 Nxc3 6 bxc3 Bg7 7 Nf3 c5 8 Rb1 O-O 9 Be2 Nc6 10 d5 Ne5 11 Nxe5 Bxe5 12 Qd2 e6 13 f4 Bc7 14 O-O exd5 15 exd5 Ba5

Both sides were happy to follow moves from Game 2 to here. Deep Fritz had played 16 d6 and wound up drawing that game. This time it tried something else and lost!

16 f5 Bxf5 17 Rxb7 Qd6 18 Bc4 Qe5 19 Rf3 Rab8

Deep Junior offered a pawn in return for an open b-file for its own rook.

20 Rxa7

According to Amir Ban, Deep Junior was in book for the first 20 moves.

Position after 15 … Ba5.

20 … Bb6 21 Ra4 Bc7 22 g3 Rb1 23 Re3 Qf6 24 Ra6 Bd6 25 Re1 Rfb8 26 Bf1 h5 27 a4 c4

Deep Junior offered a second pawn in return for greater piece movement.

28 Rc6 Ra1 29 Bxc4 Bd7 30 Rf1 Qe7

Position after 30 … Qe7.

Payback time! Deep Junior won an exchange, gaining a clear upper hand in the game.

31 Rxd6 Qxd6 32 Qf2 Qb6 33 Bf4

This move was considered fatal by the Deep Fritz team, giving Deep Junior two dominant rooks. Preferred was 33 Be3. From here on, Deep Junior made steady progress toward victory, with only minor aggravation from Deep Fritz's advancing pawns.

33 … Qxf2+ 34 Kxf2 Rb2+ 35 Ke3 Rxa4 36 Bd3 Rxh2 37 c4 Ra3 38 Kd4 h4 39 g4 Rh3 40 Be2 Rhb3 41 Ke5 Rb2 42 Re1 Raa2 43 Bd1 Ra6 44 Bc1 Rb8 45 Rg1 h3 46 Rh1 f6+ 47 Kd4 Ra1 48 Bc2 g5 49 c5 Bxg4 50 c6 Kf7 51 Rf1 Rh8 52 d6 h2 53 d7 Ke7 54 Rh1 White resigns.

Position after 54 Rh1,
White resigns.

**The Ultimate Computer Chess Challenge, Elista
Game 5, June 10, 2007
Deep Junior (W) versus Deep Fritz (B)
Queen's Gambit Declined Semi-Slav (D43)**

Deep Fritz needed a win with Black to stave off losing the match. Deep Junior needed only a draw to win the match.

1 Nf3 Nf6 2 c4 e6 3 Nc3 d5 4 d4 c6 5 Bg5

This game followed Game 1 until Deep Junior played this move. In Game 1, it chose 5 e3.

5 … h6 6 Bh4 dxc4 7 e4 g5 8 Bg3 b5 9 Be2 Bb7 10 O-O Nbd7 11 Ne5 Bg7 12 Nxd7 Nxd7 13 Bd6 a6 14 a4 e5 15 Bg4 exd4 16 e5

Deep Junior let its knight hang with 16 e5. Onlookers probably gagged when this move was made. Did Deep Junior think this didn't lose material?

**16 ... c5 17 Bf3 Nxe5 18 Bxb7 Qxd6
19 Bxa8**

Position after 19 Bxa8.

After the punching was done, Deep Junior
had a rook for three dangerous pawns.

**19 ... O-O 20 Ne4 Qc7 21 axb5
Rxa8 22 f4 gxf4 23 Qh5 Ra7
24 Rxa6 Rxa6 25 bxa6 Qc6 26 Qf5**

**Qxa6 27 Rxf4 Qg6 28 Nxc5 d3
29 Ne4 Qxf5 30 Rxf5 Ng4 31 Rb5
Bd4+ 32 Kf1 Ne3+ 33 Ke1 f5 34 Nd2
Nxg2+ 35 Kd1 Ne3+ 36 Kc1 f4
37 Rb7 Ng4 38 h3 Nh2 39 Rd7 Be3
40 Kd1 f3 41 Ne4 Kf8 42 Nf6 Bg5
43 Ne4 Ke8 44 Rd4 Be3 45 Rxc4 f2
46 Nxf2 Bxf2 47 Rf4 Bg3 48 Rd4
Drawn by agreement.**

Position after 48 Rd4,
Drawn by agreement.

**The Ultimate Computer Chess Challenge, Elista
Game 6, June 11, 2007
Deep Fritz (W) versus Deep Junior (B)
Reti Opening (A04)**

**1 Nf3 c5 2 c4 Nf6 3 g3 b6 4 Bg2 Bb7
5 O-O g6 6 Nc3 Bg7 7 d4 cxd4
8 Qxd4 d6 9 Rd1 Nbd7 10 Be3 Rc8
11 Rac1 O-O 12 Qh4 a6 13 b3 Rc7
14 Bh3 Qe8 15 g4 Qa8 16 Bd4 e6
17 g5 Ne8 18 Bxg7 Nxg7 19 Rxd6
Bxf3 20 exf3 Qxf3 21 Ne4 Nh5
22 Bg2 Qf5 23 Rcd1 Nc5 24 Nf6+
Nxf6 25 gxf6 h5 26 Rxb6 Rd7
27 Rxd7 Nxd7 28 Rxa6 Nxf6**

Deep Fritz, with three connected and
passed queenside pawns, was two pawns
down on the kingside.

Position after 28 ... Nxf6.

29 Qd4 Qb1+ 30 Bf1 Qf5

Deep Junior's 30 ... Qf5 invited a draw, but Deep Fritz's coming move 31 h3 showed it preferred to play on.

31 h3 Kg7 32 f4 Re8 33 Qe5 Qb1 34 Ra7 Qc1 35 a4 Qd1 36 Rb7 Qf3 37 Bg2 Qg3 38 Rb8 Rxb8 39 Qxb8 h4 40 Qe5 Kh7

Deep Junior, facing three passed pawns on the queenside, offered to draw the game with this move. Deep Fritz would accept, possibly overlooking that it gave Deep Junior a draw through perpetual check.

41 Qxf6 Qe3+ Drawn by agreement.

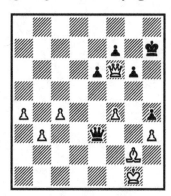

Position after 41 ... Qe3+,
Drawn by agreement.

With the match already in hand, Deep Junior was satisfied to draw this game.

Suggest Readings

Shay, Bushinsky, Showdown in Elista, ICGA Journal, Vol. 30, No, 2, pp. 121–122, June 2007.

Game 1: http://www.chessgames.com/perl/chessgame?gid=1462334, http://www.chessbase.com/newsdetail.asp?newsid=3908, http://www.telegraph.co.uk/culture/chess/malcolmpein/3665904/, Karpov-returns-in-style.html

Game 2: http://www.chessgames.com/perl/chessgame?gid=1462335, http://www.chessbase.com/newsdetail.asp?newsid=3914

Game 3: http://www.chessgames.com/perl/chessgame?gid=1462336, http://susanpolgar.blogspot.com/2007/06/deep-junior-defeated-deep-fritz.html

Game 4: http://www.chessgames.com/perl/chessgame?gid=1462337, http://www.chessbase.com/newsdetail.asp?newsid=3920

Game 5: http://www.chessgames.com/perl/chessgame?gid=1462338, http://www.chessbase.com/newsdetail.asp?newsid=3921

Game 6: http://www.chessgames.com/perl/chessgame?gid=1462367

2007: Rybka Moves to Top at the 15th WCCC

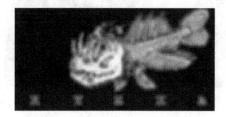

The 15th World Computer Chess Championship was staged from June 11–18, 2007 in the Science Park Amsterdam in Amsterdam, The Netherlands. The organizer was the International Computer Games Association (ICGA). The event was sponsored by the Netherland's National Computing Facilities, SARA Computing and Networks, and IBM. For the sixth time, it was held in conjunction with the Computer Olympiad.

Twelve engines took part in the round robin event, five from Germany, four from The Netherlands, two from the USA, and one from Belgium. The favorites were Rybka, Zappa, and Shredder. Conspicuously absent were Fritz, which in recent years has been mainly concerned with improving its strength when playing humans, and the defending champion Junior. The two had just finished their match in Elista and couldn't make it to the Amsterdam event.

M. Newborn, *Beyond Deep Blue: Chess in the Stratosphere*,
DOI 10.1007/978-0-85729-341-1_13, © Springer-Verlag London Limited 2011

Rybka's brains: Vasik Rajlich.
(Photo courtesy of chessbase.com)

Rybka was rated 2924 on the Swedish Rating List at the time of the championship. In second place with a rating of 2853 was Hiarcs. Shredder was in fourth place with a rating of 2837.

Rybka won the championship, securing an impressive 10 of 11 points. Rybka drew two games, one with former world champion Zappa in Round 3 and another with Loop in Round 4. Zappa, too, went undefeated, but drew four games to finish one full point behind the winner in second place. Loop finished in third place, though with only seven and a half points. It lost two games, one to Zappa and one to Shredder, who finished tied for fourth with seven points. Loop's programmer, Fritz Reul, carried out his design of the engine under the supervision of Jaap van den Herik.

Rybka capped off her rout by defeating Shredder in the final round. The latter played the Poisoned Pawn variation of the Najdorf and was neatly "outbooked" by Rybka. Shredder's book was developed by the Italian openings specialist Sandro Necchi, while Rybka's was developed by the Dutch expert Jeroen Noomen. Rybka's author Rajlich writes: "Jeroen busted out a wild Sicilian line in which White starts the festivities by sacrificing three pawns for a sizable lead in development but still nothing concrete. Rybka herself would favor Black at this point. Later in the variation, White offered a piece to keep the attack going. I'm not sure what should happen, but the entire refutation of Black's play was in the book and Black could have resigned without White playing a single new move."

Data on entries to the 15th WCCC: Name, country of origin, authors, hardware

Name	Origin	Authors	Hardware
Rybka	USA	Vasik Rajlich	Intel 2x Xeon 5355 2.66 GHz, 8 GB
Zappa	USA	Anthony Cozzie	Data not available
Loop	DEU	Fritz Reul	Intel Core 2 Quad Xeon X3200 series 3,2–3,4 GHz; Xeon Core 2 5100 series 3,0 GHz
Shredder	DEU	Stefan Meyer-Kahlen	Data not available
GridChess	DEU	Kai Himstedt, Ulf Lorenz, Thomas Gaksch, Fabien Letouzey, and Robert Hyatt	Cluster
Deep Sjeng	BEL	Gian-Carlo Pascutto	Intel 2x Xeon 5355 2.66 GHz, 8 GB
Jonny	DEU	Johannes Zwanzger	Intel Core 2 Duo 3.4GHz, 1 GB
Diep	NLD	Vincent Diepeveen	AMD K8 4x 2.4 GHz
The Baron	NLD	Richard Pijl	Data not available
IsiChess	DEU	Gerd Isenberg	Data not available
The King	NLD	Johan de Koning	Data not available
micro-Max	NLD	Harm Geert Muller	Data not available

Final standings of the 15th WCCC, Amsterdam

#	Name	1	2	3	4	5	6	7	8	9	10	11	Points	BU
1	Rybka	11bW	12wW	2wD	3bD	7wW	10bW	9wW	6bW	8wW	5bW	4wW	10.0	56.0
2	Zappa	4bD	11bW	1bD	12bW	3wW	7wD	10wW	9bW	6wD	8bW	5wW	9.0	57.0
3	Loop	5bD	4wL	11bW	1wD	2bL	12bW	7wW	10bW	9wD	6bW	8wW	7.5	58.5
4	Shredder	2wD	3bW	7wD	10bW	9wD	6bD	8wW	5bL	12wW	11wW	1bL	7.0	59.0
5	GridChess	3wD	7bW	10wD	9bW	6wD	8wD	12wW	4wW	11bW	1wL	2bL	7.0	59.0
6	Deep Sjeng	10wD	9bW	12wW	8wD	5bD	4wD	11bW	1wL	2bD	3wL	7bD	6.0	60.0
7	Jonny	8bW	5wL	4bD	11wW	1bL	2bD	3bL	12bW	10wD	9bL	6wD	5.0	61.0
8	Diep	7wL	10bD	9wW	6bD	12wW	5bD	4bL	11wW	1bL	2wL	3bL	4.5	61.5
9	The Baron	12wW	6wL	8bL	5wL	4bD	11bL	1bL	2wL	3bD	7wW	10bW	4.0	62.0
10	IsiChess	6bD	8wD	5bD	4wL	11bD	1wL	2bL	3wL	7bD	12bW	9wL	3.5	62.5
11	The King	1wL	2wL	3wL	7bL	10wD	9wW	6wL	8bL	5wL	4bL	12bW	2.5	63.5
12	micro-Max	9bL	1bL	6bL	2wL	8bL	3wL	5bL	7wL	4bL	10wL	11wL	0.0	66.0

15th WCCC, Amsterdam
Round 1, June 12, 2007
Shredder (W) versus Zappa (B)
French Defense: Tarrasch Variation. Chistyakov Defense Modern Line (C07)

1 e4 e6 2 d4 d5 3 Nd2 c5 4 Ngf3
cxd4 5 exd5 Qxd5 6 Bc4 Qd6 7 O-O
Nf6 8 Nb3 Nc6 9 Nbxd4 Nxd4
10 Nxd4 a6 11 c3 Qc7 12 Qe2 Bd6
13 h3 O-O 14 Bg5 Ne4 15 Qxe4 Qxc4
16 Rfd1 Re8 17 Rd3 h6 18 b3 Qd5
19 Qxd5 exd5 20 Be3 Bd7 21 Ne2
Bc6 22 Rad1 Rac8 23 Nd4 Bd7
24 Ne2 Bc6 25 Nd4 Bd7 26 Nf3 Bc6

Position after 32 Re1.

32 ... f4 33 Bxf4 Rxe1+ 34 Nxe1 g5
35 Bxd6 gxh4 36 Bf4 Rc5 37 d6 h5
38 Nf3 Kf7 39 Nxh4 Bc6 40 g4 hxg4
41 hxg4 Ra5 42 g5 Ke6 43 a4 Be4
44 Kf1 Bc2 45 g6 Rh5 46 g7 Kf7
47 Nf3 Rd5 48 Ne5+ Kxg7 49 Nc4
Bd1 50 Be5+ Kf7 51 f4 Bh5 52 Kf2
Rd3 53 b4 Ke8 54 b5 Bf7 55 Nb6
Be6 56 bxa6 bxa6

Position after 26 ... Bc6.

Shredder was about to win a pawn.

27 c4 Bb4 28 cxd5 Bb5 29 Rd4 Bc5
30 Rg4 f5 31 Rh4 Bd6 32 Re1

Over the next nine moves, Zappa would
win a rook for a bishop and two pawns.

Position after 56 ... bxa6.

Both side danced for the next 49 moves. Zappa then pushed a pawn to avoid a draw.

57 Ke2 Rb3 58 Bd4 Bf5 59 Kf2 Rd3 60 Be5 Ra3 61 Bd4 Bd7 62 Bc5 Rc3 63 Bb4 Rd3 64 Bc5 Kd8 65 Ke2 Bf5 66 Kf2 Rc3 67 Bb4 Rb3 68 Bc5 Bd7 69 Ke2 Bg4+ 70 Kd2 Bf5 71 Ke2 Rd3 72 Kf2 Be6 73 Ke2 Rc3 74 Bb4 Rb3 75 Bc5 Bf5 76 Bd4 Ke8 77 Kf2 Ra3 78 Ke2 Rh3 79 Bc5 Rc3 80 Bb4 Rb3 81 Bc5 Kd8 82 Bd4 Rh3 83 Be5 Ke8 84 Kd2 Rd3+ 85 Kc1 Rb3 86 Nd5 Kd7 87 Nf6+ Kc6 88 Ng8 Bg4 89 Kd2 Ra3 90 Ne7+ Kd7 91 Nd5 Be6 92 Nc3 Rb3 93 Nd1 Rb4 94 Nb2 Kc6 95 Kc3 Rb3+ 96 Kd2 Ra3 97 Bg7 Bf5 98 Be5 Bh7 99 Kd1 Bf5 100 Kd2 Rb3 101 Nc4 Kc5 102 Nb2 Rh3 103 Nd1 Rd3+ 104 Ke2 Rb3 105 Nc3

Position after 105 Nc3.

It was now or never. Zappa said "now!"

105 ... a5 106 Nb5 Kc4 107 Nd4 Rb2+ 108 Ke3 Bd7 109 Nb5 Rg2 110 Nc3 Rg1 111 Ke2 Rg2+ 112 Ke3 Rh2 113 Ke4 Kc5 114 Kf3 Rh3+ 115 Ke4 Rh1 116 Kd3 Bf5+ 117 Kd2 Rh2+ 118 Ke1 Rh3 119 Kd2 Rd3+

120 Kc1 Bd7 121 Nd1 Rf3 122 Kd2 Kb4 123 Nc3 Kc4 124 Nd1 Rd3+ 125 Ke1 Kb4 126 Ke2 Rb3 127 Nb2 Rh3 128 Nd3+ Kc4 129 Nb2+ Kd5 130 Kd2 Rh2+ 131 Ke3 Rc2 132 Nd1 Rc4 133 Kd3 Kc5 134 Nc3 Bf5+ 135 Kd2 Kc6 136 Nb5 Bd7 137 Nc3 Be6 138 Kd3 Rb4 139 Ke3 Kd7 140 Ne4 Bf5 141 Nc3 Ke6 142 Nb5 Kf7 143 Nc3 Ke8 144 Bd4 Rc4 145 Bf6 Kd7 146 Be5 Ke8 147 Bd4 Kf7 148 Be5 Bd7 149 Ne4 Rxa4

Once again, with the 50-move draw rule nearing, Zappa said "let's play on!" But the human operators soon voted to the contrary.

150 Nc5 Ra3+ 151 Kd4 Ke8 152 Kc4 a4 153 Bc3 Bc6 154 f5 Ra2 155 Nd3 Bd7 156 f6 Re2 157 Ne5 Be6+ 158 Kd3 Rf2 159 f7+ Kd8 160 Bb4 Kc8 161 d7+ Bxd7 162 Ke3 Rxf7 163 Nxf7 Kc7 164 Ba3 Drawn by agreement.

After 164 moves, the game fizzled out to a draw. Both sides were in time trouble by the end of the game, but the quality of play was excellent. This was the longest game in the 33-year history of the computer chess world championships.

Position after 164 Ba3,
Drawn by agreement.

15th WCCC, Amsterdam
Round 3, June 12, 2007
Rybka (W) versus Zappa (B)
French Defense: Rubinstein Variation (C10)

**1 e4 e6 2 d4 d5 3 Nc3 dxe4 4 Nxe4
Nf6 5 Nxf6+ gxf6 6 Nf3 Nc6 7 Bb5
Qd6 8 O-O Bd7 9 Re1 Ne7 10 Bd3
O-O-O 11 c4 Rg8**

Position after 11 ... Rg8.

Zappa invited Rybka to take a pawn in
return for an attack on the white king.
Rybka bit.

**12 Bxh7 Rh8 13 Be4 Bc6 14 Qb3
Bxe4 15 Rxe4 Qc6 16 Rg4 f5 17 Rg3
Ng6 18 Bg5 f4 19 Rg4 f5**

Position after 19 ... f5.

Zappa's kingside attack had peaked, and
the coming exchange of pieces took the
sting out of it. Zappa would settle for
winning a bishop and knight for a rook
and pawn.

**20 Bxd8 fxg4 21 Bf6 gxf3 22 Bxh8
Nxh8 23 Re1 Nf7 24 d5 exd5
25 Qxf3 Bb4 26 Qh3+ Qd7 27 Re8+
Nd8 28 cxd5 Qxh3 29 gxh3 Kd7
30 Re5 Bd6 31 Rf5 Ke7 32 h4 Nf7
33 h5 Nh6 34 Rg5 Nf7 35 Rg6 Ne5
36 Rg2 f3 37 Rg3 Kf6 38 h6 Ng6
39 Rg4 Kf5 40 h3 b6 41 Kf1 Bf4
42 h7 Be5 43 b4 b5 44 Ke1 a6
45 Kd2 Nf8 46 Rh4 Ng6 47 Rh5+ Kf4
48 Kd3 Bg7 49 d6 cxd6 50 a4 bxa4
51 Ra5 Ne5+ 52 Kc2 Nc6 53 Rxa4
Kf5 54 b5 axb5 55 Ra8 Ne5 56 h8=Q
Bxh8 57 Rxh8 Kg5 58 Kd2 b4
59 Rb8 Kh4 60 Rxb4+ Kxh3 61 Rd4
Ng4 62 Ke1 Kh4 63 Rxd6 Kg5**

Position after 63 ... Kg5.

Somewhere in here, Zappa saw it would
lose the game, but Rybka fumbled the
ball, satisfying itself with a painful draw.

Rybka's six-piece endgame tables weren't used during the game, but if they had been, a win would have been found.

64 Rd3 Kf4 65 Rd4+ Kf5 66 Ra4 Nh2 67 Ra5+ Kf4 68 Ra7 Ke4 69 Re7+ Kf5 70 Rf7+ Ke5 71 Kd2 Ke4 72 Rh7 Ng4 73 Re7+ Kf5 74 Rf7+ Ke4 75 Ke1 Ne5 76 Rf8 Nd7 77 Re8+ Ne5 78 Kf1 Kf5 79 Rf8+ Kg4 80 Rg8+ Kf4 81 Rc8 Ng4 82 Ra8 Nh2+ 83 Ke1 Ke4 84 Kd1 Ng4 85 Ra4+ Kf5 86 Ra5+ Kf4 87 Ra2 Ke5 88 Ke1 Nh2 89 Ra6 Kf5 90 Ra3 Kf4 91 Rc3 Ke4 92 Kd1 Ng4 93 Rc4+ Kf5 94 Ke1 Nh2 95 Rc5+ Kf4 96 Kd1 Ng4 97 Rc2 Ke5 98 Rd2 Nh2 99 Rd3 Kf4 100 Rd4+ Kf5 101 Rd5+ Kf4 102 Rh5 Ng4

103 Ke1 Ne5 104 Rh7 Nd3+ 105 Kf1 Kf5 106 Ra7 Kg4 107 Ra4+ Kf5 Drawn by agreement.

Position after 107 ... Kf5,
Drawn by agreement.

15th WCCC, Amsterdam
Round 4, June 13, 2007
Loop (W) versus Rybka (B)
Sicilian Defense: Canal Attack (B51)

---

1 e4 c5 2 Nf3 d6 3 Bb5+ Nc6 4 O-O Bd7 5 Re1 Nf6 6 c3 a6 7 Ba4 c4 8 d4 cxd3 9 Qxd3 g6 10 Nd4 Ne5 11 Bxd7+ Qxd7 12 Qc2 Bg7 13 Nd2 O-O 14 N2f3 Rfd8 15 Nxe5 dxe5 16 Nf3 Ne8 17 Bg5 Nd6 18 Rad1 Qc7 19 Rd3 Nc4 20 Red1 Rxd3 21 Rxd3 h6 22 Be3 f5 23 Rd1 e6 24 Bc1 Rd8

Over the coming moves, Rybka and Loop traded material, down to the point where a draw was inevitable.

Position after 24 ... Rd8.

**25 Rxd8+ Qxd8 26 Nd2 Nxd2
27 Qxd2 Qxd2 28 Bxd2 fxe4**

Rybka, though up a pawn, managed to
saddle herself with tripled pawns on the
e-file. In spite of this, she drew a difficult
position when Loop played inaccurately
on the queenside.

**29 Kf1 Kf7 30 Ke2 Kf6 31 c4 h5
32 b4 Bf8 33 c5 g5 34 a4 g4 35 a5
Ke7 36 Bg5+ Kd7 37 Ke3 Bg7
38 Kxe4 Kc7 39 Kd3 e4+ 40 Kc4 Be5
41 g3 Kc6 42 Be3 Bf6 43 Bf4 h4
44 Bd2 h3 45 Bf4 Drawn by
agreement.**

Position after 45 Bf4,
Drawn by agreement.

**15th WCCC, Amsterdam
Round 11, June 18, 2007
Rybka (W) versus Shredder (B)
Sicilian Defense: Najdorf Variation. Poisoned Pawn Accepted (B97)**

Rybka led Zappa by a point when this
final-round game was played. She needed
a win or draw to win the tournament.

**1 e4 c5 2 Nf3 d6 3 d4 cxd4 4 Nxd4
Nf6 5 Nc3 a6 6 Bg5 e6 7 f4 Qb6
8 Qd2 Qxb2 9 Rb1 Qa3 10 e5 dxe5
11 fxe5 Nfd7 12 Ne4 h6 13 Bh4 Qxa2
14 Rd1 Qd5 15 Qe3 Qxe5 16 Be2 Bc5
17 Bg3 Bxd4 18 Rxd4 Qa5+ 19 Rd2
O-O 20 Bd6 Re8 21 O-O f5 22 Qg3**

Rybka, still in book, had given her opponent a three pawn lead, but the greedy
Shredder was left with a poorly developed
queenside and a vulnerable kingside.
Rybka wasn't done giving away pieces, as
she next offered a knight! After that, she
quickly lambasted Shredder into submission. This position was arrived at in Game
3 in Elista played between Deep Junior

and Deep Fritz. Deep Fritz passed on
accepting the sacrifice and went on to lose.
Shredder will accept and lose even faster.

22 ... fxe4 23 Qg6 Rd8 24 Rf7 Qc3 25 Bg4

Position after 25 Bg4.

Last Rybka book move.

25 ... Nf8 26 Bxf8 Qa1+ 27 Rf1
Qxf1+ 28 Kxf1 Rxf8+ 29 Rf2 Nc6
30 Bh5 Rxf2+ 31 Kxf2 Ne5 32 Qe8+
Kh7 33 Ke3 b5 34 Kf4 Bb7 35 Qe7
Bd5 36 Kxe5 a5 37 g4 e3 38 g5 hxg5
39 Qxg5 Kg8 40 Qxe3 Rf8 41 Be2 b4
42 Bd3 Rf3 43 Qg5 b3 44 Bg6 Rf6
45 Qh5 Rxg6 46 Qxg6 b2 47 Qe8+
Kh7 48 Qb5 Kh6 49 Qxb2 Ba8
50 Qc1+ Kh5 51 Qf4 Bd5 52 c4 Bc6
53 Qf7+ Kg4 54 Qxe6+ Kf3 55 Qxc6+
Ke3 **Black resigns.**

Position after 55 ... Ke3,
Black resigns.

Suggest Readings

Jeroen Nooman, Jos Uiterwijk and Jaap van den Herik, "The 15th World Computer-Chess
    Championship", ICGA Journal, Vol. 30, No. 2, pp. 98–107, June 2007.
chessgames.com report on the 15th WCCC: http://www.chessgames.com/perl/chess.pl?tid=62266&
    crosstable=1
Shredder versus Zappa, Round 1, 15th WCCC: http://www.chessgames.com/perl/chessgame?
    gid=1464949
Rybka versus Zappa, Round 3, 15th WCCC: http://www.chessgames.com/perl/chessgame?
    gid=1464511
Loop versus Rybka, Round 4, 15th WCCC: http://www.chessgames.com/perl/chessgame?
    gid=1465022
Rybka versus Shredder, Round 11, 15th WCCC: http://www.chessgames.com/perl/chessgame?
    gid=1465000
Shredder website: http://www.shredderchess.com/chess-news/shredder-news/torino2006 html

2007: Zappa Upsets Rybka in Mexico City, 5.5–4.5

14

Three months following the 15th World Computer Chess Championship in Amsterdam, where Rybka finished in first place one point ahead of Zappa and where the remainder of the field trailed in the distance, these two giant chess engines went head to head in a ten-game match in Mexico City for a $10,000 prize. The event took place in the Hotel Centro Historico Sheraton; at the same time, the human world championship was held with Vishwanathan Anand, the winner. The match, played September 20–27, 2007, consisted of ten games with a time control of 60 minutes per game plus 20 seconds per move. Because of problems bringing computers into Mexico, the two participants each used a remotely located 8-core Intel Xeon X5355 processor running at 2.66 GHz.

The previous meeting of the two took place in Round 3 of the 15th WCCC. They played to a 107-move draw after Rybka, playing White, found herself unable to polish off Zappa in an endgame where she had the upper hand and Zappa saw its own demise – evidently too deep in the tree for Rybka to have seen. They also drew when they played each other in the 14th WCCC. Rybka defeated Zappa when the two met for the first time in December 2005 in the 15th International Paderborn Computer Chess Championship. Based on their overall records leading up to the match, Rybka was considered a clear favorite.

But favorites don't always win, nor does the "best" player. However, a draw in Game 1 and a victory in Game 2 supported the contention that Rybka was, indeed, the best. Then, lo and behold, three consecutive Rybka losses in Games 3 through 5 left Zappa in the lead at the match midpoint with a formidable 3.5–1.5 score. Game 6 was drawn when Zappa, playing Black, essentially played the entire game from its opening book and was satisfied to earn a half point. Zappa stumbled across a glitch in its evaluation function when in a strong position in Game 7 and settled for a second consecutive draw, maintaining its two-point lead with three games to go. Rybka fought back in Game 8 with a victory in a game where she was down an exchange at the end. In Game 9, Rybka played a Caro-Kann, following the theme played in the sixth game of the Deep Blue versus Kasparov Rematch. Unlike Deep Blue, Zappa declined the knight sacrifice when Rybka extended an invitation with 8 ... h6.

M. Newborn, *Beyond Deep Blue: Chess in the Stratosphere*,
DOI 10.1007/978-0-85729-341-1_14, © Springer-Verlag London Limited 2011

Zappa managed to stumble over another glitch in its evaluation function and found itself in a lost game, only to be rescued by a terrible 71st move by Rybka that led quickly to a drawn game. A draw in the final game would clinch the match for Zappa, and Zappa did just that, worming its way out of an inferior position to draw the game and to win the match with an impressive 5.5–4.5 score.

The games were generally long, tedious, and dramatic. Three went over 110 moves, and every one of the ten games lasted more than 50 moves. Neither side could claim a victory in fewer than 66 moves. Of the ten games, Black lost or drew all but one game: a victory by Zappa in Game 4. Six of the ten games opened with a Ruy Lopez, and two others opened with a Sicilian. A Caro-Kann in Game 9 and an English opening in Game 10 were attempts by Rybka to avoid Zappa's book lines.

Rybka versus Zappa in Mexico City, 2007: Scorecard

Name	Game 1	Game 2	Game 3	Game 4	Game 5	Game 6	Game 7	Game 8	Game 9	Game 10	Total points
Zappa	W0.5	B0.5	W1.5	B2.5	W3.5	B4.0	W4.5	B4.5	W5.0	B5.5	5.5
Rybka	B0.5	W1.5	B1.5	W1.5	B1.5	W2.0	B2.5	W3.5	B4.0	W4.5	4.5

The Openings

Six of the ten games – and the first four – were variations of the Ruy Lopez, with the same initial eight moves: 1 e4 e5 2 Nf3 Nc6 3 Bb5 a6 4 Ba4 Nf6 5 O-O Be7 6 Re1 b5 7 Bb3 d6 8 c3 O-O. These were the same moves played in Game 2 of the Deep Blue versus Kasparov Rematch. Deep Blue went on to win that game when Kasparov resigned in a position he evidently could have drawn (See Chap. 1).

Game 1: Zappa, playing White, and Rybka, Black, followed this Deep Blue versus Kasparov game to Zappa's 12th move 12 a4. The game went after move 8: 9 h3 Bb7 10 d4 Re8 11 Nbd2 Bf8 12 a4 h6 13 Bc2 exd4 14 cxd4 Nb4 15 Bb1 c5 16 d5 Nd7 17 Ra3 f5 18 exf5 Rxe1+ 19 Qxe1. The game lasted 73 moves ending in a draw, though as early as the 35th move Rybka offered Zappa the opportunity to draw by repetition. Rybka left book after her 18th move, Zappa after its 21st move. Game 1 was drawn.

Game 2: 9 h3 Na5 (Rybka had played 9 ... Bb7 and drew Game 1. Zappa, in the same position, tried an alternative.) 10 Bc2 c5 11 d4 Qc7 12 Nbd2 cxd4 13 cxd4 Bd7 14 Nf1 Rac8 15 Ne3 Rfe8 16 b3 Nc6 17 Bb2 Bd8 18 Rc1 Qa7 19 dxe5 dxe5 20 Re2 Qb7 21 a3. Rybka left book after her 21st move, Zappa after its 18th move. Game 2 was won by Rybka.

Game 3: 9 d4 (Zappa played 9 h3 in Game 1 and drew. Here it steered off with 9 d4 and won.) 9 ... Bg4 10 Be3 exd4 11 cxd4 Na5 12 Bc2 c5 13 h3 Bh5 14 g4 Bg6 15 Nbd2. Zappa left book after its 14th move, Rybka after her 15th move. Game 3 was won by Zappa.

Game 4: 9 h3 Bb7 10 d4 Re8 11 Nbd2 Bf8 12 a4 h6 13 Bc2 exd4 14 cxd4 Nb4 15 Bb1 c5 16 d5 Nd7 17 Ra3 (Game 4 followed Game 1 to here.) 17 ... c4 18 axb5 axb5 19 Nd4 Qb6 20 Nf5 Ne5 21 Rg3 g6 22 Nf3 Ned3 23 Be3 Qd8 24 Bxh6 Qf6 25 Qd2 Nxe1 26 Bxf8 Nxf3+ 27 Rxf3 Kxf8 28 Nh6 Qg7 29 Rxf7+ Qxf7 30 Nxf7 Kxf7 31 Qxb4. Rybka left book after her 27th move, Zappa after its 24th move. Game 4 was won by Zappa when it mated Rybka on the 180th move.

Game 5: After not having much success with the Ruy Lopez in Games 1 and 3, Rybka's team steered her in a different direction, a Sicilian Defense: 1 e4 c5 2 Nf3 d6 3 Bb5+ Bd7 4 Bxd7+ Qxd7 5 O-O Nf6 6 e5 dxe5 7 Nxe5 Qc8 8 Nc3 Nc6 9 Re1 Nxe5 10 Rxe5 e6. Zappa left book after its eighth move, Rybka after her seventh move. Game 5 was won by Zappa when Rybka resigned on her 129th move.

Game 6: 9 h3 Bb7 10 d4 Re8 11 Nbd2 Bf8 12 a4 h6 13 Bc2 exd4 14 cxd4 Nb4 15 Bb1 c5 16 d5 Nd7 17 Ra3 c4 18 axb5 axb5 19 Nd4 Qb6 20 Nf5 Ne5 21 Rg3 g6 22 Nf3 Ned3 23 Be3 Qd8 24 Bxh6 Qf6 25 Qd2 Nxe1 26 Bxf8 Nxf3+ 27 Rxf3 (Game 6 followed Game 4 to here. Between games, Zappa's book was modified to go in a different direction here.) 27 … gxf5 28 Rxf5 Qg6 29 Rg5 Qxg5 30 Qxg5+ Kxf8 31 Qh6+ Kg8 32 Kh2 [Last book move] Ra1 33 Qxd6 Rxb1 34 Qxb4 Rxe4 35 Qxb5 c3 36 Qxb7 Kg7 37 d6. This was Zappa's first move out of its opening book! It assigned a score of 0.0 to the position, forecasting a draw, as it did to every subsequent position. Rybka was in book until her 33rd move. Game 6 was drawn on the 52nd move.

Game 7: A second Sicilian Defense by Rybka. 1 e4 c5 2 Nf3 Nc6 (Rybka avoided the line played in Game 5, and of course, avoided the Ruy Lopez from Games 1 and 3. It was getting desperate, as to win the match, she needed to win her final three games!) 3 d4 cxd4 4 Nxd4 g6 5 Nc3 Bg7 6 Be3 Nf6 7 Bc4 Qa5 8 O-O O-O. Zappa left book after its eighth move, Rybka after her seventh. Game 7 was drawn.

Game 8: 9 Re1 d6 10 a3 Qd7 11 h3 Rae8 12 a4 b4 13 Nd5 Na5 14 Nxe7+ Qxe7 15 Ba2 Rb8 16 Nh4 Bc8 17 Bg5 Kh8 8 Nf5 Bxf5 19 exf5 Qd7 20 g4 b3 21 Bxb3 Nxb3 (Game 8; Rybka won, thus winning two, drawing one, and losing one playing this line of the Ruy Lopez as White). Rybka left book after her 15th move, Zappa after its 12th. Rybka won Game 8.

Game 9: Enough of the Ruy Lopez and the Sicilian. Rybka played a Caro-Kann Defense here. 1 e4 c6 2 d4 d5 3 Nc3 dxe4 4 Nxe4 Nd7 5 Bc4 Ngf6 6 Ng5 e6 7 Qe2 Nb6 8 Bd3 h6 9 N5f3 c5 10 dxc5 Bxc5 11 Ne5 Nbd7 12 Ngf3 Nxe5 13 Nxe5 O-O 14 O-O b6 15 Bf4. Zappa left book after its 15th move, Rybka after her 14th. Game 9 was drawn.

Game 10: Forget 1 e4. Rybka tried an English Opening with: 1 Nf3 Nf6 2 c4 e6 3 Nc3 c5 4 g3 b6 5 Bg2 Bb7 6 O-O Be7 7 Re1 d6 8 e4 a6 9 d4 cxd4 10 Nxd4 Qc7 11 Be3 Nbd7 12 f4 Rc8 13 Rc1 O-O 14 f5 e5 15 Nb3 Qb8 Rybka left book after her 15th move, Zappa also after its 15th. Game 10 was drawn.

In summary, Zappa was in book for 21, 18, 14, 24, 8, 37, 8, 12, 15, 15 moves in Games 1 through 10, an average of 17.2 moves per game. Rybka was in book for 18, 21, 15, 27, 7, 33, 7, 15, 14, 15 moves in Games 1 through 10, by some coincidence, exactly the same average as Zappa's.

Clash of the Computer Titans, Mexico City
Game 1, September 20, 2007
Zappa (W) versus Rybka (B)
Ruy Lopez: Closed variations. Flohr System (C92)

1 e4 e5 2 Nf3 Nc6 3 Bb5 a6 4 Ba4 Nf6 5 O-O Be7 6 Re1 b5 7 Bb3 d6 8 c3 O-O 9 h3 Bb7 10 d4 Re8 11 Nbd2 Bf8 12 a4 h6 13 Bc2 exd4 14 cxd4 Nb4 15 Bb1 c5 16 d5 Nd7 17 Ra3 f5 18 exf5 Rxe1+ [Last book move] 19 Qxe1 [Last book move] bxa4 20 f6 Nxf6 21 Qe6+ Kh8 22 Nh4 g5 23 Ng6+ Kg7 24 h4 Qd7 25 hxg5 hxg5 26 Rg3 Nbxd5 27 Qxd7+ Nxd7 28 Rxg5 N5b6 29 Ne4 Bxe4 30 Bxe4 Re8 31 Ne5+ Kf6 32 Ng4+ Ke7 33 Bg6 Rc8 34 Bf5 Re8 35 Bg6 Rc8

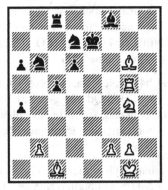

Position after 35 ... Rc8.

Rybka offered Zappa the chance to repeat the position twice, indicating her willingness to draw the game – and get out of the mess she was in! Zappa, though a pawn down, was on the attack and preferred to play on, playing 36 Ne3 and avoiding a draw.

36 Ne3 c4 37 Rh5 c3 38 bxc3 Rxc3

Rybka obtained counterplay while maintaining an extra pawn, but not enough to defeat her opponent!

39 Bb2 Rb3 40 Bd4 Rb5 41 Rh7+ Kd8 42 Bd3 Rb4 43 Nc2 Rb1+ 44 Kh2 d5 45 Bf5 Bd6+ 46 g3 Rd1 47 Bc3 Bc5 48 Ba5 Ke8 49 Bg6+ Kf8 50 Ne3 Bxe3 51 fxe3 Ne5 52 Bxb6 Nxg6 53 Ra7 Rc1 54 Rxa6 Rc4 55 Bd4 Ne7 56 Kh3 Nc6 57 Bh8 Kf7 58 g4 Nb8 59 Ra7+ Ke6 60 Kg3 Nc6 61 Ra6 Ke7 62 Ra8 Re4 63 Ra6 Kd7 64 g5 Rxe3+ 65 Kg4 Re4+ 66 Kf3 Nd4+ 67 Bxd4 Rxd4 68 Ra7+ Ke6 69 g6 Kf5 70 g7 Rf4+ 71 Kg2 Rg4+ 72 Kf3 Rg6 73 Rxa4 Rxg7 Drawn by agreement.

Position after 73 ... Rxg7,
Drawn by agreement.

Clash of the Titans, Mexico City
Game 2, September 21, 2007
Rybka (W) versus Zappa (B)
Ruy Lopez: Morphy Defense. Chigorin Defense Panov System (C99)

Rybka won a pawn in the late mid-game and went on to win a two bishops and pawns versus two bishops and pawns endgame.

1 e4 e5 2 Nf3 Nc6 3 Bb5 a6 4 Ba4 Nf6 5 O-O Be7 6 Re1 b5 7 Bb3 d6 8 c3 O-O 9 h3 Na5 10 Bc2 c5 11 d4 Qc7 12 Nbd2 cxd4 13 cxd4 Bd7 14 Nf1 Rac8 15 Ne3 Rfe8 16 b3 Nc6 17 Bb2 Bd8 18 Rc1 Qa7 [Last book move] **19 dxe5 dxe5 20 Re2 Qb7 21 a3** [Last book move] **Be6 22 Nd5 Ne7 23 Nxe7+ Bxe7 24 Nxe5**

Position after 24 Nxe5.

Rybka snatched a free Zappa pawn!

24 ... Red8 25 Qe1 b4 26 a4 Nh5 27 Nf3 Nf4 28 Rd2 Qb6 29 Be5 Rxd2 30 Qxd2 Ng6 31 Bd4 Qd8 32 Be3 Qxd2 33 Bxd2 h6 34 Kf1 Rd8 35 Be3 Bf6 36 a5 Bb2 37 Rd1 Rc8 38 Bd3 Ne5 39 Nxe5 Bxe5 40 Rb1 Rc6 41 Ke2 Bc7 42 Bd2 Bxa5 43 Ra1

43 ... Bd8 44 Bxb4 Bxb3 45 Rxa6 Rxa6 46 Bxa6

Position after 46 Bxa6.

Was Rybka's extra pawn enough to lead to victory? You'll now see Zappa's king forced to the sidelines while Rybka slowly put on the squeeze.

46 ... g5 47 Kd3 Bb6 48 f3 Kg7 49 Bc4 Ba4 50 e5 Bf2 51 Ke4 Bg3 52 Bc3 Kg6 53 Kd5 Bc2 54 Kd6 f6 55 Ke6 Bf5+ 56 Kd5 fxe5 57 Bxe5

Position after 57 Bxe5.

57 ... Be1

If Zappa had played 57 ... Bxe5, the game would likely have been drawn. Rybka took some time to nail down the victory, but there was little question about the outcome from here on.

58 g4 Bc2 59 Ke6 h5 60 Bd5 hxg4 61 hxg4 Ba4 62 Be4+ Kh6 63 Kf6 Bb4 64 f4 Bd2 65 Bg6 Bb3 66 f5 Bb4 67 Bf7 Bc2 68 Bd4 Bd1 69 Bh5 Bb3 70 Ke5 Bc4 71 f6 Ba3 72 Bb6 Bb2+ 73 Kf5 Bd3+ 74 Ke6 Bc4+ 75 Ke7 Ba3+ 76 Kd7 Bb5+ 77 Ke6 Bc4+ 78 Kf5 Bd3+ 79 Ke5 Bb2+ 80 Bd4 Ba3 81 Kd5 Kh7 82 Be3 Bc2 83 Bxg5 Bb3+ 84 Ke5 Bd1 85 Ke6 Bb3+ 86 Kd7 Ba4+ 87 Kd8 Bb4 88 f7 Ba5+ 89 Ke7 Bb4+ 90 Ke6 Bb3+ 91 Kf6 Bc3+ 92 Kf5 Bc2+ 93 Ke6 Bb3+ 94 Kd7 Ba4+ 95 Kc8 Bb4

96 Bd2 Bc5 97 g5 Bc2 98 Kd7 Ba4+ 99 Kd8 Bc2 100 Bf4 Kg7 101 Be5+ Kh7 102 Bf6 Bg6 103 Be7 Bb6+ 104 Kd7 Bxf7 105 Bxf7 Kg7 106 Ke6 Bd4 107 Be8 Bb2 108 Bf6+ Kf8 109 Bxb2 Kxe8 110 g6 **Black resigns.**

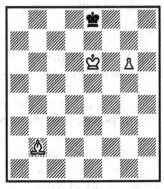

Position after 110 g6,
Black resigns.

Clash of the Titans, Mexico City
Game 3, September 22, 2007
Zappa (W) versus Rybka (B)
Ruy Lopez: Closed. Bogoljubow Variation (C91)

---

1 e4 e5 2 Nf3 Nc6 3 Bb5 a6 4 Ba4 Nf6 5 O-O Be7 6 Re1 b5 7 Bb3 d6 8 c3 O-O 9 d4

A repeat of Game 1 to here. In Game 1, Rybka played 9 ... Re8 and the game was a draw. Here Rybka found herself in trouble when she lost a passed pawn for no apparent compensation.

9 ... Bg4 10 Be3 exd4 11 cxd4 Na5 12 Bc2 c5 13 h3 Bh5 14 g4 Bg6 [Last book move] 15 Nbd2 [Last book move] Nc6 16 d5 Na5 17 a3 Re8 18 b4 Nb7 19 a4 cxb4 20 Nd4 Nc5 21 Nc6 Qc8 22 f3 Nfd7 23 axb5 Bh4 24 Rf1 Bf6 25 Rb1 axb5 26 Rxb4 Nb8 27 Nxb8 Rxb8 28 Qb1 Qd7 29 Bd3 Nxd3 30 Qxd3 Rec8 31 Rfb1 Rc3 32 Rxb5 Rbc8 33 Qe2

h6 34 Rb8 Kh7 35 Rxc8 Qxc8 36 f4 Kh8 37 Kg2 Qe8

Position after 37 … Qe8.

64 Rc6 Ra8 65 Bxd6 Bxd6 66 Nxd6 Black resigns.

Position after 66 Nxd6,
Black resigns.

Zappa was about to lock up Rybka's white bishop for the rest of the game.

38 f5 Bh7 39 Rb6 Qe5 40 Bf2 Rc2 41 Qd3 Ra2 42 Rb1 Qf4 43 Qe3 Qe5 44 Nf3 Qe8 45 Qb3 Ra8 46 Bg3 Qd8 47 Rc1 Qe7 48 Re1 Qd8 49 Rc1 Qe7 50 Rc4 Bg8 51 h4 Qd8 52 Rc6 Be7 53 g5 hxg5 54 hxg5 Rb8 55 Qc3 Ra8 56 Bf4 Bh7 57 Rc7 Rb8 58 Qc6 Qe8 59 Qxe8+ Rxe8 60 Nd2 Bg8 61 Kf3 g6 62 f6 Bf8 63 Nc4 Rd8

Zappa played very well and garnered the full point. Rybka's 38 f5! imprisoning Black's bishop basically gave White an extra piece, and eventually its superior force won Rybka's d6 pawn and the game. The final position was actually quite amusing. You have to appreciate Black's caged bishop, a relic of the 1980s when amateurs could still beat supercomputers.

After three games, the match stood tied. The mighty Rybka wasn't in for a free ride.

**Clash of the Titans, Mexico City
Game 4, September 22, 2007
Rybka (W) versus Zappa (B)
Ruy Lopez: Closed Variations. Flohr System (C92)**

1 e4 e5 2 Nf3 Nc6 3 Bb5 a6 4 Ba4 Nf6 5 O-O Be7 6 Re1 b5 7 Bb3 d6 8 c3 O-O 9 h3

Zappa lost Game 2 when it played 9 … Na5. This time it chose to develop its

queen's bishop. What followed was a wild game interspersed with long dull periods during which Rybka pressed for a win when she should have accepted a draw.

9 ... Bb7 10 d4 Re8 11 Nbd2 Bf8 12 a4 h6 13 Bc2 exd4 14 cxd4 Nb4 15 Bb1 c5 16 d5 Nd7 17 Ra3 c4 18 axb5 axb5 19 Nd4 Qb6 20 Nf5 Ne5 21 Rg3 g6 22 Nf3 Ned3 23 Be3 Qd8 24 Bxh6 Qf6 [Last book move] **25 Qd2 Nxe1 26 Bxf8 Nxf3+ 27 Rxf3** [Last book move]

Zappa had a choice here of the rook capture that it played or capturing the knight on f5. It played the wrong capture and soon found itself in deep trouble. In Game 6, this same position was reached and Zappa was booked to capture the knight as will be seen. Rybka soon traded off two rooks in return for a queen and two pawns and a clear advantage.

27 ... Kxf8 28 Nh6 Qg7 29 Rxf7+ Qxf7 30 Nxf7 Kxf7 31 Qxb4 Ra1 32 Qxb5 Rxb1+ 33 Kh2 Re7 34 Qb4 Rd7 35 Qd2 Kg8 36 Qc2 Ra1 37 Qxc4

Rybka traded off a bishop for two more pawns.

37 ... Ra8 38 b4 Rf8 39 f3 Rc8 40 Qd4 Rf7 41 h4 Rcc7 42 b5 Rc5 43 Qb4 Kh7 44 b6 Rd7 45 Qa4 Re7 46 Kg3 Rc8 47 Qb4 Rd8 48 Kf4 Bc8 49 g4 Rf8+ 50 Ke3 Rd8 51 h5 gxh5 52 gxh5

Rybka gave away her winning position with this move, according to Zappa's website. Cozzie said "Rybka missed 52 Qe1 which would have ended Black's resistance."

52 ... Bb7 53 Qb2 Rf8 54 Qh2 Rf6 55 Qh4 Ref7 56 f4 Rh6 57 Qg5 Ba8 58 Kd3 Bb7 59 Kd4 Rhf6 60 f5

Position after 60 f5.

For the next 49 moves, both sides danced. Painful!

Ba6 61 Kc3 Bb7 62 Kb4 Ba6 63 Ka5 Bb7 64 Kb5 Ba8 65 Qg6+ Kh8 66 Qg3 Bb7 67 Qf4 Rh7 68 Qd2 Rhh6 69 Qg5 Kh7 70 Kc4 Ba6+ 71 Kd4 Bb7 72 Kc3 Bc8 73 Kc2 Ba6 74 Kb2 Bb7 75 Kc1 Ba6 76 Kc2 Bb7 77 Kb2 Ba6 78 Kb3 Bb7 79 Kc2 Ba6 80 Kc1 Kh8 81 Kb1 Kh7 82 Ka2 Bb7 83 Kb3 Kh8 84 Kb4 Kh7 85 Kb5 Kh8 86 Ka4 Kh7 87 Ka5 Kh8 88 Qh4

Rybka preferred not to draw here.

88 ... Rf7 89 Qf4 Kh7 90 Kb5 Rff6 91 Qc1 Rf7 92 Qa3 Rg7 93 Qf3 Rf6 94 Qc3 Rgf7 95 Qd2 Rh6 96 Qg2 Rg7 97 Qh2 Kg8 98 Qh4 Kh7 99 Qh1 Rf7 100 Ka5 Rg7 101 Qh4

101 ... Rd7 102 Qg3 Rg7 103 Qf3 Re7 104 Kb5 Rg7 105 Qc3 Rf7 106 Qh3 Rhf6 107 Qe3 Rg7 108 Qc1 Rgf7 109 h6

Position after 109 h6.

Rybka sacked a pawn to avoid a draw by the 50-move rule. Did her scoring function really feel she would still have the better game? Maybe the passed pawns on b6 and f5 deceived Rybka on the strength of her position.

109 ... Rxh6 110 Qd2 Kg7 111 Qg5+ Kh7 112 Kb4 Rhf6 113 Kc4 Ba6+ 114 Kb3 Bc8 115 Kc3 Ba6 116 Kb2 Rh6 117 Kb3 Rg7 118 Qc1 Re7 119 Qf4 Rb7 120 f6

Position after 120 f6.

Rybka is about to lose another pawn, leaving it in several moves with two pawns versus Zappa's none.

120 ... Rf7 121 Qxd6 Rhxf6 122 Qe5 Rxb6+ 123 Kc3 Rh6 124 Kd4 Be2 125 Qe8 Bh5 126 Qd8 Bg4 127 e5 Rd7 128 Qe8 Kg7 129 Qb8 Be6 130 d6 Rh4+ 131 Ke3 Kg6 132 Qf8 Rf7 133 Qd8 Rb4 134 Qe8 Kf5 135 Qh8 Rb3+ 136 Kd4 Kg4 137 Qg8+ Kf3 138 Qa8+ Kg3 139 Qg8+ Kf2 140 Qg5 Rb4+ 141 Kc5 Rff4 142 d7 Bxd7

Position after 140 ... Bxd7.

Rybka ditched another pawn. Alternatives were much worse. One pawn remained!

143 Qh5 Rfc4+ 144 Kd6 Rd4+ 145 Ke7 Bg4 146 Qh2+ Kf3 147 e6 Re4 148 Qh1+ Kf4 149 Qc1+ Kf5 150 Qf1+ Ke5 151 Qa1+ Rbd4 152 Qg1 Bxe6

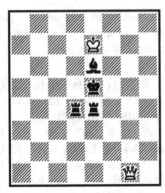

Position after 156 ... Bxe6.

No more pawns on the board. Rybka, rated over 3000, was about to lose a game when playing with the white pieces.

153 Qg5+ Bf5 154 Qg3+ Kd5+ 155 Kf6 Rf4 156 Qb3+ Kc6 157 Kg5 Bd7 158 Qc2+ Rc4 159 Qg2+ Kc5 160 Qg1+ Kd5 161 Qg2+ Ke6 162 Qg3 Rf8 163 Qh3+ Ke7 164 Qe3+ Kf7 165 Qf2+ Kg8 166 Qa2 Be6 167 Qa1 Rg4+ 168 Kh6 Rc8 169 Qa6

Zappa saw mate coming.

169 ... Bd7 170 Qa2+ Rcc4 171 Qa7 Rcd4 172 Qa2+ Kf8 173 Qb3 Ke7 174 Qa3+ Rb4 175 Qe3+ Kf6 176 Qf3+ Rgf4 177 Qc3+ Rbd4 178 Qf3

The last desperate act.

Position after 180 ... Rd8, Mate.

178 ... Rxf3 179 Kh7 Bf5+ 180 Kh8 Rd8 Mate.

**Clash of the Titans, Mexico City
Game 5, September 23, 2007
Zappa (W) versus Rybka (B)
Sicilian Defense: Canal Attack. Main Line (B52)**

The previously invincible Rybka had just lost two games in a row. This one would make it three. Rybka decided to skip playing the Ruy Lopez defense, as she had drawn and lost the two games played thus far with it. Zappa won a king and queen versus king and rook endgame here.

1 e4 c5 2 Nf3 d6 3 Bb5+ Bd7 4 Bxd7+ Qxd7 5 O-O Nf6 6 e5 dxe5 7 Nxe5 Qc8 [Last book move] **8 Nc3** [Last book move] **Nc6 9 Re1 Nxe5 10 Rxe5 e6 11 d3 Qc6 12 Re1 Be7 13 b3 O-O 14 Bb2 Rad8 15 Qe2 Nd7 16 Ne4 f5 17 Nd2 Bf6 18 Bxf6 Rxf6 19 Nf3 Qc7 20 Qd2 Nb8 21 Re3 Nc6 22 Rae1 Qd6 23 Qe2 Re8 24 Ng5 Rh6 25 h3 Nd4 26 Qd1 Qd8 27 Nf3 Nc6 28 Ne5 Qc7 29 Qc1 Rf6 30 Nxc6 Qxc6 31 Re5 Rg6 32 g3 Rh6 33 Kh2 b6 34 Qe3 Rf6 35 Re2 Qd6**

Both sides were about out of ideas.

**36 a4 h6 37 a5 g5 38 Qf3 Re7
39 Kg1 Kf8 40 Re1 Kg7 41 axb6
axb6 42 Qa8 Rf8 43 Qa1 Rf6
44 R1e2 Kf7 45 Qa8 Qd7 46 Re1 Re8
47 Qf3 Kg7 48 Kf1 Qc8 49 Kg1 Qd7
50 Kf1 Qc8 51 Ra1**

Zappa showed it wasn't interested in a
draw by repetition.

**51 … Rf7 52 Kg1 Qd7 53 Rb1 Qd6
54 Rbe1 Ree7 55 Qa8 Rf8 56 Qa6
Rd8 57 Qa1 Kg6 58 R1e2 Kf7
59 R2e3 Rf8 60 Qa4 Kf6 61 Qa6 f4**

Position after 61 … f4.

Finally a break from random motion!
Rybka was opening up the position and,
while her own pieces were relatively
immobile, activating Zappa's dangerous
rooks. Maybe Rybka intended the g-file
for her rooks.

Position after 66 Ke1.

**62 gxf4 gxf4 63 Re2 Rg8+ 64 Kf1
Rg5 65 Qc4 Rf5 66 Ke1**

Rybka chose to exchange her queen for
two Zappa rooks. If a queen is worth
nine points and a rook 5, then Rybka
calculated she gained the equivalent of a
pawn on the exchange, though Zappa
won Rybka's b-pawn shortly.

**66 … Qxe5 67 Rxe5 Rxe5+ 68 Kf1
Kg5 69 Qa6 f3 70 Qxb6 Rg7
71 Qd8+ Kg6 72 Qg8+ Rg7 73 Qb8
Rf5 74 d4 Kh5 75 Qe8+ Rg6 76 dxc5
Rxc5 77 c4 Rcg5 78 Ke1 Re5+
79 Kd2 Re2+ 80 Kc3 Rxf2 81 Qf7**

Position after 97 … Rg8.

Rfg2 **82** Qxf3+ Kh4 **83** Kb4 R2g3 **84** Qb7 h5 **85** c5 Rg7 **86** Qb6 Re7 **87** c6 Rgg7 **88** Qe3 e5 **89** Kc5 e4 **90** Kd6 Ref7 **91** b4 Rg6+ **92** Ke5 Rg5+ **93** Ke6 Rfg7 **94** Qxe4+ Kxh3 **95** Kf6 Rg4 **96** Qh1+ Kg3 **97** Qxh5 Rg8

Zappa had it all figured out here, giving up its queen for one of Rybka's rooks!

98 Qxg4+ Rxg4 **99** b5 Rc4 **100** Ke5 Rc5+ **101** Kd6 Rxb5 **102** c7 Rb6+ **103** Kd5 Rb5+ **104** Kd4 Rb4+ **105** Kc3 Rb1 **106** Kc2 Rf1 **107** c8=Q Rf3 **108** Kd2 Kf4 **109** Qc6 Rf2+ **110** Kd3 Kg5 **111** Qc1+ Rf4 **112** Ke3 Rf6 **113** Ke4+ Kg6 **114** Qc3 Re6+ **115** Kd5 Re8 **116** Qc6+ Kf7 **117** Qd7+ Re7 **118** Qf5+ Kg7 **119** Kd6 Ra7 **120** Qe5+ Kh7 **121** Ke6 Ra2 **122** Qc7+ Kg6 **123** Qc4 Ra5 **124** Qd3+ Kh5 **125** Kf6 Kh4 **126** Qc4+ Kh5 **127** Qe2+ Kh4 **128** Qe1+ Kg4 **129** Qxa5 Kf3 **Black resigns.**

Position after 129 … Kf3,
Black resigns.

Clash of the Titans, Mexico City
Game 6, September 24, 2007
Rybka (W) versus Zappa (B)
Ruy Lopez Game: Closed Variations. Flohr System (C92)

---

1 e4 e5 **2** Nf3 Nc6 **3** Bb5 a6 **4** Ba4 Nf6 **5** O-O Be7 **6** Re1 b5 **7** Bb3 d6 **8** c3 O-O **9** h3

Same as Game 2 to here. In that game Zappa played 9 … Na5 and went on to lose.

9 … Bb7 **10** d4 Re8 **11** Nbd2 Bf8 **12** a4 h6 **13** Bc2 exd4 **14** cxd4 Nb4 **15** Bb1 c5 **16** d5 Nd7 **17** Ra3 c4 **18** axb5 axb5 **19** Nd4 Qb6 **20** Nf5 Ne5 **21** Rg3 g6 **22** Nf3 Ned3 **23** Be3 Qd8 **24** Bxh6 Qf6 **25** Qd2 Nxe1 **26** Bxf8 Nxf3+ **27** Rxf3

Position after 27 Rxf3.

Same as Game 4 to here. Even though Zappa won Game 4 – though helped out by a few weak moves by Rybka as much as by its own positive play – it chose to go in a different direction here. Rather than the king capturing the bishop, Zappa chose to capture the knight.

27 ... gxf5 28 Rxf5 Qg6 29 Rg5 Qxg5 30 Qxg5+ Kxf8 31 Qh6+ Kg8 32 Kh2 [Last book move] **Ra1 33 Qxd6 Rxb1 34 Qxb4 Rxe4 35 Qxb5 c3 36 Qxb7 Kg7 37 d6**

This was Zappa's first move out of its opening book! It assigned a score of 0.0 to the position, forecasting a draw. Rybka was in book until move 33.

37 ... c2 38 Qxe4 c1=Q 39 d7 Qg1+ 40 Kg3 Rd1 41 Qf5 f6 42 Qe4 Rd2 43 d8=Q Qxf2+ 44 Kh2 Rxd8 45 Qe7+ Kg6 46 Qxd8 Qf4+ 47 Kg1 Qc1+ 48 Kf2 Qxb2+ 49 Kf3 Qc3+ 50 Ke2 Qe5+ 51 Kd1 Qa1+ 52 Kd2 Drawn by agreement.

Position after 37 d6.

Position after 52 Kd2,
Drawn by agreement.

Clash of the Titans, Mexico City
Game 7, September 25, 2007
Zappa (W) versus Rybka (B)
Sicilian Defense: Old Sicilian. Open (B35)

---

1 e4 c5 2 Nf3 Nc6 3 d4 cxd4 4 Nxd4 g6 5 Nc3 Bg7 6 Be3 Nf6 7 Bc4 Qa5 8 O-O O-O 9 Nb3 [Last book move] **Qd8 10 Be2 d6 11 f4 b6** [Last book move] **12 a3 Bb7 13 Qd3 Nd7 14 Rad1 Nc5 15 Nxc5 bxc5 16 Qd2 Nd4 17 Bd3 Rc8 18 Ne2 Qc7 19 b3 a5 20 f5 a4 21 Nxd4 cxd4 22 Bh6 axb3 23 Bxg7 Kxg7 24 cxb3 Qc3**

25 Qa2 Qa5 26 b4 Qe5 27 Qd2 Ra8 28 Ra1 Rfc8 29 Rf3 Ba6 30 Rh3 h5 31 a4 Bxd3 32 Rxd3 Rc4 33 fxg6 fxg6 34 Rf3 Rc7 35 a5 Qxe4 36 Raf1 e5 37 b5 Qd5 38 b6 Rd7 39 Qg5 Kh7 40 g4 Rg7 41 Rg3 d3 42 gxh5 Qxa5 43 hxg6+ Kg8 44 h4 e4 45 Qg4 Qxb6+ 46 Kh2 Re8 47 h5 Qb2+ 48 Kh3 Qe2 49 Qf5 d2 50 h6 Qc4

Position after 50 ... Qc4.

What motivated Zappa's next move? It gave away a winning position!

51 Ra3 Qc8 52 Qxc8 Rxc8 53 hxg7 e3 54 Rxe3 Rc1 55 Rf7 Rh1+ 56 Kg2 Rg1+ 57 Kh2 Rh1+ 58 Kg3 Rg1+ 59 Kf2 Rf1+ 60 Kxf1 d1=Q+ 61 Kf2 Qc2+ 62 Kf3 Qxg6 63 Rf4 Qh5+ 64 Kg3

64 ... Qg5+ 65 Kf3 Qh5+ 66 Kf2 Kxg7 Drawn by agreement.

Position after 66 ... Kxg7,
Drawn by agreement.

Zappa was satisfied to draw this game. With three games remaining, time was running out on Rybka.

Clash of the Titans, Mexico City
Game 8, September 26, 2007
Rybka (W) versus Zappa (B)
Ruy Lopez: Closed Variations. Martinez Variation (C84)

---

1 e4 e5 2 Nf3 Nc6 3 Bb5 a6 4 Ba4 Nf6 5 O-O Be7 6 d3 b5 7 Bb3 Bb7 8 Nc3 O-O 9 Re1 d6 10 a3 Qd7 11 h3 Rae8 12 a4 b4 [Last book move] **13 Nd5 Na5 14 Nxe7+ Qxe7 15 Ba2** [Last book move] **Rb8 16 Nh4 Bc8 17 Bg5 Kh8 18 Nf5 Bxf5 19 exf5 Qd7 20 g4 b3 21 Bxb3 Nxb3 22 cxb3 c5 23 Ra3 Ng8 24 Qe2 f6 25 Bd2 Ne7 26 d4**

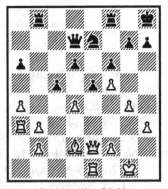

Position after 26 d4.

Rybka initiated a sequence of exchanges, capturing a bishop and two pawns and giving up a rook. The sequence also left Rybka with an important passed a-pawn.

26 ... Nc6 27 dxe5 Nd4 28 Qxa6 Nf3+ 29 Kg2 Nxe1+ 30 Bxe1 dxe5 31 Qc4 Rfd8 32 a5 Qa7 33 Bc3 Rd1 34 f3 h6 35 Qe2 Rbd8 36 Be1 R1d4 37 Ra1 Rd3 38 Bc3 R8d6 39 h4 Qa6 40 Kg3 Qb7 41 Kg2 Kg8 42 Ra3 Qa6 43 Qe4 Kh8 44 Qc4 Qb7 45 Qe4 Qa7 46 Qe2 Qa6 47 Kg3 c4

Position after 47 ... c4.

Rybka's passed a-pawn is given a defender!

48 b4 Qa7 49 Kg2 Rd1 50 Be1 Qd7 51 Kg3 R6d3 52 a6 Rxa3 53 bxa3 Rd3 54 Bf2 Qd5 55 a7 Rxa3 56 b5 Qxb5 57 Qe4 Qe8 58 Qb7 Qd8 59 Qb8 Qg8 60 g5 Ra2 61 Be1 Ra6 62 Bc3 Ra2 63 Kg4 Kh7 64 g6+ Kh8 65 Qb7 Ra3 66 Qb8 Ra2 67 Kh5 Ra3 68 Bxe5

Zappa could not have taken the bishop as it would have resulted in mate-in-nine.

68 ... Rxa7 69 Qxa7 Qc8 70 Qb8 Qxb8 71 Bxb8 Black resigns.

Position after 71 Bxb8,
Black resigns.

Clash of the Titans, Mexico City
Game 9, September 26, 2007
Zappa (W) versus Rybka (B)
Caro-Kann Defense: Karpov. Smyslov Variation (B17)

1 e4 c6

Rybka needed to win this game to win the match. After eight games of Sicilian and Ruy Lopez openings, and not having great success, Rybka tried a different approach.

2 d4 d5 3 Nc3 dxe4 4 Nxe4 Nd7 5 Bc4 Ngf6 6 Ng5 e6

Position after 6 e6.

This looks similar to the final game of the Kasparov vs Deep Blue match. Did Rybka invite Zappa to play 7 Nxe6?

7 Qe2 Nb6 8 Bd3 h6 9 N5f3 c5 10 dxc5 Bxc5 11 Ne5 Nbd7 12 Ngf3 Nxe5 13 Nxe5 O-O 14 O-O b6 [Last book move] **15 Bf4** [Last book move] **Qd4 16 Bg3 Bb7 17 c4 Qd8 18 Rad1 Qe7 19 Kh1 Rfd8 20 a3 Bd4 21 Bh4 Rd6 22 f4 Rad8 23 Bb1**

23 ... Kf8 24 Rd3 Qc7 25 b4 a5 26 Re1 Ba1 27 Rc1 Rd4 28 Rcd1 Rxd3 29 Bxd3 Bc3 30 bxa5 Bxa5 31 Bg3 Kg8 32 Bf2 Bc3 33 Bg1 Ne4 34 Qc2 Bxe5 35 fxe5 Qxe5 36 Bxb6 Rd6 37 Bg1 Qh5 38 Be3 Ng3+ 39 Kg1 Nf5 40 Bf4 Rd4 41 Be2 Qh4 42 Bc1 Qd8 43 Rf1 Qc7 44 Rf2 Rh4 45 h3 Nd4 46 Qb2 Nxe2+ 47 Qxe2 Re4 48 Qf1 Rxc4 49 Bf4 Qc6 50 Rb2 Rc3 51 Qb5 Qxb5 52 Rxb5 Bd5 53 Bd6 Rc1+ 54 Kf2 Rc2+ 55 Ke1 Rxg2 56 Rc5 g5 57 Rc3 Ra2 58 h4 f5 59 hxg5 hxg5 60 Rg3 g4 61 Rc3 Kf7 62 Be5 Kg6 63 Rc8 Rxa3 64 Rg8+ Kf7 65 Rg7+ Kf8 66 Kd2 Ra4 67 Kc3 Re4 68 Bf6 Bc4 69 Kd2 Be2 70 Rg5 Kf7 71 Bh8 f4

Position after 71 ... f4.

A sure Rybka win turns into a draw with this subtle blunder. It ensures that Zappa can do no worse than finish the match with an even score.

**72 Re5 Rxe5 73 Bxe5 f3 74 Ke3
Kg6 75 Bd6 Kf6 76 Bg3 Kf5
77 Bh2 e5 78 Bg3 Bc4 79 Bh4 Ba6
80 Bg3 Ke6 81 Be1 Kd5 82 Bh4 Bb5
83 Be1 Be2 84 Bf2 Drawn by
agreement.**

Position after 84 Bf2,
Drawn by agreement.

**Clash of the Titans, Mexico City
Game 10, September 27, 2007
Rybka (W) versus Zappa (B)
Reti Opening (A05)**

---

1 Nf3

Rybka showed that she had had it with
the openings tried so far and thus took
an entirely new path.

**1 ... Nf6 2 c4 e6 3 Nc3 c5 4 g3 b6
5 Bg2 Bb7 6 O-O Be7 7 Re1 d6 8 e4
a6 9 d4 cxd4 10 Nxd4 Qc7 11 Be3
Nbd7 12 f4 Rc8 13 Rc1 O-O 14 f5 e5
15 Nb3** [Last book move] **Qb8** [Last
book move] **16 Qe2 Rc7 17 Nd2
Rfc8 18 g4 h6 19 h4 Nh7 20 Bf2 Bc6
21 Nd5 Bxd5 22 exd5 b5 23 b3 b4
24 Qe3 Nc5 25 Ne4 Nxe4 26 Bxe4
Rd7 27 Bf3 Qc7 28 Kg2 a5 29 Kh3
Qd8 30 Qd2 Rdc7 31 Rcd1 Bf6
32 Re2 Rd7 33 Qd3 Be7 34 a3**

Position after 34 a3.

Zappa was given some space on the
queenside with this move, eventually
giving its queen and dark-squared bishop
the opportunity to gang up on Rybka
and squeak out a draw by repetition.

**34 ... bxa3 35 Ra1 Qf8 36 Rxa3 Bd8
37 Kg2 Rb8 38 Re1 Rdb7 39 c5 Rb4
40 c6 Qe7 41 Bg3 Nf6 42 g5 hxg5
43 hxg5 Ne8 44 Qd2 Rxb3 45 Rxb3
Rxb3 46 g6 Bb6**

Zappa saw a draw at this point, assigning this position and all that followed a score of 0.00.

**47 Qa2 Rb4 48 Rb1 fxg6 49 fxg6
Qg5 50 Rxb4 axb4 51 Qb1 Qd2+
52 Kf1 Qe3 53 Qf5**

Position after 53 Qf5.

While threatening mate, Rybka gave Zappa the chance to draw by repetition, throwing away possibly finishing the match with an even score.

**53 ... Qg1+ 54 Ke2 Qe3+ 55 Kd1
Qb3+ 56 Kd2 Qc3+ 57 Kd1 Qb3+
58 Ke1 Qe3+ 59 Kd1 Qb3+ Drawn by
repetition.**

Position after 59 Qb3+,
Drawn by repetition.

Suggest Readings

Anthony Cozzie, Zappa vs. Rybka, ICGA Journal, Vol. 30, No. 4, pp. 226–230, December 2007.

Zappa's website (Anthony Cozzie's commentary on the match): https://netfiles.uiuc.edu/acozzie2/www/zappa/mexico/

Rybka chess community forum: http://rybkaforum.net/cgi-bin/rybkaforum/topic_show.pl?tid=2152

Game 1: http://www.chessgames.com/perl/chessgame?gid=1473880

Game 2: http://www.chessgames.com/perl/chessgame?gid=1473881

Game 3: http://www.chessgames.com/perl/chessgame?gid=1473882

Game 4: http://www.chessgames.com/perl/chessgame?gid=1473884

Game 5: http://www.chessgames.com/perl/chessgame?gid=1473883

Game 6: http://www.chessgames.com/perl/chessgame?gid=1474491

Game 7: http://www.chessgames.com/perl/chessgame?gid=1474492

Game 8: http://www.chessgames.com/perl/chessgame?gid=1474493

Game 9: http://www.chessgames.com/perl/chessgame?gid=1474494

Game 10: http://www.chessgames.com/perl/chessgame?gid=1474495, http://rybkaforum.net/cgi-bin/rybkaforum/topic_show.pl?tid=2295

Hiarcs's website with commentary on the match: http://www.hiarcs.net/forums/viewtopic.php?t=254&postdays=0&postorder=asc&start=30

The Internet Chess Club has held annual computer competitions dating back to 1999; this marked the tenth such gathering. The seven-round tournament was held over 2 days, January 26–27, 2008, with four games on the first day and three on the second. The time control was all moves in 50 minutes plus three seconds extra per move.

The huge field of 36 contained five particularly strong entries: Rybka, Zappa, Hiarcs, Junior, and Naum. World Champion Rybka was the logical favorite, though Zappa had defeated her in head-to-head play only several months earlier. Hiarcs had finished first on tie-break points at the 17th International Paderborn CCC the previous month, having ended the competition equal in points with Rybka. Junior was always a contender; it was using the strongest computing system, a 16-core system. Naum, a dark horse, and Rybka both used 4 core Intel processors. Naum was the work of Alexander Naumov. Naumov was born in Serbia, educated at Belgrade University, and then moved to Toronto, Canada, in 1994. With such a large field and only seven rounds, the slightest misfortune could cost one the championship.

Zappa led the pack after four rounds with a perfect score, defeating Hiarcs among others. Rybka, Naum, and Glaurung were one-half point behind, Hiarcs another half point behind, and Junior yet another half point. Other than Zappa's victory over Hiarcs and a victory by Glaurung over Junior, the leading chess engines hadn't met one another in the first four rounds. Glaurung's victory over Junior was due to Internet communication problems suffered by the Israeli engine.

Rybka defeated Zappa, and Naum kept pace with a victory over Fruit in Round 5; they took the lead with 4.5/5 points. Glaurung lost to Hiarcs, who now was a half point behind the leaders. Junior was one and a half points off pace.

No sooner than Rybka had taken the lead than she was upset by Hiarcs, who moved to the top of the pack after six rounds with five points. One-half point behind were Rybka, Naum, and Glaurung, and a full point behind was Junior.

In the final round, Hiarcs had a tough opponent in Naum while Rybka faced Fruit. Hiarcs blew the championship when it lost to Naum, while Rybka won her final game, and thus shared first place with Naum. Rybka was awarded the title

M. Newborn, *Beyond Deep Blue: Chess in the Stratosphere*,
DOI 10.1007/978-0-85729-341-1_15, © Springer-Verlag London Limited 2011

based on tie-breaking points. Junior won its final round game to finish a half point behind. Glaurung and Zappa drew and both engines also finished a half point behind the leaders.

Coincidentally, Rybka and Naum had played the same opponents during the competition and had the same results with two exceptions. Rybka had defeated Zappa, while Naum had lost. Naum had defeated Hiarcs, while Rybka had lost. Five other chess engines finished within a half point of the leaders: Zappa, Glaurung, Hiarcs, Junior, and Weid.

Two unofficial games were played between Rybka and Naum following the seven-round event to break the tie; both ended in draws. The first game lasted 82 moves and the second 127 moves.

Rybka must consider herself fortunate to have won this event. One wonders whether Naum would have won the tournament outright if it hadn't lost its first-round game to unknown Symbolic by default (its Internet connection wasn't working!). Or, perhaps Junior would have won the tournament if it hadn't had to resign to Glaurung in Round 3 in an excellent position when it ran into Internet connection problems. Somewhat strangely, Glaurung also defeated Ikarus in Round 4 in similar circumstances.

Data on entries to the Internet Chess Club CCT 10: Name, author/operator, hardware

Name	Author/operator	Hardware
Rybka	Vasik Rajlich, Larry Kaufman, Nick Carlin	Intel Quad
Naum	Alex Naumov	Intel Core 2 Quad Q6600
Zappa	Anthony Cozzie, Clemens Keck, Erdogan Gunes	Intel 8x 3.0 GHz
Glaurung	Sherif Khater(Operator), Tord Romstad	Intel Core 2 Quad Q6600
Hiarcs	Mark Uniacke, Harvey Williamson, Enrico L. Carrisco	Intel 8x Xeon X5355 2.66 GHz
Junior	Amir Ban, Shay Bushinsky	Data not available
Weid	Jaap Weidemann	AMD Athlon 64 X2 3800+2 GHz
Ktulu	Rahman Paidar, Sherif Khater(Operator)	AMD Athlon 64 3500+2.2 GHz, 512 MB
LearningLemming	Sam Hamilton	Intel Core 2 Duo 2.6 GHz (1 cpu)
Arasan	Jon Dart	AMD Athlon 64 X2 4400+
E. T. Chess	Eric Triki	Intel Pentium 4 2.5 GHz
Crafty	Robert Hyatt, Tracy Riegle, Peter Skinner, Mike Byrne, Ted Langreck	Intel Core 2 Quad Xeon 2.33 GHz, 12 GB
Ikarus	Muntsin Kolss, Munjong Kolss	AMD Opteron Dual Core 2.4 GHz, 2 GB

(continued)

(continued)

Name	Author/operator	Hardware
Fruit	Fabien Letouzey, Ryan Benitez, Nolan Denson	Intel Core 2 Quad Q6600
CrashTestDummy	Richard Pijl, Arturo Ochoa(book)	AMD Opteron 270 2 GHz
Petir	Peter Alloysius, Olivier Deville	Intel Core 2 Duo E6600 2.4 GHz
Berta	Felix Schmenger	AMD Athlon 64 3000+, 512 MB
Danasah	Pedro Castro	AMD Athlon 64 X2 4600+ (1 cpu)
Booot	Alex Morozov	Intel Core 2 Duo 2.4 GHz
Rascal	Derek Mauro	Intel Core 2 Quad Q6600
Tornado	Engin Ustun	AMD Athlon 64 X2 3800+
Joker	Harm Geert Muller	Intel Core 2 Duo 2.4 GHz
Timea	Laszlo Gaspar	Intel Core 2 Quad Q6600
Telepath	Charles Roberson, James Swafford	Intel Core 2 Quad Q6600
Averno	Jose Carlos, Martinez Galan	Intel Quad
Tinker	Brian Richardson	AMD Opteron 2 GHz (1 cpu)
Twisted Logic	Edsel Apostol, N. Swaminathan	Intel Pentium 4 2.6 GHZ
Clarabit	Salvador Pallares	Intel Pentium 4 2.6 GHz 512 MB
Now	Mark Lefler	Intel Core 2 Duo 2.4 GHz
micro-Max	Harm Geert Muller	Intel Core 2 Duo 2.4 GHz
Protej	Alex Brunetti	Intel Pentium 4 1.8 GHz
Prophet	James Swafford	Intel Core 2 Duo 1.86 GHz, 2 GB
Vicki	Jaco van Niekerk	Intel Pentium 4 2.8 GHz, 1 GB
Oxygen	Robindu Guha	Intel Pentium 3 1 GHz
Symbolic	Steven J. Edwards	Data not available
ZCT	Zach Wegner, Kenny Dail	Data not available

Final standing of the Internet Chess Club CCT 10.

#	Name	1	2	3	4	5	6	7	Pts	BU
1	Rybka	20wW	15bW	13wD	9bW	3wW	5bL	14wW	5.5	29.0
2	Naum	35wL	7bW	20wW	15bW	14wW	3bD	5wW	5.5	28.5
3	Zappa	26bW	12wW	11bW	5wW	1bL	2wD	4bD	5.0	31.5
4	Glaurung	9wD	17bW	6wW	13bW	5wL	8bW	3wD	5.0	31.0
5	Hiarcs	29wW	13bW	10wW	3bL	4bW	1wW	2bL	5.0	30.5
6	Junior	32bW	16wD	4bL	25wW	12bD	10bW	9wW	5.0	25.0
7	Weid	36bL	2wL	26bW	32wW	19bW	16wW	11bW	5.0	23.5
8	Ktulu	24bW	10wL	32bW	11wD	21bW	4wL	18bW	4.5	24.0
9	LearningLemming	4bD	25wW	16bW	1wL	15bW	11wD	6bL	4.0	30.0
10	Arasan	23wW	8bW	5bL	12wL	17bW	6wL	22bW	4.0	28.5
11	E. T. Chess	30wW	14bW	3wL	8bD	13wW	9bD	7wL	4.0	28.5
12	Crafty	22wW	3bL	21wD	10bW	6wD	18bD	13wD	4.0	27.5
13	Ikarus	18wW	21bW	1bD	4wL	11bL	25wW	12bD	4.0	27.5
14	Fruit	17bW	11wL	29bW	19wW	2bL	22wW	1bL	4.0	27.5
15	CrashTestDummy	31bW	1wL	17bW	2wL	9wL	29bW	20wW	4.0	26.0
16	Petir	34wW	6bD	9wL	22bD	20wW	7bL	21wW	4.0	24.0
17	Berta	14wL	23bW	15wL	30bW	10wL	31bW	25wW	4.0	21.5
18	Danasah	13bL	4wL	33bW	24wW	23bW	12wD	8wL	3.5	24.5
19	Booot	33bW	5wL	28bW	14bL	7wL	21wD	27bW	3.5	23.0
20	Rascal	1bL	31wW	2bL	28wW	16bL	23wW	15bL	3.0	26.5

		27bW	9wL	12bD	29wW	8wL	19bD	16bL		
21	Tornado	27bW	9wL	12bD	29wW	8wL	19bD	16bL	3.0	24.5
22	Joker	12bL	27wW	25bD	16wD	32bW	14bL	10wL	3.0	22.5
23	Timea	10bL	17wL	31bW	26wW	18wL	20bL	29wW	3.0	21.0
24	Telepath	8wL	28bL	34wW	18bL	25bL	33wW	30wW	3.0	17.0
25	Averno	28wW	9bL	22wD	6bL	24wW	13bL	17bL	2.5	25.5
26	Tinker	3wL	30bD	7wL	23bL	34wW	27wL	32bW	2.5	20.0
27	Twisted Logic	21wL	22bL	30wD	31bL	28wW	26bW	19wL	2.5	18.5
28	Clarabit	25bL	24wW	19wL	20bL	27bL	32wD	33bW	2.5	17.0
29	Now	5bL	33wW	14wL	21bL	30wW	15wL	23bL	2.0	22.0
30	micro-Max	11bL	26wD	27bD	17wL	29bL	34wW	24bL	2.0	19.0
31	Protej	15wL	20bL	23wL	27wW	33bW	17wL	34bL	2.0	18.5
32	Prophet	6wL	34bW	8wL	7bL	22wL	28bD	26wL	1.5	23.5
33	Vicki	19wL	29bL	32wL	34bW	31bL	24bL	28wL	1.0	17.5
34	Oxygen	16bL	32wL	24bL	33wL	26bL	30bL	31wW	1.0	17.5
35	Symbolic	2bW	36wL						1.0	8.0
36	ZCT	7wL	35bL						0.0	7.5

Internet Chess Club CCT 10
Round 4, January 26, 2008
Zappa (W) versus Hiarcs (B)
Neo-Grunfeld, 6 O-O (D77)

Zappa and Hiarcs led the large field at this point with three points each. In their encounter a year ago at the ICC CCT 9, Zappa lost to Hiarcs when playing a Sicilian Defense. This time, Zappa tried a different approach.

1 d4 Nf6 2 Nf3 g6 3 g3 Bg7 4 c4 O-O 5 Bg2 d5 6 O-O dxc4 7 Na3 Nc6 8 Nxc4 Be6 9 b3 Bd5 10 Bb2 a5 11 Rc1 a4 12 bxa4 Ra6 13 Ne3 Bxa2 14 Ne5 Na5 15 Nd3 Ra7 16 Qc2 c6 17 Bc3 Be6 18 Nc5 Bc8 19 Rfd1 Nd5 20 Bxa5 Qxa5 21 Nc4 Qc7 22 Qb3 Nf6 23 Qb6 Qxb6 24 Nxb6 Rd8 25 d5 cxd5 26 Bxd5 Nxd5 27 Nxd5 Re8 28 Rc4

Position after 28 Rc4.

Hiarcs's pieces were tied to the sides of the board while Zappa's controlled most of the squares. Zappa gradually strengthened its position over the next 20 moves, giving its opponent little choice but to resign on the 49th move.

28 ... Bh3 29 f3 Bf8 30 Nb6 h5 31 Kf2 e5 32 g4 hxg4 33 Ncd7 Bg7 34 fxg4 f5 35 g5 f4 36 Rc7 Rd8 37 Rd6 Bxd7 38 Nxd7 Ra6 39 Rxa6 bxa6 40 Kf3 Re8 41 Ke4 Re7 42 h4 a5 43 Ra7 Kh7 44 Rb7 Kg8

Zappa was offered a draw by Hiarcs, but Zappa passed, obtaining Hiarcs's resignation five moves later.

45 Rb8+ Kf7 46 Nc5 Bf8 47 Ra8 Kg7 48 Rxa5 Re8 49 Ra7+ Black resigns.

Position after 49 Ra7+,
Black resigns.

Internet Chess Club CCT 10
Round 5, January 27, 2008
Rybka (W) versus Zappa (B)
English (A36)

Fresh from a victory over Hiarcs, Zappa now faced its biggest challenge, especially playing with the black pieces. Rybka, however, had her sights on setting the record straight regarding her recent Mexican misfortune.

1 c4 e5 2 Nc3 Nc6 3 g3 g6 4 Bg2 Bg7 5 e4 d6 6 d3 f5 7 exf5 Bxf5 8 Nge2 Nf6 9 O-O O-O 10 Nd5 Qd7 11 Nxf6+ Bxf6 12 Be3

Position after 12 Be3.

Both sides were out of book here. Zappa left book with 10 ... Qd7.

12 ... Kh8 13 Qb3 a5 14 Rfe1 Rab8 15 Rad1 Bg7 16 a3 Bg4 17 Rb1 Ne7 18 Qb5 Qxb5 19 cxb5 Nf5 20 Bd2 Bxe2 21 Rxe2 Nd4 22 Re4 Nxb5 23 a4 Nd4 24 Bxa5 Rf7 25 Bc3 Nf3+

26 Kh1 c6 27 a5 Ra8 28 Rb4 Ra7 29 Ra1 d5 30 Rb6 e4 31 Bxg7+ Kxg7 32 dxe4 dxe4 33 Bxf3 exf3

Each side had two rooks and five pawns. Rybka smartly outmaneuvered Zappa and won the endgame.

34 b4 Ra8 35 g4 Re8 36 b5 cxb5 37 Rxb5 Re2 38 Kg1 Kf6 39 h3 Rd2 40 Rab1 Ra2 41 R1b3 Kg7 42 Rb2 Rxb2 43 Rxb2 Kf6 44 Kh2 h5 45 Kg3 hxg4 46 hxg4 Kg5 47 Rb3 Kh6 48 Rb5 g5 49 Rf5 Re7 50 Kxf3 Re6 51 Rb5 Re7 52 Kg2 Kg6 53 Rb6+ Kg7 54 f3 Re2+ 55 Kg1 Re1+ 56 Kf2 Re7 57 Rb4 Kf6 58 Rb3 Kg6 59 Re3 Rc7 60 Re5 Kf6 61 Rf5+ Kg6 62 Ke3 Rd7 63 Ke4 Rc7 64 Kd4 Kh6 65 Rb5 Kg6 Kd5 Kf6 67 Kd6 Rc6+ 68 Kd7 Black resigns.

Position after 68 Kd7,
Black resigns.

Internet Chess Club CCT 10
Round 6, January 27, 2008
Hiarcs (W) versus Rybka (B)
Semi-Slav Defense: Meran. Wade Variation (D47)

Rybka led Hiarcs, Zappa, and Naum by a half point going into this penultimate round.

1 d4 d5 2 c4 e6 3 Nc3 c6 4 e3 Nf6 5 Nf3 Nbd7 6 Bd3 dxc4 7 Bxc4 b5 8 Bd3 Bb7 9 O-O a6 10 e4 c5 11 d5 Qc7 12 dxe6 fxe6 13 Bc2 c4 14 Nd4 Nc5 15 Be3 O-O-O 16 Qe2 e5 17 Nf3 Bd6 18 Rfd1 Rhe8

Position after 18 … Rhe8.

Both sides played their first 18 moves from book! In fewer than ten more moves, Rybka would find herself in a desperate situation.

19 b3 b4 20 Nd5 Bxd5 21 exd5 e4 22 Ng5 Bxh2+ 23 Kf1 c3

Rybka evidently liked the idea of a passed pawn deep in Hiarcs territory, but 23 … c3 soon led to one of the few disasters in Rybka's career.

24 Bxc5 Qxc5 25 Qxa6+ Kc7 26 Ne6+ Rxe6 27 dxe6

Position after 27 dxe6.

Hiarcs outplayed its opponent tactically after leaving book, winning a rook for a knight in the preceding moves and essentially clinching the game.

27 … Bg3 28 Qe2 Rf8 29 e7 Rf7 30 Kg1 Rxe7 31 a3 Nd5 32 Rxd5 Qxd5 33 fxg3 bxa3 34 Qe3 Qd6 35 Qxc3+ Kb7 36 Qe3 Qb4 37 Kh2 Re6 38 Rd1 Rh6+ 39 Kg1 Qb6 40 Bxe4+ Kb8 41 Qxb6+ Rxb6 42 Bxh7 Rxb3 43 Rb1 Rxb1+ 44 Bxb1

Position after 44 Bxb1.

Rybka should have resigned at this point to avoid the inevitable humiliation about to come. Nevertheless, the game continued for another 24 moves during which time Hiarcs gradually brought Rybka to her knees.

44 … Kc7 45 Kf2 Kd6 46 Kf3 Ke5 47 Ke3 Ke6 48 Kf4 g6 49 Ba2+ Kf6

50 g4 g5+ 51 Ke4 Kg6 52 Ke5 Kg7 53 Ke6 Kg6 54 Ke7 Kg7 55 Bf7 Kh7 56 Kf6 Kh8 57 Kxg5 Kg7 58 Ba2 Kf8 59 Kf6 Ke8 60 g5 Kd7 61 g6 Kc7 62 g7 Kb7 63 g8=Q Kc6 64 Qd5+ Kb6 65 Ke7 Ka6 66 Bc4+ Kb6 67 Qb5+ Kc7 68 Bd5 Kc8 69 Qb7 Mate

Position after 69 Qb7, Mate.

Internet Chess Club CCT 10
Round 6, January 27, 2008
Zappa (W) versus Naum (B)
Queen's Indian (E15)

---

1 d4 Nf6 2 c4 e6 3 Nf3 b6 4 g3 Bb7 5 Bg2 Be7 6 O-O O-O 7 Nc3 Ne4 8 Bd2 f5 9 d5 Bf6 10 Rc1 Na6 11 Be1 Nd6 12 Nd4 Nxc4 13 dxe6 Bxg2 14 Kxg2 Nc5 15 Na4 dxe6 16 Nxc5 Bxd4 17 Nxe6 Qd5+ 18 Kg1 Bxf2+ 19 Rxf2 Qxe6 20 Qb3 b5 21 Qxb5 Nd6 22 Qa6 Rf7 23 Bb4 Re8 24 Bxd6 cxd6 25 Qc4 g6 26 Qxe6 Rxe6 27 Rc2 Rfe7 28 Kf1 Re4 29 Rd2 Rd7 30 Rf3 Kf7 31 Kf2 a5 32 Rb3 Rb4 33 Rxb4 axb4 34 Ke3 Ke6 35 Rd4 Rb7 36 Rc4 Ke5 37 b3 h6 38 Kd3 g5 39 h4 Rb5 40 h5 Ra5 41 Rxb4 Rxa2 42 Rb5+ Kf6 43 Rb6 Ke5 44 Rb5+ d5 45 Rb8 Rb2 46 Re8+ Kf6 47 Rb8 Ke5 48 Re8+ Kf6 49 Rb8

Position after 49 Rb8.

Naum was given the option to draw by repetition, but passed.

49 ... g4 50 b4 Rb3+ 51 Kd4 Rxg3 52 Rg8 Kf7 53 Rg6 Rh3 54 Rxh6 g3 55 Ke3 Rh1 56 Rg6 Rxh5 57 Rxg3

57 ... Rh4 58 Rf3 Re4+ 59 Kd2 Rxb4 60 Rxf5+ Ke6 61 Rf8 Rb2+ 62 Kd3 Ra2 63 Ke3 Ke7 64 Rc8 Rb2 65 Rc6 Ra2 66 Kd4 Rxe2 67 Kxd5 Rd2+ 68 Ke5 Re2+ 69 Kd4 Rd2+ 70 Ke5 Drawn by agreement.

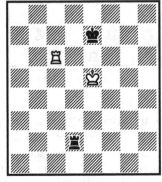

Position after 70 Ke5,
Drawn by agreement.

**Internet Chess Club CCT 10
Round 7, January 27, 2008
Naum (W) versus Hiarcs (B)
Queen's Indian (E15)**

Hiarcs led the field by a half point going into the final round. It had won five of six games, with a loss to Zappa in Round 4 as its only blemish. Rybka and Naum trailed by a half point.

Naum defeated Hiarcs in the follow game while Rybka defeated Fruit. Thus Naum and Rybka finished tied for first place on points. Two playoff games followed the regular seven rounds and both were drawn. Rybka was awarded the championship based on tie-breaking points.

1 d4 Nf6 2 c4 e6 3 Nf3 b6 4 g3 Ba6 5 b3 Bb4+ 6 Bd2 Be7 7 Bg2 c6 8 Bc3 d5 9 Ne5 Nfd7 10 Nxd7 Nxd7 11 Nd2 O-O 12 O-O Rc8 13 e4 b5

14 Re1 bxc4 15 bxc4 dxc4 16 Qa4 Bb5 17 Qc2 Re8 18 a4 Ba6 19 Rad1 Bf8 20 Nf1 Rb8 21 Ne3 Bb4 22 Bxb4 Rxb4 23 d5 Qc7 24 Qd2 Rxa4 25 dxe6

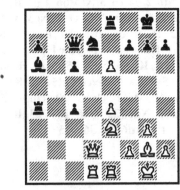

Position after 25 dxe6.

Hiarcs managed to maintain a one-pawn advantage and an exclusive monopoly on queenside pawns. But Naum's e-pawn was soon to become a major problem.

25 ... Ne5 26 Ra1 Bb5 27 Rxa4 Bxa4 28 exf7+ Qxf7 29 Ra1 Bb5 30 Qd4 Nd3 31 f4 a6 32 e5 Kh8 33 h4 Qg6 34 Kh2 Qe6 35 Ra2 c5 36 Qc3 Rd8 37 Rd2 Qf7 38 Bh3 g6 39 h5 Rd4 40 Nc2 Rd8 41 h6 Kg8 42 e6 Qe7 43 Na3

Hiarcs's one-pawn lead was about to vanish.

43 ... Re8 44 Nxc4 Nxf4 45 gxf4 Qf8 46 Kg3 Qxh6 47 Nd6

Position after 47 Nd6.

Not alone had the one-pawn advantage gone, but by this move, the game had gone and the championship as well.

47 ... Qg7 48 Qxg7+ Kxg7 49 Nxe8+ Bxe8 50 Rd7+ Kf6 51 Rxh7 c4 52 Rc7 a5 53 e7 Bf7 54 Bf1 Be8 55 Bxc4 a4 56 Rc8 Kxe7 57 Rxe8+ Kd6 58 f5 gxf5 59 Ra8 a3 60 Rxa3 Kc5 61 Ra5+ Kxc4 62 Rxf5

A rook and king versus king endgame, and certain death for Hiarcs.

62 ... Kd3 63 Rf4 Ke3 64 Ra4 Kd3 65 Kf2 Kc3 66 Ke2 Kb3 67 Rd4 Kc3 68 Re4 Kc2 69 Re3 Kc1 70 Kd3 Kb2 71 Kd2 Kb1 72 Kc3 Ka1 73 Kb3 Kb1 74 Re1 Mate.

Position after 74 Re1,
Mate.

Internet Chess Club CCT 10
Round 7, January 27, 2008
Rybka (W) versus Fruit (B)
Nimzovich-Larsen Attack (A01)

Rybka beat Fruit opening with 1 b3. Fruit's first move out of book was 3 … Nf6; Rybka's was 14 Bxc3. Rybka must have wanted to take Fruit out of book as quickly as possible as she needed a win here. Long book lines more likely lead to drawn games.

1 b3 e5 2 Bb2 Nc6 3 c4 Nf6 4 Nf3 e4 5 Nd4 Bc5 6 Nf5 O-O 7 e3 d5 8 cxd5 Nb4 9 Ng3 Nfxd5 10 Qc1 Bb6 11 Nxe4 Re8 12 Nbc3 Bf5 13 a3 Nxc3 14 Bxc3 Bxe4 15 axb4 Re6 16 h4 h6 17 Qd1 Qe7 18 h5 Bf5 19 Bc4

Position after 19 Bc4.

Fruit was willing to trade a rook for a Rybka bishop, gambling on a risky king-side attack. The attack came up short leaving Fruit down an exchange. Rybka then coasted to victory, though taking another 72 moves!

19 … Qg5 20 Bxe6 Bxe6 21 Qe2 Rd8 22 f4 Qd5 23 O-O Qf5 24 Kh2 Rd5 25 Rab1 Qxh5+ 26 Qxh5 Rxh5+ 27 Kg3 27 … Rb5 28 e4 f5 29 exf5 Rxf5

30 Rfe1 Bf7 31 Re5 Rf6 32 f5 Rd6 33 Kf4 h5 34 Rbe1 Rd3 35 R1e2 a6 36 Re7 Kf8 37 g3 Rd5 38 g4 hxg4 39 Kxg4 Rd8 40 Kg3 Rd3+ 41 Kf4 Rd8 42 d4 Rd5 43 Kg4 Rd8 44 Re1 Rd5 45 Bb2 Rd6 46 Kg5 Kg8 47 R1e4 Rd8 48 R4e5 Rd6 49 b5 Rd8 50 Bc3 axb5 51 Rxb5 Be8 52 Rbe5 Bf7 53 Bb2 Ra8 54 Rd7 c6 55 Rxb7 Bd8+ 56 Kg4 Bf6 57 b4 Bd5 58 Re1 Kh7 59 b5 cxb5 60 Rxb5 Rd8 61 Rc1 Kg8 62 Rc7 Kh7 63 Rbc5 Rd6 64 Ra7 Rd8 65 Bc3 Rd6 66 Raa5 Be4 67 d5 Rxd5 68 Rxd5 Bxc3 69 Ra3 Bxd5 70 Rxc3 Ba2 71 Kg5 Bf7 72 Rc8 Bg8 73 Rc7 Kh8 74 Rd7 Bh7 75 Rd1 Bg8 76 Rh1+ Bh7 77 Kf4 Kg8 78 Ke5 g5 79 Rh5 g4 80 Ke6 g3 81 f6 g2 82 f7+ Kg7 83 Rg5+ Kf8 84 Rd5 g1=Q 85 Rd8+ Kg7 86 f8=Q+ Kg6 87 Qf6+ Kh5 88 Rd5+ Bf5+ 89 Rxf5+ Kg4 90 Rg5+ Kh3 91 Qh8 Mate.

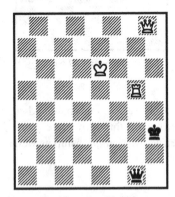

Position after 91 Qh8,
Mate.

The final 20 moves or so look more like they were played by extraterrestrials than computers.

Internet Chess Club CCT 10
Round 7, January 27, 2008
Glaurung (W) versus Zappa (B)
Queen's Gambit Declined Slav, Exchange Variation (D13)

---

1 d4 c6 2 c4 d5 3 cxd5 cxd5 4 Nf3
Nf6 5 Bf4 Nc6 6 Nc3 Bf5 7 e3 e6
8 Rc1 Bd6 9 Bxd6 Qxd6 10 Bb5 Bg4
11 O-O O-O 12 Be2 Rfc8 13 Ne1
Bxe2 14 Qxe2 a6 15 Nd3 Nb4
16 Ne5 Rc7 17 a3 Nc6 18 Nxc6 Rxc6
19 Na2 Rac8 20 Rxc6 Rxc6 21 Nb4
Rc7 22 Nd3 Qb6 23 f3 Ne8 24 Qd2
Nd6 25 Rc1 Rxc1+ 26 Qxc1 Qb3
27 Nc5 Qb6 28 Qc3 Qc7 29 Kf2 a5
30 Na4

30 ... Qxc3 31 Nxc3 Nc4 32 Nd1 b5
33 Nc3 Nxb2 34 Nxb5 Nc4 35 a4 Kf8
36 Na7 Ke7 37 Nc6+ Kd7 38 Nb8+
Kd6 39 Na6 e5 40 Nc5 f5 41 Nb7+
Kc6 42 Nd8+ Kd7 43 Nb7 e4
44 Nc5+ Ke7 45 Ke2 g5 46 g3 g4
47 f4 h6 48 Kf2 Nb2 49 Ke2 Kd6
50 Nb7+ Kc7 51 Nc5 Kb8 52 Kd2
Nc4+ 53 Ke2 Kc7 54 Ne6+ Kd7
55 Nc5+ Kd6 56 Nb7+ Ke6 57 Nc5+
Kf6 58 Kf2 h5 59 Nd7+ Ke6 60 Nc5+
Kf7 61 Ke2 h4 62 Kf2 h3 63 Ke2
Ke7 64 Nb7 Kd7 65 Nc5+ Kd6
66 Nb7+ Kd7 67 Nc5+ Ke7 68 Nb7
Ke8 69 Nc5 Kf7 70 Nd7 Ke6 71 Nc5+
Kf6 72 Nd7+ Ke7 73 Nc5 Nb2
74 Kd2 Kd6 75 Ke2 Drawn by
agreement.

Position after 30 Na4.

It was the dullest of games thus far, but
fear not, it was about to get even duller!
This could go down as one of the dullest
games in history!! Zappa seemed to have
forgotten its primary objective of shoot-
ing for a victory as it traded off its pieces
one at a time.

Position after 75 Ke2,
Drawn by agreement.

Internet Chess Club CCT 10
Playoff Game 1, January 27, 2008
Naum (W) versus Rybka (B)
Queen's Pawn Games (E00)

---

1 d4 Nf6 2 c4 e6 3 g3 Bb4+ 4 Bd2
Be7 5 Bg2 d5 6 Nf3 O-O 7 O-O c6
8 Qc2 b6 9 Bf4 Ba6 10 b3 Nbd7
11 Rd1 Rc8 12 Nc3 Qe8 13 a4 dxc4
14 bxc4 Bxc4 15 Ne4 Nxe4 16 Qxc4
Bd6 17 Ne5 f5 18 Rac1 h6

Naum's last book move was 17 Ne5 and
Rybka's was 18 ... h6.

19 Nd3 Qe7 20 f3 Bxf4 21 Nxf4 Nd6
22 Qxe6+ Qxe6 23 Nxe6 Rfe8
24 Nf4 g5 25 Ng6 Rxe2 26 Bf1 Ree8
27 Ne5 Nb8 28 f4 Kh7 29 Bd3 Kg7
30 fxg5 hxg5 31 Rf1 Rf8 32 Nf3 Kf6
33 h4 gxh4 34 Nxh4 Rce8 35 Kg2
Ke6 36 Rf2 Rh8 37 Bxf5+ Nxf5
38 Rxf5

38 ... Kd6 39 Ng6 Re2+ 40 Kf3 Rhh2
41 Nf4 Ref2+ 42 Kg4 Rh7 43 Rf6+
Kd7 44 Kf5 Kc7 45 Kg6 Rfh2
46 Ne6+ Kb7 47 Nd8+ Ka6 48 Nxc6
Nxc6 49 Rcxc6 Rd7 50 Rf4 Ra2 51 g4
Rxa4

Two pawns apiece. A tedious game
from here on where precise play was
necessary.

52 g5 Ra2 53 Rf7 Rxd4 54 Rcc7
Rd6+ 55 Kg7 Rg2 56 Rxa7+

A pawn apiece.

56 ... Kb5 57 Rf5+ Kc4 58 Rc7+ Kd4
59 Rc1 Rd7+ 60 Kg6 Rd6+ 61 Kf7
Ke4 62 Rf6 Rxf6+ 63 gxf6

A rook and pawn versus rook and pawn
endgame.

Position after 38 Rxf5.

The material was dead even, with three
pawns apiece. Material was traded off in
even exchanges until the two kings
found themselves alone.

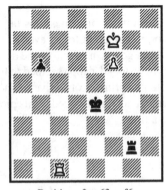

Position after 63 gxf6.

63 ... Kd5 64 Rf1 b5 65 Re1 Kd6
66 Re4 Rd2 67 Rf4 Rc2 68 Kg6
Rg2+ 69 Kf5 Rg1 70 Rd4+ Kc5
71 Re4 Rf1+ 72 Ke6 b4 73 Re5+ Kc4
74 Re2 b3 75 f7 Kc3 76 Re3+ Kc2
77 Rg3 b2 78 Rg2+ Kc1 79 Rxb2
Kxb2 80 Ke7 Kc3 81 f8=Q Rxf8
82 Kxf8 Drawn.

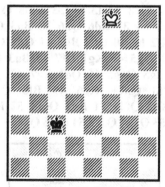

Position after 82 Kxf8,
Drawn.

Internet Chess Club CCT 10
Playoff Game 2, January 27, 2008
Rybka (W) versus Naum (B)
Queen's Gambit Accepted, classical, Rubinstein variation (D26)

The second playoff game between
Rybka and Naum also ended in a draw.
Naum's last book move was 14 ... Nf6,
Rybka's was 16 Rac1.

1 c4 e6 2 d4 Nf6 3 Nf3 d5 4 e3 dxc4
5 Bxc4 a6 6 a4 c5 7 O-O Nc6 8 Qe2
cxd4 9 Rd1 Be7 10 exd4 O-O
11 Nc3 Nd5 12 Qe4 Nf6 13 Qd3 Nb4
14 Qe2 b6 15 Be3 Bb7 16 Rac1 Rc8
17 Ne5 Re8 18 Bb3 h6 19 Bf4 Bd6
20 Bg3 Nbd5 21 Nxd5 Nxd5 22 Rxc8
Qxc8 23 Qf1 Qd8 24 Bc4 a5 25 Rc1
Re7 26 Qd3 Rc7 27 Qd1 g6 28 Bxd5
Bxd5 29 Rc3 Kg7 30 Qc2 Rxc3
31 bxc3 Bxe5 32 Bxe5+ f6 33 Bg3

Position after 33 Bg3.

The material was equal, and the odds of
anything but a draw were not good.

33 ... Qe8 34 f3 b5 35 axb5 Qxb5
36 h4 a4 37 Bd6 Qa6 38 Ba3 Qc6
39 Kf2 h5 40 Qb2 Bb3 41 Qd2 Qd5
42 Bc1 g5 43 Kg1 Kf7 44 Ba3 Qf5
45 hxg5 Qxg5 46 Qe2 Kg7 47 Qa6
e5 48 Qa7+ Kg6 49 Bf8 Qe3+
50 Kh2 Qf4+ 51 Kg1 Qc1+ 52 Kh2
Bf7 53 Qxa4 Qxc3 54 dxe5 Qxe5+

Position after 54 ... Qxe5+.

If it wasn't time to hang it up before, it
certainly was now. But the game went
on and on and on!

55 Kg1 Qe3+ 56 Kh2 Bd5 57 Qc2+
Kf7 58 Bd6 Kg7 59 Qf5 Qg5
60 Qd7+ Bf7 61 Bg3 Qe3 62 Qd6
Bc4 63 Bf4 Qd3 64 Qxd3 Bxd3

Position after 64 Bxd3.

Two hardheaded characters going at one
another.

65 g3 Kg6 66 Kg2 Bc4 67 Be3 f5

With the exception of a pawn advance
by Rybka on move 77, a painful dance
of kings and bishops went on for 60
moves. On move 127 the two sides had
no choice but to call it a draw by the 50
move rule.

68 Kf2 Be6 69 Bf4 Bd7 70 Bd2 Bb5
71 Be3 Ba6 72 Bc1 Bc4 73 Bf4
Bd5 74 Ke3 Be6 75 Bc7 Kf7 76 Kd4
Kg6 77 f4 Kf6 78 Bd8+ Kf7 79 Ke5
Bc8 80 Bg5 Bd7 81 Bf6 Bc8 82 Bh4
Be6 83 Kd6 Bc4 84 Bd8 Be2 85 Ba5
Bb5 86 Ke5 Bd7 87 Bd2 Ke7 88 Bc3
Kf7 89 Kd6 Bb5 90 Bd4 Kg6 91 Ke7
Bc6 92 Ke6 Be4 93 Kd6 Bh1 94 Bc3
Bg2 95 Be5 Be4 96 Ke6 Bb7 97 Bf6
Bc8+ 98 Ke7 Bb7 99 Be5 Bd5
100 Ke8 Bb3 101 Kd7 Bc4 102 Bd4
Bb5+ 103 Ke6 Bc4+ 104 Ke5 Bf1
105 Bc5 Bh3 106 Bb6 Bf1 107 Bf2
Bb5 108 Be1 Bd7 109 Kd6 Bb5
110 Ke6 Bd3 111 Bc3 Bc4+ 112 Kd6
Be2 113 Kd7 Kh6 114 Ba5 Bc4
115 Kd6 Kg6 116 Bb6 Be2 117 Kd5
Bd3 118 Bd8 Be4+ 119 Kd6 Bf3
120 Ke6 Be2 121 Ke5 Bd3 122 Kd6 Be4
123 Bb6 Kf6 124 Bd4+ Kg6 125 Ke6
Bd3 126 Ke7 Bc4 127 Be5 Drawn
by the 50 move rule.

Position after 127 Be5,
Drawn by the 50 move rule.

Suggest Readings

Website for the Internet Chess Club CCT 10: http://www.cctchess.com/cct10/index.html
Rybka versus Zappa, Round 5, CCT 10: http://www.chessgames.com/perl/chessgame?gid=1508827
Hiarcs versus Rybka, Round 6, CCT 10: http://www.chessgames.com/perl/chessgame?gid=1508828
Rybka versus Fruit, Round 7, CCT 10: http://www.chessgames.com/perl/chessgame?gid=1508829

2008: Rybka Retains Title at the 16th WCCC

The 16th World Computer Chess Championship was held in Beijing, China at the Beijing Golden Century Golf Club from September 28, 2008 through October 5, 2008. Beijing had hosted the 29th Olympic Games only a few weeks before, dazzling the world with its opening and closing ceremonies and everything in between. Now, the greatest electronic brains would demonstrate their awesome talent there playing mankind's ultimate mental game. The Beijing Longlife Group provided support for the event, as did the Northeastern University, the Beijing Institute of Technology, the

The Forbidden City in Beijing.

M. Newborn, *Beyond Deep Blue: Chess in the Stratosphere*,
DOI 10.1007/978-0-85729-341-1_16, © Springer-Verlag London Limited 2011

Beijing University of Post and Telecommunications, the ICGA, the University of Maastricht's ICT Competence Centre, and Tilberg University's Centre for Cognition and Communication. Ten chess engines participated in the 9-round round-robin event, including three from Germany, two from Israel, and single entries from the USA, China, The Netherlands, Great Britain, and Belgium. The rate of play was 60 moves in two hours, followed by the remaining moves in 30 minutes. Deep Blue's Feng-Hsiung Hsu attended the competition and gave a speech at the opening ceremony.

Rybka showed up to defend her title. Hiarcs was there as her major threat. Deep Junior and Shredder also attended, though, perhaps, in the twilight of their careers. On the Swedish Rating List published in the September 2008 issue of the ICGA Journal, these four chess engines were all rated at least 100 points stronger than the top human player. Rybka was rated the highest at 3238, approximately 400 points higher than the human world champion. Deep Junior, the lowest of the four, was rated at 2983. Hard to fathom! But, even with a rating of 3238, Rybka revealed that she had room to improve. In her game with Shredder in Round 2, Rybka evaluated a position as mate in 1942 moves when she meant to say mate in $(2,000-1,942)/2 = 29$!

Cluster Toga, a derivative of Fruit and second place finisher at the 2005 world championship, was a long shot for the title. Missing was Zappa, second to Rybka at the previous world championship, a 5.5–4.5 victor over Rybka in their September 2007 match in Mexico, and third to Rybka and Naum in the January 2008 ICC CCT10. Anthony Cozzie had stated that Zappa was done. In a career lasting about 5 years, it never lost a tournament game to any chess engine other than Rybka.

Jeroen Nooman. (Photo courtesy of Gian-Carlo Pascutto)

Rybka participated in the competition using a 40-processor system – five 8-processor clusters – in which all processors ran at 3 GHz or faster. One of Rybka's 8-processor clusters ran at 4 GHz, as did the eight processors of Hiarcs. China's entry in the event, Mobile Chess ran on a cell phone using a Nokia 6120c processor.

Rybka finished the nine-round event with eight points, one point better than Hiarcs, who finished one point better than Deep Junior. In the last two world championships, Rybka has now gone undefeated, winning 16 games and drawing 4. Hiarcs had a good tournament, losing only to Rybka while winning six games and drawing two. Deep Junior, winner of the world championship in 2002, 2004, and 2006, won four games, lost only to Hiarcs, and drew four. Shredder, who dominated tournaments in the early 2000s, finished in the middle of the pack, winning just two games, losing two, and drawing five. Over the course of the 9 rounds and 45 games, there were only two games won by an entry that finished lower in the standings than its opponent. In both cases, Falcon versus Cluster Toga and Sjeng versus Falcon, the engine that finished lower had the white pieces.

After six rounds, Rybka led the field with Hiarcs a half point behind. Rybka had won all but one game, and that one, against Cluster Toga, was a draw. Rybka had defeated Shredder in Round 2. Hiarcs, too, was undefeated, with four wins and two draws, one with Cluster Toga.

In Round 7, Rybka defeated Sjeng, while Hiarcs smashed Deep Junior to keep pace. Rybka met Hiarcs in the penultimate round and essentially won the game from book, relentlessly attacking Hiarcs's king who hadn't managed to castle. Rybka thus clinched the championship with one round to play, leading Hiarcs by a point and a half. In the final round, Rybka met Deep Junior. She had the Israeli chess engine by the throat when she failed to understand that a Deep Junior sacrifice led to a draw by perpetual check. That draw, coupled with a win by Hiarcs over Shredder, left Rybka ahead of second-place finisher Hiarcs by one point at the end of the competition. Rybka thus became the first engine since Cray Blitz in 1986 to successfully defend its title of world champion.

Rybka's Openings

Jeroen Noomen, the brains behind Rybka's book tried something different in this competition. Before the competition, he had concluded that the fewer moves a game follows book, the more it is to the advantage of the stronger engine (i.e., in this case, Rybka!). This makes good sense, though contrasting with commonly accepted practice. According to Noomen, the more pieces on the board, the better Rybka's chances given the strength of her search heuristics. Playing long book lines where material is traded off makes it more difficult for Rybka, with fewer pieces on the board, to find a line that achieves an advantage. In addition, the book lines stored in opening books may have many outright errors and shortcomings. Finally, lines that may have been best for Karpov, Kasparov, and Kramnik and their likes are often not optimal for chess engines playing at the 3000+ level. So leading up to the competition, Noomen found a number of "slightly offbeat, but playable" lines for Rybka to follow. Prematch testing of the idea gave very favorable results.

During the competition, Rajlich felt Rybka "had a pleasant book advantage or more in every White game and full equality or better in every game with Black." A Petrov opening when playing White (Round 1), Sicilian openings when playing White (Rounds 2, 6, and 8) or Black (Rounds 3, 5, and 9), a Ruy Lopez opening when playing White (Round 4), and a Grunfeld opening when playing Black (Round 7) covered the openings played during the competition by Rybka. Rybka won all five games with White, while winning two and drawing two with Black.

Rybka Won All Five Games When Playing White

In a Petrov played in Round 1, Rybka's 1 e4 e5 2 Nf3 Nf6 3 Nxe5 d6 4 Nc4 took The Baron out of book early and led to a victory in 54 moves. After 15 moves, each side had lost a knight and pawn.

Against Shredder's Najdorf Variation of the Sicilian Defense in Round 2, Rybka played 1 e4 c5 2 Nc3 d6 3 Nge2 Nf6 4 d4 cxd4 5 Nxd4 a6 6 h3 and defeated one of her archrivals in 66 moves. Over the first 15 moves, each side had captured two pawns and a knight.

Against Mobile Chess in Round 6, the same Najdorf Variation of the Sicilian Defense was played: 1 e4 c5 2 Nc3 d6 3 Nge2 Nf6 4 d4 cxd4 5 Nxd4 a6 6 h3 and Rybka was victorious in 37 moves.

In Round 8, Hiarcs's surprise 7 ... Rb8 took Rybka out of book with her Sicilian Defence, Kalashnikov Variation: 1 e4 c5 2 Nf3 Nc6 3 d4 cxd4 4 Nxd4 e5 5 Nb5 d6 6 N1c3 a6 7 Na3 Rb8 but Rybka was nevertheless victorious in 35 moves. Both sides were out of book by the eleventh move and only two pawns had been removed from the board.

Playing White against Jonny's Ruy Lopez Defense in Round 4, Rybka polished off Jonny in 38 moves. No piece had been removed from the board by the eleventh move when both sides were out of book. The opening: 1 e4 e5 2 Nf3 Nc6 3 Bb5 a6 4 Ba4 Nf6 5 O-O Be7 6 d3 b5 7 Bb3 O-O 8 a4 Bb7 9 Re1 Re8 10 c3 Bc5 11 Bd2.

Rybka Won Two and Drew Two When Playing Black

Playing Black against Cluster Toga in Round 3, a Sicilian Defense, O'Kelly Variation, 1 e4 c5 2 Nf3 a6 led to a draw in a game that lasted 77 moves. Each side had lost a bishop and pawn during the opening book stage of the game.

Playing Black against Falcon in Round 5, 1 e4 c5 2 Nf3 e6 3 d4 cxd4 4 Nxd4 a6 5 Bd3 Qc7 6 Nc3 Nc6 7 Be3 Nf6 8 O-O Ne5 9 h3 Bc5 10 Kh1 d6 11 f4 Ng6 12 Qe1 O-O took Rybka 51 moves to put her opponent away.

Playing Black against Sjeng's Grunfeld Opening in Round 7, 1 d4 Nf6 2 Nf3 g6 3 c4 Bg7 4 g3 d5 5 cxd5 Nxd5 6 Bg2 Nb6 7 Nc3 Nc6 8 e3 O-O 9 O-O Re8 10 d5 Na5 11 Nd4 Bd7 12 e4 Rc8 13 Bf4 c5 took Rybka 61 moves to earn its victory. Two pawns had been captured during the opening book stage of this game.

By Round 9 when Rybka played Black against Deep Junior, she had the championship locked up. The Rybka team got a bit "reckless" and played the Sicilian Defense, O'Kelly Variation, 1 e4 c5 2 Nf3 a6 3 c3 e6 4 d4 d5 5 e5 Bd7 while knowing that Deep Junior team was likely well prepared for it. The game followed the same line played in Round 3 with Cluster Toga until Deep Junior played 6 dxc5, rather than 6 Bd3 as had Cluster Toga. Deep Junior's team perhaps felt this was better than Cluster Toga's move, and perhaps it was. The Deep Junior team had seen Cluster Toga play to a draw. Deep Junior developed a strong mid-game position, but overlooked a sacrifice by Rybka, 45 … Rxg2+, that led to perpetual check and a draw in 61 moves.

Final Thoughts on Rybka's Openings

In summary, Rybka won all her games except when she played the two Sicilian Defense, O'Kelly Variation games as Black against Cluster Toga and Deep Junior. Of course, these two opponents are among the toughest. At the previous world championship, Rybka won all her games but two, drawing with Zappa in Round 3 when playing White and drawing with Loop in Round 4 when playing Black.

Perhaps Noomen's approach shows how far the game of chess is from being "solved." If he was able to steer Rybka through openings that were not mainstream and exit book lines early in the games and be successful in gaining the upper hand in such a high percentage of these games, then there evidently remains much opening theory that has yet to be developed.

Data on entries to the 16th WCCC: Name, country of origin, authors, opening book, hardware

Name	Origin	Authors	Opening book	Hardware
Rybka	USA	Vasik Rajlich	Jeroen Noomen	Cluster, 40 cores
Hiarcs	GBR	Mark Uniacke	Eric Hallsworth	Intel Skulltrail Gaming Platform, 8 core QX9775 proc. 4 GHz
Deep Junior	ISL	Amir Ban, Shay Bushinsky	Boris Alterman	Intel Xeon 7400 series (Dunnington), 12x 2.67 GHz
Cluster Toga	DEU	Kai Himstedt, Ulf Lorenz, Thomas Gaksch, Fabian Letouzey		Cluster, 24 cores
Shredder	DEU	Stefan Meyer-Kahlen	Sandro Necchi	Intel Core 2, 8x 3.16 GHz
Falcon	ISL	Omid David Tabibi	Erdogan Günez	Intel Core 2, 2x 2.1 GHz
Jonny	DEU	Johannes Zwanzger	Stefan Kleinert	Cluster, 16 cores
Sjeng	BEL	Gian-Carlo Pascutto		Intel Core 2, 4x 2.8 GHz
The Baron	NLD	Richard Pijl		AMD Opteron 270 Quad Core 2 GHz
Mobile Chess	CHN	Huang Chen		Nokia 6120c

Final standings of the 16th WCCC, Beijing

#	Name	1	2	3	4	5	6	7	8	9	Pts
1	Rybka	9wW	5wW	4bD	7wW	6bW	10wW	8bW	2wW	3bD	8.0
2	Hiarcs	4bD	7wW	6wW	10wW	8bW	9bD	3wW	1bL	5wW	7.0
3	Deep Junior	5bD	4wW	7bW	6wD	10bW	8wD	2bL	9bW	1wD	6.0
4	Cluster Toga	2wD	3bL	1wD	5bD	9wW	7wW	6bL	10wW	8bW	5.5
5	Shredder	3wD	1bL	9wD	4wD	7bD	6wW	10bW	8wD	2bL	4.5
6	Falcon	10wW	8bL	2wL	3bD	1wL	5bL	4wW	7bD	9wW	4.0
7	Jonny	8bW	2bL	3wL	1bL	5wD	4bL	9wW	6wD	10bW	4.0
8	Sjeng	7wL	6wW	10bW	9bD	2wL	3bD	1wL	5bD	4wL	3.5
9	The Baron	1bL	10wW	5bD	8wD	4bL	2wD	7bL	3wL	6bL	2.5
10	Mobile Chess	6bL	9bL	8wL	2bL	3wL	1bL	5wL	4bL	7bL	0.0

> **16th WCCC, Beijing**
> **Round 7, October 3, 2008**
> **Hiarcs (W) versus Deep Junior (B)**
> **Ruy Lopez: Schliemann Defense (C63)**

Hiarcs trailed Rybka by a half point and Deep Junior trailed by a full point when this game was played.

Hiarcs's website provides information on each move's time in seconds, its opponent's time, and its score.

#	White	Score	Time	Black	Time
1	e4	B	0	e5	16
2	Nf3	B	0	Nc6	10
3	Bb5	B	0	f5	12
4	Nc3	B	0	fxe4	11
5	Nxe4	B	0	Nf6	11
6	Qe2	B	0	d5	12
7	Nxf6+	0.01	1	gxf6	12
8	d4	0.01	2	Bg7	11
9	c4	0.01	2	Bg4	127
10	dxe5	−0.06	217	O-O	13
11	Bxc6	−0.11	470	bxc6	96
12	e6	−0.13	111	Re8	32
13	O-O	−0.11	192	Qd6	12
14	Qd3	−0.08	171	dxc4	415
15	Qxc4	0.30	186	Bxf3	18
16	gxf3	0.32	44	Qxe6	495
17	Qxe6+	0.22	1	Rxe6	103
18	Be3	0.20	1	f5	187
19	Rab1	0.20	1	Rd8	177
20	b3	0.25	1	Rd5	127
21	Rbc1	0.42	168	Be5	17
22	f4	0.38	17	Bb2	14
23	Rc4	0.50	119	a5	106
24	Re1	0.55	1	Ba3	172
25	Re2	0.54	143	Rg6+	19
26	Kf1	0.51	1	Rd1+	153
27	Re1	0.54	1	Rd5	388
28	Bc1	0.62	1	Bd6	265
29	Re8+	0.57	166	Kf7	79
30	Ra8	0.57	77	Rh6	11
31	Kg2	0.57	115	Rg6+	161
32	Kf3	0.52	1	Rh6	104
33	Ra7	0.53	112	Rxh2	120
34	Rxc6	0.50	1	Rh4	102
35	Be3	0.67	218	Rh3+	12
36	Kg2	0.64	183	Rh4	199

Position after 36 ... Rh4.

Hiarcs passed here on an opportunity to play for a draw. It soon went up a pawn and, while holding off Deep Junior's advanced h-pawn, coasted to victory from there.

#	White	Score	Time	Black	Time
37	Rca6	0.64	1	Rg4+	344
38	Kf3	0.73	1	h5	159
39	Rxa5	1.00	276	Rxa5	871
40	Rxa5	0.97	1	Kf6	94
41	Ra8	0.92	392	h4	·10
42	Rh8	1.25	254	Kg7	111
43	Rh5	1.72	222	Kg6	88
44	Rg5+	2.62	172	Rxg5	12
45	fxg5	2.63	152	h3	286
46	a4	2.88	635	f4	15
47	Ba7	4.45	210	Bb4	295
48	Bb8	5.68	133	Ba5	167
49	b4	6.33	220	Bxb4	216
50	Bxc7	12.52	105	Kxg5	19
51	a5	12.78	251	Kg6	70

Black resigns.

Position after 51 ... Kg6,
Black resigns.

16th WCCC, Beijing
Round 8, October 4, 2008
Rybka (W) versus Hiarcs (B)
Sicilian Defense (B32)

#	White	Time	Black	Score	Time
1	e4	0	c5	B	0
2	Nf3	11	Nc6	B	0
3	d4	9	cxd4	B	0
4	Nxd4	7	e5	B	0
5	Nb5	8	d6	B	0
6	N1c3	8	a6	B	0
7	Na3	8	Rb8	B	1
8	Nc4	389	Nf6	B	0

#	White	Time	Black	Score	Time
9	Bg5	167	b5	0.47	144
10	Bxf6	154	Qxf6	0.41	221
11	Ne3	9	Be7	0.46	264
12	a4	137	bxa4	0.75	223
13	Rxa4	9	Rxb2	0.83	239
14	Ncd5	153	Qg6	0.96	1

According to Noomen, Hiarcs' 7 ... Rb8
took Rybka out of book, while Rybka's
9 Bg5 took Hiarcs out of book. It wasn't
long before Rybka got the upper hand.

Position after 14 … Qg6.

Rybka felt she was ahead a pawn and coasted to victory from here. Hiarcs's uncastled king soon became exposed to a relentless attack by Rybka's pieces.

#	White	Time	Black	Score	Time
15	Bxa6	75	Bd7	1.13	104
16	Nc7+	97	Kd8	1.00	1
17	Qa1	44	Rb8	2.34	936

Hiarcs took about 15 min for this move and the next, realizing it faced serious problems.

#	White	Time	Black	Score	Time
18	Bb5	13	Bg5	2.59	903
19	Ned5	28	Ne7	3.31	152
20	O-O	57	Nxd5	3.52	40
21	Nxd5	12	Bxb5	3.85	240
22	Ra8	9	Rxa8	4.21	205
23	Qxa8+	8	Kd7	4.21	1
24	Qb7+	20	Ke6	4.14	68
25	Nc7+	11	Kf6	4.66	190
26	Nxb5	17	Qh5	4.82	64

#	White	Time	Black	Score	Time
27	Nxd6	11	Rf8	5.15	164
28	Nf5	9	Kg6	5.10	50
29	Qb6+	116	Bf6	5.16	110
30	Ne7+	68	Kh6	5.41	1
31	f3	32	Qg5	5.57	59
32	Nf5+	10	Kg6	6.35	82
33	f4	7	exf4	7.03	177
34	h4	8	Qg4	7.05	62
35	Qd6	8	Black resigns.		

Position after 35 Qd6,
Black resigns.

Rybka clinched first place in the tournament with this victory, leading the field by a point and a half with one round remaining.

16th WCCC, Beijing
Round 9, October 4, 2008
Deep Junior (W) versus Rybka (B)
Sicilian Defence, O'Kelly Variation (B28)

Rybka had the tournament wrapped up when this game was played.

1 e4 c5 2 Nf3 a6 3 c3 e6 4 d4 d5 5 e5 Bd7

Rather than playing 6 Bd3 as had Cluster Toga when playing Rybka in Round 3, Deep Junior choose to play 6 dxc5. It led to a strong position, but the Israeli chess engine overlooked a perpetual check just when it had Rybka in serious difficulties.

6 dxc5 Bxc5 7 Bd3 Qc7 8 O-O Ne7 9 Re1 Ng6 10 Nbd2 Qb6 11 Nd4 Nc6 12 N2b3 Ngxe5 13 Nxc5 Qxc5 14 Bf4 Nxd3 15 Qxd3 O-O 16 Qg3 Nxd4 17 Bd6 Qb6 18 cxd4 Rfc8 19 Be5

Position after 19 Be5.

Deep Junior, up a pawn at this point, is threatening a trivial mate-in-one!

19 ... g6 20 Qf4 Qd8 21 Re3 Rc2 22 Rh3 f5 23 Rg3 Be8 24 h4 Qe7 25 Rc1 Rac8 26 Rxc2 Rxc2 27 h5 Bf7 28 a3 b5 29 Bd6 Qd8 30 h6 Qf6 31 Bc5 Be8 32 Qb8 Kf7 33 Qd6 Rc1+ 34 Kh2 Kg8 35 Re3 Qh4+ 36 Rh3 Qf6 37 b4 Re1 38 f4 Re4 39 Qb6 g5 40 fxg5 Qf7 41 Kg1 Rg4 42 Qd8 f4 43 Rf3 Qg6 44 Be7

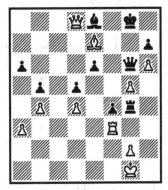

Position after 44 Be7.

Rybka now saved her own skin by sacking a rook and then checking Deep Junior until the later said enough is enough. Deep Junior had no choice but to settle for a draw in a position where its opponent could give check indefinitely.

44 ... Qb1+ 45 Rf1 Rxg2+ 46 Kxg2 Qe4+ 47 Kg1 Qe3+ 48 Rf2 Qg3+ 49 Kf1 Qh3+ 50 Ke2 Qe3+ 51 Kd1 Qd3+ 52 Rd2 Qb1+ 53 Ke2 Qe4+ 54 Kf1 Qf3+ 55 Ke1 Qh1+ 56 Kf2 Qh2+ 57 Kf3 Qg3+ 58 Ke2 Qe3+ 59 Kd1 Qb3+ 60 Rc2 Qd3+ 61 Kc1 Qxa3+ 62 Kb1 Qb3+ Drawn by agreement.

Position after 62 ... Qb3+,
Drawn by agreement.

Suggest Readings

O. David-Tabibi, The 16th World Computer Chess Championship, ICGA Journal, V. 31, No. 3, pp. 166–170, September 2008.

Rybka forum: http://rybkaforum.net/cgi-bin/rybkaforum/forum_show.pl

A discussion about Rybka's opening book by Jeroen Noomen: http://rybkaforum.net/cgi-bin/rybkaforum/topic_show.pl?tid=7738;pg=1

Hiarcs forum: http://hiarcs.net/forums/viewtopic.php?t=1677

Zappa's website: https://netfiles.uiuc.edu/acozzie2/www/zappa/

T. Karlsson, The Swedish Rating List, ICGA Journal, V. 31, No. 3, p. 191, September 2008.

chessbase.com reports on the world championship: http://www.chessbase.com/newsdetail.asp?newsid=4941

http://www.chessbase.com/newsdetail.asp?newsid=4935

2009: Rybka Tops at Internet Chess Club CCT 11

The Internet Chess Club held its 11th Computer Chess Tournament, January 26–27, 2009. Five rounds were played on the first day and four on the second. The time control was the same as it had been previously: all moves in 50 minutes plus three seconds extra per move. Rybka, the two-time world champion, returned to see if she could do better than tie for first place as she had done in the previous year's tournament. Thirty-two other entries would try to take a shot at her. However, some of her strongest rivals were missing including, in particular, Junior, Zappa, and Shredder.

Incredibly, in spite of losing a won game against Telepath in the first round on a technical communication glitch – similar to Junior's problems the previous year – Rybka won the tournament by a clear point over Fruit and Bright. Following her first-round loss, Rybka mowed down seven of her eight remaining opponents, drawing only with Crafty in Round 6. Her first round loss led to softer opponents in the following two rounds, but after that she polished off the second, third, fifth, sixth, and seventh place finishers, though not in that order. Rybka was using a powerful 52-core system with processor speeds ranging from 3.6 to 4.1 GHz.

Presented here are Rybka's victories over Fruit and Bright and her draw with Crafty. Rybka crushed both Fruit and Bright, but played to an exciting draw with Crafty. Victories over second and third place finishers Fruit and Bright were carried out playing Black, reflecting one more time Rybka's domination over the field. All three games were played out to the bitter end. Somewhat amusing was Rybka's draw with Crafty. Both sides realized the game was drawn many moves before it ended, but they played on until all material was gone and the two kings were left alone on the board.

M. Newborn, *Beyond Deep Blue: Chess in the Stratosphere*,
DOI 10.1007/978-0-85729-341-1_17, © Springer-Verlag London Limited 2011

Rybka's 52-core system.

Data on entries to the Internet Chess Club CCT 11: Name, author/operator, hardware

Name	Author/operator	Hardware
Rybka	Vasik Rajlich, Jeroen Noomen, Larry Kaufman, Lukas Cimiotti, Nick Carlin	52-core system 3.6 GHz to 4.1 GHz
Fruit	Fabien Letouzey, Ryan Benitez, Nolan Denson	Intel Core 2 Extreme QX9775 3.2 GHz
Bright	Allard Siemelink, N. Swaminathan, Wael Deeb	Intel Core 2 Quad Q6600, 2 GB
Arasan	Jon Dart	Intel Core 2 Quad Q6700 3 GHz 4GB
Crafty	Robert Hyatt, Tracy Riegle, Mike Byrne, Peter Skinner, Ted Langreck	Intel Core 2 Quad Xeon 2.33 GHz
Ikarus	Muntsin & Munjong Kolss	AMD Opteron Quad Core
Glaurung	Tord Romstad, Sherif Khater	Intel Core 2 Quad Q6600
Thinker	Lance Perkins, Kerwin Medina	Intel Core 2 Quad Q6600
Deep Sjeng	Gian-Carlo Pascutto	No data available
Twisted Logic	Edsel Apostol, Audy Arandela	No data available
The Baron	Richard Pijl, Arturo Ochoa	AMD Opteron 270 Dual Core
Telepath	Charles Roberson	Intel Core 2 Quad Q6600
Scorpio	Daniel Shawul, Andres Valverde	Intel Core 2 Quad Q6600
Ktulu	Rahman Paidar, Sherif Khater	AMD Phenom 9500 Quad Core
Deuterium	Ferdinand Mosca	Intel Core 2 Quad Q6600 (1 CPU)
Diep	Vincent Diepeveen, Andre van Ark, Arturo Ochoa, Brian Fraiser, Renze Steenhuisen	Intel 8x 2.5 GHz

(continued)

(continued)

Name	Author/operator	Hardware
ZCT	Zach Wegner, Kenny Dail	Intel 8x Xeon Mac Pro 2.8 GHz
Dirty	Pradu Kannan, Andres Valverde	No data available
Symbolic	Steven J. Edwards	Intel Mac Pro Dual Core Xeon 2.66 GHz
Gaviota	Miguel A. Ballicora	AMD Dual Core 2.4 GHz
Tornado	Engin Üstün	Intel Core 2 Quad Q8200 4 GB
Hector For Chess	Csaba Jergler	Intel Core 2 Duo 2.13 GHz
Timea	László Gáspár	Intel Core 2 Quad Q6600
Tinker	Brian Richardson	Intel Core 2 Quad Q6600 (1 cpu)
Lime	Richard Albert	Intel Core 2 Duo T5800, 3 GB
Prophet	James Swafford	Intel Core 2 Quad Q6600
Matmoi	Mathieu Pagé	AMD Athlon 64 X2 6400+ 4 GB
Neurosis	Stan Arts	Intel Pentium 4 Dual Core 3.4 GHz (1 cpu)
Clarabit	Salvador Pallares	AMD Turion 1.6x2 notebook
Noonian Chess	Charles Roberson	Intel Core 2 Duo T5500
Weid	Jaap Weidemann	AMD Athlon 64 X2 3800+
Mediocre	Jonatan Petersson	Intel Core 2 Quad Q6600

Final standing of the 11th Internet Chess Club CCT.

#	Name	1	2	3	4	5	6	7	8	9	Pts	TB
1	Rybka	12wL	16bW	26wW	3bW	9wW	5bD	7wW	2bW	6wW	7.5	39.0
2	Fruit	23bW	5bD	3wD	12bW	4wW	7bW	6wD	1wL	8bW	6.5	40.5
3	Bright	25bW	8wD	2bD	1wL	20bW	19wW	9wW	11bW	4bD	6.5	36.6
4	Arasan	30bW	13wW	11bW	7wL	2bL	8bD	15wW	9bW	3wD	6.0	37.0
5	Crafty	22bW	2wD	14bW	13wW	7bL	1wD	10bL	12wW	15bW	6.0	36.0
6	Ikarus	27wW	7bD	8bL	21wW	24bW	14wW	2bD	10wW	1bL	6.0	35.0
7	Glaurung	19bW	6wD	10bW	4bW	5wW	2wL	1bL	8bL	16wW	5.5	40.0
8	Thinker	17wW	3bD	6wW	9bL	11bD	4wD	13bW	7wW	2wL	5.5	39.0
9	Deep Sjeng	21bW	10wD	24bW	8wW	1bL	11wW	3bL	4wL	13bW	5.5	37.0
10	Twisted Logic	28wW	9bD	7wL	16bW	14bD	18wW	5wW	6bL	11wD	5.5	35.0
11	The Baron	15wW	12bW	4wL	19bW	8wD	9bL	20wW	3wL	10bD	5.0	36.0
12	Telepath	1bW	11wL	18bW	2wL	13bD	24wD	19bW	5bL	20wW	5.0	34.0
13	Scorpio	26wW	4bL	15wW	5bL	12wD	23bW	8wL	18bW	9wL	4.5	34.5
14	Ktulu	29wD	18bW	5wL	17bW	10wD	6bL	24wD	16bL	19wW	4.5	32.0
15	Deuterium	11bL	20wW	13bL	18wD	21bW	22wW	4bL	24bW	5wL	4.5	31.5
16	Diep	24bD	1wL	25bW	10wL	19wL	28bW	22bW	14wW	7bL	4.5	30.5
17	ZCT	8bL	25wD	28bW	14wL	18bL	21wL	30bW	27wW	24bW	4.5	24.0
18	Dirty	20bW	14wL	12wL	15bD	17wW	10bL	21bW	13wL	25bD	4.0	31.0
19	Symbolic	7wL	23bW	27wW	11wL	16bW	3bL	12wL	29wW	14bL	4.0	31.0

20	Gaviota	18wL	15bL	23wW	27bW	3wL	26bW	11bL	25wW	12bL	4.0	29.0
21	Tornado	9wL	28bD	29wW	6bL	15wL	17bW	18wL	30bD	27bW	4.0	25.0
22	Hector For Chess	5wL	27bL	30wW	29bD	25wW	15bL	16wL	26bW	23wD	4.0	24.0
23	Timea	2wL	19wL	20bL	30bW	29wW	13wL	27bD	28wW	22bD	4.0	23.0
24	Tinker	16wD	29bW	9wL	26bW	6wL	12bD	14bD	15wL	17wL	3.5	31.5
25	Lime	3wL	17bD	16wL	28wW	22bL	29bD	26wW	20bL	18wD	3.5	26.0
26	Prophet	13bL	30wW	1bL	24wL	27bW	20wL	25bL	22wL	28bW	3.0	24.0
27	Matmoi	6bL	22wW	19bL	20wL	26wL	30bW	23wD	17bL	21wL	2.5	27.5
28	Neurosis	10bL	21wD	17wL	25bL	30wW	16wL	29bD	23bL	26wL	2.0	25.5
29	Clarabit	14bD	24wL	21bL	22wD	23bL	25wD	28wD	19bL	30bL	2.0	25.0
30	Noonian Chess	4wL	26bL	22bL	23wL	28bL	27wL	17wL	21bD	29wW	1.5	24.0
31	Weid	32b-	-	-	-	-	-	-	-	-	0.0	4.5
32	Mediocre	31w-	-	-	-	-	-	-	-	-	0.0	4.5

Internet Chess Club CCT 11
Round 4, March 21, 2009
Bright (W) versus Rybka (B)
Caro-Kann: Advance variation (B12)

---

1 e4 c6 2 d4 d5 3 e5 Bf5 4 Nc3 e6
5 g4 Bg6 6 Nge2 c5 7 h4 h5 8 Nf4
cxd4 9 Nxg6 fxg6 10 Bb5+ Nc6
11 Bxc6+ bxc6 12 Qxd4 Qb6 13 Qd3
Bc5 14 Ke2 Qb8 15 Qxg6+ Kd7
16 Qxg7+ Ne7 17 g5

Position after 20 … Kd8.

Rybka, down two pawns, seemed to be in trouble, though her opponent's queen was overextended and its pieces were poorly organized.

17 … Qb4 18 f4 Rag8 19 Qf7 Rf8 20 Qg7 Kd8

Rybka passed on a draw while playing an innocuous move. Bright's queen, off on a fishing mission deep in enemy territory, was going to find it impossible to return to safe waters. Bright would settle with exchanging its queen for a rook on move 27.

Position after 20 … Kd8.

21 Kd1 Nf5 22 Qg6 Qd4+ 23 Bd2 Kd7 24 Kc1 Rfg8 25 Qf7+ Be7

Bright's future looked anything but bright, with its queen awaiting execution.

26 a4 Rg7 27 Qxg7 Nxg7 28 a5 Nf5 29 Ra4 Qf2 30 a6 Rb8 31 Nd1 Qg2 32 Re1

Position after 32 Re1.

Rybka continued to torture her opponent, now forcing it to give up a knight for a pawn to prevent Rybka from adding a queen to her forces. Bright could well have resigned at this point, even earlier!

32 ... Nxh4 33 Ne3 Qg3 34 Rd1 Nf3 35 Nf1 Qg2 36 b3 Nxd2 37 Nxd2 h4 38 Kb2 h3 39 Nf1 h2 40 Nxh2 Qxh2 41 g6 Rg8 42 Rad4 Rxg6 43 R1d2 Rg2 44 Rxg2 Qxg2 45 b4 Qf2 46 Rd3 Qxf4 47 Kb1 Qxe5 48 Rf3 Bf6 49 Rxf6 Qxf6 50 Kc1 Qd4 51 b5 cxb5 52 Kb1 e5 53 Kc1 e4 54 Kb1 e3 55 Ka2 e2 56 Kb3 e1=Q 57 Ka3 Qeal+ 58 Kb3 Qab2 Mate.

Position after 58 ... Qab2,
Mate.

This was Bright's only defeat in the tournament. It won five and drew three of its other games to finish tied for second place.

Internet Chess Club CCT 11
Round 6, March 22, 2009
Crafty (W) versus Rybka (B)
Caro-Kann: Classical variation (B18)

---

1 e4 c6 2 d4 d5 3 Nd2 dxe4 4 Nxe4 Bf5 5 Nc5 Nd7 6 Bd3 e6 7 Nxb7 Qc7 8 Bxf5 exf5 9 Qe2+ Be7 10 Nc5 Nxc5 11 dxc5 Nf6 12 Be3 O-O 13 O-O-O Qa5 14 Qc4 Rfb8 15 Nf3 Rb4 16 Bd2 Rxc4 17 Bxa5

The queens made a relatively early departure as did a number of pieces, setting the stage for a possible draw.

17 ... Ra4 18 Nd4 Rxa5 19 Nxc6 Rxc5 20 Nxe7+ Kf8 21 Rhe1 a5 22 a3 f4 23 g3 Re8 24 b4 axb4 25 axb4 Rc4 26 Nf5 Rxe1 27 Rxe1 g6 28 Nd6 Rxb4

Rybka pulled even on material here, though Crafty had a passed pawn on the c-file. Play from here on was very tedious.

29 f3 Rd4 30 Nb5 Rd5 31 Nc3 Rh5 32 Re2 Rh3 33 Rg2 fxg3 34 hxg3 h5 35 Nd1 h4 36 gxh4 Nd5 37 Rf2 Rxh4 38 Nb2 Ke7 39 c4 Nf4 40 Kd2 g5 41 Ke3 Ne6 42 Rc2 Ng7 43 Re2 Kd6 44 Rd2+ Ke6 45 Kf2 f6 46 Kg2 Nf5 47 Rd3 Rf4 48 c5 Nd4 49 Rc3 Nc6 50 Nc4 f5 51 Nd6 Rd4 52 Rc2 Rd5 53 Kg3 Kf6 54 Rc3 Rd1 55 f4 g4 56 Nc4 Nd4 57 c6 Nxc6 58 Ne3 Rd6 59 Nxg4+ fxg4 60 Kxg4

Position after 60 Kxg4.

Crafty exchanged its knight for the last two Rybka pawns. With six pieces remaining on the board, an endgame database could provide perfect play from here on.

60 … Nd8 61 Re3 Rd1 62 Re2 Ne6 63 Re4 Nd4 64 Re3 Rh1 65 Ra3 Rg1+ 66 Rg3 Rxg3+ 67 Kxg3

A draw was finally called for – but the game went on for 14 more amusing moves.

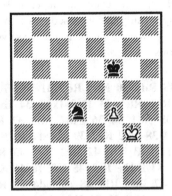

Position after 67 Kxg3.

67 … Nf3 68 Kxf3 Kg7 69 Ke4 Kf8 70 Kd5 Kf7 71 Ke5 Ke7 72 f5 Kf7 73 Kd6 Kf6 74 Kd7 Ke5 75 Ke8 Kf6 76 Kf8 Ke5 77 Kg8 Kf6 78 Kh8 Ke5 79 Kg8 Kf6 80 Kh8 Ke5 81 Kg8 Drawn by repetition.

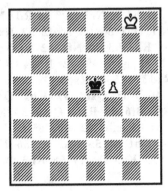

Position after 81 Kg8,
Drawn by repetition.

Fruit found itself leading the field by a half point following this sixth round with three rounds to go and an encounter with Rybka in one of them.

> **Internet Chess Club CCT 11**
> **Round 8, March 22, 2009**
> **Fruit (W) versus Rybka (B)**
> **Caro-Kann: Advance variation (B12)**

Fruit was tied with Rybka for first place when this game was played.

1 e4 c6 2 d4 d5 3 e5 c5 4 dxc5 Nc6 5 Nf3 Bg4 6 Bb5 Qa5+ 7 Nc3 e6 8 Bd2 Qc7 9 Bxc6+ bxc6 10 Na4 Bxf3 11 Qxf3 Qxe5+ 12 Be3 Be7 13 O-O Bf6 14 Rad1 Ne7 15 Bd4 Qf5 16 Qxf5 Nxf5 17 Bxf6 gxf6 18 h3 e5 19 Rd3 Nd4 20 Rxd4 exd4

Position after 20 ... exd4.

After only 20 moves, and in spite of Rybka's pawns looking like Swiss cheese, no one would give a nickel for Fruit's chances here. Fruit evidently felt it gained sufficient positional benefits from this unforced exchange.

21 Rd1 O-O-O 22 f3 Rdg8 23 Rxd4 Rg5 24 Kf1 Rhg8 25 Rd2 h5 26 Nc3 h4 27 a4 Kc7 28 Na2 Rb8 29 b3 d4 30 b4 Rd5 31 a5 Kb7 32 Nc1 Ka6 33 Nd3 Re8

Rybka was closing in for the kill with her rooks and king. Fruit was unable to carry out even the smallest of counter play in the coming moves.

34 Nf4 Rdd8 35 Nh5 f5 36 Nf4 Kb5 37 Nd3 Kc4 38 Rf2 Kc3 39 Kg1 Re3 40 Kh2

Position after 40 Kh2.

Rybka's king had maneuvered himself into the middle of the action. This was in contrast with Fruit's king who had turned to defending the edge of the board. Rybka now exchanged her rook for Fruit's knight, seeing that she could then soon advance her pawn to the eighth rank or force Fruit to give up its rook for the pawn.

40 ... Rxd3 41 cxd3 Kxd3 42 Ra2 Ke3 43 g4 d3 44 Ra3 Kf2 45 Ra1 d2 46 Rd1 Ke2 47 Rxd2+ Rxd2 48 Kg2 Ke3+ 49 Kf1 Kxf3 50 Ke1 Re2+ 51 Kf1 fxg4 52 hxg4 h3 53 Kg1 h2+ 54 Kh1 Kg3 55 b5 Re1 Mate.

Position after 55 ... Re1,
Mate.

With one round to go, Rybka led the field by a full point. She went on to win her final round game to finish the tournament a full point ahead of Fruit and Bright.

Suggest Reading

The Internet Chess Club's website for their Computer Chess Tournaments: http://www.cctchess. com/cct11/index.html

2009: Rybka Rolls Through Opposition at 17th WCCC

The 17th World Computer Chess Championship was held in the Palacio del Condestable in Pamplona, Spain, May 11–18, 2009. Ten chess engines participated in the nine-round round-robin event, including two from Germany, two from The Netherlands, and single entries from the USA, Israel, Great Britain, Hungary, Italy, and Belgium. Rybka, the defending champ and the winner for the last two years, was there to defend her title. Her main competition was expected to come from former world champions Junior and Shredder, and from Hiarcs.

A new controversial rule was imposed on the chess engines used by the participants in this competition. From the first days of major computer chess competitions, participants could bring to the table whatever system they could put together or get their hands on. In recent years, multiprocessing systems have become commonplace, especially as the computer CPUs are being designed with increasingly more processors or cores, and large clusters of cores have become available to some of the participants. The organizer of this competition imposed an 8-core limit on computers used by the participants. Some of the participants were unhappy with this arbitrarily introduced rule. In effect, it eliminated one degree of creativity open to the participants. The organizers could have put limits on memory sizes (which would limit hash table sizes) or on processor speeds, but they didn't.

Rybka figured to be as tough as ever. Entering the competition, the Swedish Rating List rated her at an astronomical 3227. That is approximately 400 points stronger than the world's best human. According to the table in Chap. 1, Rybka would win 92% of the points when playing the human world champ. Her main computer opponents in this competition were rated around 3000. Nick Carlin extended Rybka's opening book developed by Jeroen Noomen. According to Vasik Rajlich, Carlin attempted to lead Rybka to lines that terminated in "rich positions with plenty of winning chances, and to prevent opposing authors from doing the opposite."

Rybka won her first six games, including a win over the surprising second-place finisher Deep Sjeng. She then played Shredder, Hiarcs, and Junior in this order in the final three rounds, drawing with Shredder and Hiarcs while defeating Junior. In winning the championship, she finished a point and a half ahead of Deep Sjeng,

M. Newborn, *Beyond Deep Blue: Chess in the Stratosphere,*
DOI 10.1007/978-0-85729-341-1_18, © Springer-Verlag London Limited 2011

Shredder, and Junior. Shredder went undefeated in the tournament, though drawing five games. Rybka had now won three consecutive world championships.

Junior had an outstanding tournament. It trailed Rybka by one point at the end of six rounds. It moved to within a half point after winning its seventh-round game while Rybka drew. Both drew their eighth-round games. Junior, thus, was only a half point behind Rybka when the two met in a classic final round encounter that would decide the world championship. Had Junior won, it would have been world champion. However Rybka prevailed and retained the title. In winning the last three world championships, Rybka had gone undefeated. She won 23 games and drew 6. Quite a feat!

Of the ten games played between the top five finishers, it is noteworthy that the side playing Black won none. This was the second year in a row that this happened.

It is also interesting that of the 45 games played, an engine that finished the competition ahead of another engine won 33 games and drew 12, while losing none to a weaker engine. That is, there wasn't the slightest upset in the tournament. In fact, over the 2007–2010 world championships, there were only six games in which an engine that finished ahead of another engine lost a game to that engine. Moreover, it happened only once when the stronger player was playing White. This happened at the 15th WCCC when Loop, who finished third, lost a game to the fourth-place finisher Shredder. Data from world championships from 1999 through 2010 showing how stronger programs performed against weaker ones is shown below. It is separated into games in which White was the stronger player and in which Black was the stronger player. It is quite striking! Of the 360 games played in which White was the stronger player, White won 263 games, drew 77, and lost a mere 20. Of the 348 games played in which Black was the stronger player, Black won 240, drew 84, and lost 24. It shows that there was only a small advantage playing White, though clearly an advantage.

Results of games played at world championships between a stronger and a weaker player

	White is the stronger player			Black is the stronger player			Results for the stronger player		
Year	G	W	D	L	G	W	D	L	G	W	D	L
1999	58	39	15	4	47	35	7	5	105	74	22	9
2002	40	27	12	1	41	28	10	3	81	55	22	4
2003	43	36	2	5	42	29	8	5	85	65	10	10
2004	39	28	8	3	38	22	13	3	77	50	21	6
2005	32	26	6	0	34	27	5	2	66	53	11	2
2006	47	32	9	6	46	34	12	0	93	66	21	6
2007	34	21	12	1	32	23	7	2	66	44	19	3
2008	23	19	4	0	22	11	9	2	45	30	13	2
2009	22	17	5	0	23	16	7	0	45	33	12	0
2010	22	18	4	0	23	15	6	2	45	33	10	2
Totals	360	263	77	20	348	240	82	24	708	507	161	44

Four games from the championship are presented here. They are Rybka's four games against the second through fifth place finishers. Rybka defeated Deep Sjeng in Round 1. She obtained a passed a-pawn on the 16th move, and that pawn eventually led to the downfall of her opponent in a beautifully played game. The game with Shredder was a major battle in which Shredder defended against Rybka's queenside attack while maintaining a material balance that dwindled down to a drawn position. Rybka was fortunate to draw with Hiarcs. She passed up the opportunity to draw on her 29th move, only to jump on it several moves later. In Rybka's final round game with Junior, Rybka had a good start, but was in trouble at mid-game. A questionable 42nd move by Junior led to Rybka trading off her queen and a pawn for two Junior rooks and gaining the upper hand. From then on, Rybka coasted to a routine victory.

Data on entries to the 17th WCCC: Name, country of origin, authors, opening book, hardware

Name	Origin	Authors	Opening book	Hardware
Rybka	USA	Vasik Rajlich	Nick Carlin, Jeroen Noomen	Intel 8x Xeon W5580 3.2 GHz
Deep Sjeng	BEL	Gian-Carlo Pascutto	Erdogan Gunes	AMD Quad Core 3.2 GHz (rounds 1–7) Intel X5560 2.8 GHz x 8 (Rounds 8–9)
Junior	ISL	Amir Ban, Shay Bushinsky	Alon Greenfeld	Intel 8x Xeon W5580 3.2 GHz
Shredder	DEU	Stefan Meyer-Kahlen	Sandro Necchi	Intel 8x Xeon W5580 3.2GHx
Hiarcs	GBR	Mark Uniacke	Harvey Williamson, Eric Hallsworth, Sebastian Böhme, Mark Uniacke	Intel 8x Xeon W5580 3.2 GHz
Jonny	DEU	Johannes Zwanzger	Mark Roberts	No data available
The Baron	NLD	Richard Pijl	Arturo Ochoa	AMD Opteron 270 Quad Core 2 GHz
Equinox	ITA	Gian Carlo Delli Colli, Stefano Rocchi	No data available	Intel 8x Xeon X5355 2.66 GHz
Pandix 2009	HUN	Gyula Horvath	Harry Schnapp	No data available
Joker	NLD	Harm Geert Muller	No data available	Intel Core 2 Quad 2.33 GHz

Final standings of the 17th WCCC, Pamplona

#	Name	1	2	3	4	5	6	7	8	9	Pts
1	Rybka	2wW	10bW	8wW	9bW	7wW	6bW	4wD	5bD	3wW	8.0
2	Deep Sjeng	1bL	8wW	7bD	4bD	3wD	10bW	9wW	6bW	5wW	6.5
3	Junior	10bW	9wW	6bW	5wW	2bD	8wD	7wW	4bD	1bL	6.5
4	Shredder	9bW	6wD	5bD	2wD	8bW	7bW	1bD	3wD	10wW	6.5
5	Hiarcs	8wW	7bW	4wD	3bL	10wW	9bW	6wW	1wD	2bL	6.0
6	Jonny	7wW	4bD	3wL	10wW	9wW	1wL	5bL	2wL	8bW	4.5
7	The Baron	6bL	5wL	2wD	8bW	1bL	4wL	3bL	10bW	9wD	3.0
8	Equinox	5bL	2bL	1bL	7wL	4wL	3bD	10wW	9bD	6wL	2.0
9	Pandix 2009	4wL	3bL	10wD	1wL	6bL	5wL	2bL	8wD	7bD	1.5
10	Joker	3wL	1wL	9bD	6bL	5bL	2wL	8bL	7wL	4bL	0.5

17th World Computer Chess Championship, Pamplona
Round 1, May 11, 2009
Rybka (W) versus Deep Sjeng (B)
Slav Defense: Chameleon Variation (D15)

1 d4 d5 2 c4 c6 3 Nf3 Nf6 4 Nc3 a6 5 e3 b5 6 c5 g6 7 Bd3 Bg7 8 e4 dxe4 9 Nxe4 Bg4 10 Nxf6+ Bxf6 11 a4 Bxf3 12 Qxf3 Qxd4 13 axb5 O-O 14 Be2 Qb4+ 15 Kf1

Position after 15 Kf1.

Rybka would soon have a passed pawn on the a-file that eventually would turn into a queen.

15 ... Nd7 16 bxa6 Nxc5 17 Qa3 Rfb8 18 Qxb4 Rxb4 19 Ra2 Bd4 20 h4 Ne4 21 Rh3 Bxf2 22 Bd3 Ba7 23 b3 Nc3 24 Rc2 Bd4 25 Ke1 Bg7 26 Bc4 Nd5 27 Be3 e6 28 g4 Rbb8 29 Ra2 f5 30 gxf5 gxf5 31 Kf1 Kf7 32 Bf2 Be5 33 Rd3 Bd6 34 a7 Rc8 35 b4 Bxb4

Rybka fell behind by two pawns but her advanced a-pawn was too much for Deep Sjeng to handle.

36 Ra4 Be7 37 Rb3 Nc7 38 Rb7 Nd5 39 Kg2 Nc3 40 Ra5 Nb5 41 Bxb5 cxb5 42 Raxb5 Rc2 43 Rc5 Ra2 44 Rcc7 Re8 45 Rb8 e5 46 Rxe8 Kxe8 47 Rc8+ Kf7 48 a8=Q Rxa8 49 Rxa8 Black resigns.

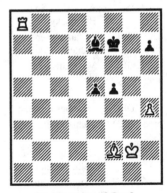

Position after 49 Rxa8,
Black resigns.

This was Deep Sjeng's only loss in the tournament. It went on to win five games and draw three in the remaining rounds.

17th World Computer Chess Championship, Pamplona
Round 7, May 16, 2009
Rybka (W) versus Shredder (B)
Queen's Gambit Declined: Ragozin Defense (D38)

Rybka had won every game until this round. Shredder trailed by a point and a half.

1 d4 d5 2 c4 e6 3 Nf3 Nf6 4 Nc3 Bb4 5 Bg5 Nbd7 6 cxd5 exd5 7 e3 c5 8 Bd3 Qa5 9 Qc2 c4 10 Bf5 O-O 11 O-O Re8 12 Nd2 g6 13 Bh3 Bxc3 14 Qxc3 Qxc3

Position after 14 … Qxc3.

Rybka gave Shredder the opportunity to exchange queens here increasing Shredder's chances to eventually escape with a draw. Shredder grabbed the opportunity, in part because it gave Rybka an isolated a-file pawn.

15 bxc3 Kg7 16 Rfb1 b6 17 g3 h6 18 Bf4 g5 19 Bd6 Nf8 20 Bg2 Ng6 21 a4 Bd7 22 Bb4 Bf5 23 Rb2 h5 24 a5 b5 25 a6 h4 26 Nb1 Bd7 27 Ra5 h3 28 Bf3 Ne7 29 Bd6 Rac8 30 Kf1 Kg6 31 Na3 Nc6 32 Raxb5 Re6 33 Bc5 Nd8 34 Rb8 Rxa6 35 Rxc8 Bxc8 36 Rb8 Bg4 37 Bxg4 Nc6 38 Rh8 Nxg4 39 Rxh3 Nd8 40 Be7 Ne6 41 Rh8 Nf6 42 Rb8 Ne4 43 f3 Nxc3 44 Ke1 f5 45 Kd2 Na4 46 Nc2 Rb6 47 Rxb6 Nxb6 48 Bc5 Kf6 49 Bxb6 axb6 50 Kc3 Ke7 51 e4 fxe4 52 fxe4 dxe4 53 d5 Ng7 54 Kxc4 Nf5 55 g4 Nh4 56 Kd4 Nf3+ 57 Kxe4 Nxh2 **Drawn by agreement.**

The game ended with material dead even.

Position after 57 … Nxh2,
Drawn by agreement.

17th World Computer Chess Championship, Pamplona
Round 8, May 17, 2009
Hiarcs (W) versus Rybka (B)
Caro-Kann Defense: Classical Variation (B18)

Rybka led Junior by a half point and Hiarcs by a full point going into this penultimate round.

1 e4 c6 2 d4 d5 3 Nc3 dxe4 4 Nxe4 Bf5 5 Ng3 Bg6 6 Nf3 Nd7 7 Bd3 e6 8 Bf4 Qa5+ 9 c3 Ngf6 10 O-O Be7 11 c4 Bxd3 12 Qxd3 O-O 13 a3 Rad8 14 h3 Qa6 15 Rfe1 c5 16 Qe2 Rfe8 17 dxc5 Nxc5 18 Rad1 Qa4 19 Ne5 Ncd7 20 Nf1 Nxe5 21 Bxe5 Qc6 22 Ne3 a5 23 Rxd8 Rxd8 24 Bc3 b6 25 Nf5 exf5 26 Qxe7 Re8 27 Qa7 Ra8 28 Qe7 Re8 29 Qa7

Position after 29 ... Qa7.

Was Rybka ready for a draw?

29 ... Ne4

29 ... Ne4 signaled she was not quite ready.

30 Bd4 Nd2 31 Re3 Ra8 32 Qe7 Nxc4 33 Rc3 Qd5 34 Bxg7

Hiarcs pulled even in material and seemed to have better pieces, but the capture gave Rybka, now facing serious problems, a second opportunity to draw, and this time she took it.

34 ... Qd1+ 35 Kh2 Nd2 36 Bh6 Nf1+ 37 Kg1 Ng3+ 38 Kh2 Nf1+ Drawn by agreement.

Position after 38 ... Nf1+,
Drawn by agreement.

Junior drew with Shredder in this round to stay one–half point off the lead.

17th World Computer Chess Championship, Pamplona
Round 9, May 17, 2009
Rybka (W) versus Junior (B)
Sicilian Defense (B40)

Rybka would win the championship if she won or drew this game. Junior would win only with a victory here.

The contempt factors set by the two sides before the game began may have ultimately led to Junior's loss. Junior had little to gain from a draw, and so the team set its contempt factor very high. Junior would then avoid a draw even if it felt it was slightly behind. It had to win this game. Conversely, Rybka's team did the opposite. Rybka was quite willing to accept a draw, as that would permit her to retain her title. Rybka would set her contempt factor to show unusually high respect for her opponent, settling for a draw even when she felt she was somewhat ahead.

1 e4 c5 2 Nf3 e6

Junior played 2 ... d6 when it drew with Rybka in their 2007 Internet Chess Club CCT 9 encounter. Here, early on, it chose a different route, hoping to do better with this choice.

3 d4 cxd4 4 Nxd4 Nf6 5 Nc3 Nc6 6 Ndb5 d6 7 Bf4 e5 8 Bg5 a6 9 Na3 b5 10 Nd5 Be7 11 Bxf6 Bxf6 12 c3 O-O 13 Nc2 Bg5 14 a4 bxa4 15 Rxa4 a5 16 Bc4 Rb8 17 b3 Kh8 18 Nce3 Be6 19 O-O g6 20 Qd3

Rybka was in book to here.

20 ... f5 21 f3 f4 22 Nc2 Ne7

Position after 22 ... Ne7.

Rybka accepted a pawn sacrifice while doubling her own pawns on the c-file, usually a pawn structure to be avoided, but not Rybka.

23 Nxe7 Bxc4 24 Nxg6+ hxg6 25 bxc4

Five captures in a row led to a one-pawn advantage for Rybka. Junior did obtain a passed a-pawn that evidently motivated the sacrifice of a pawn.

25 ... Rb2 26 Kh1 Kg7 27 Raa1 Bh4 28 Rab1 Ra2 29 Rb5 Rh8 30 Qd2 Bg3 31 Rb7+ Kf6 32 h3 Kg5 33 Rc1 Qc8 34 Rb6 a4 35 Rxd6 Qxc4 36 Rd1 Re8 37 Rb6 Qc7 38 Rb5 Kh6 39 Qd3 Qa7 40 Rbb1 Rc8 41 Rdc1 a3 42 c4

Position after 42 c4.

Junior gave up its two rooks for Rybka's queen. The remaining Rybka rooks proved too much for Junior's queen.

45 ... g5 46 Rd1 Qc7 47 c5 Qxc5 48 Rb7 Bf2 49 Rdd7 Qf8 50 Rbc7 Kh5 51 Nc3 Qg8 52 Rd6 Qh8 53 Nd5 a2 54 Ra6 Bd4 55 Rxa2 Qh6 56 Ra8 Black resigns.

At this point, Junior seemed to have a small advantage. The possibility of one more comeback in its long career loomed. However, after its next move and until the end of the game fourteen moves later, it found itself unsuccessfully trying to stave off defeat.

42 ... Qc7 43 Nb4 Rd8 44 Qxd8 Qxd8 45 Nxa2

Position after 56 Ra8,
Black resigns.

Suggest Readings

Richard Pijl, The 17th World Computer-Chess Championship, IGCA Journal, Vol. 32, No. 2, pp. 96–98, June 2009.

Rybka wins 17th World Computer Chess Championship: http://www.chessbase.com/newsdetail. asp?newsid=5444

17th World Computer Chess Championship Report: http://www.chessgames.com/perl/chess. pl?tid=68454

Rybka versus Deep Sjeng, Round 1, 17th WCCC: http://www.chessgames.com/perl/chessgame? gid=1546726

Rybka versus Shredder, Round 7, 17th WCCC: http://www.chessgames.com/perl/chessgame? gid=1546756

Hiarcs versus Rybka, Round 8, 17th WCCC: http://www.chessgames.com/perl/chessgame? gid=1546761

Rybka versus Junior, Round 9, 17th WCCC: http://www.chessgames.com/perl/chessgame? gid=1546766

http://forums.chessdom.com/viewtopic.php?f=21&t=306&start=10

http://rybkaforum.net/cgi-bin/rybkaforum/topic_show.pl?tid=11022

Rybka wins 17th World Computer Chess Championship: http://www.chessbase.com/newsdetail. asp?newsid=5444

2010: Sjeng Wins Internet Chess Club CCT 12

19

The most recent Internet Chess Club Computer Chess Tournament, CCT 12, was held as the previous year over two days, February 20–21, 2010; again five games were played on the first day and four on the second. As previously, the time control was all moves in 50 minutes plus three seconds extra per move.

A field of 28 participated with the usual engines there. However, Big Mamma was missing. Rybka passed up the event, leaving the door open for someone else to come out on top for a change. Rajlich was unable to obtain Lukas Cimiotti to operate the killer system during the dates of the competition. It was Lukas who designed the 52-core system on which Rybka has been so strong. Hiarcs, Junior, Shredder, and the up-and-coming Sjeng were the leading candidates. Given Sjeng's second-place finish in the last world championship, it might have been considered the favorite to come out on top. It was running on a large computing system consisting of three machines each running at 2.4 GHz and a fourth machine with two Intel 4 core Xeon W5590 processors running at 3.33 GHz.

Swirling around in the background for many years has been the controversy over open source chess engines and free chess engines. It came to the boil in early 2010 when some of them started playing extremely strong chess. Open source chess engines date back to GNU Chess, initially developed by Bruce Moreland in the mid-1980s. Perhaps Robert Hyatt's Crafty, arriving in the mid-1990s and a descendent of Cray Blitz, is the most well known and most widely used. In the last 5 years or so, the source code of Fabien Letouzey's Fruit has found its way into

M. Newborn, *Beyond Deep Blue: Chess in the Stratosphere*,
DOI 10.1007/978-0-85729-341-1_19, © Springer-Verlag London Limited 2011

Gian-Carlo Pascutto.
(Photo courtesy of Gian-Carlo Pascutto)

Tord Romstad. (Photo courtesy of Tord Romstad and
Gian-Carlo Pascutto)

Robert Hyatt. (Photo courtesy of Robert Hyatt)

other chess engines, most notably Cluster Toga. Another very strong derivation of an open source engine is Stockfish, derived from Glaurung by a team headed by Tord Romstad, and including Joona Kiiski and Marco Costalba. The recent derivations play chess at ratings in excess of 3000! The focus of the recent controversy are several chess programs evidently created by Russian programmers. In May of 2007, the first of these, Strelka, credited to Yuri Osipov, appeared. Some contended it was a clone of Rybka. However, Osipov contended that it wasn't Rybka, but Fruit, from which Strelka was derived. Then, in October of 2009, a slew of chess engines developed by a team calling themselves Decembrists appeared. The original Decembrists were a group of Russian soldiers and officers who revolted when Nicholas I became Tsar in 1825. The source code for the Decembrists' engines was released with the engines and the question of whether they were derived from Rybka or Fruit and how different they were became an issue. First to be released was IPPOLIT, then RobboLito, Igorrit, IvanHoe, and Firebird. Firebird became Fire at some point to avoid using the same name as Pontiac's muscle car of the same name. Houdini is the latest derivative of the open source engines and is available for free for noncommercial use. The engine's website says that "without many ideas from the excellent open source chess engines Ippolit/Robbolito, Stockfish and Crafty (in that order), Houdini would not nearly be as strong as it is now." All played very strongly, and all were freely available, possibly in conflict with the regulations surrounding open source software.

Now, after four rounds of the CCT 12, Sjeng and Hiarcs had risen to the top of the field with 3.5/4 points. They met in the fifth round and played a wild game that ended in a draw. In the following round, Sjeng defeated Shredder, while Hiarcs played to a draw with Crafty. They both obtained identical results in the next two rounds. So going into the final round, Sjeng had a half-point lead over Hiarcs. Sjeng then defeated Crafty, while Hiarcs could do no better than draw with Thinker. Sjeng thus won the tournament by a full point, clearly establishing a position as Rybka's main adversary.

Data on entries to the Internet Chess Club CCT 12: Name, author/operator, hardware

Name	Author/operator	Hardware
Sjeng	Gian-Carlo Pascutto, Sujay Jagannathan	Cluster (80–128 cores)
Hiarcs	Mark Uniacke, Robert G Osborne	Intel Skulltrail QX9775 x 2
Shredder	Stefan Meyer-Kahlen, Clemens Keck	Intel Core i9, six cores
Komodo	Don Dailey, Larry Kaufman	Intel Core 2 Quad Q6600 3.6 GHz
Scorpio	Daniel Shawul, Salvatore Spitaleri	Intel Core 2 Quad Q9650
Spark	Allard Siemelink	Quad core
Thinker	Kerwin Medina	Intel Core 2 Quad Q6600
Ikarus	Muntsin & Munjong Kolss	No data available
Crafty	Robert Hyatt, Tracy Riegle, Mike Byrne, Peter Skinner, Ted Langreck	Intel Core 2 Quad Xeon 2.33 GHz
Hannibal	Sam Hamilton, Edsel Apostol, Audy Arandela	Intel Core 2 Duo 2.93 GHz (1 cpu)
Now	Mark Lefler	No data available
Deuterium	Ferdinand Mosca	Intel Core i5 750, 6 GB
Deep Junior	Amir Ban, Shay Busihnsky	No data available
Danasah	Pedro Castro	No data available
Berta	Felix Schmenger	Intel Core i7 960, 8 GB (1 cpu)
Daydreamer	Aaron Becker	Intel Core 2 2.66 GHz
Amyan	Antonio Dieguez	Intel Celeron M 380 1.6 GHz
Telepath	Charles Roberson	No data available
Tinker	Brian Richardson	Intel Core 2 Quad Q6600 3.1 GHz (1 cpu)
The Baron	Richard Pijl, Arturo Ochoa	No data available
Dirty	Pradu Kannan, Andres Valverde	Intel Core 2 Quad Q6600 2.4 GHz
Ktulu	Rahman Paidar, Edwin Dabbaghyan	Intel processor 4.1 GHz
Gaviota	Miguel A Ballicora	AMD Dual Core 2.4 GHz
JabbaChess	Richard Allbert	Intel 2.00 GHz (1 cpu)
Butcher	Marek Kolacz	No data available
ChessPlusPlus	Mathieu Page	AMD Athlon 64 X2 6400+ 4 GB
Diep	Vincent Diepeveen, Brian Fraiser	No data available
Almond	Richard Hall	Intel Core 2 Quad Q6600 4.2 GHz (1 cpu)

Final standings of the 12th Internet Chess Club CCT

#	Name	1	2	3	4	5	6	7	8	9	Pts	TB
1	Sjeng	12wW	27bD	7bW	8wW	2bD	3wW	6bW	4bD	9wW	7.5	50.0
2	Hiarcs	14wW	15bW	3wD	27bW	1wD	9bD	4bW	6bD	7bD	6.5	49.5
3	Shredder	11bW	25wW	2bD	4wD	10bD	1bL	12wW	8wW	6bD	6.0	48.5
4	Komodo	21bW	10wW	8bD	3bD	9wD	11wW	2bL	1wD	13bW	6.0	48.5
5	Scorpio	17bL	11wL	18bL	28wW	24bW	14bW	23wW	16wW	10bW	6.0	33.5
6	Spark	9bD	7wL	21bW	22wW	8bW	10wW	1bL	2wD	3wD	5.5	48.0
7	Thinker	19wD	6bW	1bL	11wD	20bD	21wW	13bW	10wD	2bD	5.5	45.0
8	Ikarus	26wW	13bW	4wD	1bL	6wL	20wW	17bW	3bL	15wW	5.5	43.5
9	Crafty	6wD	23bD	13wW	20bW	3wD	2wD	10bL	11wW	1bL	5.0	47.0
10	Hannibal	20wW	4bL	15wW	23bW	12wW	6bL	9wW	7bD	5wL	5.0	45.5
11	Now	3wL	5bW	14wW	26wW	11bL	4bL	22wD	9bL	21wW	5.0	45.0
12	Deuterium	1bL	21wD	26bW	7bD	23wD	16wW	3bL	20wW	17bD	5.0	40.0
13	Deep Junior	16bW	8wL	9bL	24wW	23wD	15bW	7wL	22bW	4wL	5.0	41.0
14	Danasah	2bL	18wW	11bL	17wD	22bD	5wL	25bW	19wD	20bW	4.5	38.5
15	Berta	28bW	2wL	10bL	18wW	16bD	13wL	19bW	17wW	8bL	4.5	38.0
16	Daydreamer	13wL	28bW	20wL	25bW	15wD	12bL	21wW	5bL	23wW	4.5	33.5
17	Amyan	5wL	20bW	28wW	14bD	26wW	23bW	8wL	15bL	12wD	4.0	35.0
18	Telepath	27bL	14bL	5wW	15bL	25wW	22wL	20bL	-W	28bW	4.0	34.5
19	Tinker	7wD	22wL	24bW	12wL	21bL	28bW	15wL	14bD	26wW	4.0	32.0
20	BottheBaron	10bL	17wW	16bW	9wL	7wD	8bL	18wW	12bL	14wL	3.5	42.5
21	Dirty	4wL	12bD	6wL	26bW	19wW	7bL	16bL	25wW	11bL	3.5	40.0
22	Ktulu	23wD	19bW	27wL	6bL	14wD	18bW	11bD	13wL	24bL	3.5	38.5
23	Gaviota	22bD	9wD	25bW	10wL	13bD	17wL	5bL	24wW	16bL	3.5	38.0

(continued)

(continued)

#	Name	1	2	3	4	5	6	7	8	9	Pts	TB
24	JabbaChess	25wL	26bD	19wL	13bL	5wL	–W	28bW	23bL	22wW	3.5	31.0
25	Butcher	24bW	3bL	23wL	16wL	18bL	26bW	14wL	21wL	–W	3.0	35.0
26	ChessPlusPlus	8bL	24wD	12bL	21wL	17bL	25wL	–W	28wW	19bL	2.5	32.5
27	Diep	18bW	1wD	22bW	2wL	–	–	–	–	–	2.5	21.0
28	Almond	15wL	16wL	17bL	5bL	–	19wL	24wL	26bL	18wL	1.0	36.0

Internet Chess Club CCT 12
Round 5, February 20, 2010
Hiarcs (W) versus Sjeng (B)
Sicilian Defense, Najdorf (B90)

Hiarcs and Sjeng were tied for the lead each having three and a half points when this fifth-round game was played. More than the first 50 moves were in each of their opening books! It was a highly complex exciting game that wound down to a draw. The time for each move, reported on hiarc.net, show that until the 52nd move, all moves were made from book. Times from the 52nd move until the end of the game are shown along with the moves.

1 e4 c5 2 Nf3 d6 3 d4 cxd4 4 Nxd4 Nf6 5 Nc3 a6 6 Be3 e6 7 f3 b5 8 Qd2 Nbd7 9 g4 b4 10 Na4 h6 11 O-O-O Ne5 12 Qxb4 Bd7 13 Bf4 g5 14 Bd2 Be7 15 h4 Rb8 16 Qa3 gxh4 17 Bb4 Qc7 18 Bxa6 O-O 19 Rxh4 Bxa4 20 Qxa4 Qb6 21 Bb5 Nxe4 22 Rh2 Nxf3 23 Nxf3 Ra8 24 Qb3 Qxb5 25 Re1 Rxa2 26 Rxe4 Ra1+ 27 Kd2 Qf1 28 Rhe2 Rb8 29 Qc3 Rd1+

Position after 29 ... Rd1+.

This is a position to be savored.

30 Ke3 Bd8 31 Qc6 Bb6+ 32 Kf4 Qh3 33 Bxd6 h5 34 gxh5 Rf1 35 Rb4

Position after 35 Rb4.

Another position to be savored. Actually, the whole game is a gem. Now you will witness how a woman can chase a man, and how a man can escape her clutches with a little help from his good friend!

35 ... Qh4+ 36 Ke5 Qxh5+ 37 Kf4 Qh4+ 38 Ke5 Qg3+ 39 Rf4 Qg7+ 40 Rf6 Qg3+ 41 Ke4 Qg4+ 42 Rf4 Qg6+ 43 Ke5 Rd1

In retrospect, it's not that he escaped, but that she temporarily lost interest in the chase.

44 Rxf7 Rd5+ 45 Qxd5 Kxf7 46 Kf4 Qf6+ 47 Kg4 exd5 48 Bxb8 Bd8 49 Be5 Qa6 50 Rh2 Qg6+ 51 Kf4

Qe4+ **52 Kg3 {1} Ke8 {0} 53 Rh6
{116} Bg5 {0} 54 Re6+ {127} Be7 {0}
55 c3 {115} Kd7 {0} 56 Rh6 {84} Qc2
{0} 57 b4 {90} Qd3 {0}**

Position after 57 ... Qd3.

From here on, both engines take their
time in making moves.

**58 Rb6 {104} Bd8 {139} 59 Rb7+ {0}
Kc6 {50} 60 Rb8 {100} Bb6 {18}
61 b5+ {63} Qxb5 {63} 62 c4 {0} Qb1
{95} 63 cxd5+ {59} Kxd5 {29} 64 Bf4
{99} Qg6+ {16} 65 Ng5 {49} Bd4 {81}
66 Rd8+ {59} Kc4 {42} 67 Rd6 {0} Qf5
{78} 68 Nf3 {57} Bc5 {83} 69 Ne5+ {0}
Kb5 {87} 70 Rd8 {0} Qh7 {42} 71 Rb8+**

**{57} 71 ... Ka6 {70} 72 Ra8+ {53} Kb7
{28} 73 Rd8 {23} Be7 {43} 74 Rd3 {69}
Ka6 {151} 75 Rd7 {0} Qh4+ {66} 76 Kf3
{0} Kb5 {56} 77 Be3 {54} Bb4 {87}
78 Rd5+ {0} Ka4 {55} 79 Rd3 {75} Qf6+
{81} 80 Ke4 {56} Qe7 {62} 81 Bd4 {0}
Qh4+ {77} 82 Kd5 {69} Qd8+ {24}
83 Ke4 {67} Qg5 {14} 84 Bc3 {65} Qh4+
{23} 85 Kd5 {50} Qh1+ {32} Drawn
by agreement.**

Position after 85 ... Qh1+,
Drawn by agreement.

The two engines remained alone in first
place after this draw. Four rounds
remained.

Internet Chess Club CCT 12
Round 6, February 21, 2010
Sjeng (W) versus Shredder (B)
Sicialian Defense, Najdorf (B90)

Shredder figured to be Sjeng's most dangerous opponent yet to be encountered.

1 e4 c5 2 Nf3 d6 3 d4 cxd4 4 Nxd4 Nf6 5 Nc3 a6 6 f3 e6 7 Be3 b5 8 Qd2 Nbd7

This position was reached in Sjeng's game with Hiarcs in the previous round (and on the previous pages), though with colors reversed.

9 a3 Bb7 10 O-O-O Ne5 11 g4 Nfd7 12 Rg1 Nb6 13 f4 Nec4 14 Qe1 Qc7 15 f5 e5 16 Nb3 Na4 17 Nxa4 bxa4 18 Nd2 Nxe3 19 Qxe3 h6 20 Qh3 Rc8 21 Bd3 d5 22 f6

Position after 22 f6.

Sjeng offered a pawn to Shredder, eventually winning it back on its 32nd move.

22 ... gxf6 23 Qf3 dxe4 24 Nxe4 Bxe4 25 Qxe4 Qc6 26 Rde1 Bc5 27 Rgf1 Ke7 28 c3 a5 29 Kc2 Rhg8 30 Qf4 Qe6 31 Qxa4 Rxg4 32 Qxa5 Bb6 33 Qb5 Rc5 34 Qa6 Rg2+ 35 Re2 Rxe2+ 36 Bxe2 f5

Position after 36 ... f5.

With four pawns apiece and material equal, Sjeng went on to win the ensuing battle to promote a pawn.

37 Qa4 e4 38 Qb4 Kf8 39 a4 Kg7 40 Rg1+ Kf6 41 Rd1 Qc6 42 Bb5 Qc7 43 Qd4+ Re5 44 Qd2 e3 45 Qe2 Re4 46 Rd7 Qf4 47 b4 Bc7 48 a5 Re7 49 Rxe7 Kxe7 50 Kb3 Qe5 51 Bc4 f4 52 a6 Qf5 53 a7 Qb1+ 54 Ka4 Qe4 55 Qd3 Qa8 56 Qd4 Bb8 57 Qc5+ Bd6 58 Qb6 Be5 59 Qa5 Bb8 60 axb8=R Qxb8 61 Qf5 Qc7 62 Qxf7+ Kd8 Black resigns.

Position after 62 ... Kd8,
Black resigns

Internet Chess Club CCT 12
Round 9, February 21, 2010
Sjeng (W) versus Crafty (B)
Ruy Lopez (C78)

Sjeng led Hiarcs by a half point going
into this final round.

**1 e4 e5 2 Nf3 Nc6 3 Bb5 a6 4 Ba4
Nf6 5 O-O b5 6 Bb3 Bb7 7 d3 Be7
8 c3 O-O 9 Re1 h6 10 a4 b4 11 Nbd2
d5 12 exd5 Nxd5 13 Ne4 Kh8**

Position after 13 … Kh8.

Crafty buried its king in the corner where
it hid for most of the game. There were a
number of moves between here and when
Crafty finally felt the need to move its
king where it should have done so.

**14 d4 exd4 15 cxd4 Nf6 16 Ng3 Bd6
17 Ne5 Bxe5 18 dxe5 Qxd1 19 Bxd1
Nd5 20 Bd2 Rad8 21 Rc1 Nd4 22 a5
Ne6 23 Be2 Rfe8 24 Bc4 Ndf4
25 Bxf4 Nxf4 26 Bxf7 Nxg2 27 Bxe8
Nxe1 28 Rxe1 Rxe8 29 f4 c5 30 Nf5
Bd5 31 Nd6 Re7 32 Kf2**

Position after 32 Kf2.

Sjeng's king had the right idea, becoming a force in the coming moves, while
Crafty's king continued to cower in the
corner.

**32 … Bb3 33 Ke3 Rc7 34 Ne4 c4
35 Kd4 Bc2 36 e6 c3 37 bxc3 Re7
38 Kd5 b3 39 Kd6 Re8 40 e7 b2
41 Nc5 b1=Q 42 Rxb1 Bxb1**

Position after 42 … Bxb1.

Sjeng coasted to victory from this point on.

43 Nxa6 Bg6 44 Nc7 Rb8 45 f5 Bf7 46 a6 Rb1 47 a7 Rd1+ 48 Kc6 Ra1 49 a8=R+ Rxa8 50 Nxa8 h5 51 Nc7 h4 52 e8=Q+ Bxe8+ 53 Nxe8 Kg8

The king finally moved, but it was way too late.

54 Nxg7 Kxg7 55 c4 Kf6 56 c5 Ke5 57 h3 Kxf5 58 Kd6 Kf6 59 c6 Kf5 60 c7 Ke4 61 c8=Q Kd4 62 Qg4+ Ke3 63 Kc5 Kd2 64 Qe4 Kc3 65 Qe2 Kb3 66 Qd2 Black resigns.

Position after 66 Qd2,
Black resigns.

Sjeng finished the tournament undefeated with six victories and three draws,
a most impressive result!

Suggest Readings

Hiarcs's website reporting on the games: http://www.hiarcs.net/forums/viewtopic.php?t=3106&
    postdays=0&postorder=asc&start=0&sid=5fba06d72244d0eca5060dbe518271f4

A February 2010 interview with Gian Carlo Pascutto by Frank Quisinsky: http://www.schach-
    welt.de/spezial/computerschach-/interviews-/gian-carlo-pascutto.html

An interview with Tord Romstad (Norway) Joona Kiiski (Finland) Marco Costalba (Italy)
    Programmers of Stockfish: http://www.schach-welt.de/spezial/computerschach-/interviews-/
    tord-romstad-and-team.html

Home page for Ippolit: http://ippolit.wikispaces.com/

Strelka = Rybka 1.0: http://rybkaforum.net/cgi-bin/rybkaforum/topic_show.pl?tid=1655

Arne Moll, "Chess Engine Controversy," March 29, 2010: http://www.chessvibes.com/reports/
    chess-engine-controversy/

Home page for the Houdini Chess Engine: http://www.cruxis.com/chess/houdini.htm

Website for Stockfish: http://www.chess.com/download/view/stockfish-16

The 18th World Computer Chess Championship was held in the Shiinoki Cultural Center in Kanazawa, Japan, September 24–October 1, 2010. It was hosted by the Japan Advanced Institute of Science and Technology (JAIST). Ten chess engines participated in the nine-round round-robin event, including three from the USA, three from Germany, two from Hungary, and single entries from Israel and Hungary. Rybka was there to defend her title, now 3 years running. Rondo, a derivative of Zappa, Deep Junior, and Shredder figured to be the main threats. Rondo was the work of Zach Wegner, a student of Anthony Cozzie. Missing was Deep Sjeng.

For this championship, the hardware limitation placed on the entries at the last championship was removed. Instead, a separate special competition in which all participants used essentially the same hardware was held. Rybka passed up this competition which was won by Shredder. The rate at which moves were made was also sped up to all moves in one hour 45 minutes plus 15 seconds per move. Essentially games were limited to lasting at most four hours.

Rybka, Rondo, Shredder, Jonny, and Deep Junior took advantage of the rule change and came with powerful systems. According to Lucas Cimiotti, who cooked up Rybka's 200 processor system for Rajlich, it consisted of "11 Nehalem EP 8 core computers, 2 Westmere 8 core computers, and 8 Westmere 12 core computers. Most computers have 24 Gb RAM, one has 32 Gb and a few have only 12 or 16 Gb. Mainboards are: 1 Intel, 1 Tyan, 3 Supermicro, and 16 Asus. Computers are connected by normal 1 gigabyte ethernet." As for a count of the nodes searched per second, Cimiotti added that "this is a rather difficult question. Rybka doesn't count nodes in the way other engines do. Parts (or all - I don't know) of the quiescence search are simply not counted. So you get a node count which really looks low. The node count for multiprocessor systems is calculated by the node count of the parent task multiplied by a factor which is the effective speedup for the number of cores. So the node count you get when running Rybka is more like a performance index. In the cluster this only applies to the master computer. The total node count the cluster indicates is the master's node count multiplied by the number of computers in the cluster. In a normal middle game position the cluster gives a node count of

M. Newborn, *Beyond Deep Blue: Chess in the Stratosphere*,
DOI 10.1007/978-0-85729-341-1_20, © Springer-Verlag London Limited 2011

13,000 to 18,000 kn/s - but to compare this to other engines, you'll probably have to multiply this by (I guess) 20." Quite impressive also was Jonny's system involving 100 nodes of a 253–node supercomputer at the University of Bayreuth in Bayreuth, Germany. Each node contained eight cores running Intel E5520 2.27 GHz processors. The system was searching on average a billion positions per second, with a peak rate about two and a half million!

Through the first four rounds, none of the heavyweights meet. With the exception of a loss by Deep Junior to Thinker, and three draws by Pandix Breakthrough with Rybka, Rondo, and Shredder, the leaders – Rybka, Rondo, Deep Junior, and Shredder – defeated their weaker rivals and were drawing away from the others. Rybka, Rondo, and Shredder led with three and a half points with Deep Junior a half point behind.

In Round 5, the two titans, Rybka and Rondo, met, wrestled for 83 moves and then called it a draw. With draws by Deep Junior and Shredder, the three-way tie for first place with Deep Junior a half point off the pace remained intact.

The leadership narrowed to Rybka and Rondo after the sixth round. Rondo defeated Shredder, and Deep Junior lost to Jonny. Rybka had a breather, romping over last place finisher Hector for Chess. Thus, Rybka and Rondo led Shredder by a point, while Deep Junior fell behind by a point and a half.

Rybka and Rondo won their games in Round 7 as did Shredder who defeated Deep Junior. Meanwhile, Thinker won its fourth game in a row and found itself one point off the lead and tied with Shredder.

Going into the final two rounds, Rybka and Rondo, tied for first place and leading the field by a point, faced strong opponents. Rybka had the advantage, though, playing Deep Junior as Black and Shredder as White; Rondo would play Black against both Thinker and Deep Junior.

In Round 8, Rybka, playing Black, defeated Deep Junior to take a clear one-point lead over Rondo, who suffered its first loss of the competition, losing to Thinker. Rondo, Shredder and Thinker, who was doing surprisingly well, were all one point behind.

The final round had the potential of being a real thriller, but it required Shredder to defeat Rybka. If that had happened, and if Rondo had defeated Deep Junior, and Thinker had defeated Pandix Breakthrough, the nine rounds would have ended with four programs tied for the championship! The odds, however, were not good. Rybka had to lose! However, Rybka handled Shredder in style to capture its fourth consecutive world championship, a clear one and a half points ahead of Rondo and Thinker. Shredder finished two points off the lead.

Data on entries to the 18th WCCC: Name, country of origin, authors, opening book, hardware

Name	Origin	Authors	Opening book	Hardware
Rybka	USA	Vasik Rajlich	Jiri Dufek	Intel 11 Nehalem EP 8 Cores, 2 Westmere 8 Cores, and 8 Westmere 12 Cores, 2.93–3.6 GHz Westmere, 2.93–3.6 GHz
Rondo	USA	Zach Wegner	Erdogan Gunes	Intel 32 Core Nehalem-EX 7560
Thinker	USA	Kerwin Medina	Anson Williams, Nelson Hernandez	Intel 4 Core i7
Shredder	DEU	Stefan Meyer-Kahlen	Sandro Necchi	Intel 12 Core Xeon
Jonny	DEU	Johannes Zwanger	Mark Roberts	100 Intel 8 Core E5520, 2.27 GHz
Pandix Breakthrough	HUN	Gyula Horvath	Gyula Horvath	Intel 4 Core Xeon (4 Cores in use)
Deep Junior	ISL	Amir Ban, Shay Bushinsky	Alon Greenfeld	Intel 12 Core Xeon
Darmenios	POL	Dariusz Czechowski	Dariusz Czechowski	Intel 4 Core Xeon (1 Core in use)
Fridolin	DEU	Christian Sommerfeld	Erdogan Gunes	Intel 4 Core Xeon (1 Core in use)
Hector for Chess	HUN	Csaba Jergler	Csaba Jergler	Intel 4 Core Xeon (1 Core in use)

Final standings of the 18th WCCC, Kanazawa

#	Name	1	2	3	4	5	6	7	8	9	Pts
1	Rybka	8bW	3wW	6bD	5wW	2bD	10bW	9wW	7bW	4wW	8
2	Rondo	9bW	5bW	10wW	6wD	1wD	4wW	8wW	3bL	7bD	6.5
3	Thinker	7wW	1bL	4bL	8bW	10wW	9bW	5bW	2wW	6wD	6.5
4	Shredder	10bW	6bD	3wW	9wW	5wD	2bL	7wW	8bW	1bL	6
5	Jonny	6bW	2wL	9wW	1bL	4bD	7wW	3wL	10bW	8bW	5.5
6	Pandix Breakthrough	5wL	4wD	1wD	2bD	7bD	8wW	10wW	9bD	3bD	5
7	Deep Junior	3bL	9bW	8wW	10wW	6wD	5bL	4bL	1wL	2wD	4
8	Darmenios	1wL	10bW	7bL	3wL	9wW	6bL	2bL	4wL	5wL	2
9	Fridolin	2wL	7wL	5bL	4bL	8bL	3wL	1wL	6wD	10bD	1
10	Hector for Chess	4wL	8wL	2bL	7bL	3bL	1wL	6bL	5wL	9wD	0.5

18th WCCC, Kanazawa
Round 5, September 27, 2010
Rondo (W) versus Rybka (B)
Sicilian (B40)

Rondo, Rybka, and Shredder were all tied for first place when this game was played. All three drew their games, including this one between Rondo and Rybka. Deep Junior kept pace a half point off the lead when it drew its game too. This was to be the game of the tournament.

1 e4 c5 2 Nf3 e6 3 b3 b6 4 Bb2 Bb7 5 Nc3 Nc6 6 d4 cxd4 7 Nxd4 Nf6 8 Nxc6 Bxc6 9 f3 Bc5 10 Qd2 O-O 11 O-O-O d5 12 exd5 Nxd5 13 Nxd5 Bxd5 14 h4 Qe7 15 Kb1 Rfd8 16 Bd3 a5 17 Qg5 f6 18 Qh5 h6 19 Qg6 Kf8 20 Qh7 Qf7 21 Rd2 a4 22 Rhd1 Bc6 23 Be4 Rxd2 24 Rxd2 Bxe4 25 Qxe4 Qe8 26 Bd4 Bxd4 27 Qxd4 b5 28 Qd6+ Kg8 29 Kb2 a3+ 30 Kc1 Kh8 31 Qc7 Qh5 32 Rd4 Rg8 33 Qd6 e5 34 Re4 Qg6 35 Re2 Ra8 36 Qc6 Rb8 37 Qc7 Qe8 38 Rd2 b4 39 Rd5 Rc8 40 Qd7 Qf8 41 Kd2 Re8 42 Ke3 Rb8 43 h5 Re8 44 g4 Rc8 45 Kd2 Qg8 46 Qd6 Re8 47 Ke3 Rc8 48 Rc5 Rxc5 49 Qxc5

Trades were made tit-for-tat to this point.

49 ... Qb8 50 Qc6 Qd8 51 Ke2 Qf8 52 Qc7 Qa8 53 Qc4 Qb7 54 Qc5 Kh7 55 c4 bxc3 56 Qxc3 e4

57 Qc2 f5 58 gxf5 exf3+ 59 Ke3 Kh8 60 Qc4 Qa7+ 61 Kxf3 Qd7 62 Qe4 Qd1+ 63 Qe2 Qd8 64 Kg3 Qg5+ 65 Qg4 Qd2 66 Qxa2 67 f6 Qc2 68 f7 Qc7+ 69 Kg4 Qc8+ 70 Kg3 Qf8 71 Qf2 a2 72 Qxa2 Qxf7

The game lasted another ten moves with both sides prepared to draw.

73 Qa8+ Kh7 74 Qe4+ Kh8 75 Qf3 Qc7+ 76 Kg4 Qd7+ 77 Qf5 Qd1+ 78 Qf3 Qg1+ 79 Kf5 Qg5+ 80 Ke6 Qd8 81 Qd5 Qf6+ 82 Kd7 Qf4 83 Qa8+ Kh7 Drawn by agreement.

Position after 83 Kh7,
Drawn by agreement.

A real battle, leaving unclear which of these two giants would finish on top.

18th WCCC, Kanazawa
Round 6, September 29, 2010
Rondo (W) versus Shredder (B)
Sicilian (B56)

1 e4 c5 2 Nf3 d6 3 d4 cxd4 4 Nxd4
Nf6 5 Nc3 Qc7 6 Bg5 e6 7 Bxf6 gxf6
8 Qf3 Be7 9 O-O-O a6 10 Qg3 Nc6
11 Qg7 Rf8 12 Nb3 Qb6 13 Rd2 Bd7
14 Kb1 O-O-O 15 Qh6 Rh8 16 Qh5
Rdg8 17 f4 Rg7 18 g3 Kb8 19 Be2
Rhg8 20 Rhd1 Qc7 21 Rd3 Nb4
22 Rd4 Nc6 23 R4d2 Be8 24 a3 Bd7
25 Bf3 Qb6 26 Rd3 Be8 27 Ne2 Na7
28 Ned4 Bd7 29 Nd2 Be8 30 f5 Qd8
31 Be2 Nc6 32 Nc4 Ne5 33 Rc3 Bd7
34 Rb3 Ba4 35 Rb4 Bd7 36 Nb6 Be8

37 Bxa6 Nc6 38 Nxc6+ Bxc6 39 Bc4
Qe8 40 Qf3 exf5 41 Bd5 fxe4 42 Qc3
e3 43 Qxe3 Rg4 44 Bxc6 Qxc6
45 Qxe7 Rxb4 46 Nd7+ Kc8
47 Nxf6 Rb6 48 Nxg8 Qc3 49 Qe8+ Kc7
50 Qxf7+ Kb8 51 b3 d5 52 Qxd5 Rc6
53 Qe4 Rc8 54 Ne7 Black resigns.

Position after 54 Ne7,
Black resigns.

Position after 36 ... Be8.

Rondo played some strong tactical chess
over the next ten moves or so to wrap up
the game.

In winning this game, Rondo kept pace
with Rybka, who easily won her game
over last-place finisher Hector for Chess.

18th WCCC, Kanazawa
Round 8, September 30, 2010
Deep Junior (W) versus Rybka (B)
Sicilian, Taimanov Variation (B48)

Deep Junior's results thus far were disappointing, and they would soon get even more so. At the last world championship, Deep Junior played Rybka in the final round. It trailed the champion by a half point, and it could have been world champion with a victory. It pressed too hard, and went on to lose the game. This year, it was well out of contention with two rounds to go, but it had the potential of playing the role of spoiler here.

1 e4 c5 2 Nf3 e6 3 d4 cxd4 4 Nxd4 Nc6 5 Nc3 Qc7 6 Be3 a6 7 Qd2 Nf6 8 O-O-O Be7 9 f3 O-O 10 g4 b5 11 g5 Nh5 12 Nce2 Nxd4 13 Qxd4 f5 14 Bh3 f4 15 Bf2 Bxg5 16 Qc5 Qxc5 17 Bxc5 Re8 18 Rhg1 Be7 19 Bxe7 Rxe7 20 e5 g6 21 Bg4 Ng7 22 Nxf4 Bb7 23 Rd6 a5 24 a3 Rf8 25 Nd3 Nf5 26 Bxf5 Rxf5 27 f4 Rh5 28 h3 Bc6 29 Rg3 Kf8 30 Kd2 Ke8 31 Kc3 Kd8 32 Nc5 Rf5 33 Rd4 Kc7 34 Kd2 Ref7 35 Nd3 Rh5 36 c4 Rh4 37 Kc3 bxc4 38 Kxc4 Kb6 39 Kc3 Rf8 40 Rd6 Rf5 41 Rd4 Kb5

Rybka preferred not to draw. Small positional gains gradually gave Rybka an advantage until it finally outmaneuvered Deep Junior and won its a-pawn on move 60.

42 Rc4 Ka6 43 Rd4 Kb6 44 b3 Kb5 45 a4+ Kb6 46 Rc4 Rf8 47 Kd2 Bd5 48 Rc5 Rb8 49 Kc3 Bc6 50 Kb2 Rh8 51 Ka3 Rf8 52 Rc2 Rf5 53 Rc3 h6 54 Re3 g5 55 fxg5 Rxg5 56 b4 Ka7 57 Rc5 Rg1 58 Rxa5+ Kb6 59 Ne1 Rh1 60 Rc5 R4xh3 61 Nc2 h5 62 Rcc3 Rxe3 63 Nxe3 Ra1+ 64 Kb2 Rxa4 65 Nc2 Be4 66 Rh3 Bxc2 67 Kxc2 Rxb4 68 Rxh5

Position after 68 Rxh5.

Rybka struggled over the next 17 moves to capture Deep Junior's pawn on e5. Once captured, the victory was routine.

68 ... Kc5 69 Rh3 Kd5 70 Re3 Rf4 71 Kb3 Rc4 72 Rd3+ Rd4 73 Re3 Kc6 74 Rc3+ Kb7 75 Re3 Kc7 76 Kc3

Position after 41 Kb5.

**76...Rd1 77 Kc4 Rd2 78 Kc3 Rd5
79 Kc2 Kc8 80 Re2 Kd8 81 Kb3 Ke7
82 Kc4 Kf8 83 Re3 Kg7 84 Rg3+ Kh6
85 Rg1 Rxe5 86 Rg2 Rg5 87 Rd2
d5+ 88 Kc5 Rg4 89 Re2 Rc4+
90 Kb5 Re4 91 Rg2 Kh5 92 Kc5 d4
93 Kc4 e5 94 Kd3 Re3+ 95 Kd2 Ra3
96 Rg8 e4 97 Re8 Ra2+ 98 Ke1 e3
99 Re4 Rd2 100 Kf1 Kg5 White
resigns.**

Position after 100 ... Kg5,
White resigns.

18th WCCC, Kanazawa
Round 9, October 1, 2010
Rybka (W) versus Shredder (B)
Catalan, Open (E04)

If anyone had any doubts about Rybka's
domination of the field, this game – and
the previous one – should have dispelled
them.

1 d4 Nf6 2 c4 e6 3 g3 d5 4 Nf3 dxc4

A standard opening that gives up a pawn.
In this case, Rybka played down a pawn
until the 41st move. It went up a pawn
on the 45th move and then coasted to
victory in a smartly played endgame.

**5 Bg2 a6 6 O-O Nc6 7 e3 Bd7 8 Qe2
b5 9 b3 cxb3 10 axb3 Be7 11 Nc3
Bd6 12 Bb2 O-O 13 Rfc1 Nd5 14
Ne4 Re8 15 Nc5 Bc8 16 Ne1 Bf8 17
Ned3 Ra7 18 Qe1 Nb8 19 Ne5 Qe7
20 e4 Nb6 21 Bf1 f6 22 Ned3 Rd8 23
Bg2 Qe8 24 e5 f5 25 h4 Nd5 26
Bxd5 Rxd5 27 Nf4 Rd8 28 d5 exd5**

**29 e6 d4 30 Qe5 Be7 31 Ncd3 Bd6
32 Qxd4 c5 33 Nxc5 Nc6 34 Qe3
Bxf4 35 Qxf4 Rd5 36 Qf3 Bxe6 37
Nxe6 Qxe6 38 Re1 Qf7 39 Re8+
Qxe8 40 Qxd5+ Rf7**

Position after 40 ... Rf7.

Rybka drew even in material here and
went up a pawn shortly.

41   Rxa6   Nb4   42   Ra8   Nxd5
43 Rxe8+ Rf8 44 Re5 Rd8 45 Rxf5 g6
46 Rg5 Kf7 47 h5 Rd6 48 Kf1 Ke7
49 hxg6 hxg6 50 Ke2 Ke8 51 Kf3 Kd7
52 Ke4 Kc6 53 Bd4 Re6+ 54 Re5
Rd6 55 Re8 Nf6+ 56 Bxf6 Rxf6 57 f4
Kc5 58 Ke5 Rf7 59 Rb8 Rd7 60 Rg8
Rd3 61 Rxg6 Rxb3 62 Rg8 Re3+
63 Kf6 Rf3 64 f5 Kc6 65 g4 Ra3 66 g5
Ra6 67 Kg6 Kd5+ 68 f6 Rb6 69 Kf5
Rb7 70 g6 Kc5 71 f7 Kb4 72 f8=Q+
Kb3 73 Qd6 Ra7 74 Qe6+ Kb4
75 Qe1+ Kb3 76 Rh8 Kc4 77 Qc1+ Kb4
78 Rh3 Ka5 79 Qa3+ Kb6 80 Qd6+
Kb7 81 Rh7+ Ka8 82 Qd8 Mate.

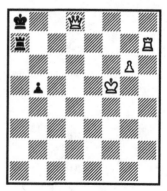

Position after 82 Qd8,
Mate.

Suggest Readings

The results were given daily on the ICGA website: http://ticc.uvt.nl/icga/cg2010results/
    TournamentResults.html
Communications with Vasik Rajlich, Lucas Cimiotti, Zach Wegner, and Johannes Zwanger.

And Beyond Rybka?

21

As the first decade of the twenty-first century and this book come to an end, Rybka's reign at the top of the world of chess-playing entities is now four years old. History has shown that staying there for much longer is a tough task. A number of chess engines have risen to the top including Chess 4.0, Kaissa, Belle, Cray Blitz, Hitech, Deep Blue, Fritz, Shredder, Junior, Hydra, Zappa, and now Rybka. All but Hitech and Hydra established their positions at world championships. None but Cray Blitz held the title for more than four years. Cray Blitz did so for six years. However, though champion for the longest time, it was best by the narrowest of margins. Fritz won the title in 1995 and held it for four years until Shredder took it away in 1999. Junior, the comeback kid, captured the title three times, in 2002, 2004, and 2006, each time only to be relieved of it the following year.

Right now, it's difficult to see who might replace Rybka and when that might happen. Quite likely Shredder, Junior, Hiarcs, Zappa, and Fritz have had their day. Sjeng is a possibility, though it is not exactly a spring chicken either. To remain on top takes a tremendous amount of energy, and it is hard to sustain such a level for too many years.

The likelihood of the human world chess champion defeating the best chess-playing engine is approaching zero quickly. The ratings of the top six engines, according to the ICGA Journal of March 2010 are as shown on the next page. These engines are rated about 200–400 points stronger than the world's best human.

In Chap. 2, a table showing data on the top-rated engine on the Swedish Rating List on alternate years from 1986 through 2000 was presented. It showed that over that period of time the rating of the top engine increased by 718 points while processor speeds increased by a factor of 37.5. On the next page, the table from Chap. 2 is extended to include data from the next decade. It shows that ratings, from the year 2000 through 2010, increased by 506 points, and processor speeds increased by a factor of 5.4. Overall from 1986 through 2010, ratings increased by 1224 points! That gives an average rating improvement of approximately 50 points per year. It should be pointed out that the processors used for testing, in general, were not the fastest available when the testing was done. In major competitions, multiple processor

M. Newborn, *Beyond Deep Blue: Chess in the Stratosphere*,
DOI 10.1007/978-0-85729-341-1_21, © Springer-Verlag London Limited 2011

The top-rated engines on the Swedish
Rating List March 2010

#	Name	Rating
1	Rybka	3227
2	Naum	3149
3	Shredder	3124
4	Fritz	3117
5	Zappa	3068
6	Hiarcs	3039

Swedish Rating List's top-rated engine in March of alternate years from 1986 to 2010

Engine	Computer	Year	Rating	Increase
Deep Rybka 3	Intel Q6600 2 GB 2,400 MHz	2010	3227	+292
Rybka 2.3.1	AMD Athlon 256 MB 1,200 MHz	2008	2935	+083
Fruit 2.2.1	AMD Athlon 256 MB 1,200 MHz	2006	2852	+034
Shredder 8.0	AMD Athlon 256 MB 1,200 MHz	2004	2818	+088
Fritz 7.0	AMD Athlon 256 MB 1,200 MHz	2002	2730	+009
Fritz 6.0	AMD K6-2 128 MB 450 MHz	2000	2721	+132
Fritz 5.0	Intel Pentium MMX 200 MHz	1998	2589	+149
M_Chess_Pro 5.0	Intel Pentium 80 MHz	1996	2440	+095
Mephisto Genius 2.0	Intel 486/50 66 MHz	1994	2345	+086
Mephisto Lyon	Motorola 68030 36 MHz	1992	2259	−073
Mephisto Portorose	Motorola 68030 36 MHz	1990	2332	+195
Mephisto MM4	Hitachi Turbo 16 K, 6301Y 12 MHz	1988	2137	+134
Mephisto Amsterdam	Motorola 68000 12 MHz	1986	2003	

versions of the engines were often used yielding even stronger performances. The testing usually involved hundred of games for each engine, and the statistical error was typically around 30–35 rating points too high or low. From 1986 to 2010, computer speeds used for the testing went from 12 to 2,400 MHz, a speedup by a factor of 200! In addition, processors went from 32 bits to 64 bit word sizes, and memory sizes went from a few megabytes to a few gigabytes. Of course, faster processors were not the only reason for the improvement.

Endgame tables, now widely available for all positions with six or fewer pieces on the board, will soon be available for all seven-piece endgames. As memory sizes increase, a larger number of these tables can be kept in main memory during the game. In the meanwhile, they can be called in from slower memory as needed.

Opening books will improve and get larger. Shredder's website currently advertises a "Huge Book" with 16 million moves. It occupies approximately a gigabyte of space. An older Rybka 3 opening book is marketed with over three million positions occupying 260 megabytes. A newer Rybka 4 Aquarium Opening Book is advertised as containing over 18 million positions. The Fritz Powerbook 2009 is advertised as having 27 million opening positions. In comparison, Belle's opening book in the mid-1980s contained about a half million moves; Fritz's Powerbook 2009 is about 50 times larger. Chess engines will eventually write their own books. Just as there are six-piece endgame tables, there will likely be opening books named by the depth that each position in the table has been checked out. We will have, let's say, a BOOK12, a BOOK13, etc.

Currently Rybka is playing two classes above the top human player, assuming a class covers about 200 rating points. The criticism of play by both Rybka and Zappa at their 2007 match in Mexico suggests there remains much room for improvement. In the coming years, the improvement of chess engines will continue, if for no other reason, as a result of progress in computer hardware. Research carried out by Ken Thompson, Ernst Heinz, your author, and several others suggests that the improvement will continue if for no other reason as processor speeds increase. Along with faster processors, computers with many processors will effectively permit very large game trees to be searched. Over the next decade, the engines will reach ratings of as much as 3500. They will be as much stronger than the world human champion as is the world human champion over the typical Expert level player. Hard to imagine, eh?

To make man versus machine games interesting, a number of possibilities are possible and more are surfacing. One can proportion the time each side is given based on ratings. In horse racing, weight is a great equalizer. Horses that compete in many of the major races are assigned weights that their jockeys must carry based on their record: the stronger their record, the greater their weight. The assigned weights are meant to give all entries an equal chance of winning. Weights range from about 110 to 130 pounds. The jockeys usually weigh about 110 pounds, and they carry the extra weight in lead blocks in their saddles. It's hard to imagine that 20 pounds can make much difference to a 1000-pound horse, but many races come down to winning or losing by a nose! For a 1000-pound horse, carrying an extra 20 pounds might be considered equivalent to a human long distance runner carrying an extra 2–3 pounds on his jaunt. Would any runner be happy with that? In chess, time is also an equalizer. Given what we've learned from computer chess, if doubling the processor speed leads to a 100 point rating improvement, then a 100 point rating difference should lead to a two–to–one time split to give each side equal chances.

Rather than giving the weaker player more time, one can give him or her a material advantage at the beginning of the game. Currently, the top computers seem to be able to beat grandmasters with a one-pawn spot. One can also give the weaker player the white pieces. This is a small advantage. One might construe from the recent results of chess engines that winning with Black is getting increasingly difficult.

Will the game ever be solved? Recently checkers was. Jonathan Schaeffer at the University of Alberta used the same approach used to develop endgame databases for chess on the game of checkers. He found that with perfect play, the game is a draw.

Of course, checkers is orders of magnitude simpler than chess, so it doesn't follow that given checkers has been solved, chess will ever follow.

A half century ago, researchers were not sure how good chess engines could get, and how to design them. Some originally thought they had to be designed using a special chess language and modeled to play like humans. As of today, the best chess engines are written in anything but a special language, and there is little interest in finding out how humans play. Research in this area was initially motivated by an attempt to understand what intelligence is all about. As of today, we still don't have a good definition of the word intelligence. To that degree, work on computer chess hasn't solved the fundamental question: what is the definition of intelligence.

As I grow older, I am concerned that my time above the surface of this beautiful planet will end without several questions related to intelligence being answered – in particular the following three!

First: what can humans do that computers cannot? Whenever somebody conjures up an example, we find that computers can, in fact, do it. Fairly bright people used to argue that humans had some mystical "intuition" that allowed them to play great chess and that could never be programmed. It was this attribute that would prevent computers from ever reaching the grandmaster level until it was understood and programmed. Nobody mentions this any longer. But can computers be programmed to appreciate a beautiful painting or symphony that evokes tears? Yes, these are judgments that they can make. Even now, they can compose music that is hard to distinguish from the leading composers. They can also play chess and make moves that are undistinguishable from those of the top grandmasters. However, they have yet to pass the Turing Test in which a man and a machine, hidden from view, are asked questions by a third person who tries to determine which he is getting answers from. Progress on this issue is tested annually, this year at the upcoming Loebner Prize Competition in Artificial Intelligence to be held this October at the California State University in Los Angeles. IBM's new question answering system called Watson is surprising some with its brilliance. One wonders, whether computers will ever have a sense of being alive.

Second: by how much have we underestimated the intelligence of the animals with whom we share this planet? Have we put ourselves on too tall of an intellectual pedestal with no other living creature measuring anywhere near us? Historically we have. But now we are finding many contradictions to this contention. As a child, I was taught that we distinguish ourselves from animals in our use of tools: we do and they don't. Today, that sounds absurd, as we know animals use all kinds of tools to acquire food and build homes. It was said that they have no sense of themselves. And a soul? If they had a soul – I'm not sure what that is! – we might find it more difficult to rationalize eating them. In underestimating the intelligence of other creatures, we have vastly overestimated our own. We are only a few hundred years away from the days of burning witches. We are not that far from the days when we imagined ourselves at the center of the universe. And we were living in caves only several thousand years ago.

Terra Cotta Army, Xi'an, China.

Third: is there intelligent life beyond the earth? We must make a greater effort to at least search Mars for a starting point. There is no question more intriguing than whether life exists elsewhere in this universe, and if so, what is it like – whether it has or ever had any intelligence as we understand it. Here on earth, we recently uncovered the vast Terra Cotta Army buried near Xi'an, China. It's hard to fathom that no one knew about this treasure until it was accidently discovered several decades ago. I have observed that nature moves very quickly in hiding the present. While the surface of Mars shows no signs of life, is it not possible that there are unimaginable treasures only meters under the surface? Moreover, the existence of water on Mars has been detected by NASA's Phoenix lander in 2008. This, of course, has long been thought to be a necessary prerequisite for life, although we have also found that living creatures can exist in the most extreme environments.

And so this book comes to an end. Deep Blue's triumph was a major milestone in the history of the study of intelligence. Somewhat more than a decade later its successors have confirmed that milestone and are now playing far stronger chess. Moreover, in spite of their great improvement, there remains considerable room for even greater improvement. However, the questions just raised, when answered, will resolve even more fundamental issues. I'm eagerly waiting. With my years getting fewer, I make a final plea to my scientific colleagues to try to answer these questions while I'm still here!

My cat Linda resigning prematurely.

Suggest Readings

Papers concerned with chess engine strength as a function of search depth:

Ken Thompson, Computer chess strength, Advances in Computer Chess 3, M. R.B. Clarke (ed.), Pergamon, pp. 55–56, 1982.

Robert Hyatt and Monty Newborn, Crafty goes deep, ICCA Journal, Vol. 20, No.2, pp. 79–86, June 1997.

Ernst A. Heinz, Dark Thought goes deep, ICCA Journal, Vol. 21, No. 4, pp. 228–244, December 1998.

Monty Newborn, A hypothesis concerning the strength of chess programs, ICCA Journal, Vol. 8, No. 4, pp. 209–215, December 1985.

Larry Kaufman, The Rybka vs. Ehlvest Pawn-Handicap Match, ICGA Journal, Vol. 30, No. 1, pp. 49–51, March 2007.

Jonathan Schaeffer, Yngvi Bjornsson, Neil Burch, Akihiro Kishimoto, Martin Muller, Rob Lake, Paul Lu and Steve Sutphen, Solving Checkers, International Joint Conference on Artificial Intelligence (IJCAI), pp. 292–297, 2005.

Water discovered on Mars (An article by David A. Fahrenthold): http://www.washingtonpost.com/wp-dyn/content/article/2008/08/01/AR2008080102856.html

Life without Light (By Robin Meadows in the Zoogoer, May/June 1996): http://nationalzoo.si.edu/Publications/ZooGoer/1996/3/lifewithoutlight.cfm

Life in Extreme Environments: http://www.astrobiology.com/extreme.html

Shredder's opening book: http://www.shredderchess.com/online-chess/online-databases/openingdatabase-info.html

Rybka 3's opening book: http://www.amazon.com/ChessCentral-Rybka-3-Opening-Book/dp/3866810962

Rybka Aquarium opening book: http://chessok.com/shop/index.php? main_page=product_info&products_id=352

Fritz Powerbook 2009: http://www.chesscentral.com/Fritz_Powerbook_2009_p/fritzpb-09.htm

Appendix I

A Look at the Books

The book lines for the 118 games presented in this book are given in the form of a game tree on the following pages. Each line terminates after ten moves by each side with an indication of results, the chapter and the game in the chapter where the game appears, followed by the year when it was played, the round or game, and participants. Games are arranged chronologically at each node with more recent games following older ones.

Of the 118 games, White won 42, 58 were drawn, and 18 were won by Black. As the book was being written, games were selected based on their significance to the outcome of each tournament and to highlight the leading programs. There was no conscientious effort to bias the data in favor of one color or the other.

Several lines transposed into one another, but the tree keeps the lines separate. This was the case with lines 34 and 40, lines 76 and 94, and lines 95, 97, and 98.

Lines 17 through 21 were identical for the first ten moves. White went on to win two of the games, draw two and lose one. The games were played between 2003 and 2005. Two years later in 2007, White chose to steer the game in a different direction on its eighth move, playing 8 Qd2. This alternate move led to two White victories. However, an analysis of games on chessgames.com played from 2007 on and between two players with ratings over 2600 show no strong results for White.

There were six initial moves made by White in the games: 1 e4, 1 c4, 1 Nf3, 1 d3, 1 d4, and 1 b3. The results for each of these moves are as shown here.

M. Newborn, *Beyond Deep Blue: Chess in the Stratosphere*,
DOI:10.1007/978-0-85729-341-1, © Springer-Verlag London Limited 2011

Summary of the outcomes of the 118 games presented in this book
as a function of their opening move

Move	Games	White wins	Drawn	Black wins
1e4	71	24	34	13
1c4	3	1	2	0
1Nf3	12	4	7	1
1d3	1	0	1	0
1d4	30	12	14	4
1b3	1	1	0	0

There were 21 different lines that resulted after two White moves and one Black move. The lines and the results for each line are shown below. It is clear that various lines of the Sicilian Defense were played by far the most. Queen's Pawn Openings accounted for the next most often selected lines.

Summary of the outcomes of 118 games presented in this book as a function of the first three moves

1	... 1	2	Games	White wins	Drawn	Black wins
e4	c5	c3	2	1	1	0
		Nc3	2	0	1	1
		Nf3	39	13	21	5
	e5	Nf3	18	8	5	5
		Bc4	1	1	0	0
	c6	d4	7	1	4	2
	e6	d4	2	0	2	0
c4	e5	Nc3	2	0	2	0
	e6	d4	1	0	1	0
Nf3	d5	d4	2	2	0	0
		93	2	1	1	0
	c5	93	1	1	0	0
		c4	2	0	1	1
	Nf6	c4	4	0	4	0
d3	e5	Nf3	1	0	1	0
d4	d5	c4	9	5	2	2
		nf3	1	1	0	0
	Nf6	c4	17	4	11	2
		Nc3	1	1	0	0
		Nf31	1	1	0	0
	c6	c4	1	0	1	0
b3	e5	Bb2	1	1	0	0

Tree of moves played in the 118 games presented in this book

#	1		2		3		4		5		6		7		8		9		10		R	Game
1	e4	c5	2 c3	d5	3 exd5	Qxd5	4 d4	Nf6	5 Nf3	Bg4	6 Be2	e6	7 h3	Bh5	8 O-O	Nc6	9 Be3	cxd4	10 cxd4	Bb4	W	1996: G 1 DB v GK, Philly
2													7 O-O	Nc6	8 Be3	Bb4	9 cxd4		10 a3	Ba5	D	1996: G 3 DB v GK, Philly
3			2 Nc3	Nc6	3 f4	g6	4 Nf3	Bg7	5 Bb5	Nd4	6 O-O	Nxb5	7 Nxb5	d6			9 Nc3		10 d3	Bb7	B	1999: R 5 Junior v Fritz, 9th WCCC
4							4 Bc4	e5	5 d3	Be7	6 Nd2	Bg5	7 h4	Bxd2+	8 Bxd2	Nf6	9 O-O	Nbd7	10 f4	Bg4	D	2003: R 5 Deep Junior v Fritz, 11th WCCC
5			2 Nf3	d6	3 d4	cxd4	4 Nxd4	Nf6	5 Nc3	a6	6 Be3	e5	7 Nb3	Be6	8 f3	Be7	9 Qd2	Nbd7	10 g4	b5	W	1999: R 7 Ferret v Fritz, 9th WCCC
6																Nbd7	9 g4	b5	10 g5	b4	D	2004: G 3 Hydra v Shredder, Abu Dhabi
7																	9 Qd2	Be7	10 g4	O-O	D	2006: R 3 Junior v Shredder, 14th WCCC
8															8 g4	h6	9 Qd2	Nbd7	10 O-O-O	Bd7	D	2003: R 7 Deep Junior v Shredder, 11th WCCC
9																b5					W	2004: G 1 Hydra v Shredder, Abu Dhabi
10																Nfd7	9 Qd2	Nb6	10 O-O-O	N8d7	D	2004: R 9 Deep Junior v Fritz, 12th WCCC
11											6 f4				8 Qd2	Nbd7	9 g4	b4	10 Na4	h6	D	2010: R 5 Hiarcs v Sjeng, ICCT 12
12											6 f4	e5	7 Nf3	Nbd7	8 a4	Be7	9 Bd3	O-O	10 O-O	exf4	D	2002: P 2 Junior v Shredder, 10WCCC
13											6 Be2	e5	7 Nb3	Be7	8 O-O	O-O	9 Kh1	Nc6	10 Be3	Be6	D	2003: G 6 Deep Junior v Kasparov, NY
14																b6	9 Kh1	Nbd7	10 Be3	Bb7	W	2004: G 7 Hydra v Shredder, Abu Dhabi
15												e6	7 O-O	Be7	8 f4	O-O	9 Kh1	Nc6	10 Be3	Qc7	D	2004: R 6 Fritz v Shredder, 12th WCCC
16																	9 a4	Nc6	10 Be3	Qc7	D	2004: G 5 Hydra v Shredder, Abu Dhabi
17											6 Bg5	e6	7 f4	Be7	8 Qf3	Qc7	9 O-O-O	Nbd7			W	2003: R 5 Shredder v Brutus, 11th WCCC
18																					D	2003: P 1 Shredder v Deep Fritz, 11th WCCC
19																					D	2004: R 5 Shredder v Deep Junior, 12th WCCC
20																					B	2004: G 2 Shredder v Hydra, Abu Dhabi
21															Qb6	8 Qd2	Qxb2	9 Rb1	Qa3	10 e5	h6	W	2005: R 11 Shredder v Junior, 13th WCCC
22																8 Qd2	Qxb2	9 Rb1	Qa3	10 e5	dxe5	W	2007: G 3: Deep Junior v Deep Fritz, Elista
23																				dxe5	W	2007: R 11 Rybka v Shredder, 15th WCCC
24											6 Bc4	e6	7 O-O	Be7	8 Bb3	Qc7	9 Re1	Nc6	10 Re3	O-O	W	2006: G 6 Deep Fritz v Kramnik, Bonn
25											6 f3	e6	7 Qd2	b5	8 O-O-O	Nbd7	9 Re1	Bb7	10 O-O-O	Ne5	W	2010: R 6 Sjeng v Shredder, ICCT 12
26										Nc6	6 Bg5	e6	7 Bxf6	gxf6	8 Qd2	a6	9 O-O-O	Bd7	10 Bxf6		B	2003: R 6 Brutus v Junior, 11th WCCC
27										g6	6 Be3	Bg7	7 f3	O-O	8 Qd2	Nc6	9 O-O-O	d5			B	2005: R 9 Shredder v Zappa, 13th WCCC
28																		Nxd4	10 Bxd4	Be6	D	2006: R 4 Shredder v Zappa, 14th WCCC
29										Qc7						Nxd4	9 O-O-O	a6	10 Qg3	Nc6	W	2010: R 6 Rondo v Shredder, 18th WCCC
30					3 Bb5+	Nc6	4 O-O	Bd7	5 Re1	Nf6	6 c3	a6	7 Ba4	c4	8 d4	cxd3	9 Qxd3	g6	10 Nd4	Ne5	D	2007: R 4 Loop v Rybka, 15th WCCC

(continued)

(continued)

#	Moves	Result	Game
31	e6 3 d4 Bd7 4 Bxd7+ Qxd7 5 O-O Nf6 6 e5 dxe5 7 Nxe5 Qc8 8 Nc3 Nc6 9 Re1 Nxe5 10 Rxe5 e6	W	2007: G 5 Zappa v Rybka, Mexico
32	…cxd4 4 Nxd4 a6 5 Bd3 Bc5 6 Nb3 Ba7 7 c4 Nc6 8 Nc3 d6 9 O-O Nge7 10 Re1 O-O	D	2003: G 2 Deep Junior v GK, NY
33	…7 Qe2 d6 8 Be3 Nc6 9 Nc3 b5 10 Bxa7 Rxa7	D	2004: G 6 Shredder v Hydra, Abu Dhabi
34	…Nc6 5 Nc3 a6 6 Be2 d6 7 Be3 Nf6 8 f4 Bb4 9 O-O Qc7 10 Qe1 O-O	B	2005: R 5 Shredder v Fruit, 13th WCCC
35	…6 Be2 a6 7 O-O Nf6 8 Be3 Bb4 9 Na4 O-O 10 c4 Bd6	D	2004: G 8 Shredder v Hydra, Abu Dhabi
36	…6 Be3 a6 7 Qd2 Nf6 8 O-O-O Bb4 9 f3 Ne5 10 Nb3 b5	D	2006: R 6 Junior v Rybka, 14th WCCC
37	…Be7 8 Bg5 a6 9 f3 O-O 10 g4 b5	B	2010: R 8 Deep Junior v Rybka, 18th WCCC
38	…Nf6 5 Nc3 e5 … 8 Bg5 a6 9 Na3 b5 10 Nd5 Be7	W	2009: R 9 Rybka v Junior, 17th WCCC
39	…Nf6 5 Nc3 Nc6 … 9 f3 Bc5 10 Qd2 O-O	D	2010: R 5 Rondo v Rybka, 18th WCCC
40	…Nc6 5 Nc3 d6 6 c4 … 9 Nc2 Be7 10 Be2 b6	D	2003: G 4 Deep Junior v GK, NY
41	…g6 5 Nc3 Bg7 6 Be3 … 9 Nb3 Qd8 10 Be2 d6	D	2007: G 7 Zappa v Rybka, Mexico
42	…Nf6 5 Nb5 d6 6 N1c3 a6 7 Na3 Rb8 … 9 Bg5 b5 10 Bxf6 Qxf6	W	2008: R 8 Rybka v Hiarcs, 16th WCCC
43	…e5 … 6 dxc5 Bxc5 7 Bd3 d5 8 exd5 cxd5 9 Re1 Ng6 10 Nbd2 Qb6	D	2008: R 9 Junior v Rybka, 16th WCCC
44	e5 2 Nf3 Nc6 3 Nc3 Nf6 4 d4 exd4 5 Nxd4 Bb4 6 Nxc6 bxc6 7 Bd3 d5 8 exd5 cxd5 9 O-O O-O 10 Bg5 c6	D	1996: G 5 DB v GK, Philly
45	…Nxe4 4 Bd3 d5 5 Nxe5 Nd7 6 Nxd7 Bxd7 … 9 Nc3 Qxd4 10 Nxd5 Bc6	D	2006: G 4 Deep Fritz v Kramnik, Bonn
46	…Nc6 3 Bb5 a6 4 Ba4 Nf6 5 O-O Be7 6 Re1 b5 7 Bb3 d6 8 c3 O-O 9 h3 … 10 d4 Re8	W	1997: G 2 DB v GK, NY
47	…a6 … 7 Bb3 … 9 h3 Bb7 10 d4 Re8	W	2003: R 4 Brutus v Fritz, 11th WCCC
48	…	D	2007: G 1 Zappa v Rybka, Mexico
49	…	B	2007: G 4 Rybka v Zappa, Mexico
50	…	D	2007: G 6 Rybka v Zappa, Mexico
51	…b5 … Na5 10 Bc2 c5	B	2003: R 1 Deep Junior v Ruy Lopez
52	…	W	2007: G 2 Rybka v Zappa, Mexico
53	…9 d4 Bg4 10 Be3 exd4	W	2007: G 3 Zappa v Rybka, Mexico
54	…O-O 8 a4 b4 9 d3 d6 10 a5 Be6	B	1999: R 2 Fritz v Shredder, 9th WCCC
55	…6 Qe2 b5 7 Bb3 d6 8 c3 O-O 9 d4 Bg4 10 Rd1 exd4	W	1999: R 7 Shredder v Junior, 9th WCCC
56	…6 d3 b5 7 Bb3 Bb7 8 Nc3 O-O 9 Re1 d6 10 a3 Qd7	W	2007: G 8 Rybka v Zappa, Mexico
57	…b5 6 Bb3 Bb7 7 d3 Be7 8 c3 O-O 9 Re1 h6 10 a4 b4	W	2010: R 9 Sjeng v Crafty, ICCT 12
58	…Nf6 4 O-O Nxe4 5 d4 Nd6 6 Bxc6 dxc6 7 dxe5 Nf5 8 Qxd8+ Kxd8 9 Nc3 h6 10 b3 Ke8	D	2002: G 1 Deep Fritz v Kramnik, Bahrain
59	…f5 4 Nc3 fxe4 5 Nxe4 Nf6 … 7 Nxf6+ gxf6 8 d4 Bg7 9 c4 g4 10 dxe5 O-O	W	2008: R 7: Hiarcs v Deep Junior, 16th WCCC
60	…3 Bc4 Bc5 4 b4 Bxb4 5 c3 Ba5 6 d4 exd4 7 O-O Nge7 8 cxd4 d5 9 exd5 Nxd5 10 Ba3 Be6	D	1999: R 6 Ferret v Shredder, 9th WCCC
61	…3 d4 exd4 4 Nxd4 Bc5 5 Nxc6 Qf6 6 Qd2 Be6 7 Nc3 Ne7 8 Qf4 Be6 9 Qxf6 gxf6 10 Na4 Bb4+	B	2002: G 3 Deep Fritz v Kramnik, Bahrain

62			2 Bc4	Nf6	3 d4	exd4	4 Nf3	Nc6	5 e5	d5	6 Bb5	Ne4	7 Nxd4	Bd7	8 Bxc6	bxc6	9 O-O	Bc5	10 f3	Ng5	W	2006: R 3 Shredder v Rybka, 14th WCCC
63		c6	2 d4	d6	3 Nf3	Nf6	4 Nc3	Bg4	5 h3	Bh5	6 Bd3	e6	7 Qe2	d5	8 Bg5	Be7	9 e5	Nfd7	10 Bxe7	Qxe7	D	1997: G 4 DB v GK, NY
64				d5	3 Nc3	dxe4	4 Nxe4	Nd7	5 Ng5	Ngf6	6 Bd3	e6	7 N1f3	h6	8 Nxe6	Qe7	9 O-O	fxe6	10 Bg6+	Kd8	W	1997: G 6 DB v GK, NY
65									5 Bc4	Ngf6	6 Ng5	e6	7 Qe2	Nb6	8 Nb3	h6	9 N5f3	c5	10 dxc5	Nxc5	D	2007: G 9 Zappa v Rybka, Mexico
66								Bf5	5 Ng3	Bg6	6 Nf3	Nd7	7 Bd3	e6	8 Bf4	Qa5+	9 c3	Ngf6	10 O-O	Be7	D	2009: R 8 Hiarcs v Rybka, 17th WCCC
67					3 e5	Bf5	4 Nc3	e6	5 g4	Bg6	6 Nge2	c5	7 h4	h5	8 Nf4	cxd4	9 Nxg6	fxg6	10 Bb5+	Nc6	B	2009: R 4 Bright v Rybka, ICCT 11
68						c5	4 dxc5	Nc6	5 Nf3	Bg4	6 Bb5	Qa5+	7 Nc3	e6	8 Bd2	Qc7	9 Bxc6+	bxc6	10 Na4	Bxf3	B	2009: R 8 Fruit v Rybka, ICCT 11
69					3 Nc2	dxe4	4 Nxe4	Bf5	5 Nc5	Nd7	6 Bd3	e6	7 Nxb7	Qc7	8 Bxf5	exf5	9 Qe2	Qe2+	10 Nc5	Nxc5	D	2009: R 6 Crafty v Rybka, ICCT 11
70		e6	2 d4	d5	3 Nd2	c5	4 Ngf3	cxd4	5 exd5	Qxd5	6 Bc4	Qd6	7 O-O	Nf6	8 Nb3	Nc6	9 Nbxd4	Nxd4	10 Nxd4	a6	D	2007: R 1 Shredder v Zappa, 15th WCCC
71					3 Nc3	dxe4	4 Nxe4	Nf6	5 Nxf6+	gxf6	6 Nf3	Nc6	7 Bb5	Qd6	8 O-O	Bd7	9 Re1	Ne7	10 Bd3	O-O-O	D	2007: R 3 Rybka v Zappa, 15th WCCC
72	1 c4	e5	2 Nc3	Nf6	3 Nf3	Nc6	4 g3	d5	5 cxd5	Nxd5	6 Bg2	Nb6	7 O-O	Be7	8 d3	O-O	9 a4	a5	10 Be3	Ra6	D	1997: P Shredder v Ferret, 9th WCCC
73				Nc6	3 g3	g6	4 Bg2	Bg7	5 e4	d6	6 d3	f5	7 exf5	Bxf5	8 Nge2	Nf6	9 O-O	O-O	10 Nd5	Qd7	W	2008: R 5: Rybka v Zappa, ICCT 10
74		e6	2 d4	Nf6	3 Nf3	d5	4 e3	dxc4	5 Bxc4	a6	6 a4	c5	7 O-O	Nc6	8 Qe2	cxd4	9 Rd1	Be7	10 exd4	O-O	D	2008: P 2 Rybka v Naum, ICCT 10
75	1 Nf3	d5	2 d4	e6	3 g3	c5	4 Bg2	Nc6	5 O-O	Nf6	6 c4	dxc4	7 Ne5	Bd7	8 Na3	cxd4	9 Naxc4	Bc5	10 Qb3	O-O	W	1996: G 2 GK v DB, Philly
76				c6	3 c4	e6	4 Nbd2	Nf6	5 e3	Nbd7	6 Bd3	Bd6	7 e4	dxe4	8 Nxe4	Nxe4	9 Bxe4	O-O	10 O-O	h6	D	1996: G 4 GK v DB, Philly
77										c5	6 b3	Nc6	7 Bb2	cxd4	8 exd4	Be7	9 Rc1	O-O	10 Bd3	Bd7	W	1996: G 6 GK v DB, Philly
78			2 g3	Bg4	3 b3	Nd7	4 Bb2	e6	5 Bg2	Ngf6	6 O-O	c6	7 d3	Bd6	8 Nbd2	O-O	9 h3	Bh5	10 e3	h6	W	1997: G 1 GK v DB, NY
79					3 Bg2	Nd7	4 h3	Bxf3	5 Bxf3	c6	6 d3	e6	7 e4	Ne5	8 Bg2	dxe4	9 Bxe4	Nf6	10 Bg2	Bb4+	D	1997: G 5 GK v DB, NY
80		c5	2 g3	Nf6	3 c4	e6	4 Nc3	d5	5 cxd5	Nxd5	6 Bg2	Nc6	7 O-O	Be7	8 d4	O-O	9 e4	Nxc3	10 bxc3	b6	W	2003: R 3 Fritz v Shredder, 11th WCCC
81			2 c4	Nf6	3 Nc3	e6	4 g3	b6	5 Bg2	Bb7	6 O-O	a6	7 Re1	Be7	8 e4	d6	9 d4	cxd4	10 Nxd4	Qc8	B	2003: P 2 Deep Fritz v Shredder, 11th WCCC
82					3 g3	b6	4 Bg2	Bb7	5 O-O	g6	6 Nc3	Bg7	7 d4	cxd4	8 Qxd4	d6	9 Rd1	Nbd7	10 Be3	Rc8	D	2007: G 6 Deep Fritz v Deep Junior, Elista
83		Nf6	2 c4	e6	3 Nc3	d5	4 d4	c6	5 e3	Nbd7	6 Qc2	Bd6	7 Be2	O-O	8 O-O	dxc4	9 Bxc4	Qe7	10 Ne2	e5	D	2006: R 4 Rybka v Zappa, 14th WCCC
84													7 Bd3	O-O	8 O-O	dxc4	9 Bxc4	b5	10 Bd3	Bb7	D	2007: G 1 Deep Junior v Deep Fritz, Elista
85									5 Bg5	h6	6 Bh4	dxc4	7 e4	g5	8 Bg3	b5	9 Be2	Bb7	10 O-O	Nbd7	D	2007: G 5 Deep Junior v Deep Fritz, Elista
86						c5	4 g3	b6	5 Bg2	Bb7	6 O-O	Be7	7 Re1	d6	8 e4	a6	9 d4	cxd4	10 Nxd4	Qc7	D	2007: G 10 Rybka v Zappa, Mexico
87	1 d3	e5	2 Nf3	Nc6	3 c4	Nf6	4 a3	d6	5 Nc3	Be7	6 g3	O-O	7 Bg2	Be6	8 O-O	Qd7	9 Ng5	Bf5	10 e4	Bg4	D	1997: G 3 GK v DB, NY
88	1 d4	d5	2 c4	c6	3 Nc3	Nf6	4 e3	e6	5 Nf3	Nbd7	6 Qc2	Bd6	7 Be2	O-O	8 O-O	dxc4	9 Bxc4	a6	10 e4	e5	B	2002: P 1 Shredder v Junior, 9th WCCC
89													7 g4	dxc4	8 Bxc4	b6	9 e4	e5	10 g5	Nh5	W	2003: G 1 GK v Deep Junior, NY
90												b6	7 cxd5	exd5	8 Bd3	Be7	9 Bd2	O-O	10 g4	Nxg4	B	2003: G 3 GK v Deep Junior, NY
91					3 Nf3	Nf6	4 Nc3	a6	5 e3	b5	6 c5	g6	7 Bd3	Bg7	8 e4	dxe4	9 Nxe4	Bg4	10 Nxf6+	Bxf6	W	2009: R 1 Rybka v Deep Sjeng, 17th WCCC

(continued)

(continued)

No.	Moves	Result	Game
92	dxc4 3 Nf3 Nf6 4 e3 e6 5 Bxc4 c5 6 O-O a6 7 dxc5 Qxd1 8 Rxd1 Bxc4 9 Kf1 b5 10 Be2 Bb7	W	2002: G 2 Kramnik v Deep Fritz, Bahrain
93	3 e4 b5 4 a4 c6 5 Nc3 b4 6 Na2 Nf6 7 e5 Nd5 8 Bxc4 e6 9 Nf3 a5 10 Bg5 Qb6	W	2006: G 2 Deep Fritz v Kramnik, Bonn
94	e6 3 Nf3 c5 4 cxd5 exd5 5 g3 Nc6 6 Bg2 Nf6 7 O-O Be7 8 Nc3 O-O 9 Bg5 cxd4 10 Nxd4 h6	D	2002: G 4 Kramnik v Deep Fritz, Bahrain
95	Nf6 3 Nf3 e6 4 Nc3 Nbd7 5 Bg5 c6 6 e3 Qa5 7 cxd5 exd5 8 Bd3 Ne4 9 Qc2 c4 10 Bf5 O-O	D	2009: R 7 Rybka v Shredder, 17th WCCC
96	c6 3 Nc3 Nf6 4 e3 e6 5 Nf3 Nbd7 6 Bd3 dxc4 7 Bxc4 b5 8 Bd3 Bb7 9 O-O a6 10 e4 c5	W	2008: R 6 Hiarcs v Rybka, ICCT 10
97	2 Nf3 Nf6 3 c4 e6 4 Nc3 c6 5 Bg5 Nbd7 6 Qc2 h6 7 g4 Ne4 8 Rg1 e5 9 cxd5 cxd5 10 g5 hxg5	W	2005: R 7 Zappa v Junior, 13th WCCC
98	Nf6 2 c4 e6 3 Nf3 d5 4 Nc3 Be7 5 Bg5 h6 6 Bh4 O-O 7 e3 Ne4 8 Bxe7 Qxe7 9 cxd5 Nxc3 10 bxc3 exd5	W	2002: G 5 Deep Fritz v Kramnik, Bahrain
99	Bb4 5 e3 O-O 6 a3 Bxc3+ 7 bxc3 c5 8 Bb2 Nc6 9 Rc1 Re8 10 Bd3 dxc4	D	2006: G 5 Kramnik v Deep Fritz, Bonn
100	Be7 5 Bg5 h6 6 Bh4 O-O 7 e3 b6 8 O-O dxc4 9 Bxc4 Nd5 10 Bxe7 Qxe7	D	2002: G 8 Kramnik v Deep Fritz, Bahrain
101	b6 4 g3 Ba6 5 b3 Bb4+ 6 Bd2 Be7 7 Bg2 c6 8 Bc3 d5 9 Ne5 Nfd7 10 Nxd7 Nxd7	B	2002: G 6 Kramnik v Deep Fritz, Bahrain
102	Bb7 … 8 Nc3 … d5	W	2008: R 7 Naum v Hiarcs, ICCT 10
103	Bb7 5 Bg2 Be7 6 O-O O-O 7 Nc3 Ne4 8 Nc3 O-O 9 O-O Na6 10 Bc1 d5	D	2006: R 6 Zappa v Junior, 14th WCCC
104	b6 4 g3 Bb7 5 Bg2 Be7 6 O-O O-O 7 Nc3 Ne4 8 Bd2 f5 9 d5 Bf6 10 Rc1 Na6	D	2008: R 6 Zappa v Naum, ICCT 10
105	Ne4 8 Qc2 Nxc3 9 Qxc3 c5 10 Rd1 d6	B	2002: R 7 Deep Fritz v Kramnik, Bahrain
106	3 Nc3 Bb4 4 f3 d5 5 a3 Be7 6 e4 dxe4 7 fxe4 e5 8 d5 Bc5 9 Bd3 Ng4 10 Nf3 Bc5	B	2002: R 4 Deep Junior v Shredder
107	4 e3 … 6 cxd5 exd5 7 Ne2 Bd6 8 O-O O-O 9 a3 c6 10 Qc2 Bxh2+	D	2003: G 5 GK v Deep Junior, NY
108	e6 3 Nc3 Bb4 4 e3 O-O 5 Bd3 d5 6 Nf3 c5 7 O-O Nc6 8 a3 Bxc3 9 bxc3 dxc4 10 Bxc4 Qc7	D	2004: G 4 Shredder v Hydra, Abu Dhabi
109	d5 4 Bg2 dxc4 5 Qa4+ Nbd7 6 Qxc4 a6 7 Qd3 c5 8 cxd5 Bxc5 9 Nf3 O-O 10 O-O Qe7	D	2006: G 1 Kramnik v Deep Fritz, Bonn
110	d5 … 6 Nc3 Nc6 7 Qc2 c5 8 Nf3 b6 9 Ne5 Nd5 10 Nc3 Bd7	D	2006: G 3 Kramnik v Deep Fritz, Bonn
111	4 Nf3 … 5 Bg2 dxc4 6 O-O Nc6 7 Qa4 cxb3 8 Nf3 b5 9 b3 cxb3 10 axb3 Be7	W	2010: R 9 Rybka v Shredder, 18th WCCC
112	Bb4+ 4 Bd2 Be7 … 6 bxc3 b6 7 Bg2 Bb7 8 Qc2 b6 9 Bf4 Ba6 10 b3 Nbd7	D	2008: P 1 Naum v Rybka, ICCT 10
113	g6 3 Nc3 d5 4 cxd5 Nxd5 5 e4 Nxc3 6 bxc3 Bg7 7 Nf3 c5 8 Rb1 O-O 9 Be2 Nc6 10 d5 Ne5	D	2007: G 2 Deep Fritz v Deep Junior, Elista
114	…	W	2007: G 4 Deep Fritz v Deep Junior, Elista
115	2 Nc3 d5 3 f3 c6 4 e4 dxe4 5 fxe4 e5 6 Nf3 Bb4 7 e5 Nfd7 8 f4 Qh4+ 9 g3 Qd8 10 Bd3 c4	W	2005: R 3 Zappa v Fruit, 13th WCCC
116	2 Nf3 g6 3 g3 Bg7 4 c4 d5 5 cxd5 Nf6 6 O-O dxc4 7 Na3 O-O 8 Nxc4 Be6 9 b3 Bd5 10 Bb2 a5	W	2008: R 4 Zappa v Hiarcs, ICCT 10
117	c6 2 c4 d5 3 cxd5 cxd5 4 Nf3 Nf6 5 Nc3 Nc6 6 Bf4 Bf5 7 e3 e6 8 Rc1 Bd6 9 Bxd6 Qxd6 10 Bb5 Bg4	D	2008: R 7 Glaurung v Zappa, ICCT 10
118	1 b3 e5 2 Bb2 Nc6 3 c4 Nf6 4 Nf3 e4 5 Nd4 Bc5 6 Nf5 d5 7 e3 O-O 8 cxd5 Nb4 9 Ng3 Nfxd5 10 Qc1 Bb6	W	2008: R 7 Rybka v Fruit, ICCT 10

W = White win, B = Black win, D = Draw, G = Game, R = Round, P = Playoff, v = vs.

Appendix II

When the End Is Near

Of the 118 games presented in the chapters of this book, 18 ended with six or fewer pieces on the board. In these cases, a six-piece endgame table would have known the outcome. The 18 games, when they each reached a state with six pieces on the board and how much longer the game went on, are summarized on the next page and then individually examined on the following pages of this appendix.

In addition to these 18 games, 9 others ended with no more than seven pieces on the board. These games will be solvable in a number of years when seven-piece endgame tables become available. Ten others finished with eight or fewer pieces, out of reach for endgame table solutions for now. Thirty-seven of the 118 games ended with no more than eight pieces on the board.

The amount of memory for endgame tables grows quickly as the number of pieces on the board increases. There are tables available online at http://kirill-kryukov.com/chess/tablebases-online/. The six-piece tables occupy about a terabyte of memory (1,000 GB). There are 295 different such endgames. The KBNP versus KQ six-piece table is the largest of them, occupying 16.49 GB of memory. At the other extreme, the KNN versus KNN occupies only about 2 MB of memory. Five-piece tables occupy about 7 GB, although compression techniques used by Shredder squeeze them into a modest 157 MB. With the current disk sizes in the range of several hundred gigabytes, and main memories in the range of several gigabytes, decisions must be made by the chess programmers regarding how their programs should handle the endgame tables during a game. In particular, decisions must be made on which tables to leave permanently in memory (3, 4, and 5 piece) and which ones should be dragged into main memory and when. For example, should they be brought into memory when found in the search tree at some particular depth?

Memory space required by endgame table in http://
kirill-kryukov.com/chess/tablebases-online/

Pieces	Approx. memory required
3	100 KB
4	30 MB
5	7 GB
6	1 TB

Summary of the 18 games that reached the point where there were six or fewer pieces on the board

Game	White pieces	Black pieces	Ending entered	Game ended	Result
Ferret (W) vs. Shredder (B): 9th WCCC	KRP	KRP	66	70	Draw
Zappa (W) vs. Fruit (B): 13th WCCC	KPP	KPP	67	75	1–0
Kramnik (W) vs. Deep Fritz (B): 2006, G1	KNP	KBP	45	47	Draw
Shredder (W) vs. Zappa (B): 15th WCCC	KBN	KBP	163	164	Draw
Rybka (W) vs. Zappa (B): 15th WCCC	KRP	KNP	63	107	Draw
Zappa (W) vs. Rybka (B): Mex. 2007, G1	KRP	KRP	73	73	Draw
Rybka (W) vs. Zappa (B): Mex. 2007, G2	KBBP	KB	105	110	1–0
Rybka (W) vs. Zappa (B): Mex. 2007, G4	KQ	KRRB	152	180	0–1
Zappa (W) vs. Rybka (B): Mex. 2007, G5	KQPP	KR	98	129	1–0
Zappa (W) vs. Rybka (B): Mex. 2007, G7	KRR	KQP	66	66	Draw
Hiarcs (W) vs. Rybka (B): ICC CCT 10	KBPP	KP	57	67	1–0
Zappa (W) vs. Naum (B): ICC CCT 10	KRP	KRP	60	70	Draw
Naum (W) vs. Hiarcs (B): ICC CCT 10	KRB	KPP	58	74	1–0
Rybka (W) vs. Fruit (B): ICC CCT 10	KRP	KBP	70	91	1–0
Naum (W) vs. Rybka (B): ICC CCT 10	KRP	KRP	63	82	Draw
Crafty (W) vs. Rybka (B): ICC CCT 11	KRP	KRN	60	81	Draw
Sjeng (W) vs. Crafty (B): ICC CCT 12	KPPP	KPP	54	66	1–0
Deep Junior(W) vs. Rybka (B): 18th WCCC	KR	KRPP	85	100	0–1

9th WCCC, Round 6, June 18, 1999
Ferret (W) versus Shredder (B)

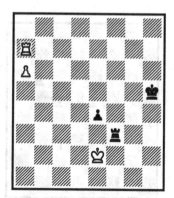

Position after 66 … Kxh5.

67 Ra8 Rf7 68 Ke3 Re7 69 Rb8 Kg6 70 Rb6+ Kf5 Drawn by agreement.

==============================

13th WCCC, Round 3, August 15, 2005,
Zappa (W) versus Fruit (B)

Position after 67 … dxe2.

68 Kxe2 Kf5 69 Kd3 Ke5 70 Ke3 Kf5 71 Kd4 Ke6 72 Ke4 Kf6 73 Kf4 Kg6 74 Ke5 h4 75 g4 Kg5 Black resigns.

Man/Machine, Game 1, Nov. 25, 2006
V. Kramnik (W) versus Deep Fritz (B)

Position after 45 Kxb6.

45 … Bf2+ 46 Kc6 Be1 47 Nxe5 Kxe5 Drawn by agreement.

==============================

15th WCCC, Round 1, June 12, 2007
Shredder (W) versus Zappa (B)

Position after 163 Nxf7.

163 … Kc7 164 Ba3 Drawn by agreement.

15th WCCC, Round 3, June 12, 2007
Rybka (W) versus Zappa (B)

Position after 63 Rxd6.

63 … Kg5 64 Rd3 Kf4 65 Rd4+ Kf5
66 Ra4 Nh2 67 Ra5+ Kf4 68 Ra7
Ke4 69 Re7+ Kf5 70 Rf7+ Ke5
71 Kd2 Ke4 72 Rh7 Ng4 73 Re7+
Kf5 74 Rf7+ Ke4 75 Ke1 Ne5 76 Rf8
Nd7 77 Re8+ Ne5 78 Kf1 Kf5
79 Rf8+ Kg4 80 Rg8+ Kf4 81 Rc8
Ng4 82 Ra8 Nh2+ 83 Ke1 Ke4
84 Kd1 Ng4 85 Ra4+ Kf5 86 Ra5+
Kf4 87 Ra2 Ke5 88 Ke1 Nh2 89 Ra6
Kf5 90 Ra3 Kf4 91 Rc3 Ke4 92 Kd1
Ng4 93 Rc4+ Kf5 94 Ke1 Nh2
95 Rc5+ Kf4 96 Kd1 Ng4 97 Rc2
Ke5 98 Rd2 Nh2 99 Rd3 Kf4
100 Rd4+ Kf5 101 Rd5+ Kf4
102 Rh5 Ng4 103 Ke1 Ne5 104 Rh7
Nd3+ 105 Kf1 Kf5 106 Ra7 Kg4
107 Ra4+ Kf5 Drawn by
agreement.

Clash of the Computer Titans,
Game 1, September 20, 2007
Zappa (W) versus Rybka (B)

Position after 73 Rxa4.

73 … Rxg7 Drawn by agreement.

================================

Clash of the Titans, Mexico City
Game 2, September 21, 2007
Rybka (W) versus Zappa (B)

Position after 105 Bxf7.

105 … Kg7 106 Ke6 Bd4 107 Be8 Bb2
108 Bf6+ Kf8 109 Bxb2 Kxe8 110 g6
Black resigns.

**Clash of the Titans, Mexico City
Game 4, September 22, 2007
Rybka (W) versus Zappa (B)**

Position after 152 ... Bxe6.

**Clash of the Titans, Mexico City
Game 5, September 23, 2007
Zappa (W) versus Rybka (B)**

Position after 98 Qxg4+.

153 Qg5+ Bf5 154 Qg3+ Kd5+
155 Kf6 Rf4 156 Qb3+ Kc6 157 Kg5
Bd7 158 Qc2+ Rc4 159 Qg2+ Kc5
160 Qg1+ Kd5 161 Qg2+ Ke6
162 Qg3 Rf8 163 Qh3+ Ke7
164 Qe3+ Kf7 165 Qf2+ Kg8 166 Qa2
Be6 167 Qa1 Rg4+ 168 Kh6 Rc8
169 Qa6 Bd7 170 Qa2+ Rcc4
171 Qa7 Rcd4 172 Qa2+ Kf8
173 Qb3 Ke7 174 Qa3+ Rb4
175 Qe3+ Kf6 176 Qf3+ Rgf4
177 Qc3+ Rbd4 178 Qf3 Rxf3
179 Kh7 Bf5+ 180 Kh8 Rd8 Mate.

98 ... Rxg4 99 b5 Rc4 100 Ke5 Rc5+
101 Kd6 Rxb5 102 c7 Rb6+ 103 Kd5
Rb5+ 104 Kd4 Rb4+ 105 Kc3 Rb1
106 Kc2 Rf1 107 c8=Q Rf3 108 Kd2
Kf4 109 Qc6 Rf2+ 110 Kd3 Kg5
111 Qc1+ Rf4 112 Ke3 Rf6 113 Ke4+
Kg6 114 Qc3 Re6+ 115 Kd5 Re8
116 Qc6+ Kf7 117 Qd7+ Re7
118 Qf5+ Kg7 119 Kd6 Ra7
120 Qe5+ Kh7 121 Ke6 Ra2
122 Qc7+ Kg6 123 Qc4 Ra5
124 Qd3+ Kh5 125 Kf6 Kh4
126 Qc4+ Kh5 127 Qe2+ Kh4
128 Qe1+ Kg4 129 Qxa5 Kf3 Black
resigns.

Clash of the Titans
Game 7, September 25, 2007
Zappa (W) versus Rybka (B)

Position after 66 ... Kxg7.

Drawn by agreement.

============================

Internet Chess Club CCT 10
Round 6, January 27, 2008
Hiarcs (W) versus Rybka (B)

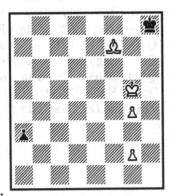

Position after 57 Kxg5.

**57 ... Kg7 58 Ba2 Kf8 59 Kf6 Ke8
60 g5 Kd7 61 g6 Kc7 62 g7 Kb7
63 g8=Q Kc6 64 Qd5+ Kb6 65 Ke7
Ka6 66 Bc4+ Kb6 67 Qb5+ Kc7
68 Bd5 Kc8 69 Qb7 Mate**

Internet Chess Club CCT 10
Round 6, January 27, 2008
Zappa (W) versus Naum (B)

Position after 60 Rxf5+.

**60 ... Ke6 61 Rf8 Rb2+ 62 Kd3 Ra2
63 Ke3 Ke7 64 Rc8 Rb2 65 Rc6 Ra2
66 Kd4 Rxe2 67 Kxd5 Rd2+ 68 Ke5
Re2+ 69 Kd4 Rd2+ 70 Ke5 Drawn
by agreement.**

============================

Internet Chess Club CCT 10
Round 7, January 27, 2008
Naum (W) versus Hiarcs (B)

Position after 58 ... gxf5.

**59 Ra8 a3 60 Rxa3 Kc5 61 Ra5+
Kxc4 62 Rxf5 Kd3 63 Rf4 Ke3
64 Ra4 Kd3 65 Kf2 Kc3 66 Ke2 Kb3**

**67 Rd4 Kc3 68 Re4 Kc2 69 Re3 Kc1
70 Kd3 Kb2 71 Kd2 Kb1 72 Kc3 Ka1
73 Kb3 Kb1 74 Re1 Mate.**

**Internet Chess Club CCT 10
Round 7, January 27, 2008
Rybka (W) versus Fruit (B)**

Position after 70 Rxc3.

**70 ... Ba2 71 Kg5 Bf7 72 Rc8 Bg8
73 Rc7 Kh8 74 Rd7 Bh7 75 Rd1 Bg8
76 Rh1+ Bh7 77 Kf4 Kg8 78 Ke5 g5
79 Rh5 g4 80 Ke6 g3 81 f6 g2 82 f7+
Kg7 83 Rg5+ Kf8 84 Rd5 g1=Q
85 Rd8+ Kg7 86 f8=Q+ Kg6 87 Qf6+
Kh5 88 Rd5+ Bf5+ 89 Rxf5+ Kg4
90 Rg5+ Kh3 91 Qh8 Mate.**

**Internet Chess Club CCT 10
Playoff Game 1, January 27, 2008
Naum (W) versus Rybka (B)**

Position after 63 gxf6.

**63 ... Kd5 64 Rf1 b5 65 Re1 Kd6
66 Re4 Rd2 67 Rf4 Rc2 68 Kg6
Rg2+ 69 Kf5 Rg1 70 Rd4+ Kc5
71 Re4 Rf1+ 72 Ke6 b4 73 Re5+
Kc4 74 Re2 b3 75 f7 Kc3 76 Re3+
Kc2 77 Rg3 b2 78 Rg2+ Kc1
79 Rxb2 Kxb2 80 Ke7 Kc3 81 f8=Q
Rxf8 82 Kxf8 Drawn.**

**Internet Chess Club CCT 11
Round 6, March 22, 2009
Crafty(W) versus Rybka (B)**

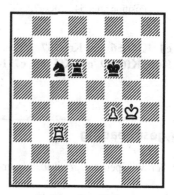

Position after 60 Kxg4.

60 ... Nd8 61 Re3 Rd1 62 Re2 Ne6 63 Re4 Nd4 64 Re3 Rh1 65 Ra3 Rg1+ 66 Rg3 Rxg3+ 67 Kxg3 Nf3 68 Kxf3 Kg7 69 Ke4 Kf8 70 Kd5 Kf7 71 Ke5 Ke7 72 f5 Kf7 73 Kd6 Kf6 74 Kd7 Ke5 75 Ke8 Kf6 76 Kf8 Ke5 77 Kg8 Kf6 78 Kh8 Ke5 79 Kg8 Kf6 80 Kh8 Ke5 81 Kg8 Drawn by repetition.

Internet Chess Club CCT 12
Round 9, February 21, 2010
Sjeng (W) versus Crafty (B)

Position after 54 ... Kxg7.

55 c4 Kf6 56 c5 Ke5 57 h3 Kxf5 58 Kd6 Kf6 59 c6 Kf5 60 c7 Ke4

61 c8=Q Kd4 62 Qg4+ Ke3 63 Kc5 Kd2 64 Qe4 Kc3 65 Qe2 Kb3 66 Qd2 Black resigns.

18th WCCC
Round 8, September 30, 2010
Deep Junior(W) versus Rybka (B)

Position after 85 ... Rxe5.

86 Rg2 Rg5 87 Rd2 d5+ 88 Kc5 Rg4 89 Re2 Rc4+ 90 Kb5 Re4 91 Rg2 Kh5 92 Kc5 d4 93 Kc4 e5 94 Kd3 Re3+ 95 Kd2 Ra3 96 Rg8 e4 97 Re8 Ra2+ 98 Ke1 e3 99 Re4 Rd2 100 Kf1 Kg5 White resigns.

Suggest Reading

http://en.wikipedia.org/wiki/Endgame_tablebase

Chess Engines and Human Participants in the Games Presented in This Book

Listed along the left column are the names of the players of the games that appear in the book. The top column lists the chapters in the book. Entries in the table correspond to the number of games played by a player appearing in the corresponding chapter.

	1	2	3	4	5	6	7	8	9	10	11	12	13	14	15	16	17	18	19	20
Deep Blue	12																			
G. Kasparov	12			6																
Fritz/Deep Fritz		3		8		5	2				6	6								
Shredder		4	3			5	2	8	3	3			2					1	1	2
Junior/Deep Junior		2	3		6	4	2		2	3		6				2		1		1
Ferret		3																		
V. Kramnik			8						6											
Ruy Lopez					1															
Brutus/Hydra					3		8													
Fruit									2						1		1			
Zappa/Rondo								3	3			2	10	4						1
Rybka										3		3	10	5	2	3	4			3
Loop												1								
Hiarcs														3	2		1	1		
Naum														4						
Glaurung														1						
Bright																1				
Crafty																1		1		
Deep Sjeng																	1	3		

**Web sites of the participants in games presented
in this book are listed below if available**

Deep Blue: www.research.ibm.com/deepblue
Kasparov, Garry: www.kasparov.com
Fritz: www.chesscentral.com/Fritz11-p/fritz-11.htm
Junior: http://www.chesscentral.com/Deep-Junior-Chess-Software-p/1191188.htm
Shredder: www.shredderchess.com
Kramnik, Vladimir: www.kramnik.com
Zappa: https://netfiles.uiuc.edu/acozzie2/www/zappa/
Fruit: www.fruitchess.com
Rybka: www.rybkachess.com/index.php?auswahl=Computer+chess
Hiarcs: www.hiarcs.com
Naum: www.superchessengine.com/naum.htm
Crafty: www.craftychess.com
Sjeng: http://www.lokasoft.nl/deepsjengintro.htm

Index